The State's Power to Tax in the Investment Arbitration of Energy Disputes

International Arbitration Law Library

VOLUME 58

Editors

Professor Julian D.M. Lew QC has been involved with international arbitration for more than forty years as counsel, as arbitrator and as an academic. He is the founder and has been the Head of the School of International Arbitration, Centre for Commercial Law Studies, Queen Mary University of London since its creation in 1985. He is now an independent international arbitrator at 20 Essex Street, London.

Stavros Brekoulakis is Professor at Queen Mary University of London and an associate member of 3 Verulam Buildings (Gray's Inn). He is a leading academic in international arbitration and has led, or been involved in, several projects with ICCA, ICC Commission and ILA. He also acts as an independent arbitrator and has been appointed as chairman, sole arbitrator, co-arbitrator and emergency arbitrator under the rules of all the major arbitration rules.

Introduction

Since its first volume published in 1993, this authoritative practitioner-oriented series has published in-depth and analytical works on niche aspects of international arbitration, authored by specialists in the field.

Objective

This authoritative and established series covering in-depth analyses of niche areas appeals to both practitioners and academics. The series includes specific monographs and PhD dissertations of high quality, which are practical and cover issues not fully explored in general texts.

Frequency

A volume is published whenever an interesting topic presents itself.

The titles published in this series are listed at the end of this volume.

The State's Power to Tax in the Investment Arbitration of Energy Disputes

Outer Limits and the Energy Charter Treaty

Cornel Marian

Wolters Kluwer

Published by:
Kluwer Law International B.V.
PO Box 316
2400 AH Alphen aan den Rijn
The Netherlands
E-mail: international-sales@wolterskluwer.com
Website: lrus.wolterskluwer.com

Sold and distributed in North, Central and South America by:
Wolters Kluwer Legal & Regulatory U.S.
7201 McKinney Circle
Frederick, MD 21704
United States of America
Email: customer.service@wolterskluwer.com

Sold and distributed in all other countries by:
Air Business Subscriptions
Rockwood House
Haywards Heath
West Sussex
RH16 3DH
United Kingdom
Email: international-customerservice@wolterskluwer.com

ISBN 978-94-035-1752-0

e-Book: ISBN 978-94-035-1803-9
web-PDF: ISBN 978-94-035-1851-0

To Klara and my family, who never cease to inspire me.

Table of Contents

Foreword

It strikes me how immensely the international legal field has expanded and evolved since my own modest entry into it in the early 1950s. While sadly armed interventions still abound, long gone are the days of 'gunboat diplomacy' to protect investments. The display of force in the event of nationalization is a distant memory. Yet, the economic forces at play giving rise to economic confrontations have hardly changed. In fact, with globalization, the strains on the fragile diplomatic system have magnified and multiplied. In the field of energy, needs have soared and the demand for investment funds has grown immensely for the development, maintenance and distribution of sustainable energy. To become available, they need fair treatment.

The state's power to tax is a timely and necessary contribution to the research on the rising tide of energy disputes involving states. With a focus on the Energy Charter Treaty (ECT), this work explores the delicate balance between states' power to tax on the one hand and investment protection on the other. I have sometimes pondered the controversy regarding the suspended EU-US free trade agreement. On one side, I have seen a demand for states to have a maximum of fiscal and regulatory freedom, and opposition to subject the exercise of such freedom to arbitration. On the other side, I have watched in the real world a closure of nuclear power plants in both Germany and Sweden. If prompted by new regulation or by taxation that has become prohibitive, is it not fair that international investment losses can be subject to arbitration?

The present work analyzes the existing case law to provide a way forward. It uses the *Yukos* ECT award to jump-start an important journey to answer what a tax is under international law, what a bona fide exercise of such tax power is, what the limits to the power to tax are, and how these issues are closely intertwined. The work tackles the challenges posed by the renewable energy industry in its efforts to establish itself as a valuable long-term alternative to non-renewable energy sources. It also offers a rich inventory of existing and new questions that arise from the need for investment funds, as reflected in energy disputes.

In the late 1950s, the circle of international legal researchers and practitioners was relatively small. In my own country, Sweden, I was often lonely in a growing field. With this memory, I am delighted to see that the author finalized his dissertation for

Frankfurt University at the Lauterpacht Centre of the University of Cambridge. Having myself been a student of Hersch Lauterpacht and a close friend of his son, Eli Lauterpacht, I am happy to see the Lauterpacht name inspire new researchers across the world in tackling the expansion and evolution of international law. I welcome Cornel Marian and his work.

Hans Blix
Director General Emeritus of the International Atomic Energy Agency
Associate Professor of International Law at Stockholm University
Stockholm, 2019

Preface

The issues surrounding international investment arbitration, energy law, and taxation have witnessed detailed studies with respect to these individual fields. Efforts have been made, at any given time, even with respect to an interdisciplinary review of any of these subjects. Given the extensive materials already available, I am called to defend the decision to explore a further contribution to these fields.

Why focus an entire study on the impact of the state's power to tax on investment protection in the energy sector?

This book contributes to the interdisciplinary review of these three important subject matters. I aim to dissect and analyze the emerging case law from international tribunals reviewing investor protection mechanisms and taxation measures arising in the context of energy-related disputes. The book reviews the rising number of tax-related investment arbitrations arising not only from the Energy Charter Treaty but also from the investment protection instruments that carry an impact on the energy sector.

The need for alternative and sustainable sources of energy poses a monumental and time-pressing challenge. As the tide of an entire industry changes, states seek to find alternative, environmentally friendly solutions to carbon-heavy energy use. States need to do this fast. The budgets of even the most developed countries have witnessed setbacks, be it due to the aftermath of the economic recession of 2008, the Eurozone austerity measures, the impending impact of Brexit, or the trade conflict between the two largest world economies (United States (US) and China). It comes as no surprise that confronted with shrinking budgets, states venture audaciously into taxation incentive schemes that aim to inject capital without direct monetary contribution from the states themselves.

The result has seldom been positive. A high number of investment disputes has already arisen. The rosy outlooks of incentive schemes, be it being cost based instead of revenue based, appear attractive politically, but when applied to financial realities, they leave states strained for cash. The rapid change in the case law carries a direct impact on the interpretation of what investor rights are protected but more importantly also on the outer limits of a state's power to tax. The book affords considerable attention to the *Yukos* awards that set in motion an interdisciplinary review of the outer limits of the state's power to tax, including defining what bona fide taxation measures are and the prophetic words of the late Professor Wälde, who called for a systematization of the red flags occurring in the state's investment policy with regard to taxation.

The book does not seek to provide a predictive measure for any decision-maker. Instead, it seeks to analyze the existing case law so as to develop a theoretical framework, which in part may not only aid states in developing their tax-specific investment incentive schemes but also assist investors in completing a necessary level of due diligence against possible adverse tax measures. The approach chosen by me is to explore the substantive rights offered to investors resulting from the state's power to tax. Such review is specifically limited to energy-related disputes as the state's power to tax encounters specific challenges when linked to the energy resources and a sovereign right to dispose of such resources.

The overlap between arbitration and taxation is nothing new. Arbitration, by default, is a procedural mechanism. Some original cases have confronted adverse tax measures, resolved by international arbitration. Arbitration's cross-border procedural peculiarities have generated increasing interest from taxation practitioners, who aim to resolve cross-border disputes arising from avoidance of double taxation. While an interdisciplinary review of taxation and arbitration in the context of double taxation is interesting and peripherally relevant even for investment protection schemes, this book focuses on investment protection as a substantive right protected by investment treaties. The review of the taxation schemes becomes relevant for purposes of identifying the theoretical framework for the state's power to tax, including the outer limits of such powers, a subject matter that goes unchallenged in the context of double taxation disputes.

If I were to summarize this book's goals, it would be for the book to contribute to connecting, rather than disintegrating, the seemingly distinct subject matters of investment arbitration, energy law, and taxation in an effort to combat further fragmentation. It does neither search nor formulate a universal principle. By drawing heavily on the existing case law, I adopt a pragmatic approach and construct the law contextually. Whether I succeed or fail in this goal, it is but for the reader to decide.

Stockholm, 2020

List of Abbreviations

AB	Aktiebolag. Private Limited Liability Company in Sweden
AC	Alternating Current
AG	Aktiengesellschaft. Private limited liability company in Germany
ASIL	American Society of International Law
BEPS	Base Erosion and Profit Shifting
BIT	Bilateral Investment Treaty
BV	Besloten vennootschap met beperkte aansprakelijkheid. Private Limited Liability Company in the Netherlands
CIS	Confederation of Independent States
CPI	Consumer Price Index
CSP	Concentrated Solar Power
CTA	Competent Tax Authority
DC	Direct Current
DTT	Double Taxation Treaty
EEC	European Energy Charter, signed at Hague December 17, 1991
ECT	The Energy Charter Treaty, signed December 1994, entered into force on April 1998
EU	European Union
EUR	Euros
EURATOM	The European Atomic Energy Community
FDI	Foreign Direct Investment
FET	Fair and Equitable Treatment
Ff.	and following
GAAT	General Agreement on Trade and Tariffs
IBA	International Bar Association

IBFD	International Bureau of Fiscal Documentation (the preeminent independent non-profit foundation that provides tax research, international tax information, education and government consultancy)
IAEA	International Atomic Energy Agency
ICC	International Chamber of Commerce (International Court of Arbitration)
ICJ	International Court of Justice
ICSID	International Centre for the Settlement of Investment Disputes
IEA	International Energy Agency
IEC	International Energy Charter, adopted and signed in the Hague, May 21, 2015
ILA	International Law Association
ILC	International Law Commission
IMU	Imposta municipale propria. Italian Municipal Property Charge/Tax
INECEL	Instituto Ecuatoriano de Electrificación: Ecuador's state-owned entity under the Ministry of Natural Resources and Energy responsible for power generation, transmission, and distribution
Interpretative Law	Ecuador Law No. 2004-41 (2004)
IRC	US Internal Revenue Code
IRENA	International Renewable Energy Association
IRS	United States Internal Revenue Service: the US federal taxation authority
LCIA	London Court of International Arbitration
LLC	Limited Liability Company
LSG	Legal Subgroup members to the Energy Charter Treaty
MAP	Mutual Agreement Procedure (procedure under double taxation treaties to resolve disputes, usually by referring matters to competent authorities)
MENA	Middle East and North Africa
MFN	Most-Favored-Nation
MIT	Multilateral Investment Treaties
MPEPIL	Max Planck Encyclopedia of Public International Law
NAFTA	North American Free Trade Agreement
NT	National Treatment
Occidental or Oxy	Occidental Petroleum
OECD	Organisation for Economic Co-operation and Development
OEPC	Occidental Exploration and Production Company
OPEC	Organization of the Petroleum Exporting Countries
PE	Permanent Establishment
PCA	Permanent Court of Arbitration

PEEREA	The Protocol on Energy Efficiency and Related Environmental Aspects to the ECT, signed and entered into force on 16 April 1998
PPA	Power Purchase Agreement
PSA	Production-Sharing Agreement
PSC	Production-Sharing Contract
PV	Photovoltaic (Solar Cell Conversion)
REIO	Regional Economic Integration Organization
RES	Renewable Energy Sources
Restatement	Restatement (Third) of the Foreign Relations of the United States
S.A.	Société anonyme or società anonima. Private company in French and Italian
SAA	Swedish arbitration act. Lag (1999: 116) om skiljeförfarande
SCC	Stockholm Chamber of Commerce (Arbitration Institute)
Sp.	Spanish
Specified Inclusion	Any of the provisions of ECT Article 21(2)-(6)
SRI	*Servicio de Rentas Internas* (Ecuador Internal Tax Authority)
TASA	Tassa servizi indivisibili (TASI). Italian municipal property tax/charge on services
Taxation Article	ECT Article 21
Taxation or Tax Exclusion	The first sentence of ECT Article 21(1)
Taxation Subgroup	European Energy Charter Conference Subgroup on Taxation. The Taxation Subgroup served as the drafting discussion group for the drafting and the finalization of the Taxation Article
T-bonds	Treasury bonds
TFEU	Treaty on the Functioning of the European Union
Trade Amendment	Amendment to the Trade-Related Provisions of the Energy Charter Treaty
TVPEE	Tax on the Value of Production of Electrical Energy
UC	Umbrella clause
UN	United Nations
UNCITRAL	United Nations Commission on International Trade Law
US	United States
US Proposal	The US Proposal to the Taxation Article, formally adopted on June 19, 1992
USMCA	United States, Mexico and Canada Agreement, signed on November 30, 2018, in effect from July 1, 2020
UNTS	United Nations Treaty Series
VAT	Value-added tax
VCLT	Vienna Convention on the Law of the Treaties
WTO	World Trade Organization

YNG	Yuganskneftegaz, the corporate owner of a large Siberian oil field and the most valuable asset in the Yukos portfolio
Yukos	OAO NK Yukos Oil Company OJSC

List of Figures

List of Tables

Acknowledgments

The book constitutes a revised form of my final dissertation at the Faculty of Law of the University of Frankfurt. I am grateful to my advisors and members of the academic committee, Professors Rainer Hofmann, Kaj Hobér, and Stefan Kadelbach for extensive feedback and detailed discussions. This book would not have seen the light of day had it not been for the Lauterpacht Center at Cambridge University where I completed the final stages of my writing. Thank you to Professors Eyal Benvenisti and Jorge Viñuales for helpful feedback. Thank you also to the following research centers: the Energy Charter Secretariat (Vitali Hiarlouski, who has helped guide me through the *travaux* and other critical sources, and Alejandro Carballo Leya for lending me his advice and spearheading the efforts of making the Energy Charter Treaty (ECT) *travaux* public), the University of Neuchâtel, and the Swiss Institute of Comparative Law, who all have generously opened the doors for me to complete my research and writing. I gratefully acknowledge the help of John Frederick, Ryan Posey, Luca Castiglione, Ander Garcia, Carlos Rodriguez Estanga, Olga Kuchmiienko, Karl Ömer Rösch and Charlotte van den Berg.

Little may have been accomplished without the love, affection and unfettered support through the long nights and early mornings of research and writing. Thanks to my wife, Klara, whose own doctorate studies emboldened me to pursue my own; I owe her so very much for challenging me and pushing me to my very best. Thanks to my mother, Natalia, whose hard work knows no bounds, to my father, Nicolae, to my uncle, Grigore, and to my sister, Viorica, who all taught me that scholarly research is a marathon rather than a sprint; I remain eternally grateful to them. The views presented in this book are my own. The errors, if any, are solely those of mine.

Today, the state resorting to absolutely legal market mechanisms, is looking after its own interests. I consider this to be quite logical.[1]

Vladimir Putin, 2004

The precepts of international law need not only to be interpreted in the light of the ideals and ethico-legal principles which are at their basis. They need also to be seen within the sociological context of economic interests, social tensions, and aspirations for power, which are the motivating forces in the international field, and which give rise to the factual situations forming the raw material for regulation by international law.[2]

Hans Morgenthau, 1940

[...] the power to tax involves the power to destroy [...][3]

McCulloch v. Maryland, 1819

1. Yukos Universal Limited v. the Russian Federation, Final Award, PCA Case No. AA 227, July 18, 2014, para. 43 [hereinafter "*Yukos* Award"].
2. Hans Morgenthau, *Positivism, Functionalism and International Law,* 34 Am. J. Int'l L. 283, 269 (1940).
3. McCulloch v. Maryland, 17 U.S. 316, 431 (1819).

CHAPTER 1
Introduction

§1.01 THE ENERGY SECTOR AT A CROSSROADS

Energy constitutes a fundamental resource for human existence and development.[4] With population growth and human progress, energy consumption of low-cost, high-polluting sources of energy has risen gradually in the past century often without environmental concerns. The effects of climate change have made themselves known across the economic, political, and social spectrums, thereby calling for a reevaluation of the status quo, conservation and transition to sustainable sources of energy.

Several forces impose further obstacles. In the decades to come, the world's energy consumption will continue to increase sharply.[5] As demand rises, a unique opportunity to invest in new energy sources arises. However, due to the initial investment costs and the new technology to make use of new sources of energy, the incentive to switch to new energy sources has been lackluster. In a similar manner, climate change and the impact of fossil fuels on climate change are putting pressure on industry production to modify its core production features. Some backlash is witnessed from existing market actors that view change as threatening their modes of operations.

Today more than ever, states are called upon to exercise a more active role in energy policy. Not only are states expected to regulate the efficient and safe production and distribution of energy to end users, but they are also asked to incentivize increased production of energy and the transition to clean energy. Yet, states have few instruments at their disposal to address the challenges affecting the energy sector. Across the spectrum, developed and less-developed countries alike encounter the pressures of scarce budgets. Countries that carry budget surpluses have few incentives to invest in

4. R.F.M. Lubbers, A European Energy Community, Memorandum, June 25, 1990 at 2 (noting that "Energy is the key to economic development and the driving force behind modern society") [hereinafter "the Lubbers Memorandum"].
5. US Energy Information Administration, EIA, projects that world energy consumption will increase by 56% by 2040, July 25, 2013; http://www.eia.gov/ (Accessed: May 30, 2020).

clean solutions. Some of these, including those who benefit from the current levels of consumption, are making a change but the change is again not fast enough to meet the existing challenges.[6]

One inherent instrument available to states is the power to tax. Taxes and similarly related measures are, by definition, mandatory contributions levied by the state for the support of public needs.[7] The power to tax is derived from a state's inherent sovereign power to exercise policy over its own territories.[8] With the aid of taxation policy, the state may regulate a sector, promote economic activity, and shape sector-specific policies, including subsidizing and incentivizing economic activity.[9] In a similar manner, states may restrict economic activity either by means of a specific legislative intent or by outcome of an incidental effect. Such restrictions on economic activity may materialize by acts of a state withdrawing existing tax-benefit schemes or reducing the tax benefits over time.

Against the background of exercising its regulatory powers, states or state actors may even target economic actors or specific sectors with nationalizing, expropriating or expropriatory-like measures to adversely affect investments. Motivation for nationalization may be manifold: it may be conducted with a noble cause such as to serve a public interest, but it may also be less noble. Customary international law recognizes the state's sovereignty to expropriate as it deems fit; however, if expropriation or nationalization were in fact to occur, customary international law dictates that "prompt, adequate and effective compensation" shall be paid.[10]

That states nationalize or expropriate is nothing new.[11] Historical examples of expropriatory takings have been traditionally blatant: the state expropriates actual property such as mines, oil fields or withdrawing the rights or concessions to explore such properties.[12] Over time, international jurisprudence has expanded so as to recognize that a state's expropriatory conduct may occur even by other measures such

---

6. UAE to invest USD 163 billion in renewable energy projects: Oil-rich Gulf state aims to meet almost half of its power needs from green sources and reduce fossil-fuel use, Al Jazeera, Jan. 10, 2017; at: http://www.aljazeera.com/news/2017/01/uae-invest-163b-renewable-energy-projects-170110160613154.html.
7. *Tax, Black's Law Dictionary* (11th ed. 2019) (quoting 1 Thomas M. Cooley, *The Law of Taxation* § 1, at 61-3 (Clark A. Nichols ed., 4th ed., 1924) ("Taxes are the enforced proportional contributions from persons and property, levied by the state by virtue of its sovereignty for the support of government and for all public needs")).
8. *Id. See, e.g.*, Eiser Infrastructure Limited and Energia Solar Luxembourg S. v. Spain, Award, ICSID Case Nr. ARB/13/36, May 4, 2017 at para. 270.
9. *See* William Park, *Tax Arbitration and Investor Protection, in Investment Protection and the Energy Charter Treaty* 118 (Graham Coop and Clarisse Ribeiro eds., 2008).
10. Case of the Norwegian Claims Against the United States (1922), 1 UN Rep. Int'l Arb. Awards 307, 343 (1922) (the tribunal determined that the Norwegian shipowners were entitled to "just compensation"). *See generally* Frank G. Dawson and Burns H. Weston, "*Prompt, Adequate and Effective*": *A Universal Standard for Compensation*, 30 Fordham L. Rev. 734-5 (1962) (discussing the Hull formula and the opposition to the Hull formula by Soviet scholars post-1917).
11. *See generally* The Lena Goldfields Arbitration, The Times (London), Sept. 3, 1930, p. 7 (publishing the award as read before the House of Commons). *See also id.* 12-13.
12. *See, e.g.*, V.V. Veeder, *The Lena Goldfields Arbitration: The Historical Roots of Three Ideas*, 47 Int'l & Comp. L.Q. 747, 748-50 (1998). *See also* V.V. Veeder, *Lloyd George, Lenin and Cannibals: The Harriman Arbitration: The 1999 Freshfields Lecture*, 16(2) Arb. Int'l 115, 116-18 (2000).

as legislative acts and policy initiatives.[13] Taxes, taxation measures and policy initiatives pertaining to taxation may not be deemed ultimately as direct takings. Measures having *the effect* of expropriation or nationalization are now recognized as constituting an important albeit inexact form of expropriation: indirect expropriation.

The inquiry into the effects of any given taxes may also be relevant for purposes of determining whether a breach has occurred with regard to other investment protection undertakings, such as the protection against non-discriminatory measures, ensuring that the fair and equitable treatment is afforded or that the investor enjoys the most-favored-nation (MFN) treatment[14] that would otherwise be afforded to others. In such manner, an evident point of tension emerges. On the one hand, the power to tax is inherently ingrained in the sovereignty of the state. On the other, the effects of the state's exercising its power to tax have a meaningful bearing on existing or potential investments. This tension is particularly acute in the context of energy matters where the state is called to take a proactive role at all levels of government and enjoys sovereignty over its natural resources.[15]

§1.02 A FLEDGING ECT DURING AN ENERGY CRISIS

These pressing concerns are of vital importance for examining the future of the energy sector with the ECT at the center of these inquiries. The ECT's purpose is to promote long-term cooperation in the energy field with a set of defined objectives focusing on trade, cooperation, and energy efficiency/environmental protection.[16] The ECT was developed thirty years ago, at the end of the Cold War, when geopolitical concerns differed greatly from those confronted by the energy sector today.

The vision for an energy treaty emerged during the meeting of the European Council in Dublin in June 1990 when the Dutch Prime Minister noted that economic recovery in the newly liberalized Eastern Europe and the soon to be former Soviet Union would benefit from cooperation in the energy sector.[17] The European Council welcomed the proposal and invited the Commission of the European Communities to investigate the best means to achieve greater cooperation in the energy sector affecting this group of states. A regime was adopted to attain equitable rules and regulations for the various private and state actors involved in the production, distribution and

13. *See* Burns H. Weston, *Constructive Takings under International Law: A Modest Foray into the Problem of Creeping Expropriation*, 16 Va. J. Int'l L. 103, 176 (1975).
14. For the origins of the MFN treatment and non-discrimination principle as developed in GATT/WTO jurisprudence, *see generally* Kaj Hobér, *WTO and Russia, in Contemporary Issues in International Arbitration and Mediation: The Fordham Papers 2014*, 223-51, 227-8 (Arthur W. Rovine ed., 2014).
15. *See, e.g.*, United Nations, Paris Agreement, Preamble (2015).
16. *See* ECT Art. 2 referring to the objectives and principles of the European Energy Charter. *See also* European Energy Charter, Title 1.
17. Final Act of the European Energy Charter Conference, *Background*, *in* the Energy Charter Secretariat, *The Energy Charter Treaty and Related Documents: A Legal Framework for International Energy Cooperation* 23 (2004).

consumption of energy resources.[18] The ECT's fundamental aim was "to strengthen the rule of law on energy issues, by creating a *level playing field* of rules to be observed by all participating governments, thus minimizing the risks associated with energy-related investments and trade."[19]

The ECT has, from the outset, witnessed its share of setbacks. Despite a highly active participation by the US in the drafting process of the ECT, the US delegation acceded to the 1991 European Energy Charter (EEC) but declined to sign the 1994 ECT in its original form, the 1994 Protocol on Energy Efficiency or the 1998 Amendment. The US delegation's main misgivings were with the "lack of sound, stable legal regimes to facilitate investment."[20] But, the US's statement of non-signing goes further than that.[21] By referring to the "devil in the details," the US position expressly referred to the discrepancies in the *taxation* measures as not being specific and clear enough to exclude state and local indirect taxes from the scope of the treaty as one of the reasons for non-signature.[22]

Considering the ECT's purpose to bring together on energy issues the two warring sides of the Cold War, the Russian decision to withdraw from the ECT offers an equaling telling lesson. In the case of the Russian withdrawal, tax considerations are even more determinative than the examples provided by the US on local taxations. Russia, after having signed but never ratified the ECT, withdrew from the ECT immediately after the three adverse *Yukos* ECT awards were rendered. The *Yukos* awards, which cumulatively are the largest award against a state in history, declined to view the Russian tax measures as bona fide exercises of the power to tax.

But the US and Russia are not alone in their criticism of the ECT and its tax provisions. In 2015, Italy withdrew from the ECT citing budgetary concerns, but in effect resulting from the wave of renewable energy cases that have similarly affected Spain and the Czech Republic.[23] The same cases witnessed tax issues to be a central matter in the disputes.

In other words, taxation issues matter. They matter for purposes of treaty accession, treaty withdrawal, and most importantly, the disputes arising in the energy context (renewable and non-renewable energy alike).

18. *See also* Andrey Konoplyanik, *A Common Russia–EU Energy Space: The New EU–Russia Partnership Agreement, Acquis Communitaire and the Energy Charter*, 27:2 J. Energy & Natural Resources 258-91, at 290 (2009).
19. Energy Charter Secretariat, *Explanatory Note, in The Energy Charter Treaty and Related Documents: A Legal Framework for International Energy Cooperation* (Energy Charter Secretariat ed., 2004) at 14 (emphasis added).
20. William Fox, *The United States and the Energy Charter Treaty: Misgivings and Misperceptions, in The Energy Charter Treaty: An East-West Gateway for Investment & Trade* 194-201, at 194, 197, 200-01 (Thomas W. Wälde ed., 1996). *Cf.* Kaj Hobér, *The Energy Charter Treaty: A Commentary* 58-9 (2020) (noting that "[f]or the United States it was important to be involved in the negotiations leading to the European Energy Charter and the ECT, and to monitor the development, so as not to leave the CIS market to West European countries and companies").
21. *See generally* Shaun Donnelly, *United States: Statement on the European Energy Charter Treaty*, I.L.M. 34:2 at 556-8 (Mar. 1995).
22. Fox, *supra* note 20, at 196-7 (discussing the State Department Position Paper, US Problems with the European Energy Charter Treaty Text (released in Lisbon on Dec. 16-17, 1994)).
23. *See* Kyriaki Karadelis, *Italy to Quit Energy Charter Treaty*, Global Arb. Rev., Apr. 23, 2015.

Despite any setbacks and shortcomings to meeting the goals set by the Paris Agreement, the ECT remains a vital treaty on energy in an age when energy and climate issues require future investments and considerable commitments by the states.[24] To achieve these aims, the adoption of the International Energy Charter (IEC) seeks to abandon the Cold War bipolar model of cooperation in favor of an inclusive approach. Recent Energy Charter Secretariat initiatives, as observed by the issuance of the Bucharest Declaration, sought to update and renew the investment protection regime so that it fits the needs and challenges of this century, including those resulting from the focus on renewable energy, incorporating the increased role of the European Union, and addressing the shifting geopolitical tides in the Middle East.[25]

Not only the ECT but also the investment arbitration regime has met considerable criticism from legal scholars and the public at large for overburdening developing economies. As such criticism goes, the developing states, which are already in dire conditions, are the ones bearing the lion's share of the investment disputes seemingly defending against opportunistic and onerous investment protections that often aim to circumvent domestic mechanisms without adequate representation of their interests among the decision-makers.[26] Although such overreaching criticism does have its degree of credence, not keeping states responsible for unlawful takings sets a highly dangerous precedent that carries ramifications for domestic policy and international law alike. On the one hand, private investors have been able to bring claims directly against states. On the other hand, states are increasingly more creative in the strategies they adopt to expropriate investments as noted in the *Yukos* disputes. Issues of taxation, particularly pertaining to energy and natural resources, rest at the center of the debate regarding the formal validity of the investment protection regime.

While there is considerable work on the state power to tax and on energy, there is little research on the intersection between the state power to tax, international investment energy law and dispute resolution. The late Professor Thomas Wälde of the University of Dundee spearheaded much of the early foundational research on the ECT, including on issues relating to dispute resolution and investment protection. Professor Wälde succeeded in bringing together different actors involved in the field and developing objective research on all facets of the ECT.[27] He highlighted that for a very complex field, international investment energy law has been subject to research with

24. For a critical position of ECT, *see generally* Sarah Keay-Bright and Steivan Defilla, *Energy Charter Treaty Review Should End Protection for Fossil Fuels*, Energy Post, Mar. 20, 2019 (Sarah Keay-Bright was previously the head of energy efficiency sector at the Energy Charter Secretariat, and Steivan Defilla was a former director of the Secretariat).
25. Energy Charter Conference, Bucharest Energy Charter Declaration, Nov. 27, 2018; https://energycharter.org/ (Accessed: May 30, 2020) [hereinafter the "Bucharest Declaration"].
26. *See generally* Michael Waibel et al., *the Backlash Against Investment Arbitrations: Perceptions and Reality, in the Backlash against Investment Arbitration* (Waibel et al. eds., 2010), xxxvii-li, at xl and xli-xlvii (discussing the "tenuous relationship" between FDI in developing countries and BITs as well as inadequate representation of developing countries as two main reasons for backlash). *See also* Kevin Gallagher and Elen Shresta *Investment Treaty Arbitration and Developing Countries: A Re-appraisal*, 12(6) J. Word Invest. & Trade 919-28.
27. *See generally* Andrey Konoplyanik, *Professor Wälde: In Memoriam of the Friend, in Liber Amicorum: Thomas Wälde Law Beyond Conventional Thought* 123-5 (Jacques Warner and Arif Ali eds., 2009).

too many important questions being left unresolved.[28] Taxation remains one of these issues.

The existing research is still limited to the ECT's past aims, but increasingly shifting toward the Treaty's future application. In fact, the rapid increase in the number of arbitrations in this specialized subject matter has defined the area as highly *dynamic* and particularly ideal for in-depth research, despite the uncertainty with the future of the ECT. Regardless of the long-term vision for the ECT, the current ECT taxation case law provides conclusive lessons in balancing the investor protections with the state power to tax for both improving the current regime, drafting future treaties, and developing tax-specific legislation, the starting inquiry being the ECT article covering taxation issues, ECT Article 21.

§1.03 THE TAXATION ARTICLE

ECT Article 21 ("Taxation Article" or "ECT Taxation Article") remains at the center of this book; the original text as below:

ARTICLE 21

TAXATION

(1) Except as otherwise provided in this Article, nothing in this Treaty shall create rights or impose obligations with respect to Taxation Measures of the Contracting Parties. In the event of any inconsistency between this Article and any other provision of the Treaty, this Article shall prevail to the extent of the inconsistency.

(2) Article 7(3) shall apply to Taxation Measures other than those on income or on capital, except that such provision shall not apply to:
   (a) an advantage accorded by a Contracting Party pursuant to the tax provisions of any convention, agreement or arrangement described in subparagraph (7)(a)(ii); or
   (b) any Taxation Measure aimed at ensuring the effective collection of taxes, except where the measure of a Contracting Party arbitrarily discriminates against Energy Materials and Products originating in, or destined for the Area of another Contracting Party or arbitrarily restricts benefits accorded under Article 7(3).

(3) Article 10(2) and (7) shall apply to Taxation Measures of the Contracting Parties other than those on income or on capital, except that such provisions shall not apply to:
   (a) impose most favoured nation obligations with respect to advantages accorded by a Contracting Party pursuant to the tax provisions of any convention, agreement or arrangement described in subparagraph (7)(a)(ii) or resulting from membership of any Regional Economic Integration Organization; or

28. Professor Wälde described the ECT's perception as "a complex instrument hermetically protected from easy access and understanding, and basically inaccessible to non-specialists." Thomas Wälde, *International Investment Under the 1994 Energy Charter Treaty, in The Energy Charter Treaty: An East-West Gateway for Investment & Trade* 268 (Thomas Wälde ed., 1996).

(b) any Taxation Measure aimed at ensuring the effective collection of taxes, except where the measure arbitrarily discriminates against an Investor of another Contracting Party or arbitrarily restricts benefits accorded under the Investment provisions of this Treaty.

(4) Article 29(2) to (6) shall apply to Taxation Measures other than those on income or on capital.

(5) (a) Article 13 shall apply to taxes.

(b) Whenever an issue arises under Article 13, to the extent it pertains to whether a tax constitutes an expropriation or whether a tax alleged to constitute an expropriation is discriminatory, the following provisions shall apply:

(i) The Investor or the Contracting Party alleging expropriation shall refer the issue of whether the tax is an expropriation or whether the tax is discriminatory to the relevant Competent Tax Authority. Failing such referral by the Investor or the Contracting Party, bodies called upon to settle disputes pursuant to Article 26(2)(c) or 27(2) shall make a referral to the relevant Competent Tax Authorities;

(ii) The Competent Tax Authorities shall, within a period of six months of such referral, strive to resolve the issues so referred. Where nondiscrimination issues are concerned, the Competent Tax Authorities shall apply the non-discrimination provisions of the relevant tax convention or, if there is no non-discrimination provision in the relevant tax convention applicable to the tax or no such tax convention is in force between the Contracting Parties concerned, they shall apply the non-discrimination principles under the Model Tax Convention on Income and Capital of the Organisation for Economic Co-operation and Development;

(iii) Bodies called upon to settle disputes pursuant to Article 26(2)(c) or 27(2) may take into account any conclusions arrived at by the Competent Tax Authorities regarding whether the tax is an expropriation. Such bodies shall take into account any conclusions arrived at within the six-month period prescribed in subparagraph (b)(ii) by the Competent Tax Authorities regarding whether the tax is discriminatory. Such bodies may also take into account any conclusions arrived at by the Competent Tax Authorities after the expiry of the six-month period;

(iv) Under no circumstances shall involvement of the Competent Tax Authorities, beyond the end of the six-month period referred to in subparagraph (b)(ii), lead to a delay of proceedings under Articles 26 and 27.

(6) For the avoidance of doubt, Article 14 shall not limit the right of a Contracting Party to impose or collect a tax by withholding or other means.

(7) For the purposes of this Article:

(a) The term "Taxation Measure" includes:

(i) any provision relating to taxes of the domestic law of the Contracting Party or of a political subdivision thereof or a local authority therein;
and

(ii) any provision relating to taxes of any convention for the avoidance of double taxation or of any other international agreement or arrangement by which the Contracting Party is bound.

(b) There shall be regarded as taxes on income or on capital all taxes imposed on total income, on total capital or on elements of income or of capital, including taxes on gains from the alienation of property, taxes on estates, inheritances and gifts, or substantially similar taxes, taxes on the total amounts of wages or salaries paid by enterprises, as well as taxes on capital appreciation.

(c) A "Competent Tax Authority" means the competent authority pursuant to a double taxation agreement in force between the Contracting Parties or, when no such agreement is in force, the minister or ministry responsible for taxes or their authorized representatives.

(d) For the avoidance of doubt, the terms "tax provisions" and "taxes" do not include customs duties.

§1.04 THE ORIGINS AND THE GOALS OF THE INQUIRY

The book has been inspired by two sources:

(1) the *Yukos* ECT case that, incidentally as of February 2020, is back in the public light after the Hague Court of Appeal reversed the lower court's ruling setting aside the final award by addressing specifically the Taxation Article;[29] and

(2) the statements of the late Professor Thomas Wälde, who in the 2008 plenary lecture before the American Society for International Law, called for a systematization of the red flags arising from the conduct of the state in taxation matters viewed against investment protection mechanisms.[30]

Based on these two originating factors, the book sets out three goals:

(1) to review and map out existing case law and scholarly work pertaining to the treatment of tax measures in the context of energy disputes with a focus on the ECT cases;

(2) to evaluate the limits to the state's power to tax as the states address current challenges for the energy sector, and

(3) to develop new initiatives for the future so as to offer a useful instrument for states in drawing their taxation policy and investment incentives.

29. *Yukos* Award, para. 43; Yukos Universal Limited v. the Russian Federation, Interim Award on Jurisdiction, PCA Case No. AA 227, Nov. 30, 2009 [hereinafter "*Yukos* Decision on Jurisdiction"]. Case C/09/477160/HA ZA 15-1 (Neth.), Hague District Court, Apr. 20, 2016, paras. 5.4-5.98 [hereinafter the "*Yukos* District Court Judgment"]. Hague Court of Appeal (Gerechtshof Den Haag) (Neth.), Case nr. 200.197.079/01, Judgment, Feb. 18, 2020; rev.d *Yukos* District Court Judgment, paras. 9.2.1, 9.3.2, 9.9 [hereinafter the "*Yukos* Court of Appeal Judgment"].

30. Thomas Wälde, *National Tax Measures Affecting Foreign Investors Under the Discipline of International Investment Treaties*, Proceedings of the Annual Meeting, Am. Soc'y Int'l L. Proc., vol. 102. Apr. 9-12, 2008 at 59.

§1.05 THE RESEARCH QUESTION, THE FIVE SUB-INQUIRIES AND THE ADOPTED INDUCTIVE APPROACH

In addressing these goals, this book sets out to answer one overarching research question:

What are the outer limits to the state power's power to tax in investment arbitration when reviewed expressly in the context of the energy disputes and the ECT?

The inquiry will address whether a balance may be discerned between, on the one hand, a state's unrestricted power to tax and, on the other hand, the investors' expectations in having their investments protected as these relate to the energy sector. In addressing this main question, this book will progressively answer the following five sub-inquiries in the following chapters:

(1) What are the origins of the ECT and specifically the Taxation Article?
(2) What are the key elements of a tax and how have they materialized in the first investment cases?
(3) What is the formal structure of the ECT Taxation Article and are there means to systematize the various elements of the Taxation Article and the taxation articles of other investment treaties?
(4) How do taxation provisions interplay with substantive standards of investment protection, as reviewed by international arbitral tribunals, in the ECT and other energy-related international instruments? In particular, how has the *Yukos* arbitration changed the framework of taxation issues in investment arbitration and what have been some of the lessons for the states? On the basis of the existing ECT case law, are there any emergent points of tension in the national and cross-border taxation regulatory measures that are energy and drawing on the additional BIT-related case, are these points of tension ECT-specific or as part of a particular pattern linked to taxation? If they are not ECT-specific, does the ECT and non-ECT (BIT) case law allow for the observed points of tension to be reconciled with regard to: (a) the consultation of domestic law and the (b) interplay between jurisdiction and merits in the context of the tax exclusion, inclusion, merits, and valuation review?
(5) May the points of tension arising out of the existing case law be streamlined to modernize the current language in the ECT, set out a benchmark for tax legislation against investment commitments, and further improve the taxation provisions in investment treaties?

In conducting the analysis, the book relies heavily on the four "distinct features" of the inductive approach to international law:[31]

31. *See generally* Georg Schwarzenberger, *The Inductive Approach to International Law* (1965). *See also* Georg Schwarzenberger, *The Inductive Approach to International Law*, 60(4) Harv. L. Rev. 539-70 (1947). NB: Despite both the book and the articles having the same titles, it is the book that is being referenced below as per italicized text.

(1) reliance on the "near-universality" of Article 38 of the Statute of the World Court;[32]
(2) evidence of the "means for the determination of rules of law" by various agencies and institutions bearing an effect on the development of the particular rule;[33]
(3) assumption that "the rules of international law [are] the only binding norms of international law unless evidence is forthcoming that a principle, which has been abstracted from such rules, has itself acquired the character of an overriding rule";[34] and
(4) awareness of the existing variations in the application of international law when reviewed in different contexts and organization levels of the international society (unorganized, partly organized and fully organized).[35]

While remaining within the confines of the International Court of Justice (ICJ) Statute of Article 38(1) reflecting the status of arbitral decisions as "subsidiary means of determination of rules of law," the review of the case law remains cognizant of the increasing role precedent carries in investment law: whether it is assessing a *jurisprudence constante* or arguably even making new law by means of interpretation of open-ended principles embossed in the bilateral investment treaties (BITs).[36]

Careful attention is attributed to *treaty practice* and specifically the conscious choice that states make in drafting typical formulations for purposes of defining long-range interests that are jointly accepted and may be further adopted on the basis of reciprocity.[37] Whenever matters of treaty interpretation arise, this book's methodology relies heavily on the Vienna Convention on the Law of the Treaties (VCLT).[38] The aim of the analysis below is to interpret the provisions of ECT Article 21 governing the state's power to tax in accordance with VCLT Articles 31(1) and 33.[39] Treaties are

32. Schwarzenberger 1965, *supra* note 31, at 5 and 19.
33. *Id.* 5 and 19-22.
34. *Id.* 5 and 85-97.
35. *Id.* 6, 165-92.
36. *See generally* Stephan Schill, *Sources of International Investment Law*, *in The Oxford Handbook of the Sources of International Law* 1095-115, at 1103-5 (Samantha Besson and Jean d'Aspremont eds., 2017) (discussing the shift in burden of proof when departing from "established precedent" and "the role of investment tribunals as law-makers" when interpreting "vague and open-ended principles ... such as FET, full protection and security, indirect expropriation, or national treatment, into concrete rules that limit how executive, legislator, and judiciary in host States ought to conduct themselves in relation to foreign investors").
37. Schwarzenberger 1965, *supra* note 31, at 33.
38. United Nations, *Vienna Convention on the Law of Treaties*, May 23, 1969, U.N.T.S., vol. 1155, p. 331, Art. 31(1) [hereinafter "VCLT"].
39. Although VCLT remains the premier instrument for treaty interpretation, several major jurisdictions, including the United States (US), have not ratified the treaty. *See, e.g.*, Commentary to the Restatement (Fourth) of Foreign Relations Law: Jurisdiction Treaties § 106 Tentative Draft No 2 (2017), Oct. 2017 Update. *See also* Evan Criddle, *The Vienna Convention on the Law of Treaties in U.S. Treaty Interpretation*, Virginia J. Int'l L. 44:2 at 433-4 (2004). Recent drafting of the Restatement of the Foreign Relations Law has sought to align the US federal jurisprudence to the VCLT mechanisms. *See* Restatement (Fourth) of Foreign Relations Law: Jurisdiction Treaties § 106 Tentative Draft No 2 (2017), Oct. 2017 Update. *See also* VCLT Art. 33.

reviewed critically under the assumption that they incorporate and reflect a sense of multilateralism.[40]

§1.06 DATA: ECT AWARDS, OTHER DOCUMENTS, AND NATIONAL LEGISLATION

In terms of research materials and data, the book relies on the compilation of agreements and protocols constituting the ECT, the legislative history, and arbitral and court decisions arising from 129 pending or completed arbitration cases under the ECT. These are all known and pending cases as of March 15, 2020. In addition, the book examines non-ECT Cases that are closely reflected in the ECT practice. For ECT cases, the reviewed documents include a total of 104 awards and court decisions covering 40 concluded ECT tax-related arbitrations or arbitrations with a decision on merits, 92 arbitration orders and awards. The book has also reviewed the thirty-seven drafts leading to the current version of the ECT, which are publicly available, together with the respective volumes of the *travaux* available at the ECT Secretariat. For non-ECT cases, thirty cases, twenty-eight involving Ecuador and two involving Russia, were evaluated. Three BITs (Canada-Ecuador, US-Ecuador and Denmark-Russia), which have influenced heavily the ECT jurisprudence, are discussed in detail. The book relies on data from the United Nations Conference on Trade and Development (UNCTAD)'s Investment Policy Hub for purposes of reviewing cumulative existing and terminated BITs, including analyzing their tax provisions.

§1.07 DELIMITATIONS: DOUBLE TAXATION, COMPETITION ISSUES AND TRANSIT OUTSIDE THE SCOPE OF THIS STUDY

The book examines the treatment of taxation measures under the ECT and other related bilateral instruments pertaining to energy. The state's power to tax is then discussed in the context of the contravening commitments of the state to guarantee certain measures of protection to investors. It does not aim to provide a comprehensive review of taxation and arbitration as two separate subjects. For this reason, the study sets out three main delimitations: double taxation, EU and competition law, and transit falling outside the scope of this inquiry. For the first limitation, the growing body of literature in the context of DTTs focuses on ensuring adequate protections from double or multiple taxation at the national level. Some mechanisms, such as the referral to the competent tax authorities (CTA), originate from DTTs; however, this book treats investment arbitration and tax arbitrations as two separate subjects where the later falls outside the scope of the inquiry. For the second limitation, the book does not delve

40. Schill, *supra* note 36, at 1095-115 and 1100-01.

into EU law as a general inquiry or the additional mechanisms derived from prohibitions against state aid, whether at the EU level or otherwise, nor on the interrelationship between tax and state aid, which may materialize in recent intra-EU disputes.[41] For the third limitation, the book will similarly not examine issues affecting transit, which have already been subject to separate academic research,[42] and trigger a distinct set of practices falling outside of the inquiry of the investment arbitration regime, outside of the inquiry of the crossover between energy and investment protection.

§1.08 STRUCTURE

To answer the research question, this book addresses the seven sub-inquiries in respective chapters. In Chapter 2, it examines the background to the ECT and the ECT Taxation Article. Chapter 3 addresses the essential elements of a tax and how tax-related issues materialized in the early arbitrations. In Chapter 4, the work delves into the ECT Taxation Article and develops a catalog system for taxation provisions. In Chapter 5, the discussion turns to the existing case law with a detailed analysis of the select BIT tax-related cases and ECT case law and a consolidation of the unifying issues pertaining to taxation matters: power to tax, limitations to such power, procedural issues, definitional concerns, and the scope of the individual provisions. Chapter 6 draws on the lessons learnt to identify best practices and offer solutions for legislators and treaty negotiators. Chapter 7 concludes the book with the answer to the research question by means of answering each sub-inquiry and summarizing the driving concerns for future points of inquiry on the implications of the outer limits to the state power to tax.

41. *See generally* Ioan Micula, Viorel Micula, S.C. European Food S.A, S.C. Starmill S.R.L. and S.C. Multipack S.R.L. v. Romania, ICSID Case No. ARB/05/20. *See also* Jerome Monsenego, *Selectivity in State Aid Law and the Methods for the Allocation of the Corporate Tax Base* (Wolters Kluwer 2018). Against the background of *Achmea*, the intra-EU jurisdictional objection has been universally denied in ECT case law. *See, e.g.*, Rockhopper Italia S.p.A, Rockhopper Mediterrane and Ltd and Rockhopper Exploration plc v. Italian Republic, Decision on the Intra-EU Jurisdictional Objection, ICSID Case No. ARB/17/14, June 26, 2019, paras. 152-75. *See also OperaFund* Award, paras. 378-88 and Vattenfall et al v. Germany, Decision on the *Achmea* issue, ICSID Case no. ARB/12/12, Aug. 31, 2018, paras. 92-231. On issues of taxation, the EU Member States have delegated, for their most part, their competency to the European Union on narrow matters, primarily linked to *indirect* taxes that may be deemed to affect free movement of goods and supply of services that fall within the scope of the EU. *See generally* TFEU Art. 113 and CFEU Art. 17 ("No one may be deprived of his or her possessions, except in the public interest and in the cases and under the conditions provided for by law, subject to fair compensation being paid in good time for their loss").

42. *See, e.g.*, Katja Yafimava, *The Transit Dimension of EU Energy Security: Importance of Russian Gas Transit Across Ukraine, Belarus, and Moldova* (2011).

CHAPTER 2
The Energy Charter Treaty and Its Provisions on the State's Power to Tax

§2.01 GENERAL

In exploring the proper balance between the state power to tax and investment protection, the sub-inquiry of this chapter focuses on the *origins* of the ECT (or "Treaty") and specifically those of the Taxation Article. It further inquires into how the historical origins of the ECT and the Taxation Article correlate to the tension between the two conflicting forces: the power to tax and investment protection obligations.

§2.02 EMERGENCE OF THE ECT

[A] ECT Against Other Investment Protection Mechanisms of Its Day

The ECT and specifically the Taxation Article are better understood against the Treaty's historical background. The ECT emerged from the last vestiges of the Cold War when it became apparent that meaningful cooperation between Eastern and Western Europe on matters relating to energy was attainable. In the late 1980s, Russia and the former Eastern Bloc were in desperate need of foreign direct investment (FDI) while being rich in natural resources.[43] Western Europe, in turn, required energy resources aimed at diversifying its sources of energy and possessed the financial resources to make

43. Lubbers Memorandum, *supra* note 4, at 2 (highlighting that "many possibilities" exist on the production side in Russia and Central and Eastern Europe but that there is a "desperate need of capital and technology" in these countries). *See also* James P. Dorian and Eugene M. Khartukov, *International Oil and Gas Investment in the CIS States, in The Energy Charter Treaty: an East-West Gateway for Investment & Trade* 37-51 (Thomas W. Wälde ed., 1996).

long-term investments. This combination between supply and demand for both investment and energy served as the primary catalyst for the ECT.[44]

ECT's emergence resembles a prolonged accretion due to the maturation of public international law and the consolidation of geopolitical forces, rather than a sudden burst.[45] The EEC, which served as the ECT's foundation, was signed on December 17, 1991.[46] It was one of the first international undertakings entered into by the Russian Federation as a new state. For many former Soviet Republics, it was the first internationally agreed treaty as independent entities.[47] The run-up process to the negotiation of the ECT finds its roots in the investment protection regime movement shaped to a great extent by the post-World War II BITs.[48] Following World War II, the world witnessed an increase in trade and investment.[49] The trade regime developed in parallel a regime of bilateral and multilateral treaties that gradually incorporated provisions on protection of property and guarantees to do business in the given states.[50]

The early 1990s witnessed several multilateral investment initiatives, some successful and some less so.[51] These initiatives built on the initial agreements that protected trade. A separate set of agreements emerged providing for protection of

44. Energy Charter Secretariat, The Energy Charter Treaty and Related Documents: A Legal Framework for International Energy Cooperation, Introduction, p. 13. The solution has been described as a "win-win" for all. *See also* Kaj Hobér, Investment Arbitration and the Energy Charter Treaty, 1 J. Int'l Dispute Settlement 153-90, 154 (2010). *See* Julia Doré, *Negotiating the Energy Charter Treaty, in The Energy Charter Treaty: An East-West Gateway for Investment & Trade* 138 (Thomas W. Wälde ed., 1996) (referring to "the general euphoria of the opening of Eastern Europe" in which the "Lubbers Plan" was discussed that was "in the interest of all sides"). *See also* Crina Baltag, *The Energy Charter Treaty: The Notion of Investor* 8-9 (2012).
45. *See generally* Lubbers Memorandum, *supra* note 4, at 1. The impact of the recession caused by the energy crisis of 1970s and the subsequent fluctuations in the energy market were considerable concerns in the early 1990s. For a comprehensive review of the energy problem in the 1990s, *see* Robert Marbro, a Dialogue Between Oil Producers and Consumers: the Why and the How, Oxford Institute for Energy Studies, 1992; https://www.oxfordenergy.org/(Accessed: May 30, 2020). Jeswald W. Salacuse, *The Energy Charter Treaty and Bilateral Investment Treaty Regimes, in The Energy Charter Treaty: An East-West Gateway for Investment & Trade* 321-3 (Thomas W. Wälde ed., 1996).
46. Concluding Documents of the Hague Conference on the European Energy Charter, Dec. 16-17, 1991, in The Energy Charter Treaty and Related Documents: A Legal Framework for International Energy Cooperation 209-21 (Energy Charter Secretariat ed., 2004) [hereinafter the "Energy Charter"].
47. *See generally* Andrei A. Konoplyanik and Friedrich von Halem, *The Energy Charter Treaty: A Russian Perspective, in The Energy Charter Treaty: An East-West Gateway for Investment & Trade* 156-78, 165 (Thomas W. Wälde ed., 1996).
48. Salacuse, *supra* note 45, at 321 (quoting IEA Chief Legal Counsel to say that the investment protection provisions in the ECT "resemble provisions in bilateral investment treaties although their draft has not been based on any single negotiating party's treaty practice"). *See* Craig S. Bamberger, *The Energy Charter Treaty—A Description of Its Provisions* 15 (OECD 1994).
49. *See, e.g.*, World Trade Organization, World Trade Report 2013 at 55; http://www.wto.org (Accessed: May 30, 2020).
50. *See* Salacuse, *supra* note 45, at 323 (discussing the US perspective and particularly how the bilateral investment treaties find their roots in the treaties of friendship, commerce, and navigation).
51. *See, e.g.*, United States Trade Representative, Request for Comments on Negotiating Objectives Regarding Modernization of the North American Free Trade Agreement With Canada and Mexico, 82 FR 23699, May 23, 2017; http://www.federalregister.gov (Accessed: May 30, 2020).

investments and, uniquely and perhaps unappreciated at the time, the opportunity of investors to enforce such rights against the states by means of international arbitration.[52]

The North American Treaty Agreement (NAFTA) and the Multilateral Agreement on Investment (MAI) are two examples from the early 1990s with different track records. The NAFTA was an example of a successful multilateral initiative covering a specific geographic scope, that is, North America. NAFTA entered into force on January 1, 1994, covering only three countries (US, Canada, and Mexico) but applying to a broad set of operations without a sector-specific limitation like energy in the case of the ECT. USMCA replaces NAFTA while retaining the investor-state dispute settlement (ISDS) provisions in a revised form despite criticism from the public.[53] MAI was an unsuccessful initiative to cover investment matters. Arising in the move to codify existing practice, MAI aimed at uniformly covering all investments across sectors and across a broad geographic base. It served as an uncompleted example of multilateral investment initiative, as negotiations ceased when the host state, France, expressed its intent not to support the project.[54] In the current discussion of finding multilateral initiatives, MAI provides a stark reminder of the difficulties involved in reaching consensus among many actors on what constitutes adequate protection for foreign investments.

While covering investment protections, both NAFTA and MAI contain taxation commitments with similar structures. NAFTA set out specific and detailed obligations on the application of the taxation exception.[55] The structure of MAI was slightly less complex, and even in the negotiation stages it adopted a carve-out and a clawback similar to the provisions in the ECT.[56]

Signed on December 17, 1994, in Lisbon, the ECT differed from existing bilateral treaties in being multilateral in nature and covering a specific sector, that is, "energy" (Figure 2.1).

52. Asian Agricultural Products Ltd v. Republic of Sri Lanka, 6 ICSID Review FILJ 526 (1991; 30 ILM 577 (1991). *See generally* Jan Paulsson, *Arbitration Without Privity, in The Energy Charter Treaty: an East-West Gateway for Investment & Trade* 422-3 and 425-9 (Thomas W. Wälde ed., 1996).

53. North American Free Trade Agreement, 32 I.L.M. 289, Preamble (1993) [hereinafter "NAFTA"]. Agreement between the United States of America, the United Mexican States, and Canada ("USMCA") became effective on July 1, 2020. *See* Office of the U.S. Trade Rep., Exec. Office of the President, United-States-Mexico-Canada Agreement Text (2020), Dec. 13, 2019 text; available at https://ustr.gov/ [hereinafter "USMCA"]. *Compare* USMCA Chap. 14 *with* NAFTA Chap. 11. For general ISDS criticism in the USMCA negotiations, *see, e.g.*, Tom Jones, *Academics Urge Trump to Ditch ISDS in NAFTA*, Global Arb. Rev., Oct. 27, 2017.

54. MAI was the product of the negotiations of the Organisation for the Economic Co-operation and Development (OECD) between 1995 and 1998. The negotiations ceased in December 1998. Rudolph Dolzer and Christoph Schreuer, *Principles of International Investment Law* 10 (2nd ed., 2012).

55. NAFTA Art. 2103.

56. OECD, the Multilateral Agreement on Investment, MAI Negotiating Text, Apr. 24, 1998, Chap. VIII; http://www.italaw.com (Accessed: May 30, 2020). *See also* OECD, the Multilateral Agreement on Investment, Report by the Chairman of the Negotiating Group, DAFFE/MAI(98) /17, May 4, 1998, at 46; http://www.oecd.org (Accessed: May 30, 2020).

Figure 2.1 Sectoral and Geographic Coverage of Various Treaties, Including ECT, on Energy Matters

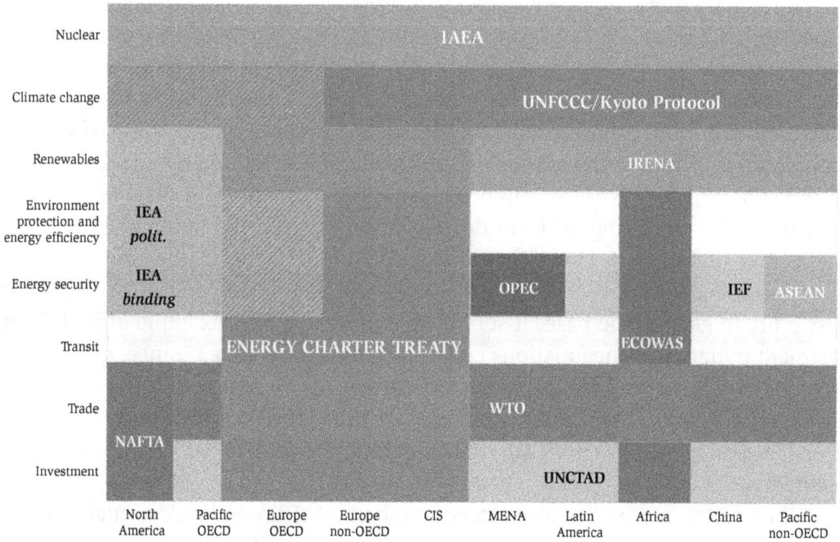

Source: Author's Own.

Abbreviations:
IAEA: International Atomic Energy Agency
IRENA: International Renewable Energy Agency
IEF: International Energy Forum
ASEAN: Association of Southeast Asian Nations
ECOWAS: Economic Community of West African States
UNFCCC: United Nations Framework Convention on Climate Change
polit.: political (non-binding)
Source: Energy Charter Secretariat, reproduced with permission from the ECT Secretariat.

Besides the highly criticized ISDS article, the ECT contains provisions on a wide range of operations and energy-related matters, including transit, trade, energy security and environmental protection.[57] The ECT has a wide geographic application given its fifty-four members, including the EU and European Atomic Energy Community (EURATOM), from both Organisation for Economic Co-operation and Development (OECD) and non-OECD Member States.[58] An additional forty-two members are observers, including the US and China.[59] ECT's scope of application overlaps with other

57. *See* Figure 2.1 (reproduced also in Irina Pominova, "Risks and Benefits for the Russian Federation from Participating in the Energy Charter: Comprehensive Analysis," Energy Charter Secretariat Knowledge Center 2014).
58. As of Feb. 18, 2019; *see generally* Energy Charter Secretariat. Members and Observers to the Energy Charter Conference; http://energycharter.org (Accessed: May 30, 2020). Cf. The Secretary-General of ECT Secretariat addressed the misconceptions that "the ECT is only

treaties and organizations, including International Renewable Energy Association (IRENA), International Energy Agency (IEA) and World Trade Organization (WTO). But perhaps what makes the ECT particularly noteworthy is its broad scope of application covering the energy sector and the multilateral investment protection regime.

Considering its origins of bridging the bipolarity of the Cold War, the ECT carries the "universal scope" of binding all Contracting States.[60] In such manner, states could face a claim along the lines of the highly debated NAFTA provisions.[61] What was noteworthy was the Western states could be the subject of a lawsuit, a fact that Professor Wälde argued in 1995 was "certainly not intended when the Charter Process was started by the European Community" and "has not been fully appreciated."[62] As the energy sector involves state sovereignty over natural resources and complex chains and capital-intensive investments for the exploration of such resources, investment protection mechanisms such as bilateral treaties and the dispute resolution mechanism in said treaties play a critical role in the sector.

[B] The Historical Context That Gave Rise to the ECT

What started in 1991 as an initiative to bring the East and West together in terms of energy has morphed into something different than what was once envisioned. Early on, the initiative focused on linking Russia and former Soviet Republic's energy resources to the Western markets. Yet, at the time of the signing in 1994, some critical states such as the US, Norway and Russia abstained from signing or ratifying the treaty. Additional initiatives have been drawn to improve the treaty, but those initiatives failed short of addressing the fundamental reservation that the US had on the level of investment protection and the binding obligations of the treaty.

It soon became clear in the negotiation process that the path would be lengthy for the Russian Federation to align with its Western counterparts on investment protection. The negotiating states drafted the ECT with the aim of having it applied to "fully developed market econom[ies]" even when Russia and the remaining Soviet Blocs

applicable to a particular geographic area" by highlighting that: (1) "from the beginning it was designed as a truly global framework without geographical restraints" and (2) the International Energy Charter declaration has "expand[ed] to states in South and East Asia, Latin America and Africa." Cara Downing, Discussing the Energy Charter Treaty—Q&A with Dr Urban Rusnák, Secretary-General, Energy Charter Treaty Secretariat, Norton Rose Fulbright, Oct. 2018; available at: https://www.nortonrosefulbright.com/ (Accessed: May 30, 2020).

59. Energy Charter Secretariat. Members and Observers to the Energy Charter Conference; http://energycharter.org (Accessed: May 30, 2020).
60. *See generally* Thomas Wälde, *International Investment under the 1994 Energy Charter Treaty, in The Energy Charter Treaty: An East-West Gateway for Investment & Trade* 252 (Thomas Wälde ed., 1996).
61. *See, e.g.*, Eiser Infrastructure Limited and Energia Solar Luxembourg S.à.r.l. v. Spain, Award, ICSID Case No. ARB/13/36, May 4, 2017, where the two corporate investors were incorporated in England and Luxembourg, respectively, and the respondent was the Kingdom of Spain, both Western countries.
62. *See generally* Wälde, *supra* note 60, at 252.

faced a lengthy path to reach such a threshold.[63] As Russia was not a member of the General Agreement on Tariffs and Trade (GATT), the Western countries proposed a "two-level approach": where GATT Rules would apply to GATT Member States and a distinct separate regime would apply to non-GATT Member States.[64] The US insisted on a "roll-back principle," which was the basis of NAFTA, where non-conforming measures are gradually phased out after several years in place.[65] In stark contrast, Russia insisted on a "standstill" principle where the exceptions provided by the international agreement would be deemed closed.[66] Several compromises were reached to draw Russia into the signing of the Treaty. Eventually, the Russian Federation signed the ECT but stopped short of its ratification for reasons linked to the finalization of the additional protocols.

The issue took a dramatic turn when the former shareholders of Yukos brought claims against Russia, invoking the ECT investment protection provisions of the ECT. The Russian Federation's defense built on the argument that the state was not subject to the ECT because it did not ratify the treaty and the provisional application of the Treaty did not apply.[67] This defense was not successful in the arbitration[68] but it gave grounds to set aside the award in the Hague District Court.[69] In connection to the tribunal delivering an unfavorable jurisdictional decision, the Russian Federation withdrew from the application of the Treaty, by formally invoking ECT Article 45(3) covering provisional application.[70] But as found by the arbitral tribunal, the Russian Federation remains bound by the substantive provisions of the treaty for a period of twenty years.[71]

By the late 2000s, a critical sentiment *against* an ISDS regime began permeating the public debate.[72] Countries such as Spain, Italy, and the Czech Republic rolled back state-sponsored subsidies and incentives intended to promote investments in the renewable energy sector. In a similar turn of events, Italy had withdrawn from the ECT citing budgetary reasons. Considering though that Italy's contributions to the ECT Secretariat are nominal against its national budget, the actual reason for Italy's withdrawal from the ECT seems linked to other factors (e.g. the avoidance of further liability from the renewable energy disputes).[73] Much like Italy, Spain is now exposed to considerable pressure to evaluate its ECT commitments. After Spain lost an

---

63. *See* Konoplyanik and von Halem, *supra* note 47, at 175.
64. *Id.* 168.
65. *Id.* 172. *See* Sébastien Miroudot, *Investment, in Preferential Trade Agreement Policies for Development: A Handbook* 314 (Jean-Pierre Chauffour and Jean-Christophe Maur eds., 2011).
66. Konoplyanik and von Halem, *supra* note 47, at 175.
67. *Yukos* Decision on Jurisdiction, paras. 244-398.
68. *Id.* paras. 393-8.
69. Case C/09/477160/HA ZA 15-1, Apr. 20, 2016, Hague District Court, paras. 5.4-5.98.
70. *See* Energy Charter Treaty, Art. 45(3). *See also* Alison Ross, *Russian Withdrawals from Energy Charter Treaty*, Global Arb. Rev., Aug. 7, 2009.
71. *See* ECT Art. 45(3). *Yukos* Decision on Jurisdiction, paras. 339-45.
72. *See generally* Louis T. Wells, *Backlash to Investment Arbitration: Three Causes, in The Backlash Against Investment Arbitration* 341-52 (Michael Waibel, Asha Kaushal et al. eds., 2010).
73. *Italy to quit Energy Charter Treaty*, Global Arb. Rev., Apr. 23, 2015. *See also* MENA Chambers, Note 12—Italy's Withdrawal from the Energy Charter Treaty, May 5, 2015; http://www.menachambers.com (Accessed: Jan. 1, 2017).

arbitration, the European Commission instructed Spain not to pay out the order as paying the award would contradict intra-EU competency, argued vehemently as a defense.[74]

Against this backdrop, the Energy Charter Conference sought the modernization of the ECT to be in line with the aims and objectives of the twenty-first century. Under the initiative of the IEC, a non-binding commitment has been reached of moving toward finding solutions to amending the ECT to meet the current challenges. The new initiative moves away from reflecting the ECT as a by-product of the Cold War. It sees the US back at the negotiation table. In the aftermath of *Yukos*, the Russian Federation is notably absent from the discussions and the future of the ECT remains uncertain.[75]

§2.03 KEY DATES

Given the rich and complex negotiation history leading to the signing of the ECT, the elements of the treaty need to be outlined:

- June 25-26, 1990: Lubbers Memorandum.
- December 17, 1991: European Energy Charter adopted in the Concluding Document of the Hague Conference on the European Energy Charter signed at The Hague during the Hague Session on December 16-17, 1991 ("Hague I"). December 17, 1994. Final Act of the European Energy Charter Conference, as opened for signature in Lisbon on December 17, 1994, and corrected by the Protocol of Correction of August 2, 1996, included the final version of the ECT.
- April 16, 1998: ECT entered into force.
- April 16, 1998: Energy Charter Protocol on Energy Efficiency and Related Environmental Aspects (PEERA) entered into force.
- April 24, 1998: Final Act of the International Conference and Decision by the Energy Charter Conference in respect of the Amendment to the Trade-Related Provisions of the ECT entered into force on January 21, 2010.
- May 20, 2015: IEC signed at The Hague ("Hague II").

The ECT timeline may be divided into several stages. For purposes of this analysis, five stages are drawn out:[76]

74. Douglas Thompson, *EU Warns Spain Not to Pay Solar Awards*, Global Arb. Rev., Jan. 19, 2018 (discussing the decision by the European Commission finding that the actions of Spain were compatible with European legislation on state aid). *See* European Commission, Reasoned Decision on State Aid SA.40348 (2015/NN), C(2017) final, Nov. 10, 2017.
75. *See generally* Ina Kotova, *A Treaty à la Carte? Some Reflections on the Modernization of the Energy Charter Process*, 9 J. World Energy L. & Bus. 359 (2016).
76. *Cf.* Johann Robert Basedow, *The EU in the Global Investment Regime: Commission Entrepreneurship, Incremental Institutional Change and Business Lethargy* Chapter 6 (Routledge, 2017) (discussing four stages of the negotiation process). *See also* Fox, *supra* note William Fox, *The United States and the Energy Charter Treaty: Misgivings and Misperceptions, in The Energy Charter Treaty: an East-West Gateway for Investment & Trade* 194-201, at 200 (Thomas W. Wälde ed., 1996) (discussing that it was questionable whether the US will participate in the second-stage Treaty negotiations intended to cover all actions after Dec. 17, 1991). *See* Doré,

(1) Pre-negotiation phase to the European Energy Charter capturing the major geopolitical forces and individual initiatives, including the "Lubbers Plan," as well as the international instruments covering the end of hostilities of the Cold War and the commencement of closer collaboration, such as the Paris Charter, Bonn Declaration and the Sofia (pre-1991).
(2) The drafting and the signing of the European Energy Charter setting the objectives for the ECT (1991).
(3) The drafting of protocols and negotiation process of the ECT that included the drafting of the relevant protocols (1991-1994).
(4) The signing, correction and the immediate amendments to the ECT (commonly described as the after-stage in the negotiation process)[77] (1994-1998).
(5) The post-signing transformative stage: run-up, negotiation and the drafting of the IEC, including the work for next stages (1998-present).

§2.04 THE FIVE STAGES OF THE NEGOTIATION PROCESS

[A] The Lubbers Plan and the Pre-negotiation Phase

Several initiatives were made in the past to induce collaboration between the East and the West, including from the Soviet delegation in 1977 for the convocation of "an all-European conference on energy."[78] These were not so successful. More than a decade later, the ECT managed to change the energy landscape in part due to the timing being ripe for full collaboration with the West.

The ECT, in its current form, originated from the Memorandum of then Dutch Prime Minister, Ruud Lubbers, to the European Council session in Dublin on June 25-26, 1990.[79] The driving force behind the "Lubbers Memorandum" or the "Lubbers Plan" was "[the] concern for the long-term energy supply."[80]

The Lubbers Memorandum sets out three clear objectives for the European cooperation in the energy field: "environmental protection, guaranteed supplies and stable political relations."[81] It is easy to miss the environmental protection aim of the ECT, as early initiatives have not focused on this issue. However, as the Memorandum was drafted less than five years after the Chernobyl nuclear disaster, its emphasis also lay with environmental pollution and safety, particularly nuclear safety.[82] With the

---

supra note 44, at 138 (discussing two stages: (1) the first stage where interest in the "Lubbers Plan" was addressed and (2) the second stage where the states agreed on the European Energy Charter).

77. *See* Fox, *supra* note 20, at 200.
78. *See* Konoplyanik and Halem, *supra* note 47, at 156-7.
79. Final Act of the European Energy Charter Conference, *the Energy Charter Treaty and Related Documents: a Legal Framework for International Energy Cooperation* (Energy Charter Secretariat, 2014). *See also* Ruud Lubbers, *Foreword, in The Energy Charter Treaty: An East-West Gateway for Investment & Trade* xiii (Thomas W. Wälde ed., 1996).
80. Lubbers Memorandum, *supra* note 4, at 2. *See also* Konoplyanik and von Halem, *supra* note 47, at 156.
81. Lubbers Memorandum, *supra* note 4, at 2 and 7.
82. *See id.* 7 (noting "[w]hatever the case, it is important that we weigh up the advantages and disadvantages, taking account not only of the need for energy but also of the safety standards at

focus on "long-term energy supply," an emphasis on new forms of energy may be discerned[83] even when the technology for renewable was at least a decade from providing commercially sound solutions.

At its core, the Lubbers Plan was uniquely ambitious: it went beyond being a mere "progra[m] for modernization of [the] Soviet energy industries on the basis of international cooperation."[84] For all intents and purposes, the Lubbers Plan was a macroeconomic program aimed at stabilizing the former Soviet economy.[85] The Memorandum served as the platform for a high-level discussion among the UK, Germany, and Denmark heads of government. The European Council also invited the Commission of the European Communities ("European Commission") to investigate the means for a close cooperation between the East and West.[86]

The initiative attracted the support of the European Commission President Jacques Delors for the Conference on Security and Co-operation in Europe (CSCE) meeting in Paris in November 1990.[87] The meeting in Paris culminated in the Charter of Paris for a New Europe that served as an official declaration of the end of the Cold War.[88] The Charter of Paris set out in motion the unification tendencies for Eastern and Western Europe; it ensured pan-European and cross-border economic activity that would bring Europe closer together and thereby prevent the formation of any future "Berlin Walls."[89] In all, the Charter addressed a wide range of issues, including the cooperation on energy matters, as follows:

> We are determined to give the necessary impetus to co-operation among our States in the fields of energy, transport and tourism for economic and social development. We welcome, in particular, practical steps to create optimal conditions for the economic and rational development of energy resources, with due regard for environmental considerations.[90]

What followed in 1991 was the refining of the outline of the Lubbers Plan in the negotiations leading up to the signing of a Concluding Document of the Hague Conference on the European Energy Charter in December 1991 ("Hague I").[91] Although

existing nuclear power stations in Western, Central and Eastern Europe"). *See also* Nathalie L.J.T. Horbach, *Nuclear Protocol of the Energy Charter Treaty*, 13 *J. Energy Natural Res. L.* 163-4 (1995).

83. Horbach, *supra* note 82, at 164.
84. Andrei Konoplyanik, *Lubbers Plan: Soviet Energy as a Standpoint for Improving Economic Reforms in the USSR*, 13:3 Energy J. 281-94, 81-2 (1992).
85. *Id.*
86. Final Act of the European Energy Charter Conference, *the Energy Charter Treaty and Related Documents: A Legal Framework for International Energy Cooperation* (Energy Charter Secretariat ed., 2004).
87. *Id.* xv. *See also* the Energy Charter Treaty, Preamble at 39.
88. *See generally* Konoplyanik and von Halem, *supra* note 47, at 156-7.
89. *Id.* 157. The Lubbers Memorandum, too, contained a clear reference to the avoidance of future walls referencing the avoidance of any Berlin-type walls in the future. *See* Lubbers Memorandum, *supra* note 4, at 2.
90. *See* Conference on Security and Co-operation in Europe, Charter of Paris for a New Europe 9; http://www.osce.org/mc/39516 (Accessed: Oct. 31, 2019).
91. The Lubbers Memorandum proposed that the European Energy Community be granted "its own structure [...] with one possible structure would be in the form of a charter." Lubbers Memorandum, *supra* note 4, at 2.

non-binding in nature, the EEC set out the general objectives for a comprehensive treaty that would later become the ECT.[92] The ECT, which was finalized in December 1994 and entered into force in April 1998, appeared as an appendix to the Final Act of the Energy Charter Conference.[93]

[B] The EEC as the Foundational Document for the ECT

By the time the EEC was being negotiated and drafted, the tensions of the Cold War were fading. The Charter was initially designed and viewed as a European exercise but soon, under pressure from the US, it expanded to include all OECD countries, including non-European members.[94] Under a Spanish proposal, the Charter aimed to involve the states of North America, viewed as critical for the European energy framework.

The negotiations of the EEC took five months. The initiatory conference was held from July 15-17, 1991, and it involved all OECD members at the time of the agreement with the exception of South Korea and New Zealand. Additional countries, including Organization of the Petroleum Exporting Countries (OPEC) members and the Maghreb countries, appeared in an observer capacity during the initial conference.[95]

The EEC generated three main objectives that shaped the future ECT: (1) development of trade in energy consistent with major multilateral agreements; (2) cooperation in the energy field; and (3) energy efficiency and environmental protection.[96] For purposes of how to implement these objectives, the Charter focused on the need for states to "take coordinated action to achieve greater coherence of energy policies, which should be based on the principle of non-discrimination and on market-oriented price formation, taking due account of environmental concerns."[97] Such coordinated action was intended to be taken only within the limits of State sovereignty and sovereign rights over energy resources.[98]

Upon reviewing in retrospect the objectives and the means of implementation of the Charter, one deduces a general and ambitious framework for the Member States without particularly specific obligations. The Charter reads more like a memorandum of understanding than a binding instrument.[99] It set out possible areas of cooperation and committed states to negotiate in good faith a basic agreement and protocols on

92. Wälde, *supra* note 60, at 252.
93. *See* Final Act of the European Energy Charter Conference, *The Energy Charter Treaty and Related Documents: a Legal Framework for International Energy Cooperation* (Energy Charter Secretariat, 2004).
94. Doré, *supra* note 44, at 139-40.
95. *See also id.* 140.
96. Concluding Document of the Hague Conference on the European Energy Charter, Dec. 17, 1991, in Energy Charter Secretariat, The International Energy Charter Consolidated Energy Charter Treaty, 29-31 (2016); http://www.energycharter.org (Accessed: May 30, 2020).
97. *Id.* 31.
98. *Id.*
99. *Compare* Charter of the United Nations, June 26, 1945, 59 Stat. 1031, T.S. No. 933, 3 Bevans 1153 (entered into force on Oct. 24, 1945) *with* Memorandum of Understanding, Memorandum of Understanding on Exchange of Information in Matters Relating to Securities and Futures, Sept. 23, 1986, United States-United Kingdom, 25 I.L.M. 1431.

areas that would include *inter alia* horizontal and organizational issues, transportation, energy efficiency, transport of oil, and transfer of technology.[100] As the Charter served only as a non-binding instrument, what followed with the negotiations of the ECT greatly exceeded the complexity of the negotiations of the Charter.

[C] The Negotiations and Drafting of the ECT

[1] Binding Nature of the Treaty and the Matter of Protocols

From the moment the EEC was signed, it took precisely three years to agree on the terms of the ECT. Once the drafting process commenced, the ECT became a multifaceted and multitiered approach. As it sought to address the "new" realities of the early 1990s, it confronted the unchartered relationship between Russia, the former Soviet Republics, and the West on the issues of energy.

Even where the negotiations were multilateral, much attention was attributed to the Russian Federation and the US, which were the main players in this East-West undertaking.[101] Ironically, neither of these two countries currently adhere to the ECT in its current form. The US did not sign the ECT citing concerns of its non-binding obligation. The Russian Federation, having signed the treaty, withdrew from provisional application after the Yukos affair.[102] The ECT remains a complex and often maze-like international instrument due to its complex drafting history and ambitious goals.

The work on a first agreement was already in progress at the time of the signing of the EEC.[103] The Charter was concluded on December 17, 1991, and the most considerable structural modifications to the treaties came from the first to the second draft in September 1991 when the agreement itself was modified from a protocol to an actual agreement. By the time the Charter was concluded in December 1991, work had been progressing on a fourth draft that captured in essence the parties' obligations. In the course of three years, from the signing of the Charter to the completion of the Final Act that would constitute the actual ECT, twenty-seven distinct drafts were circulated modifying the respective chapters and capturing the broad undertakings by the Contracting States.

The ECT followed a parallel drafting process where the Treaty was being negotiated alongside several protocols covering issues pertaining to the nuclear sector, energy efficiency, and hydrocarbons.[104] Such approach ensured that the Treaty could

100. Concluding Document of the Hague Conference on the European Energy Charter, Dec. 17, 1991, in Energy Charter Secretariat, The International Energy Charter Consolidated Energy Charter Treaty, 34-5 (2016); http://www.energycharter.org (Accessed: May 30, 2020).
101. Fox, *supra* note 76, at 194-5. For the challenges and the priorities confronting the Russian delegation, *see* Konoplyanik and von Halem, *supra* note 47, at 165-6.
102. The Russian Federation remains bound by the ECT for the next twenty years in accordance with ECT Art. 45(3).
103. International Energy Agency, The Energy Charter Treaty: a Description of its Provisions, 1995.
104. *See generally* Doré, *supra* note 44, at 140-1.

be signed and that "key areas" were addressed.[105] Of these envisioned three protocols, only one, the protocol on energy efficiency, became a final document. Negotiations on a protocol for nuclear energy seized when it became clear that coverage of the sector would duplicate the work being done at the International Atomic Energy Agency (IAEA).[106] During the same period between 1991 and 1994, the IAEA prepared an international nuclear safety convention that covered "land-based civil nuclear power plants."[107]

Work on the hydrocarbon protocol was also suspended when it became clear that the issues covered by the protocol touched upon "fundamental principles" of the ECT that were ultimately best addressed in the body of the actual Treaty.[108] The hydrocarbon protocol triggered two issues on which opinion among drafters was divided and which eventually led to the suspension of the talks. First, the hydrocarbon protocol placed into the limelight the European initiative to introduce third-party access to pipelines on fair terms and conditions. The drive for such approach ultimately subsided after the ECT adopted an understanding to the treaty as a whole that Contracting States will not be mandated to provide third-party access.[109] Second, the actual protocol circulated by the Norwegian delegation, which presided over the working group, was prone to follow the objectives of the ECT per se closely.[110] Despite the early positive feedback on the drafts,[111] the hydrocarbon protocol was scrapped in part as it did not sufficiently address the principle of non-discrimination.[112] As the work on several protocols was either suspended or progressed in parallel, the attention turned to trade and transit of energy resources as key instruments of the treaty.

[2] Trade and Transit as Decisive Topics

On issues of trade, the ECT confronted a trying reality shaped by the difficulty of integrating Russia in the global regime. For starters, although the GATT Regime was in existence, Russia, a key player, sat outside the GATT block for the ECT. Second, the

105. *See* Horbach, *supra* note 82, 168.
106. Doré, *supra* note 44, at 140-1. Horbach, *supra* note 82, at 164-5 & 68. Work on the Vienna Nuclear Safety Convention did not commence until 1993, late in the drafting of the ECT's Nuclear Protocol. *Id.* 172.
107. Horbach, *supra* note 82, at 164.
108. *Id.* 142-3.
109. The Energy Charter Treaty, Understanding with Respect to the Treaty as a Whole, 2016, at 37. *See also* Doré, *supra* note 44, at 142.
110. Doré explains the position of the Norwegian delegation being shaped by its interests in the state-owned Statoil. Doré, *supra* note 44, at 142-3.
111. *See generally* Greek Delegation Proposal, Comments to the draft Jan. 21, 1992 ("the draft prepared by the Norwegian working team meets our basic requirements") *Cf.* Ministry of Denmark, Comments on the Energy Charter Treaty, Hydrocarbon Protocol, Jan. 15, 1992 ("Generally we think that the draft Protocol, dated November 28th 1991, is a good basis for further work in this field. The draft is, however, very detailed in a number of areas, where a more simple approach would be useful." *See generally* Energy Charter Secretariat, Preparation of a Common Position on the Draft Hydrocarbons Protocol (Presidency Comments), Jan. 17, 1992 ("Generally, points I and VI to XI of the Draft protocol are related to the Basic Agreement and should not be discussed at this stage").
112. Doré, *supra* note 44, at 142-3.

GATT/WTO framework was itself undergoing parallel negotiations to fundamentally realign the trade regime. In 1994, when negotiations for the ECT took place, the reality of Russia being a member of the GATT/WTO was an improbable, if at all conceivable, vision. Today, the Russian Federation is a member of the WTO after withdrawing from the ECT.

A common concern that permeated throughout the negotiation process and the various drafts has been the relationship between GATT and the early draft versions of the ECT.[113] In the multilateral context where states seek to balance their aims and objectives against those of the community of states, the Russian Federation sought the "balance of interests" between its interests as a potentially capital-importing country and those of foreign counterparts providing foreign investment.[114] For investment protection, this "balance of interest" meant providing a concrete undertaking but that undertaking to be heavily reliant on national obligations. The Russian Federation sought to adhere to the "national treatment" standard afforded by its national legislation where the exact same level of protection was afforded to domestic and foreign investors.[115] It later opposed the position proposed by the West, which relied heavily on the GATT standards and afforded equal treatment for foreign investors. As its representatives put it, the Russian Federation feared a higher treatment of protection that foreign investors would receive compared to domestic investors.[116]

At the time of the drafting of the ECT, the Russian Federation and the other former Soviet Republics remained outside of the GATT Regime. While some progress had been made for some of the former Soviet Republics to join the GATT Regime,[117] the negotiations for the Russian Federation to join GATT continued to stall.[118] The provisions of the ECT, as found in ECT Article 4 opted for a broad obligation on the GATT Contracting States not to derogate, as between each other, from the provisions of GATT and Related Instruments. ECT Article 4 was drafted in such a manner that it would even cover the new WTO Provisions, which would eventually replace the existing GATT Regime.[119] These concerns were reflected even in the drafting of the Taxation Article.

113. European Energy Conference Secretariat, Note to the Secretariat to the Basic Agreement for the European Energy Charter of Jan. 20, 1992, 4/92, Jan. 21, 1992, para. 4.

114. Konoplyanik and von Halem, *supra* note 50, at 171-2.

115. For "national treatment," *see* Dolzer and Schreuer, *supra* note 54, at 198-206.

116. Konoplyanik and von Halem, *supra* note 47, at 171 (Konoplyanik notes that the Russian Federation provides "national treatment" to capital investments in such manner that domestic and foreign investments are not treated differently, whereas the GATT Rules focus on non-discrimination and MFN whereby the level of protection among foreign investors should be the same).

117. *See* Energy Charter Secretariat, Trade Amendment: Explanatory Note; http://www.energycharter.org (Azerbaijan, Belarus, Bosnia and Herzegovina, Turkmenistan and Uzbekistan are ECT signatories that have not acceded to the WTO).

118. For a comprehensive discussion on Russia's trade talks to join GATT/WTO, *see* World Trade Organization, Report of the Working Party on the Accession of the Russian Federation to the World Trade Organization, WT/ACC/RUS/70WT/MIN(11)/2, Nov. 17, 2011. *See also* "Russia Becomes WTO Member After 18 years of talks," Brit. Broadcasting Co. (BBC), Dec. 16, 2011.

119. ECT Art. 4. Craig S. Bamberger, *Overview, in The Energy Charter Treaty: An East-West Gateway for Investment & Trade* 1-34, 3 (Thomas W. Wälde ed., 1996). Energy Charter Secretariat, *Amendment to the Trade-Related Provisions of the Energy Charter Treaty, in Energy Charter*

At its core, the ECT drafting process aimed at "avoiding interference with or duplication of activities" between its own regime and that of GATT.[120] While the non-derogation obligation was limited to GATT Contracting countries, it indirectly imposed obligations of "best efforts" concerning energy tariffs and transit among all ECT Contracting States. The regime envisioned that the Russian Federation and the former Soviet Republics would eventually be members of GATT. The interim provisions applied as long as one of the Contracting Party is not party to the GATT and Related Instruments,[121] which by its structure bound states to GATT provisions as long as they were not GATT/WTO Member States. They also allowed for a limited exception for trade between non-GATT Member States that were former Soviet Republics.[122] These provisions, which applied specific tariff rules on a provisional basis, translated into a continued debate on the scope of the ECT obligations against the GATT/WTO regime.

[D] Efficiency Protocol, Signing and Ratification and Correction and Amendments

[1] Protocol: Energy Efficiency/PEERA

Already at the beginning, the Lubbers Memorandum delineated concerns with the adverse environmental impacts of energy and the importance of "clean energy."[123] "Environmental pollution" required, according to Lubbers, that "energy supply must also be safeguarded and new forms of energy production must be developed and used in an environmentally sound way."[124] Energy efficiency appeared as one of the three objectives of the Hague Conference in 1991.[125]

The right to regulate over environmental aspects, while linked to the state's power to tax, has been tied to national sovereignty over natural resources, as captured in ECT Article 18. ECT Article 19 went further and incorporated specific provisions on

Treaty and Related Documents: A Legal Framework for International Energy Cooperation modified April 1998; in force Jan. 21, 2010, 164-204 (ECT Secretariat ed., 2004) [hereinafter "Trade Agreement"].

120. Bamberger, *supra* note 119, at 3.

121. ECT Art. 29(1) ("The provisions of this Art. shall apply to trade in Energy Materials and Products while any Contracting Party is not a party to the GATT and Related Instruments").

122. *See, e.g.*, Art. 29(2)(b). Trade between former Soviet Republics could be governed by an agreement between subject to whichever was earlier of two triggering factors: a time limitation ("until Dec. 1, 1999") or triggering factor ("the admission of the Contracting State to GATT").

123. Lubbers Memorandum, *supra* note 4, at 2. For the discussions on the environmental impact, *see generally* Clare Shine, *Environmental Protection under the Energy Charter Treaty, in The Energy Charter Treaty: An East-West Gateway for Investment and Trade* (Thomas Wälde ed., 1996). *See also* Antonia Layard, *The European Energy Charter Treaty—Tipping the Balance between Energy and the Environment*, European Energy and Environmental L. Rev. 4:5, 150-6 (1995).

124. *Id.*

125. Concluding Document of the Hague Conference on the European Energy Charter, *in Energy Charter Treaty and Related Documents: A Legal Framework for International Energy Cooperation* 209-22; at 215 (ECT Secretariat ed., 2004).

environmental protections, including a distinct dispute resolution clause for environmental provisions only.[126] ECT Article 19 bound states to "strive" to reduce "in an economically efficient manner" environmentally harmful practices.[127] It lacks any provisions on liability for environmental pollution and damage.[128] Although in the 1990s these provisions were perhaps *avant garde*, they lack any considerable "bite" when reviewed against the current debate on climate change.

In the early discussions, it was proposed and adopted that environmental issues of "principal and general nature" were to be adopted in the treaty, whereas "environmental issues which are common to more than one sector" should be dealt with in a separate protocol.[129] The result was the Protocol on Energy Efficiency and Related Environmental Effects (PEEREA): it was the only protocol that witnessed broad acceptance at the time of the signing of the treaty with forty signatories, including the EU signing it. PEEREA was and remains non-binding on the parties. It lacks any "targets, standards or concrete commitments to improve energy efficiency."[130] It provided "a menu of good practices" and a "forum in which to share experiences and policy advice."[131] Despite its limitations viewed against current demands, PEEREA remains an important contribution to energy efficiency.

[2] Signing and Ratification

The first major setback to the Energy Secretariat came in the disappointing news that the US would not sign the Treaty. The Secretariat became aware of the decision not to sign the treaty on December 7, 1994. A day before the US announcement, the Dutch Ambassador Charles Rutten, Chairman of the Energy Charter Plenary Session, praised the parties for reaching a compromise.[132] The discussion took a turn for the worse when the Secretary-General, Clive Jones, learned of the official position of the US State Department articulated in a "decision paper" to the National Security Council.[133] The position was confirmed the same day by Shaun Donnelly, the US Deputy Assistant Secretary of State, and generated a strong response from the Secretary-General.[134] From the follow-up brief, repeated efforts were made to meet and communicate with US

126. ECT Art. 19(2).
127. ECT Art. 19(1).
128. *See* Shine, *supra* note 123, at 538.
129. European Energy Charter Conference Secretariat, Basic Agreement for the European Energy Charter, 31/92 BA 13 at 49 (detailing the Netherlands proposal); http://www.energycharter.org.
130. *See* Energy Charter Secretariat, *An introduction to the Energy Charter Treaty, in Energy Charter Treaty and Related Documents: A Legal Framework for International Energy Cooperation* 16 (ECT Secretariat ed., 2004).
131. *Id.*
132. European Energy Charter, Report by the Chairman of the Negotiating Conference, Ambassador Charles Rutten, to the Signature Conference, Dec. 6, 1994.
133. European Energy Charter Conference Secretariat, the Note of Secretary General Clive Jones for the Attention of Ambassador Rutten, Dec. 7, 1994/832.
134. European Energy Charter Conference Secretariat, the Note of Secretary General Clive Jones for the Attention of Ambassador Rutten, Dec. 7, 1994 (different unmarked correspondence from the same day).

senior officials. By December 12, 1994, no formal declaration had come forward. Finally, during the Ministerial Signature Conference, Deputy Assistant Secretary Donnelly addressed the representatives of all states highlighting the shortcomings of the current draft. Essentially, the official position was that the treaty did not provide "a high standard of protection" for its investors.[135]

Given the US's prominent role in the discussions, its decision not to sign the Treaty, which it shaped, raises one notable concern. Were the deviations in the treaty text so fundamental as to prevent signature? The answer is likely no, but they may be rooted in the handling of the MFN clause. Fourteen years after the US announcement, Craig Bamberger who served as the principal legal adviser to the negotiations wrote:

> I never heard an explanation of how the United States proposed to deal with the "Jackson-Vanik" amendment in order to be able to grant unconditional most favored nation treatment to former Communist bloc countries that became parties to the Energy Charter Treaty.[136]

Under the Jackson-Vanik Amendment, a country in breach of human rights standards could only attain "conditional" MFN status, which contradicted the ECT MFN provisions. Although Bamberger does not assert that the tensions in the ECT with the Jackson-Vanik Amendment[137] were the sole reason for the US not adopting the ECT, the direct conflicts arising out of a broad multilateral MFN clause had without a doubt effectively prevented the US from agreeing to the ECT.[138]

The US's prevalence in negotiations was felt in the context of the amendments of the "transit protocol"(Transit Protocol). After the ECT's entry into force, the Contracting Parties sought to extend the provisions of ECT Article 7 by means of a Transit Protocol.[139] In 2002, the Contracting Parties circulated a draft[140] but eventually the support behind the draft dwindled; in 2011, work on the Transit Protocol was suspended. In the end, the US never signed the Treaty referring to various reasons, including the shortcomings in the ECT final version to account for the specifics of the

135. Shaun Donnelly, United States: Statement on the European Energy Charter Treaty, International Legal Materials, 34:2 at 556-8 (March 1995).
136. Craig S. Bamberger, *The Negotiation of the Energy Charter Treaty, in Investment Protection and the Energy Charter Treaty* (Graham Coop and Clarisse Ribeiro eds., 2008) at xxxix-l.
137. 19 U.S.C. §§ 2432(a)-(e)(1990). The amendment served as an official legislative mechanism to address the concern over the Soviet Union's and other Eastern Bloc's introduction of exit taxes for Jewish émigrées. The Jackson-Vanik Amendment, introduced in 1974, allowed for the liberalization of trade with Eastern Bloc countries, by preserving control mechanisms over human rights breaches and emigration violations. It enabled the US's ability to sanction Russia and other Eastern European countries for human rights breaches, including for exit "tax" penalties applied on Russian émigrées. The Jackson-Vanik Amendment remained in effect until 2012 when it was repealed by the Magnitsky Act. *See* Russia and Moldova Jackson-Vanik Repeal and Sergei Magnitsky Rule of Law Accountability Act of 2012, Pub. L. 112-208, Dec. 14, 2012.
138. *See also* Fox, *supra* note 76, at 197-8 (confirming the same approach).
139. Energy Charter Secretariat, Decision of the Energy Charter Conference: Mandate for Negotiations on a Multilateral Transit Framework, CCDEC 1999 14 TTG, Dec. 7, 1999; http://www.energycharter.org (Accessed: May 30, 2020).
140. Energy Charter Secretariat, Draft of the Final Act of the Energy Charter Conference, Oct. 31, 2003; http://www.energycharter.org (Accessed: May 30, 2020).

US local taxation. Failure of the US to sign the treaty may have led to loss of momentum but did not lead to the ECT's paralysis.[141]

[E] Modernization

[1] Energy Charter Conference as the Platform for Modernization and Change

The Treaty is not meant to be static. Besides the abandoned Transit Protocol, the Treaty included a set of corrections[142] and a Trade Amendment that harmonized the treatment of WTO and non-WTO members.[143]

The Treaty envisions a flexible framework by which the Contracting States would meet periodically at a conference to tackle a set of "functions."[144] Fourteen in number, these functions undertaken by the Energy Charter Conference cover a broad range of aims and seek to complement the objectives for the Energy Charter Secretariat. In general terms, the functions may be divided into three groups: (1) supervisory-administrative, (2) facilitative of the Treaty and future modifications, and (3) policy-oriented.

The *administrative* functions are supervisory in nature and they envision setting out the priorities and programs of work for the Secretariat.[145] These duties include "approv[ing] the annual accounts and the budget for the Secretariat,"[146] as well as the other fundamental decisions for the "establishment and functioning of the Secretariat," including the appointment of the Secretariat's Secretary-General.[147] The supervisory function covers even such tasks as setting out and agreeing to contractual or other terms that may be necessary for the operation of the Charter and its Secretary, such as the terms of headquarters or defining privileges and immunities.[148]

The Conference's *core* functions serve to implement the purposes of the Charter by means of the operations of the Treaty and its Protocols.[149] At the core, the basic scope is to ensure that the Charter Conference "carr[ies] out the duties assigned to it by the Treaty and any Protocols."[150] These duties include *executing* the facilitation of the

141. *See* Fox, *supra* note 76, at 200-01 (noting that "[...] while the ECT may suffer from the absence of US participation, such an absence may not significantly harm the ECT in its implementation").
142. The Protocol of Correction to the Energy Charter Treaty, PV/EECH/X 1, Aug. 2, 1996; http://www.energycharter.org (Accessed: May 30, 2020).
143. Final Act of the International Conference and Decision by the Energy Charter Conference in Respect of the Amendment to the Trade Provisions of the Energy Charter Treaty, Apr. 24, 1998; in effect Jan. 21, 2010; http://www.energycharter.org (Accessed: May 30, 2020) [hereinafter "Trade Amendment"].
144. *See* ECT Art. 34(1) and 34(3).
145. ECT Art. 34(3)(d), (e), (f) and (n). *See also* ECT Art. 35.
146. ECT Art. 3 (3)(d).
147. ECT Art. 34(3)(n).
148. ECT Art. 34(3)(f).
149. ECT Art. 34(3)(a), (b) and (c).
150. ECT Art. 34(3)(a).

Charter's objectives.[151] The duties also cover the review and the facilitation of the implementation process linked to the principles of the Charter, Treaty and its Protocols.[152] In practical terms, the Conference authorizes and approves terms of reference for the negotiation of protocols,[153] authorizes the negotiations of any Declarations that aim to complement the Treaty,[154] makes decisions, if any are necessary, on accessions to the Treaty,[155] reviews and adopts any amendments,[156] modifications or technical changes,[157] and association agreements[158] to the Treaty.

The Conference also retains basic *policy* functions. If one doubted the initial aim of the treaty to integrate former Soviet Bloc countries, ECT Article 34 dispels any such concerns. Article 34(3)(g) expressly provides the Conference with the function of "encourag[ing] co-operative efforts aimed at facilitating and promoting *market-oriented reforms* and *modernization of energy sectors* in those countries of Central and Eastern Europe and the former Union of Soviet Socialist Republics undergoing economic transition."[159]

By relying on this triad of functions, the Conference with the assistance of the Secretariat may adopt timely and necessary changes to carry out the objectives of the Charter and the Treaty. On several occasions, the Conference along with the Secretariat has undertaken such steps aimed at addressing the challenges facing the energy market in Eastern Europe and the subsequent challenges covering the energy industry worldwide.

[2] IEC as the Future Unveiled

Several attempts have, in the past, been launched to modernize the ECT. Two major developments may be noted after the Treaty and the protocols went into force. These are: (1) the failed bilateral discussions over transit between the EU and Russia, including disagreement over the Regional Economic Integration Organization (REIO) clause and (2) the revised framework for a new charter having a broad membership beyond Eastern Europe and Russia.[160]

Concerning the failed bilateral negotiations on transit, it may be noted that transit has been at the heart of the heated ECT negotiations with Russia.[161] From the early drafting of the ECT, the provisions on transit were contentious and remained to be

151. ECT Art. 34(3)(c).
152. ECT Art. 34(3)(b).
153. ECT Art. 34(3)(h).
154. ECT Art. 34(3)(i).
155. ECT Art. 34(3)(j).
156. ECT Art. 34(3)(l).
157. ECT Art. 34(3)(m).
158. ECT Art. 34(3)(k).
159. ECT Art. 34(3)(g) (emphasis added).
160. *See generally* Kotova, *supra* note 75, at 358-9.
161. *See generally* Tarcisio Gazzini, *Energy Charter Treaty: Achievements, Challenges and Perspectives, in Foreign Investment in the Energy Sector Balancing Private and Public Interests* 115 (Eric De Brabandere and Tarcisio Gazzini eds., 2014).

regulated in the separate Transit Protocol. Despite signing the treaty, Russia's rectification of the treaty was conditional on the ratification of the Transit Protocol in such manner that those two legal instruments were in the Russian view, back-to-back obligations.[162] The aim of the Transit Protocol was to clarify the provisions of ECT Article 7 regarding transit; so the withdrawal of the Russian Federation inevitably made the Transit Protocol obsolete.

The limitations on transit were twofold: negotiation-driven and practice-driven. In terms of negotiations, the European Union could not agree with Russia on several key issues, the most important being the treatment of the energy flows within the European Union that was deemed to be an REIO.[163] European Union adopted the position that transit obligations bound the REIO as a whole and not the individual Member States, an issue that was unacceptable to the Russian Federation.[164] Any work on the Transit Protocol was suspended in 2003 only to be recommenced after the Russian Federation withdrew from the provisional application of the ECT. Further negotiations on the draft Transit Protocol were short-lived.

In terms of practice, the challenges of uninterrupted and unimpeded transit were too ambitious to overcome when put into practice. Transit and supply interruptions occurred repeatedly throughout the 1990s and 2000s that the ECT regime was not capable of addressing. Of these supply crises, the most alarming interruption occurred in January 2009 when Gazprom suspended the supply to Ukraine for two weeks, thereby disrupting not only Ukrainian energy use but also a large portion of the European markets.[165] The ECT has viewed the development as a dispute arising out of a pure commercial contract; however, the inability of the ECT regime to avoid the uninterrupted and unimpeded supply highlighted the limitation of the transit provision with regard to key energy suppliers across the Russian and the Confederation of Independent States (CIS) region.

As to the revised framework for the new path forward, the focus has been on a new charter. In 2010, the Energy Charter Secretariat contextualized the decision previously reached in Rome[166] for the modernization of the Energy Charter Process.[167]

162. Konoplyanik refers to the Russian Duma formulating in 2001 a formal position that "a successful finalization of the transit protocol would be a pre-condition to ECT ratification by Russia." Andrei Konoplyanik, *Russia-EU, G-8, ECT and Transit Protocol*, 4 Russian/CIS Energy & Mining L. J. 9 (2006).

163. Gazzini, *supra* note 161, at 115-18. The other two contested matters were "long-term capacity booking and creation of transit infrastructure and the cost-reflectiveness of tariffs arising from auctions." *See generally* Energy Charter Secretariat, Transit Protocol; http://www.energycharter.org (Accessed: May 30, 2020).

164. Gazzini, *supra* note 161, at 117 discussing Art. 20 of the Draft Energy Charter Protocol Final Act of the Energy Charter Conference, Appendix 1, Oct. 31, 2003; http://www.energycharter.org (Accessed: May 30, 2020).

165. Simon Pirani, Jonathan Stern and Katja Yafimava, *The Russo-Ukrainian Gas Dispute of January 2009: A Comprehensive Assessment*, Oxford Institute for Energy Studies Paper NG 27.

166. *See generally* The Energy Charter Conference, Joint Statement, Dec. 9, 2009; http://www.energycharter.org (Accessed: May 30, 2020) [hereinafter "Rome Statement on Modernization"].

167. Energy Charter Secretariat, Decision and Road Map for the Modernization of the Energy Charter Process, Nov. 24, 2010; available at http://www.energycharter.org (Accessed: May 30, 2020) [hereinafter "Road Map for Modernization of the Energy Charter" or the "Road Map"].

Although there were seven diverse areas with firm objectives, the key driver in the road map for the modernization initiative has been the "targeted expansion and consolidation of its geographical scope."[168] The future of the Russian Federation remained uncertain after the formal announcement that Russia had ended the provisional application of the treaty, but at this time the Russian Federation has exercised caution in participating in the ECT modernization efforts.

The IEC has three main objectives: trade, cooperation, and energy efficiency and environmental protection.[169] Of these three objectives, energy efficiency and environmental protection retain central attention, given the means of implementation and the legislative history leading up to the drafting of the IEC.[170] On trade, the IEC revisits the alignment of the energy obligations with WTO obligations as well as emphasis on non-proliferation obligations. On cooperation, the IEC adopts ambitious and wide goals for collaboration between future signatories.

Recent events revealed that the ECT modernization process has stalled by criticism, and increasing interest by the European Commission to play an active role in the modernization initiative.[171] The European Commission has sought and received a mandate for entering in negotiations for modernizing the ECT on the EU's behalf.[172] On November 27, 2018, ECT Member States adopted the Bucharest Declaration by which it issued a statement by which Member States "strongly commit to start discussions on the modernization of the ECT and will undertake every effort to reach a final conclusion on the most suitable policy options in a timely and proper manner, reflecting the new realities of the energy sector and investment policy and serving the interests of the Energy Charter constituency."[173] The same day, the Energy Charter Secretariat approved a list of topics that are subject for modernization.[174] Although taxation is not expressly listed under the treaty, the right to regulate constitutes an important aim of the modernization efforts and is contained in the list of modernization topics.[175] Recent negotiations for the amendment of the treaty reveal a strong interest for the Contracting States to include the "right to regulate" in the Preamble and possibly in a standalone article.[176] In parallel to the initiative to strengthen the state's right to

---

168. Road Map, Area A at 3.
169. *See* IEC, Objectives, pp. 13-15.
170. *See* IEC, Implementation and Legislative History, at 16-20 and 22-5.
171. *See* Tom Jones, *EU states give green light for ECT renegotiation*, Glob. Arb. Rev., July 17, 2019.
172. EU Council, Council adopts negotiation directives for modernization of Energy Charter Treaty, Press Release, July 15, 2019. *See also* European Commission, Recommendation for a Council Decision authorizing the entering into negotiations on the modernization of the Energy Charter Treaty, COM(2019)final. May 14, 2019. *See even* European Union et al, Statement Submitted to the Energy Charter Treaty (ECT) Secretariat pursuant to Art. 26(3)(b)(ii) of the ECT replacing the statement made on Nov. 17, 1997 on behalf of the European Communities, Official Journal of the European Union, L115/1, May 2, 2019, 1-3 (the modification clarifies by which the EU will act as a respondent, instead of the respective Member States).
173. Energy Charter Conference, Bucharest Energy Charter Declaration, Nov. 27, 2018; https://energycharter.org/ (Accessed: May 30, 2020).
174. Energy Charter Secretariat, Approved Topics for the Modernization of the Energy Charter Treaty, Nov. 29, 2018 (announcing the topics agreed on Nov. 27, 2018).
175. *Id.*
176. *See, e.g.*, Energy Charter Secretariat, Decision of the Energy Charter Conference, CCDEC 2019 08 STR, Brussels, Oct. 6, 2019 at 155-16 (Albania, Azerbaijan, European Union, Georgia,

regulate, taxation may commonly adopt regulatory functions, beyond pure revenue generation, by which the cost of a targeted behavior may be increased or reduced.[177] In such manner, taxation matters may fall within the aim of the ongoing modernization initiatives and would be ripe for revisions.[178]

§2.05 THE FRAMEWORK OF THE ECT AND ITS TAXATION ARTICLE

[A] Purpose of the ECT

The overriding purpose of the treaty is defined in ECT Article 2 further complemented by the Preamble to the treaty.[179] ECT Article 2 incorporates the "purpose" of the treaty as "establish[ing] a legal framework in order to promote long-term cooperation in the energy field, based on complementarities and mutual benefits, in accordance with the objectives and principles of the [European Energy] Charter."[180]

The purpose of the Treaty, as formulated in ECT Article 2, accomplishes two functions: (1) it sets out the principle of mutual benefit between Contracting States and (2) it incorporates the Charter into the ECT. The first function closely follows the aims of the Lubbers Memorandum to add a "win-win" strategy for all Contracting States: the non-Soviet states to obtain access to natural resources in the former Soviet Bloc, while the latter would receive investment in the much-needed energy sector.

The second function aims to incorporate the non-binding obligations of the Charter to serve as an underlying obligation for the Contracting States. The Preamble reinforces the function of the ECT "to establish the structural framework required to implement the principles enunciated in the European Energy Charter"; in setting the key objectives of the EEC, the Charter refers to deriving its authority from "within the framework of State sovereignty and sovereign rights over energy resources and in a spirit of political and economic co-operation."[181] Since 2015, a new initiative commenced to modernize the treaty, of which the first step has been to draft a Charter. Until the IEC materializes into a viable treaty, the purpose of the EEC and the ECT, namely to integrate the post-Soviet Bloc into the Western regime through a mutually beneficial strategy, remains the driving purpose of this current version of the ECT.

Luxembourg, Switzerland, and Turkey all welcomed the adoption of the right to regulate in the Preamble, except Japan; Georgia, Luxembourg, Switzerland, and Turkey welcomed the adoption of a separate article on the right to regulate).

177. *See, e.g., id.* 2 (Azerbaijan notes that specific topics for the discussion may still be linked to the ECT Art. 21, particularly on the NT of taxpayers prior to the Azerbaijan's WTO accession).
178. *See infra* §8.02.
179. *See generally* Lucy Reed and Lucy Martinez, *The Energy Charter Treaty: an Overview*, 14 ILSA J. Int'l & Comp. L. 405-31, 406 (2008).
180. ECT Art. 2.
181. ECT, preamble, para. 5. *See also id.* para. 6 ("wishing to implement the basic concept of the European Energy Charter initiative ...").

[B] The Taxation Article Within the ECT

The final form of the Treaty, which was sent for ratification, is divided into eight parts, with fourteen annexes, which cover the exclusions and the reservations of the signatories, adding to the complexity of the treaty. Its aim is to be flexible while accounting for the needs of various entities. In the end, the treaty is plagued with complexities as a result of a lengthy and uneven negotiation process.

The Taxation Article contains the main provisions covering the State's power to tax, but the reference to the taxation power appears in one notable context relating to sovereignty over natural resources. ECT Article 18 stipulates that states shall have decision-making power over the resources within its jurisdiction that includes the power "to specify and enjoy any taxes" for the exploration and exploitation of these resources.[182] The checks-and-balance relationship between ECT Articles 18 and 21 incorporates the title II of the Energy Charter Conference whereby states shall facilitate "the development and diversification of resources [while] the signatories undertake to avoid imposing discriminatory rules on [...] taxation."[183]

The complexity of the ECT Taxation Article finds its root-cause in the negotiation history,[184] despite it having received considerably less attention in the negotiation process.[185] Unlike the transit and trade provisions that were negotiated by senior trade and foreign ministers and even encountered the scrutiny of national parliaments, it was the finance ministries who essentially negotiated the contents of the article with the aim of avoiding dual obligations arising out of double taxation obligations and MFN clauses.[186]

Craig Bamberger, who chaired the legal advisory committee of the Energy Charter Conference, observed that "the article did not experience meaningful [c]onference review in its final form, and due to its overriding paragraph (1) exclusion, it may have unanticipated limiting effects on rights and obligations under other provisions of the Treaty."[187] It was effectively negotiated by representatives of finance ministries.[188] As further noted by Bamberger, the Taxation Article had a "defensive" purpose. It sought primarily to avoid the application of MFN provisions to tax obligations in the context of the ECT investor-state regime.[189]

The first draft incorporated a reference to taxation for purposes of double taxation. It only incorporated a vague obligation for the states to negotiate around any

182. ECT Art. 18(3).
183. Concluding Document of the Hague Conference on the European Energy Charter, Dec. 16-17, 1991.
184. *See* Sophie Nappert, *Square Pegs and Round Holes: The Taxation Provision of the Energy Charter Treaty and the Yukos Awards*, Paris J. Int'l Arb. (2015:1) 7-28, at 8.
185. *See infra* Chapter 4.
186. Bamberger, *supra* note 119, at 24.
187. *Id.*
188. Craig Bamberger, *Overview*, *in The Energy Charter Treaty: An East–West Gateway for Investment and Trade* 1-34, 24 (Thomas Wälde ed., 1996); Stadtwerke Munchen GmbH, RWE Innogy GmbH and Others v. Kingdom of Spain, Award, ICSID Case No. ARB/15/1, Dec. 2, 2019, paras. 172-3. *See also* Hobér, *supra* note 20, at 356-7.
189. Bamberger, *supra* note 119, at 24.

conflicting issues linked to double taxation.[190] The April 9, 1992 draft extended the protections against double taxation provisions and introduced an exclusion for domestic law that constitutes "arbitrary and unjustifiable discrimination."[191] The Japanese delegation aimed to have the provisions limited to double taxation issues and "tax evasion."[192]

The drafters did not pursue the incorporation of the "tax evasion" in the treaty in the later drafts. The focus remained on the avoidance of double taxation issues that was later extended to resolve any conflicts resulting from membership in a customs union or different treatment based on residency.[193] The pivotal change occurred with the June 19, 1992 draft,[194] when the US delegation introduced its proposal that would serve as the basis for the final version of the Taxation Article ("US Proposal").[195] The US Proposal led to the formation of the taxation subgroup ("Taxation Sub-Group") that was tasked to address eight objectives linked to *inter alia* removal of any conflicts between tax treaties and the ECT.[196] Subsequent changes preserved the format and the complexity of the Taxation Article. Other tax-related proposals arose but did not gain any traction.[197]

In fact, the January 1992 legal memorandum from the US to the UK delegation, later forwarded to the Energy Charter Secretariat, lay behind the US Proposal for the exclusion of tax matters ("Carve-Out") and the current version of the Taxation Article, as below:

> In assessing tax discrimination, MFN is never a relevant criterion. A carve-out for tax discrimination (i.e., national treatment) when a tax treaty is in force is necessary. In addition, even where there is no tax treaty, it should be clear that when we talk about "discrimination," we mean when the two parties whose treatment is being compared are in the same, or similar circumstances. It must also be made clear that when we speak of tax discrimination, we are not talking about situations where a distinction in treatment exists between domestic and foreign

190. Draft Treaty, Basic Protocol to the European Energy Charter, Aug. 20, 1991, Art. 14. For the ECT drafts, *see* Energy Charter Secretariat, Travaux préparatoires; http://www.energycharter.org (Accessed: May 30, 2020).
191. European Energy Charter, Basic Agreement for the European Energy Charter, BA 12 22/92, Apr. 9, 2012 at 56-7.
192. *Id.* 56.
193. European Energy Charter Conference Secretariat, Legislative History to Basic Agreement, BA-13 37/92, June 19, 1992, Art. 20(2), at 78.
194. The US Proposal appears in the June 15, 1992 draft from the Working Group II, *see* European Energy Charter Conference Secretariat, June 15, 1992, Working Group II, Room Document 9.
195. European Energy Charter Conference Secretariat, Legislative History to Basic Agreement, BA-13 37/92, June 19, 1992, at 81-2.
196. *Id.* 81.
197. One of these was the proposal from the Ukraine delegation, supported by the Russian delegation, a tax cap on non-subsidies electricity supply. The proposal dwindled after it was referred to a separate group on electricity. *See* Memorandum from Sydney Fremantly, UK Minister for Energy to Charles Rutten, Chairman of the Energy Charter Conference, June 19, 1992.

persons necessary to ensure adequate tax collection. Reflecting these points will require amendment to the proposed text.[198]

The contents of the US-UK memorandum confirm Craig Bamberger's observations that the focus of the Taxation Article was to resolve the uncertainties linked to the MFN clause.

The US Proposal included the near-opposite use of terms in the carve-out and clawback than in the final version of the treaty. It adopted "direct taxes and taxes on capital gains" in the carve-out and used the term "taxation measures" in the expropriation clawback.[199] Following the input from the Taxation Subgroup, the draft of October 21, 1992, incorporated the definition of the term "Taxation Measure," linking it to domestic law and tax treaties. In the October 21, 1992 draft, the carve-out incorporated the term "Taxation Measure" as appearing in the final version, albeit not capitalized. It also preserved the term "taxation measure" for purposes of the provisions on expropriation permitting the review of expropriation measures despite the carve-out.

The change from "taxation measures" to "tax" in the expropriation subparagraph occurred between the third version and the fourth version of the compromised text.[200] In the July 7, 1993 draft, the term "tax" replaced the term "taxation measures" without a formal comment for the change.[201] The reasons for the change are difficult to pinpoint in the *travaux.*[202] Some suggestions have linked the change to the definition of taxation measures as a list that was meant to be inclusive.[203] Another hypothesis has linked it to the potential uncertainties resulting from the referral to the CTAs mechanisms.[204]

Regardless of the reasons for the change, it remains difficult to trace the exact reason for the adoption of the term "tax" in the expropriation clawback. All the subsequent drafts adopted this new version despite some observed commentary to the contrary.[205] The capitalization of key terms and the current numeration of articles were

---

198. Memorandum of Conrad Ouelette, Department of Treasury, to Dorothy Mercer Jan. 8, 1992 appended in Memorandum from David Brown, Director, US Dep't of State, Office of Global Energy Bureau of Economic and Business Affairs to Sydney Fremantle, UK Dep't of Energy, Jan. 13, 1992.
199. *Id.* 81 (direct tax being labelled as "taxes on income and [sic] capital gains or on the taxable capital of corporations"). *See generally* MENA Chambers, Note 13—Making Sense of the Taxation Provisions of the Energy Charter Treaty, July 22, 2015; http://www.menachambers.com (Accessed: Jan. 1, 2017), no longer online, copy with the author.
200. *Compare* European Energy Charter Conference Secretariat, Draft Treaty to Basic Agreement—Third Version, CONF-60 46/93, June 1, 1993, at 54 *with* European Energy Charter Conference Secretariat, Draft Treaty to Basic Agreement—Fourth Version, CONF-64 55/93, July 7, 1993, at 51.
201. European Energy Charter Conference Secretariat, Draft Treaty to Basic Agreement—Fourth Version, CONF-64 55/93, July 7, 1993, at 49-53.
202. *See, e.g., Yukos* Award, para. 1415 ("the Tribunal does not find much helpful guidance in the *travaux préparatoires* of the ECT").
203. *See, e.g., Yukos* Award, para. 1380 (summarizing the claimant's reliance on the comments of the French delegation to the memorandum of the Legal Subgroup (LSG)).
204. *See* MENA Chambers, *supra* note 199, para. 54 (discussing Memorandum from the Chairman of the Legal Sub-Group to the Chairman of Working Group II, dated Mar. 5, 1993).
205. Handwritten comments on Nov. 15, 1994; *see* the addition of the word "measures" after "taxes" with the addition: "includes conventions treaties. carve-out in [ECT Article 21](1) is for tax

formalized only with the June 25, 1994 draft.[206] A final point of tension in the final hours before signing the Treaty was whether the provisions of ECT Article 29(2) to (6) should be subject to the same exceptions as ECT Article 7, as per ECT Article 21(2). In the end, the final draft did not subject the interim provisions of ECT Article 29(2)-(6) to the DTT and tax collection exceptions; thus, it was extracted as a provision standing on its own.[207]

What remains disconcerting is that the proposal for the Taxation Article came from the US delegation that in the end abstained from signing the treaty. The seemingly miscellaneous article did not retain much importance, perhaps until the *Yukos* disputes when the Russian Federation used it as a shield. The Taxation Article's complex wording and limited negotiation has provided parties with substantial room to formulate persuasive arguments around the chapter's scope of application. Matched by the initiative of states to attract investment in the energy sector by means of tax incentives schemes, the Taxation Article opens the inquiry into the powers of the state and outer limits of the state to shape fiscal policy against previous commitments to investors.[208]

§2.06 SUB-CONCLUSION TO THE CHAPTER

The sub-inquiry for this chapter focused on the origins of the ECT and the Taxation Article, which balances two conflicting forces: the state's power to tax and the protection of investor rights. The sub-inquiry started with a review of the origins of the Cold War and delves further into specifically the reasons behind the Taxation Article.

The final days of the Cold War defined the ECT. During this time, the proverbial East and West sought to come together in a partnership on energy. The contribution of this chapter has been a deep dive into the Lubbers Memorandum. Although previous studies have considered the Lubbers Memorandum, this book has delved into the original memorandum to extrapolate the original intent behind the ECT. This intent centered on three key pillars: (1) environmental protection, (2) guaranteed supplies and (3) stable political relationships, of which environmental protection reemerges in the context of the climate change debate confronted today. The path from the Lubbers Memorandum to the final provisions of the ECT unveiled the tensions between the need to access energy resources and the ability to regulate the interrelationship of previously quasi-belligerent states during the Cold War. This tension between access and regulation translated directly into the state's broad power by means of taxes, with

measures—which more than tax." Whose comments it was cannot be verified. Energy Charter Treaty, Travaux préparatoires, Notes to the Nov. 15, 1994 draft, on file with the author.

206. European Energy Charter Conference Secretariat, Final Act of the Conference on the Energy Charter Treaty, Interim Text, June 25, 1994, at 33-7.

207. European Energy Charter Conference Secretariat, Fax Consultations: Message No: 276L, Nov. 22, 1994 containing Memorandum of Craig Bamberger to Legal Subgroup Members, Nov. 21, 1994.

208. For a discussion on the preferred means to incentivize economic activity by means of taxation instruments, *see generally* Ruth Mason, *Federalism and the Taxing Power*, 99 Cal. L. Rev. 975, 977-9 & 985 (2011).

the subsequent inquiry on what are limitations to such power (not addressed by the Treaty).

In turn, the Taxation Article is closely linked to the MFN provision. The roots of the Taxation Article draw on the need to limit contradictory obligations resulting from the prevailing MFN commitments. In relying on the US-UK legal memorandum, I have proposed that the origins behind the Taxation Article lie in the initial drafters' abandoned attempt to limit the contradictory obligations arising out of the MFN clause. As a result, the broad power to tax adopted in ECT Article 21(1) became subject to a set of complex and intricate inclusions and limitations to such inclusions, which are examined below in Chapter 4. However, prior to embarking on a clear cataloging of the Taxation Article, this book examines the elements of a tax in Chapter 3. At the core, the Taxation Article aimed to clarify, not confuse, the relationship between the ECT and existing treaties, including DTTs. It sought to define a clear demarcation for investor protection mechanisms and tax. But as the subsequent case law discussion in Chapter 5 reveals, the complexity of the Taxation Article has left too many issues unresolved, including on the scope of its coverage arising from the basic meaning of the term "tax."

CHAPTER 3

Much Ado about Tax

§3.01 TAXES WITHIN THE STATE'S MACROECONOMIC TOOLS: IMPETUS FOR GROWTH OR OBSTACLE TO PROGRESS?

The next sub-inquiry sets out to assess: what are the key elements of a tax, and how do they interact with investment protections mechanisms as observed in the first international arbitrations? The sub-inquiry is placed against the ECT backdrop of seeking to adopt a "level playing field" for member countries on foreign investment in the energy sector.

The power to tax constitutes one of the two aspects of fiscal policy; the other being the spending power of a state. States have two means by which they exercise control over their macroeconomics: monetary policy and fiscal policy. Whereas monetary policy consists of managing the money supply and interest rates, fiscal policy captures the tax and spending power of a national government. Fiscal policy is the fundamental tool by which a state affects macroeconomic conditions such as aggregate demand and economic growth, as well by extension investment (both foreign and domestic).[209] However, by imposing taxes, governments affect economic policy by determining how much to tax, what to tax, and how to collect the taxed proceeds. Putting aside the debate on whether investment treaties attract foreign investment,[210] it is generally accepted that a nation's tax policy unequivocally affects FDI.[211]

209. N. Gregory Mankiw, *Macroeconomics* 17-3 (10 ed., 2019); *see also* Troy Segal, *Monetary Policy v. Fiscal Policy: What Is the Difference*, Investopedia, Apr. 10, 2019; http://www.investopedia .com (Accessed: May 30, 2020).

210. *See generally* Lisa Sachs and Karl Sauvant, *BITs, DTTs and FDI flows: An Overview, in The Effect of Treaties on Foreign Direct Investment: Bilateral Investment Treaties, Double Taxation Treaties and Investment Flows* (Karl Sauvant and Lisa Sachs eds., 2009).

211. *See generally* OECD, Tax Effects on Foreign Direct Investment, Policy Brief, Feb. 2008, at 2 ("Studies examining cross-border flows suggest that on average, FDI decreases by 3.7% following a 1 percentage point increase in the tax rate on FDI").

The state regulates private actors by means of tax in two ways; by means of (1) "tax expenditures" (or "incentives/deductions") and (2) "tax penalties."[212] Through administrative agencies or other state authorities, states may freely impose taxes on nationals and non-nationals ("aliens" or "foreigners") alike, subject to certain practical and legal limitations.[213] By extension, states may tax both domestic and foreign investors. The limits of taxation power on nationals and domestic investors would be found in the very limits to the state's power to tax: in the case of national investors, it would be covered in national administrative and constitutional law.

By its nature, taxation involves a complicated calculus that includes a taking. Be it by taxing property, income, capital gains or property bought, governments use tax proceeds to cover public expenditures. However, tax proceeds may also be used for economic programs that generate growth: be it in established or emerging areas. Tax too little and the government ends up with a budget deficit where the government's expenses exceed its revenue. Tax too much and businesses start to balk because of reduced income. Taxation carries the inherent *balancing act* of determining how much one may extract without hindering growth.[214] It shapes a nation's financial health for the foreseeable future.[215] In so far as commonality, the buzzwords for the power to tax are ubiquitous: "[t]axes are the price we pay for civilized society";[216] "[t]he power to tax involves the power to destroy[...]";[217] "... nothing is certain, except death and taxes."[218] National conflicts and crises have commonly commenced over taxes; examples of even military confrontations are widespread.[219]

As international arbitration seeks to curb contentious disputes by means of peaceful resolution,[220] taxation issues commonly emerge in investment cases. With the emergence of disputes from the renewable energy sector, tax-related investment

212. Mason, *supra* note 208, at 977-8 & 984-92.
213. *See infra* Chapter 3.03.
214. William Park refers to the Louis XIV's Finance Minister, Jean-Baptiste Colbert, who stated "plucking the goose as to obtain the largest amount of feathers with the smallest amount of hissing." *See* Park, *supra* note 9, at 144.
215. The Ottoman Empire infamously took on so much public debt that by 1881 it was forced to transfer its authority of tax collection to European creditors, thereby gaining the label "the sickman of Europe." *See* DC Blaisdell, *European Financial Control in the Ottoman Empire: A Study of the Establishment, Activities, and Significance of the Administration of the Ottoman Public Debt* 93-5 (1929); https://archive.org/details/in.ernet.dli.2015.216049 (Accessed: May 30, 2020).
216. Compania General de Tabacos de Filipinas v. Collector of Internal Revenue, 275 US 87 at 100 (1927) (Holmes J., dissenting).
217. McCulloch v. Maryland, 17 U.S. 316, 431 (1819).
218. The quote is commonly attributed to Benjamin Franklin. *See* F.R. Shapiro. *Yale Book of Quotations* 288 (2006).
219. William Park, *supra* note 9 at 144 n. 86 (discussing the "fiscal perennial" of taxation's "enhanced role" in wartime). *See also* Grant Dorfman, *The Founders' Legal Case: "No Taxation Without Representation,"* 44 Hous. L. Rev. 1377-412, at 1388 (discussing the phrase "no taxation without representation" and the origins of the American Revolutionary War). The German Peasant War of 1524-5 and the Irish Tithe War of 1830-8 are but a few examples of armed resistances against the state for the power to impose taxes.
220. *See generally Arbitrating for Peace: How Arbitration Made a Difference* (Ulf Franke, Annette Magnusson and Joel Dahlquist eds., 2016).

arbitrations have appeared to be on the rise.[221] One possible explanation, which goes beyond the practical considerations of the parties, concerns "the absence of legal means of asserting [investor]'s rights against the state authorities." Not only is the power to tax a "determined exercise of state powers" but states also rarely consent to limiting such power.[222] In examining the impact of taxation measures as these affect investment by aliens and specifically foreign investors, three inquiries are undertaken as to: (1) the definition of tax (subject matter) and the taxpayers whom the state may tax and what the common basis for taxation (jurisdiction), (2) the detailed discussion of the limits to the state's power to tax, (3) several early arbitrations that examined these limits, and (4) the conclusion by answering the initial sub-inquiry of this section.

§3.02 DEFINITIONAL CONUNDRUMS OF WHAT IS A TAX?

[A] Definition

What is a tax? The ordinary meaning of the term carries particular importance despite remaining elusive.[223]

The term "tax" is the generic term capturing the government revenue collection arm of its fiscal policy. As a broad term, it appears as both a verb and a noun.[224] The focus of the inquiry is into "tax" as a noun, yielding itself to several often overlapping definitions. The International Bureau of Fiscal Documentation (IBFD) clarifies that "there is *no single definition* of a tax and definitions tend to vary according to the context."[225] In pure tax law terms, IBFD refers to the OECD "working definition" that defines tax as:

> compulsory unrequited payment to general government.[226]

---

221. For a discussion on this phenomenon, *see* Peter D. Cameron, *International Energy Investment Law: The Pursuit of Stability* para. 5.17 (2010) (citing to Sebastien Manciaux, *Changement de Législation Fiscal et Arbitrage International*, Revue de l'Arbitrage 2001:2, 311-42). However, note the ECT cases and namely the rise of disputes arising from the renewable energy sector and involving the Czech Republic, Italy, and Spain that have triggered the ECT provision on taxation, *see infra* §§5.04-5.06.
222. *Id.*
223. *See* Geoffrey Morse, David Williams and Sandra Den, *Davies: Principles of Tax Law* 1-01, 1-02 (Sweet & Maxwell, 8th ed., 2016) (noting that "'what is a tax' is surprisingly difficult to answer" referring to describing "an elephant to a child").
224. *Oxford English Dictionary*, 2020.
225. IBFD International Tax Glossary 464 (7th ed., 2015).
226. *Id.* (discussing the OECD definition). *See also* OECD, Negotiating Group on the Multilateral Agreement on Investment (MAI), Expert Group No.3 Expert Group No.3 on Treatment of Tax Issues in the MAI, DAFFE/MAI/EG2(96)3, Apr. 19, 1996 at paras. 1, 9-11. *Cf. Black's Law Dictionary* defining a tax as:

> A charge, usu. monetary, imposed by the government on persons, entities, transactions, or property to yield public revenue. • Most broadly, the term embraces all governmental impositions on the person, property, privileges, occupations, and enjoyment of the people, and includes duties, imposts, and excises. Although a tax is often thought of as being pecuniary in nature, it is not necessarily payable in money.
> *Tax, Black's Law Dictionary* (11th ed. 2019).

The payment is "unrequited" in that "benefits provided by government to taxpayers are not normally in proportion to their payments."[227] According to the OECD definition, the term excludes "fines unrelated to tax offences and compulsory loans paid to the government."[228]

IBFD's definition thereby sets out that a tax is:

> a government levy that is not in return for a specific benefit and is not imposed by way of a fine or penalty (e.g. for non-compliance with the law), except in some cases where it corresponds to tax-related offences.[229]

Both the IBFD and OECD definitions of "tax" are contrasted with other "borderline cases" of certain fees and charges.[230] IBFD, on the one hand, contrasts taxes to "user charges and fees" by drawing that "although compulsory, [these] are generally requited in the sense that there is a link between the amount paid and the benefit provided."[231] OECD, on the other hand, notes that compulsory social security fees and vehicle license fees are "universally regarded as taxes," but "the strength of the link between the fee and the service provided may vary considerably, as may the relation between the amount of levy and the cost of providing the service."[232]

For purposes of classification, the OECD also organizes taxes in six major categories (e.g., series/classifications):

(1) Taxes on income, profits and capital gains (Series 1000);
(2) Social security contributions (Series 2000);
(3) Taxes on payroll and workforce (Series 3000);
(4) Taxes on property (Series 4000);
(5) Taxes on goods and services (Series 5000), including taxes on production, sale transfer and leasing, as well as value-added tax (VAT) and sales tax; and
(6) Other taxes (Series 6000).

227. OECD, Negotiating Group on the Multilateral Agreement on Investment (MAI), Expert Group No.3 Expert Group No. 3 on Treatment of Tax Issues in the MAI, DAFFE/MAI/EG2(96)3, Apr. 19, 1996 at para. 1, 9-11. *See also* IBFD International Tax Glossary 464 (7th ed., 2015).
228. OECD, Negotiating Group on the Multilateral Agreement on Investment (MAI), Expert Group No.3 Expert Group No.3 on Treatment of Tax Issues in the MAI, DAFFE/MAI/EG2(96)3, Apr. 19, 1996 at para. 2.
229. IBFD, *supra* note 227, at 464 (discussing the OECD definition). *See also* OECD, Negotiating Group on the Multilateral Agreement on Investment (MAI), Expert Group No.3 Expert Group No.3 on Treatment of Tax Issues in the MAI, DAFFE/MAI/EG2(96)3, Apr. 19, 1996 at paras. 1, 9-11.
230. OECD, Negotiating Group on the Multilateral Agreement on Investment (MAI), Expert Group No.3 Expert Group No.3 on Treatment of Tax Issues in the MAI, DAFFE/MAI/EG2(96)3, Apr. 19, 1996 at para. 1, 9-11. *See* IBFD, *supra* note 227, at 464. *See also* Peter Harris and David Oliver, *International Commercial Tax* 9 (2010) ("... not all government levies are taxes").
231. IBFD, *supra* note 227, at 464.
232. OECD, Negotiating Group on the Multilateral Agreement on Investment (MAI), Expert Group No.3 Expert Group No.3 on Treatment of Tax Issues in the MAI, DAFFE/MAI/EG2(96)3, Apr. 19, 1996 at paras. 7 and 9. *Cf.* IBFD, *supra* note 227, at 464 (noting that "whether social security contributions constitute a tax is a debated issue" even for compulsory contributions).

OECD determines several factors where a levy[233] would be unrequited thus deemed a tax, including whether the charge exceeds the cost associated with any services involved, whether the payer is not the beneficiary of any benefit involved, or whether a benefit is offered in the first place and when the benefits are not proportional to the levy charged.[234]

By means of example, the following are not taxes:

- court fees; driving license fees; harbor fees; passport fees; radio and television license fees are *"non-tax revenues"*/non-taxes as the public authorities are deemed to provide a service to the taxpayer;
- permission to perform such activities as distributing films; hunting, fishing; providing entertainment or gambling facilities; selling alcohol or tobacco; permission to own dogs or to use or own motor vehicles or guns; severance taxes are viewed as taxes falling within the 5000 Class,[235] as the fee is deemed unrequited either because the public authority is not providing a service or that the service is not proportional to the levy.

The determinative factor is whether there is any return benefit associated with the levy: a levy which carries a benefit would constitute a fee, not a tax.

[B] Tax Subjects

Who would then be subject of taxation measures by the government? The tax subject is everyone whom the state may tax, that is, all taxpayers. A state may tax any subject falling within its jurisdiction unless excluded otherwise. A state has a broad power to tax its individuals and even aliens, especially those who have taken up residence in the country.[236] It may tax anyone within its borders: not only its nationals but also foreigners. A person traveling through Country X is likely to pay sales tax or VAT on goods purchased in Country X, or be exempt from such tax depending on the status of the individual area where the purchase is made (e.g., duty-free area at the airport), the nature of the purchase and the individual (their residence and/or direction of travel). The state may equally impose *charges* for travel: imposed on the airline, these charges may be further passed by the airline to the traveler. A state is unlikely to tax the traveler on all foreign-source income on the sole basis that the individual is only traveling

233. The definition of a "levy" covers imposition of both a "tax" and a "fine." *See Levy, Black's Law Dictionary* (11th ed. 2019) ("the imposition of a fine or tax; the fine or tax so imposed").
234. OECD, Negotiating Group on the Multilateral Agreement on Investment (MAI), Expert Group No.3 Expert Group No.3 on Treatment of Tax Issues in the MAI, DAFFE/MAI/EG2(96)3, Apr. 19, 1996 at para. 9. *See also* Harris and Oliver, *supra* note 230, at 9 ("The charge must vary in some respect to the service received and not according to some general notion of ability to pay. There must be some connection between the cost of the service to be provided by the government and the amount of revenue to be raised (but a reasonable profit is okay)").
235. OECD, Negotiating Group on the Multilateral Agreement on Investment (MAI), Expert Group No.3 Expert Group No. 3 on Treatment of Tax Issues in the MAI, DAFFE/MAI/EG2(96)3, Apr. 19, 1996 at para. 11.
236. *Oppenheim's International Law*, §404.

through the airport.[237] However, it may do so in the event the individual has resided in the country for a determined period of time (e.g. 30, 90 or 180 days). The same applies to corporations which have local operations in a country despite being based abroad. A state may tax a foreign company which has local presence, or "permanent establishment" (PE). Although the main rule is that six months of local presence is required, it is not uncommon that rules for determining permanent establishment to be triggered already at 30 days of local presence where the state has the right to determine whether the presence of a legal entity may in fact constitute PE despite being on paper less than 6 months.[238]

[C] Jurisdiction to Tax

For purposes of determining the jurisdiction to tax, there are three levels of taxation: subnational, national, and international (Figure 3.1).[239] Subnational taxation comprises of the level of taxation at the local level; national taxation being the taxation at the national level and international taxation covering all issues that extend beyond the national border such as extraterritorial taxation, interplay between any two or more states' conflicting taxation regulations (double taxation).

Figure 3.1 The Three Levels of the Jurisdiction to Tax

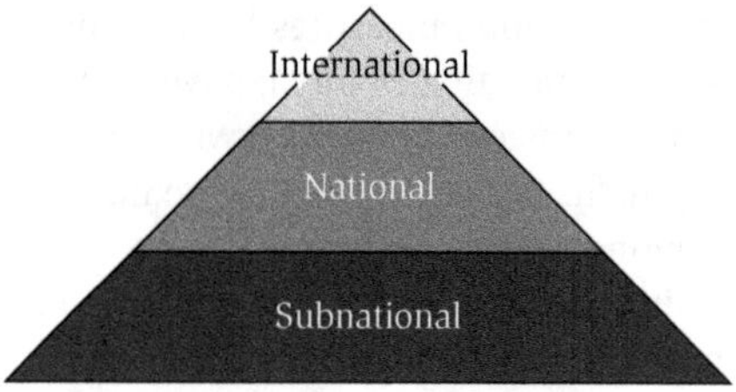

Source: Author's Own.

237. *See* Reuven S. Avi-Yonah, *International Tax as International Law*, Tax L. Rev. 57(4) 483-501 at 498 (2004) ("Can a country simply decide to tax nonresidents that have no connection to it on foreign source income? The answer is clearly no, both from a practical perspective and, I would argue, from a customary international law perspective").
238. Tax Code of the Russian Federation, Art. 306(3) (triggered when "entrepreneurial activities begin to regularly carried out through a division of that organization"). *See also* Federal Arbitrazh Court of the district of Moscow (Russ.), June 11, 2015, Case no. A40-138879/14 ("Oriflame decision") (denying the deduction of licensing and trademark payments of Russian subsidiary to Dutch parent company).
239. *See generally* Walter Hellerstein, *Jurisdiction to Tax Income and Consumption in the New Economy: A Theoretical and Comparative Perspective*, 38 Ga. L. Rev. 1-70, 3 (2003-2004). In the US domestic context, *see* Frederick N. Judson, *A Treaties on Power of Taxation, State and Federal, in the United States* 404 (The Lawbook Exchange 2007) (noting that "due process of law in State taxation therefore requires that the tax shall be levied for a public purpose and upon persons or property within the jurisdiction of the State").

A state's jurisdiction sets out the state's competence to regulate the activities of natural and legal persons.[240] The state may impose levies on natural or juridical persons at all of these three levels "so long as there is some kind of real link between the state and the proposed taxpayer, whether it be, for example, nationality or domicile."[241] The jurisdiction to tax is inherently tied to state sovereignty.[242] In accordance with the UN General Assembly Resolution 3281, a state retains the right to choose its economic system.[243] A state also has full permanent sovereignty over its wealth, natural resources and economic activity,[244] including the right "to regulate and exercise authority over foreign investment within its national jurisdiction in accordance with its laws and regulations and in conformity with its national objectives and priorities.[...]"[245]

Besides sovereignty over fiscal/economic policy and national resources, the other theories on which the jurisdiction to tax is grounded on are "the realistic or empirical theory," "the ethical or retributive theory," and the "contractual theory."[246] A further helpful distinction is between substantive jurisdiction and enforcement jurisdiction. Substantive jurisdiction comprises of the ability of the state "to impose tax on the subject matter of the exaction."[247] Enforcement jurisdiction concerns "the power of the state to compel collection."[248] The two bases of international law that justify jurisdiction, nationality and territoriality[249] are incorporated in international tax law similarly

240. Malcolm Shaw, *International Law* 486 (8th ed., 2017). The concept of sovereignty in the context of taxation powers is further reinforced by the shielding of consuls and diplomats from local taxes. *See* Vienna Convention on Consular Relations, 596 UNTS 261, entered into force on Mar. 19, 1967, Art. 49. *See also* Vienna Convention on Diplomatic Relations, 500 UNTS 95, entered into effect on Apr. 24, 1964, Arts. 23 & 34. *See generally* L. Oppenheim et al., *Oppenheim's international law* 1101-02 & 1148 (1996).

    International organizations also benefit from tax exemptions on the basis that taxing such entities would "hinder" [their] "functionality." *See generally* Jan Klebbers, International Institutions, in *The Cambridge Companion to International Law* 231-2 (James Crawford and Martti Koskenniemi eds., 2012).
241. Shaw, *supra* note 240, at 486.
242. *See* James Crawford, *Brownlie's Principles of Public International Law* 456-7 (7th ed., 2012). *See also* Christopher Staker "Jurisdiction" in Malcolm Evans ed. *International Law* 289-315 at 291 (5th ed., 2018) ("English-language monographs typically devote a chapter to the topic [...] continental monographs, on the other hand, have tended to adopt a rather different approach, regarding jurisdiction as an aspect of statehood or territory or the law of the sea or of some other aspect of international law"). *See also* A.R. Albrecht, "The Taxation of Aliens under International Law" 29 Brit. Y.B. Int'l L. 145-85, at 145-9 (1952). *See also* Rutsel Sivestre J. Marta, *The Jurisdiction to Tax in International Law: Theory and Practice of Legislative Fiscal Jurisdiction* 22-3 (1989). Albrecht's article is heavily relied on by the tribunal in Burlington Resources v. Ecuador, Decision on Liability, ICSID Case No. ARB/08/5 (Dec. 14, 2012), para. 391.
243. United Nations General Assembly Resolution 3281 (XXIX): Charter of Economic Rights and Duties of States," Official Records of the General Assembly: Twenty-Ninth Session, Supplement No. 31 (A/9631), Article. 1 at 50-5 (1974).
244. *Id.* Art. 2(1).
245. *Id.* Art. 2(2).
246. Albrecht, *supra* note 242, at 145-9. Marta, *supra* note 242, at 18-23.
247. Hellerstein, *supra* note 242, at 3, 4-7, 14-20.
248. *Id.* 3, 8-13 and 21-8.
249. The bases of jurisdiction under international law extend beyond the nationality and territoriality and may additionally include: (1) passive personality principle, (2) protective principle,

in two distinct bases for jurisdiction.[250] The first, *residence*, entails the state to tax the residents of its territory (and in the case of the US of its citizens) on their worldwide income.[251] The second, *source*, enables states to tax income derived from sources within its jurisdiction.[252] The free movement of capital as a result of globalization and lessening exchange controls led to most countries adopting a combination of both systems for purposes of asserting tax jurisdiction.[253]

Residency of individuals is often defined by the number of days in a year or consecutive years an individual resides in a state. For corporations, there are two tests to assert residency. The first is the seat of the company, namely where the company is incorporated. The second is the "less formal definition" based on other circumstances such as control of the company or meeting of the management team.[254]

Source focuses on the origin of the income to be taxed. For passive income (income derived from "investments not controlled by the taxpayer"), the source of the payer often determines the source of the income.[255] For active income (income derived from wages and controlled activities by the taxpayer), substantive rules apply so that:

- income from royalties is sourced where the intellectual property is protected,[256] and
- income from services is sourced where the services are rendered.[257]

The distinction in the treatment of active as opposed to passive income would determine what exemptions and deductions could be taken, passive income being far more restrictive in its coverage of deductions and exceptions. Source rules counteract the challenges arising from taxation on the basis of territoriality, including the difficulty

(3) universality principle. *See, e.g.*, Shaw, *supra* note 240, at 488-513. It may also be categorized in different forms. *See* Staker, supra note 242, at 291. *Cf. Id.* 486, 488 and 515 (discussing (1) legislative, executive and judicial; (2) civil; (3) criminal; and (4) extraterritorial jurisdiction).

250. Reuven S. Avi-Yonah, *Advanced Introduction to International Tax Law* 8 (2015). *See also* Asif Qureshi, *The Public International Law of Taxation: Text, Cases and Materials* 49-52 (1994).
251. Note that the US is unique in that it taxes its citizens on worldwide income regardless of residency; such rule dates back to the American Civil War. Avi-Yonah, *supra* note 250, at 10.
252. *Id.* For an overview of source-based taxation and the principle of non-discrimination (particularly as it materialized in ECJ jurisprudence), *see generally* Ruth Mason and Michael S. Knoll, *What Is Tax Discrimination?*, 121 Yale L.J. 1014, 1026-33 (2012).
253. Avi-Yonah, *supra* note 250, at 10.
254. *See* Avi-Yonah, *supra* note 250, at 9-11.
255. *See, e.g.*, Nielsen, Administrator v. Johnson, Treasurer, 279 U.S. 47 (1929) (inheritance tax was upheld when the tax was imposed on a Danish national without connection to the US as a result of the inherited property being located in Iowa. Inheritance tax was upheld despite US-Denmark treaty providing for the exclusion of any levies on property removed from one Contracting State to another).
256. Royalties may be considered "passive income" when "not derived from the ordinary trade or business." *See, e.g.*, 26 U.S. Code § 1411(c)(1)(A)(i) (Title 26 in the US Code is designated as the Internal Revenue Code) [hereinafter "IRC"]. Royalties from mineral rights may be treated as either passive or active income depending on the business organization. In general, "direct participation" in the business is not necessarily required by the landowner for the income to be treated as "active." *See* Richard D. Blau, Bruce N. Lemons, Thomas P. Rohman, Excess passive investment income—Passive investment income defined generally—Royalties, 1 S Corporations Federal Taxation § 8:65, para. 7 (2019), Westlaw SCORP.
257. Avi-Yonah, *supra* note 250, at 13-14.

linked to define the source of income. It does so by the establishment of rules, often embodied in tax treaties that set out the treatment of "various categories of income."[258]

[D] Definitional Conundrums in a Crosslinguistic Setting

In the absence of a defined term for the noun "tax" in a treaty, an additional layer of complexity arises when the term is used in compound form, and especially when that compound form is applied in or translated into different languages. Drafters may further seek to narrow the generic term "tax" by implementing various constructions to refer to government measures of taxation rather than the generic act of taxation. The compound noun may commonly include a noun-noun compound form or even adjective-noun form in English: "tax measures," "taxation measures," "tax provisions," "taxation provisions" or even the less common "taxational measures."

Each compound form requires an examination of its ordinary meaning. In treaty contexts, whenever ambiguity arises, the formal rules of VCLT Article 33(1) ought to be applied with an inquiry of whether the treaty gives the terms a specific meaning or not.[259] In many such instances, these forms may be used as synonyms, particularly when they are otherwise not given a specific meaning in the treaty. The compound form of the term may change the formal meaning of the term independent of the specific meaning of the individual terms. For example, the term "repressive tax" is not a tax that is repressive but it is a tax on activities that are aimed to be repressed, such as luxury items or unwanted behavior (e.g., "sin tax").[260]

"Tax measures," "taxation measures" or "taxational measures" may commonly be used interchangeably as the compound forms have very little distinction. "Tax" would refer to the generic meaning of the term. "Taxation" retains the form of a noun but adopts the function of referring to the act of "fixing the sum."[261] 'Taxational' is the adjective form of the term.[262] In all these three forms, the terms refer to the same denotation with a varying degree of commonality and should be considered synonyms.

Synonyms are, in the "strict[]" form, terms that "have the same sense (in the same language)."[263] However, they may also refer to terms near in meaning. Synonyms may "hav[e] the same general sense, but possess[] each of their meanings which are not shared by the other or others, or having different shades of meaning or implications appropriate to different contexts."[264] "Tax measures," "taxation measures" and "taxational measures" are in their form *strict* synonyms. Tax provisions and tax measures

258. Avi-Yonah, *supra* note 237, at 490-1, 500-1("arbitrary rules embodied in tax treaties ... may form part of customary international law," but in the US, legislation may override customary international law and treaties. Nonetheless, customary international law may be used in the absence of treaties and legislation).
259. VCLT Article 31(1) sets out that: "[a] treaty shall be interpreted in *good faith* in accordance with the *ordinary meaning* to be given to the terms of the treaty *in their context* and *in the light of its object and purpose*."
260. *See, e.g., Repressive tax, Black's Law Dictionary* (11th ed. 2019).
261. *Oxford English Dictionary*, 2020 ("taxation").
262. *See Oxford English Dictionary*, 2020 ("taxational").
263. *Oxford English Dictionary*, 2020 ("synonym").
264. *Id.*

are also synonyms but not in the strict meaning of the term. The terms "tax provisions" and "tax measures" contain differences; these have "different shades" but carry the same "general sense." Whereas "tax provisions" refer to the drafted text of a law or administrative act, "tax measures" are linked to the actual acts undertaken by the state. The latter (e.g., "tax measures") may encompass the former ("tax provisions") but otherwise should carry the same meaning. Unless some distinction is required between a drafted instrument giving rise to a specific need for characterizing the text as an actual act of the state, "tax provisions" and "tax measures" may be used interchangeably as synonyms.

Translations of compound words in different languages may generate further confusion as different meanings may be attributed to the individual components of the compound noun in different languages.[265] When the compound noun term is not formally defined in the treaty, small deviations may impact the understanding particularly when the term has an outcome-determinative meaning. Near-synonyms of compound words in one language may not necessarily serve as near-synonyms in others, or not be translated as such. Such discrepancy would be complicated if the treaties have the same weight in their two different translations. In such crosslinguistic framework, additional care should be exercised when drafting, translating and interpreting the terms.

§3.03 DEFINING THE LIMITS ON THE STATE'S TAXATION POWER

[A] The Limits to a State's Power to Tax

As the state may tax anyone within its borders, territoriality is the first conceived limit of the state's power to tax. However, a state may commonly exercise its power under certain occasions even beyond its borders.

Not only are taxpayers subject to national taxation, but due to overlapping principles for assessing taxes, taxpayers may also be subject to double or multiple taxation. International law seeks only to mitigate such adverse effects by: (1) "double taxation" treaties (DTTs) reducing or minimizing the overlap and (2) "negative principle" by which enforcement of fiscal and penal laws of an individual state is restricted in the other state.[266]

Other than formal limits on the jurisdiction of the state's taxing power, the limits on a state's power to tax are fourfold:

---

265. *See generally* Gonia Jarema, *Compound Representation and Processing: A Cross-language Perspective, in The Representation and Processing of Compound Words* 56-62 (Gary Libben and Gonia Jarema eds., 2006) (discussing that the structure of the compound nouns may impact their use and understanding in different languages).

266. James Crawford and Martti Koskenniemi, *Introduction, in The Cambridge Companion to International Law* 9 (James Crawford and Martti Koskenniemi eds., 2012). *See also Oppenheim's International Law* § 371 ("whatever may be the rule of international law as to the duty of the states (and their courts) to recognize the effects of foreign legislation within the foreign country concerned, it would appear that there is no such obligation with respect to foreign legislation, whatever the place of its purported effect, which is in itself contrary to international law").

- national constitutional law;
- customary international law;
- treaty limitations; and
- administrative considerations.[267]

These four elements cover a wide range of issues, all of which are relevant for the practice of arbitral tribunals. These are discussed below[268] but a sense of pragmatism needs to be accounted when reviewing the application of these limits. For example, a case that carries a direct impact on the state power to tax has emerged from Amsterdam where, in 2010, a series of letters from the Amsterdam City Archives, due to be destroyed, revealed an unreasonable exercise of the state power to tax returning Holocaust survivors.[269] The letters, tracing back to the period of 1945-1947, unveiled 217 cases where the city enforced the collection of back-payments for property taxes, penalty fees, and gas bills for the period during World War II on individuals who were sent to concentration camps. The letters were desperate requests for extensions, delays of payments, and cancellation of accumulated taxes, fees and penalties while the inhabitants were deported. In 1947, a local court ruled that the City of Amsterdam was entitled to full payment of the retroactive taxes and fees, despite contrary advice from the City Attorney.[270] The outcome of the revelation has been a wide campaign that culminated in a public apology and compensation by the City of Amsterdam in 2016. The faulty decision of the City of Amsterdam against its own citizens is a notable reminder on the limits to a state's power.

[B] National Constitutional Law and Administrative Considerations

[1] Constitutional Limits

Regardless of the contextual definition for tax, a tax involves a mandatory contribution, or a taking, to the government. National constitutional norms define the primary limitations under the domestic regime. Constitutional norms set out the inquiry on the authority of the state including how the government derives its powers and may exercise the power to tax.[271] Whether it is by checks and balances in a traditional

267. Harris and Oliver, *supra* note 230, at 44. For a "classic" US perspective on the domestic limits of due process to tax procedure, *see generally* Judson, *supra* note 239, at 372-403.
268. *See infra* 3.03[B] ff.
269. Amsterdam compensates Jews after the revelations of a temporary worker (Dutch "Amsterdam compenseert Joden na onthulling door uitzendkracht"), Radio N1, May 17, 2016; available at: https://www.nporadio1.nl/radio-eenvandaag/onderwerpen/356547-amsterdam-compenseert-joden-na-onthulling-door-uitzendkracht (Accessed: May 30, 2020). *See also* 'The Tax Man Scoffs at Genocide: Amsterdam Holocaust Survivors Were Forced to Pay Back Taxes', Washington Times, Apr. 19, 2014; https://www.washingtontimes.com/news/2014/apr/19/amsterdam-holocaust-survivors-were-forced-pay-back/ (Accessed: May 30, 2020).
270. Amsterdam City Council Decision nr. 42, Besluitenboek, vol. 488, 510, Sept. 24, 1947. *See also* Decision Nr. 518 (Neth.), Preliminary referral decision, Amsterdam City Hall, Sept. 12, 1947, Gementeblad afd. 1, 848-50.
271. *See, e.g.*, The Swedish Instrument of Government (Sw. "Regeringsformen"), 1974:152, 9 kap. US Constitution, Art. I Sect. 8 ("The Congress shall have Power To lay and collect Taxes,

Montesquieu balance-of-powers regime or simply by a judicial review of constitutional acts, the constitutional framework constitutes a *self-check* within its own legal framework.

Taxation powers under national constitutional theory are rooted in the *social contract* theory.[272] Under this theory, the individual enters into a contract *voluntarily* with other individuals to adhere to a set of rules unrelated to "divine right, necessity custom, convenience, or psychological compulsion."[273] Under the social contract theory, an individual only transfers some limited authority to the state and the state may exercise only such authority authorized by the people. Taxes then become a contribution to the pool of resources for the benefit of everyone and not one individual in particular as it would be the case for an insurance scheme. The individuals adhere to pay a portion of their income to maintain and preserve such common interests (infrastructure, schools, army, and pension for the elderly).[274] The principle of social theory stands at the root of the American democracy and has influenced political thought in France[275] and Germany up until the 1800s;[276] it then has retreated, less so in the US, in favor of utilitarianism, including Marxism.[277]

Social contract theory yields itself to limits, as contract limitations set out conceptual demarcations. However, such demarcation is complicated by the lack of clarity on what encapsulates the social contract. The national constitution would often serve as the binding mechanism for the social contract, but often its text alone may not be sufficient for establishing the scope of consent granted by a citizen taxpayer to the state.

In such manner, the constitutional limits are subject to two layers. The operative text of the national constitution forms the first layer of limitations to the government powers to tax, as defined under national law. National constitutional regimes sanction unlawful conduct in breach of its own norms as these may change over time.[278] Any tax

Duties, Imposts and Excises, to pay the Debts and provide for the common Defence and general Welfare of the United States; but all Duties, Imposts and Excises shall be uniform throughout the United States"); *see also* Mason, *supra* note 208, at 994-6 (discussing US constitutional limits). *See also* the Constitution of the Russian Federation, arts. 57 (imposing the obligation on citizens to pay taxes), 71 and 72 (setting out the primary jurisdiction at the federal level and joint jurisdiction on the subjects of the Russian Federation).

272. Arguments have been made that a social contract may be deduced even in a transnational context. *See, e.g.*, Allisons Christians, *Sovereignty, Taxation and Social Contract*, 18 Minnesota J. Int'l L. 99 (2009) ("[t]o identify grounds upon which one state can or should intervene in the tax policy decisions of another is essentially to identify and define a code of conduct for tax system design in an international social contract").
273. *See generally* Patrick Riley, *Social Contract and its Critics, in The Cambridge History of Eighteenth-Century Political Thought* (Mark Goldie and Robert Wokler eds., 2006), 347-75 at 347.
274. *Id.* 350 (discussing the writings of Francisco Suárez: "men can be 'gathered together' into 'one political body' only by 'special volition, or common consent'; the people cannot 'manifest' consent 'unless the acts are voluntary'").
275. For French contrarianism before and after Rousseau, including the radicalization of contractarianism theory, *see id.* 358-69.
276. *See id.* 347, 369.
277. *Id.* 347 and 373-5.
278. For example, the US Constitution has originally restricted the power to tax "direct taxes apportioned under the states" thereby limiting the power of the US federal government to

measures shall be subject to existing regimes under national law. The proper forum for such scrutiny is often the national court, be it an ordinary court or a constitutional court.

Behind the limits derived from the national constitutional regimes rests a second layer rooted in the principle that stands at the core of legitimacy and reasonableness of tax legislation. It is what Alexander Hamilton defined in Federalist No. 30 as "confidence in [government's] engagements." Such confidence is intended to apply to foreigners and nationals alike, as below:

> The power of creating new funds upon new objects of taxation, by its own authority, would enable the national government to borrow as far as its necessities might require. Foreigners, as well as the citizens of America, could then reasonably repose confidence in its engagements; but to depend upon a government that must itself depend upon thirteen other governments for the means of fulfilling its contracts, when once its situation is clearly understood, would require a degree of credulity not often to be met with in the pecuniary transactions of mankind, and little reconcilable with the usual sharp-sightedness of avarice.[279]

Confidence or trust,[280] as observed by Alexander Hamilton and then adhered to by the US Supreme Court in *McCulloch v. Maryland*, draws the red line between legitimate exercise of government authority and abuse:

> That the power to tax involves the power to destroy; that the power to destroy may defeat and render useless the power to create; that there is a plain repugnance in conferring on one Government a power to control the constitutional measures of another, which other, with respect to those very measures, is declared to be supreme over that which exerts the control, are propositions not to be denied. But all inconsistencies are to be reconciled by the magic of the word CONFIDENCE. Taxation, it is said, does not necessarily and unavoidably destroy. To carry it to the excess of destruction would be an abuse, to presume which would banish that confidence which is essential to all Government.[281]

---

impose broad income taxes. *See* US Constitution, Art. I, Section 2, Clause 3. *See also* Pollock v. Farmers' Loan & Trust Company, 157 U.S. 429 (1895), aff'd, 158 U.S. 601 (1895). The Sixteenth Amendment reversed such precedent. It legitimized "income tax" and extended the power to collect income tax irrespective of the source of the income and without regard to previous limits that it be apportioned between the states. US Constitution, Sixteenth Amendment (ratified 1913).

279. Federalist No. 30 *Concerning the General Power to Tax* (Alexander Hamilton). The Federalist Papers had the primary objective to convince the voters of the State of New York to ratify the US Constitution and serve as a collection of critical essays from the time of the drafting of the US Constitution, *see* Gregory E. Maggs, *A Concise Guide to the Federalist Papers As A Source of the Original Meaning of the United States Constitution*, 87 B.U. L. Rev. 801 (2007). The "thirteen other governments" refer to the governments of the thirteen original states, which at the time were acting independently from each other. *See also* Ruth Mason, *supra* note 208, at 1035 (2011) (discussing Federalist No. 31 granting broad powers to tax).

280. *See also* Judson, *supra* note 239, at 2 (discussing the "fatal defect" of the Articles of Confederation not to enable the federal government to collect revenue by means of federal taxation).

281. McCulloch v. Maryland, 17 U.S. 316, 431 (1819) (emphasis in the original). Federalist Nos. 30 and 31. *See also See even* Magdalena Andersson, Speech by Minister for Finance at Stockholm Tax Conference concerning capacity building (May 30, 2018); https://www.government.se/

The holding sets out the principles behind determining what taxes are authorized or needed, as well as extrapolates when the actions of the state go beyond what is authorized, accepted or necessary. Abusive exercise of government authority when taxing would thereby be unlawful under national constitutional norms.[282]

These principles, which incorporate the limits to the absolute power to tax, could be incorporated in domestic law, as it is in the US. When domestic principles fail, the analysis needs to extend beyond domestic practice. For example, national constitutions may authorize unlimited taxation powers, even guised as some version of the social contract between the citizen taxpayer and the state.[283] On a pure national level, courts may scrutinize these constitutional norms under basic principles of justice and otherwise binding norms. International tribunals may, if properly authorized to review such actions, exercise authority to review such otherwise binding national norms against overriding principles of justice inherent in constitutional protections. In such manner, the textual review of national regimes serves as a relevant but not sufficient determination of any breach of taxation powers.

Figure 3.2 below reveals the inherent structural limits at the national level derived from constitutional norms. The power to tax is inherent in the state's sovereignty but such power may only be exercised within the limits of the national regime, set out by national constitutions. National courts retain the authority to examine any breaches of constitutional norms and to invalidate such breaches; investment tribunals have never stood as appellate bodies on national constitutional matters. What investment tribunals are called to rule on are breaches of treaty provisions after Contracting States expressly consent to international tribunals exercising jurisdiction of such disputes. The consent to international dispute settlement is derived from the same source as the power to tax: the sovereignty of the state. There are then two limits derived from constitutional norms: (1) those directly derived from constitutional norms and (2) those extending beyond the domestic constitutional norms. The former are textual readings in the ordinary work of the court, where the acts of legislative or administrative agencies are reviewed against existing constitutional norms. The latter are principles that would transcend existing domestic constitutional norms. The analysis is ultimately an exercise in determining where the purview of domestic constitutional norms ends and what lies beyond that.

---

speeches/ ("well, it's about trust. Trust between the legislator and the taxpayer"). *But cf* Judson, *supra* note 239, at 5 (arguing that Hamilton's position was for "unrestrained" taxation powers).

282. *See generally* Thomas Cooley, *Remedies of Illegal Taxation*, Am. L. Register 29 (1881), 1-16 (detailing the scrutiny by the US courts of taxation measures adopted prior to the passage of the Sixteenth Amendment).

283. *See, e.g.*, 1977 Soviet Constitution Art. 14 (emphasis added):

> [...] The state exercises control over the measure of labour and of consumption in accordance with the principle of socialism: "*From each according to his ability, to each according to his work.*" It fixes the rate of taxation on taxable income.
>
> Socially useful work and its results determine a person's status in society. By combining material and moral incentives and encouraging innovation and a creative attitude to work, the state helps transform labor into the prime vital need of every Soviet citizen.

Figure 3.2 The Power to Tax at the National Level

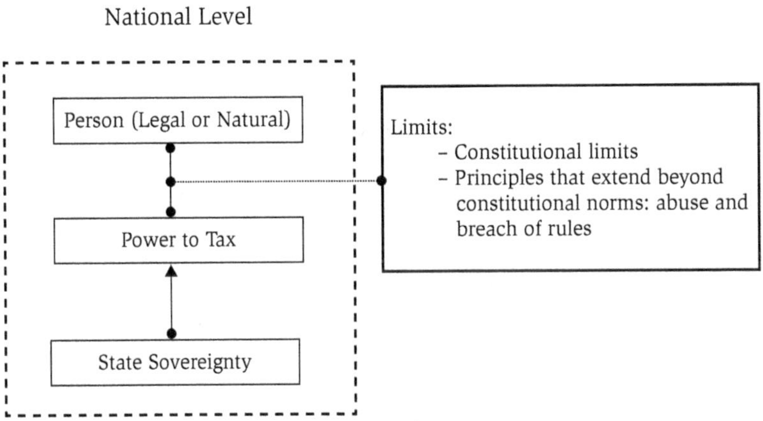

Source: Author's Own.

The principle of abuse also links well to the public international law principle of abuse of rights, namely where the state may exercise such powers in a manner that "impedes the enjoyment by other States of their own rights or for an end different from that for which the right was created" that would be the subject of the following sections on customary international law and treaties.

[2] Administrative Considerations

Adam Smith introduced four basic principles of taxation: proportionality, certainty, efficiency, and minimization of deadweight loss.[284] A tax shall be proportional based on what the individual is earning; shall be "certain, not arbitrary," timely so the taxpayer can meet his or her obligations; and should maximize the payment to the public treasury without impacting the ability to pay.[285] OECD has further clarified these principles to include: neutrality, efficiency, certainty and simplicity, effectiveness and fairness, as well as flexibility.[286] These principles, together with the requirement of confidence in the state, shape the application of the tax law. Across jurisdictions, tax administration falls upon administrative agencies. Taxation is also commonly viewed as an arm of domestic administrative law, subject to specific administrative laws[287] and

284. Adam Smith, *An Inquiry into the Nature and Causes of the Wealth of Nations*, Book V Chap. II Part II (Edwin Cannan ed., Methuen & Co. 1904)(1776); at https://www.econlib.org/ (Accessed: May 30, 2020).
285. *See id.*
286. OECD, *Addressing the Tax Challenges of the Digital Economy* 30-1 (2014).
287. *See, e.g.*, Sweden, Taxeringslag (1990:324) ("Tax Assessment Act"); in the US on the federal level, the United States Tax Court, Rules of Practice and Procedure shall apply. *See also* United States Tax Court, Rules of Practice and Procedure, Rule 1(b).

supplemented by criminal legislation covering tax evasion and tax avoidance.[288] The OECD principles for taxation are therefore well engrained in tax practice: be it in how administrative rules are formulated, applied or interpreted.

Administrative costs are "normally" linked to "how much scope there is for the tax to be incorporated in existing systems of administration and control."[289] The lion's share of existing environmental energy-related taxes are transaction-based: either levied on "value of goods and services" or determined on the basis of "incomes paid or received."[290] One way to decrease the administrative costs is to link new operations to "corresponding operations already undertaken for existing taxes."[291] However, new environmental taxes based on emissions require, at a minimum, an assessment of three items: (1) "measurement costs per source," (2) "the number of emissions sources" and (3) "scope for integration with normal commercial activities."[292] When reviewed in the context of subsidies or tax exemptions, a similar administrative-burdensome analysis needs to be undertaken for the *sources*, *quantities*, and *commercial link*. In part as a result of this triad of costs, there exists a fundamental limitation linked to efficiency and effectiveness. The principles of efficiency and effectiveness, as derived from national administrative law, dictate against the prosecution of tax breaches that are prohibitively expensive and do not advance overriding public purposes.[293]

Although these principles may often stand in contradiction with administrative limitations, new technology and access to information has made previously daunting information-gathering tasks accessible and affordable. In the last decade, new technology and new bank regulations have made access to information much easier. In the current age, pressures on government regimes from investigative journalists have incentivized the curtailing of complex tax-minimization schemes across jurisdictions.[294] However, even as old barriers come down, new barriers are coming up. The digital economy, for example, poses new challenges and is becoming increasingly difficult to subject to taxation.[295] In such instances, the principles of efficiency remain relevant for containing the state's power to tax and inadvertently serve as an important consideration for investment protection regimes.

288. *See, e.g.*, Sweden, Skattebrottslag (1971:69) ("Tax Penal Code").
289. Stephen Smith, *"Green" Taxes and Charges* 19 (1995).
290. *Id.*
291. *Id.*
292. *Id.*
293. *But see* Judson, *supra* note 239, at 405 (discussing in the domestic context that "public purpose is implied in the conception of a tax").
294. *See generally* Nicola Slawson, *Mossack Fonseca law firm to shut down after Panama Papers tax scandal*, The Guardian, Mar. 14, 2018. *See also* Andrew P. Morriss and Lotta Moberg, *Cartelizing Taxes: Understanding the OECD's Campaign Against "Harmful Tax Competition,"* Columbia J. Tax L. 4:1, 33-40 (2013).
295. OECD, Addressing the Tax Challenges of the Digital Economy, Action 1—2015, Final Report, OECD Publishing, Paris; http://www.oecd.org/ctp/tax-challenges-digital-economy-discussion-draft-march-2014.pdf (Accessed: May 30, 2020).

[C] Customary International Law

The second limit to the state's power to tax is found in customary international law. In the investment protection regime, several areas of customary international law are relevant as, for example, expropriation or denial of justice.[296] For purposes of taxation, the critical areas of customary international law may be considered: expropriation, sovereignty over natural resources, customary minimum standard, the principle of non-discrimination, and abuse of rights.

Under the Statute of the ICJ Article 38(1)(b),[297] customary law is defined in terms of what the court shall apply, as below:

> international custom, as evidenced by general practice accepted as *law*.

In such manner, customary international law comprises of two elements: (1) general practice and (2) acceptance as law ("opinion juris").[298] The first prong captures uniform general practice over some period of time. Practice needs to be "uniform, extensive and representative in character."[299] Also, only public acts count as practice.[300] However, a state persistently and openly dissenting may be deemed not to be bound by such practice, also known as the "persistent dissenter rule."[301]

The relationship between the first and the second prong remains debated. General practice is often deemed to suffice for establishing a binding obligation.[302] A different position insists on the existence of both prongs for a finding of a binding obligation.[303] Such a view is usually preferred by investment arbitration

296. *See* Dolzer and Schreuer, *supra* note 54, at 17.
297. *Cf.* Patrick Dumberry, *The Formation and Identification of Rules of Customary International Law in International Investment Law* 18 n. 15 (2016) (discussing the criticism and the limitations in the use of the ICJ Statute Art. 38(1)).
298. *See generally* Tullio Treves, *Customary International Law*, Max Planck Encyclopedia of Public International Law, Nov. 2006.
299. *See* International Law Association, Committee on Formation of Customary (General) International Law, Final Report, 2000, Section 12; http://law.umich.edu (Accessed: May 30, 2020) [hereinafter "ILA Final Report on the Formation of Customary International Law"]. *See also* Maurice Mendelson, *The Formation of Customary International Law*, Hague Academy of Int'l L. Collected Courses 272, 155-410 at 197-227 (1998).
300. ILA Final Report on the Formation of Customary International Law, Sect. 5.
301. ILA Final Report on the Formation of Customary International Law, Sect. 15.
302. ILA Final Report on the Formation of Customary International Law, Sect. 16.
303. *See generally* Dumberry, *supra* note 297 at 30-5. *See also* Christopher Greenwood, "Sources of International Law: An Introduction," Outline of the UN Library Presentation, 2008; available at: http://legal.un.org/avl/pdf/ls/greenwood_outline.pdf (May 30, 2020) ("A new rule of customary international law cannot be created unless both of these elements are present"). *Cf.* ILA Final Report acknowledges the different views:

> The view has already been expressed in this Statement that the subjective element is not in fact usually a necessary ingredient in the formation of customary international law—certainly on the part of any given State which is allegedly bound by the putative customary rule. But whether or not this approach is accepted, what seems clear is that, if there is a good deal of State practice, the need (if such there be) also to demonstrate the presence of the subjective element is likely to be dispensed with. [...] But whatever the theory, the result is the same: the more the practice, the less the need for the subjective element.

tribunals.[304] Regardless of the necessity versus the sufficiency of the two prongs to each other, the second prong, referred to also as "opinio juris," requires a "belief that this practice is rendered obligatory by the existence of a rule requiring it."[305] Consent by the state is often not necessary.[306] A substantial manifestation of acceptance may establish acceptance, even in the case of lack of practice.[307]

Customary international law is notoriously difficult to determine. Sending flowers at the death of a high official may be deemed customary, but it does not rise to the level of a general practice that is accepted as law. Conversely, relieving foreign diplomats from customs duties for goods imported for personal use would constitute a binding obligation under customary international law regardless of whether the state has entered or not into a treaty on diplomatic protection.[308] The difference goes beyond what is deemed as general practice and extends into what is accepted as law. The gesture of the flowers emerge as a courtesy protocol; abstaining from sending such flowers may be perceived as an insult or a sign of unamiability but is unlikely to start a diplomatic crisis. Whereas the imposition of customs duties on diplomatic officers when they arrive into the country to complete their work would inadvertently open diplomats to the risk of unequal and disproportionate taxation, as well as retaliation.

Taxation measures per se are not subject to customary international law unless they infringe on other binding norms established by customary international law. In the investment regime, the main concern centers on the adverse impact on the property of individuals inadvertently triggered by expropriation or denial of benefits. In the taxation context, this may materialize in a creeping expropriation without adequate compensation. Restatement (Third) of the Foreign Relations of the United States ("Restatement") reveals state practice that attempts to clarify customary international law. Restatement §712 comment g notably specifies that:

> A state is responsible as for an expropriation of property [...] when it subjects alien property to taxation, regulation, or other action that is confiscatory, or that prevents, unreasonably interferes with, or unduly delays, effective enjoyment of an alien's property or its removal from the state's territory. [...] A state is not responsible for loss of property or for other economic disadvantage resulting from bona fide general taxation, regulation, forfeiture for crime, or other action of the kind that is commonly accepted as within the police power of states, if it is not discriminatory, [...] and is not designed to cause the alien to abandon the property to the state or sell it at a distress price.[309]

Due to the complexity of assessing customary international norms, the limits arising from customary international law on taxation are difficult to delineate. An international minimum standard may nonetheless be deemed to exist under customary

304. Dumberry, *supra* note 297, at 35.
305. *Id.* (quoting North Sea Continental Shelf Cases (Federal Rep. of Germany-Denmark), ICJ, Reports of Judgments Advisory Opinions and Orders, Judgment, Feb. 20, 1969, para. 77) at 1.
306. ILA Final Report on the Formation of Customary International Law, Sect. 18.
307. ILA Final Report on the Formation of Customary International Law, Sect. 19.
308. ILA Final Report on the Formation of Customary International Law, Sect. 17 (ii) Commentary.
309. Restatement (Third) of the Law of Foreign Relations of the United States §712 (Am. Law Inst. 1987) [hereinafter "Restatement"].

international law,[310] regardless of whether fair and equitable treatment (FET) or protection against unlawful expropriation is incorporated in treaties.[311] Drawing on the *Neer* standard, a "precise" formula may be neither helpful nor exhaustive, as codification of all future elements may be difficult to attain. Moreover, states may engage in wrongful conduct aimed at circumventing express written norms with conduct that otherwise may, or in fact does, violate general principles accepted as law.[312]

The lack of a "precise" formula and the concerns with codification accentuate the uncertainty in the scope and use of customary international law in investment law, but especially when it comes to taxation matters. Customary international law does not in itself fill a gap. Analogies to customary international law do not replace the exercise of interpreting the treaty provisions;[313] this is reviewed below.

[D] Treaties

The relationship between treaties and customary international law remains tenuous.[314] In many respects, treaties do not constitute "a source of law so much as a source of obligation under law."[315] In agreeing to certain terms between each other, states may or may not codify customary international law.[316] However, a treaty whether bilateral[317] or multilateral[318] and even in the context of a succession of treaties[319] is not presumed to create international law. In some limited cases, however, multilateral treaties may assist in "crystalliz[ing]" emerging rules.[320]

---

310. *See generally LFH Neer and Pauline Neer (US v Mexico)* (1926) 4 RIAA 60, 61-2, para. 4:

> Without attempting to announce a precise formula, it is in the opinion of the Commission [...] to hold (first) that the propriecy of governmental acts should be put to the test of international standards, and (second) that the treatment of an alien, in order to constitute an international delinquency, should amount to an outrage, to bad faith, to wilful neglect of duty, or to an insufficiency of governmental action so far short of international standards that every reasonable and impartial man would readily recognize its insufficiency. Whether the insufficiency proceeds from deficient execution of an intelligent law or from the fact that the laws of the country do not empower the authorities to measure up to international standards is immaterial.

311. *See generally* Martins Paparinskis, *The International Minimum Standard and Fair and Equitable Treatment* 155-9 (2013).
312. *See generally* US Department of Justice, Office of Legal Counsel, Memorandum for William Haynes III, Jan. 9, 2002 and US Department of Justice, Memorandum for Alberto Gonzales, Counsel for the President, Aug. 1, 2002 (setting out that waterboarding is not torture).
313. *See* Dolzer and Schreuer, *supra* note 54, at 107 (discussing Sporrong & Lönnroth v. Sweden that held that there was no expropriation when the City of Stockholm subjected two properties to twenty-three- and eight-year-long expropriation permits but never exercised the right to expropriate).
314. *See generally* Dolzer and Schreuer, *supra* note 54, at 17.
315. Greenwood, *supra* note 303, at 2.
316. ILA Final Report on the Formation of Customary International Law, Sect. 20 and 21.
317. ILA Final Report on the Formation of Customary International Law, Sect. 20.
318. ILA Final Report on the Formation of Customary International Law, Sect. 24.
319. ILA Final Report on the Formation of Customary International Law, Sect. 25.
320. ILA Final Report on the Formation of Customary International Law, Sect. 26.

Treaties constitute written agreements between two or multiple states.[321] Upon entering into force, treaties set out binding obligations on Contracting States that must be performed in good faith.[322] Unless stated otherwise, they apply on the territory of the state.[323] Treaties may also be sector- and country-specific that may be in the interest of the Contracting States. Their provisions may incorporate international customary law obligations in its provisions. For example, ECT Article 8 sets out a general provision on transfer of technology. Article 8(2) imposes an obligation on the ECT Member States to eliminate "existing [obstacles] and create no new obstacles for the transfer of technology" for the specific energy materials and products subject to two narrow limitations.[324] In a similar manner, Article 8(1) sets out a general obligation to "promote access and transfer of technology on a commercial and non-discriminatory basis." Whereas Article 8(2) and part of Article 8(1) incorporate sector-specific and subject-specific obligations that could hardly rise to the level of international customary law, the "non-discrimination" standard that appears in Article 8(1) incorporates general obligations of non-discrimination under international customary law. It has the potential of shaping future standards for transfer of technology.

Against this background, investment treaties oblige states to afford foreign investors a certain degree of investor protection. Whether bilateral or multilateral in form, treaties may contain different degrees of investment protection standards depending on the agreed commitment of states. NAFTA and ECT are primary examples of multilateral investment treaties (MITs): whereas NAFTA combines only three Member States, the ECT applies to fifty-two states, EU and EURATOM. There exist some 2,913 bilateral agreements in place of which 2,353 are in force.[325] They contain treaty-specific standards of protections, including protection against expropriation, discrimination, affording national treatment or FET, and offer the opportunity for private parties to bring a claim against the host state.[326] Approximately 10% of the treaties contain tax-specific provisions.[327]

Not only do investment treaties codify investment protections standards[328] but they also can shape the formation of customary international law.[329] As customary international law contains a requirement of general practice being accepted as law, treaties by their codification of practices may give rise to accepted standards emerging from treaty practice. To take the above discussed example, although sending flowers

321. VCLT Art. 2(1)(a).
322. VCLT Art. 26.
323. VCLT Art. 29.
324. ECT Art. 8(2). The two limitations are: "subject to non-proliferation and other international obligations."
325. *See* UNCTAD, International Investment Agreements Navigator, Cataloguing the treaties; https://investmentpolicy.unctad.org/international-investment-agreements (Accessed: May 30, 2020).
326. *See generally* Paulsson, *supra* note 52, at 426-7 (particularly discussing the BITs entered by the USSR).
327. UNCTAD, International Investment Agreements Navigator, Cataloguing the Treaties; https://investmentpolicy.unctad.org/international-investment-agreements (Accessed: May 30, 2020).
328. Stephen M. Schwebel, *The Influence of Bilateral Investment Treaties on Customary International Law*, 98 Am. Soc'y Int'l. L. Proc. 27-8 (2004).
329. *Id.*

for a funeral per se will not formally qualify as customary international law, codifying expropriation in a treaty dispels any doubts that unlawfully expropriation violates customary international law.[330] In such case, treaties may also clarify what standard of compensations is due and on what basis it shall be assessed.

DTTs relieve certain individuals from being taxed twice by two different states if certain criteria are met. They aim to avoid, reduce or align conflicting and potentially contradictory taxation rules of one or multiple states applied to the same tax subject. DTTs are intended to address instances when the same individual falls subject to different jurisdictions and reconciliations of tax obligations is necessary. The modern DTTs could be traced to the 1928 Model Tax Treaties developed by the League of Nations[331]; these treaties being rooted in the 1899 double taxation agreement between the Austro-Hungarian Empire and Prussia that precipitated several bilateral treaties and eventually the first multilateral tax treaty, the Rome Convention.[332]

Sovereignty remains a core prerogative of DTT,[333] but the actual power of the state goes often unexplored.[334] The power to tax sits firmly in the nature of the autonomous tax system. DTTs do not aim to harmonize tax laws; their aim is modest in seeking to "disentangle" the applicable tax base and assign it between several jurisdictions.[335] How this is accomplished remains exclusively at the domestic level, but the treaty regime may regulate the "interfaces" between the respective "autonomous national tax systems."[336] One of these interfaces may be stipulated in the DTT such as how the CTAs may coordinate with each other. Figure 3.3 captures the relationship of the migratory individuals and the movable tax base that may be the subject of multiple conflicting jurisdictions; in which case, the state may in reliance on

330. Although few would argue against unlawful expropriation being part of customary international law, the nature of compensation ("just," "adequate," "appropriate") is tied to the Hull formula. *Id.* 29.
331. League of Nations, Double Taxation and Tax Evasion, Report Presented by the General Meeting of Government Experts on Double Taxation and Tax Evasion, Publications of the League of Nations v. II, 49 (1928); https://www.uni-heidelberg.de/ (Accessed: May 30, 2020).
332. *See generally* Sunita Jogarajan, *Double Taxation and the League of Nations* 1-6 (2018) (referring to the 1899 Prusso-Austro-Hungarian Treaty, Preussiches Gesets, betreffend die Vermeidung von Doppelbesteuerungen (1900) (Prussia), Anlage B Schlussprotokoll, III and Convention for the Purpose of Avoiding Double Taxation between Austria, Hungary, Italy, Poland, Romania and the Kingdom of the Serbs, Croats and Slovenes, Rome, concluded Apr. 6, 1922, reproduced in League of Nations, Double Taxation and Fiscal Evasion: Collection of International Agreements and International Legal Provisions for the Prevention of Double Taxation and Fiscal Evasion 73-5 (1928), in force between Austro-Hungary and Italy).
333. Thomas Rixen, *From Double Tax Avoidance to Tax Competition: Explaining the Institutional Trajectory of International Tax Governance*, 18(2) Rev. Int'l Pol. Econ. 197-227 at 206-7 & 209 (2010). *See generally* Peter Dietsch, *Rethinking Sovereignty in International Fiscal Policy*, Rev. Int'l Studies 37, 2107-20 at 2112-14 (2011).
334. *See* Ben J. M. Terra & Peter J. Wattel, *European Tax Law* 715 (5th ed., 2008):

> The most important function of international tax law is to distinguish between your tax jurisdiction and mine, to divide the tax market; to distinguish between income (tax base) essentially attributable to your jurisdiction and tax base essentially attributable to my jurisdiction, and to not simply yield if you claim something I consider mine.

335. Rixen, *supra* note 333, at 209.
336. *Id.*

a treaty seek to "disentangle" the tax base and consent to assign it to different jurisdictions.

Figure 3.3 The Power to Tax in the DTT Context

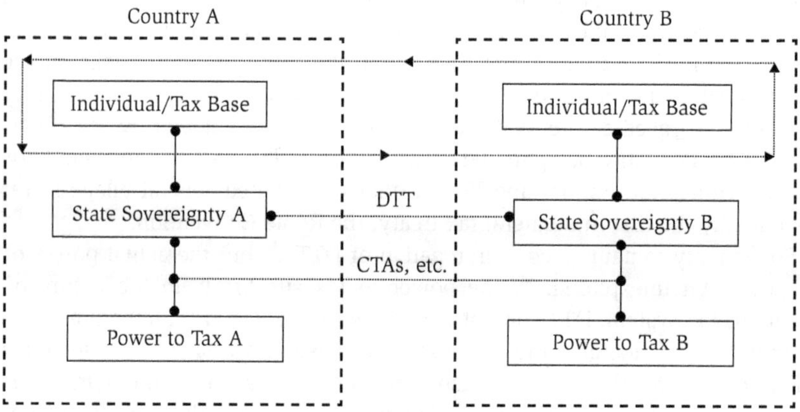

Source: Author's Own.

§3.04 A REVIEW OF THE EARLY TAX-RELATED ARBITRATIONS

[A] General Considerations

Tax disputes have arisen ever since states have exercised taxation powers.[337] In the past, resistance to unfair taxation occurred by means of armed conflict and even threats or actual secession.[338] In some early investment cases, foreign investors used arbitration, where possible, to address any infringement on their rights. Before the rapid rise in investor-state arbitration, five non-energy related arbitration set out the framework for addressing infringement by states by means of taxation powers; they incorporated the broad powers to tax and confronted the issues of limitations to such powers. These five cases are: *Brewer, Moller and Co. ("Brewer")* Case,[339] *Cook v. Mexico*,[340] *Kügele v.*

337. *See, e.g.*, Simon P. Anderson et al, *The Efficiency of Indirect Taxes Under Imperfect Competition*, J. Pub. Econ. 231-51, at 232 (2001) (discussing how in the Mesopotamian city of Lagash, the tax records were kept on soft clay to preserve the records of taxes owed and paid).
338. For an economic model of secession, *see* James M. Buchanan and Roger L. Faith, *Secession and the Limits of Taxation: Toward a Theory of Internal Exit*, Am. Econ. Rev. 77: No. 5, 1023-31 (1987).
339. Brewer, Moller and Co. Case, UN Rep. Int'l Arb. Awards (1903 Mixed Claims Commission, Germany-Venezuela), X, 423 [hereinafter "Brewer"]. *See also* Mixed Claims Commission Germany-Venezuela, Constituted under the Protocols of Feb. 13 and May 7, 1903, X, 357-476.
340. George Cook v. United Mexican States, Oct. 8, 1930, concurring opinion by American Commissioner Oct. 8, 1930, pages 61-8, in UN Rep. Int'l Arb. (General Claims Commission (Agreement of Sept. 8, 1923, as extended by the convention signed Sept. 2, 1929) (Mex., US.),

Polish State,[341], *Revere Copper and Brass Inc. v. Overseas Private Investment Corporation,*[342] and *Too v. Greater Modesto Insurance Company and the United States.*[343]

[B] *Brewer*

In *Brewer*, German investors brought a claim against Venezuela following the Venezuelan civil war, which led to the expropriation of property.[344] There were two cases brought by Brewer, Moller & Co., the first case dealing with municipal taxes. The main finding of the 1903 Mixed Claims Commission was that "[t]axes apparently legally levied and paid without protest [cannot] be recovered."[345] Although the second part of the holding focused on the need to raise an objection, the holding's first part concerned itself with the presumption of validity and the non-discrimination limit as below:

> The umpire is unable to see any ground whatever on which to sustain this claim. The uniform presumption of the regularity and validity of all acts of public officials applies to this case, and there is not the slightest evidence or attempt to prove that these taxes were illegally levied. There is a statement in the expediente that only warehouses owned by Germans fell under the operation of this law. If it were shown that this tax was specially levied upon Germans owning warehouses, because they were Germans, or that for any other reason they were unlawfully classified, the allegation might need further consideration; but it so clearly appears that the tax is a general one, and that the classification is made upon a basis of the values of property, that it excludes any such inference.[346]

The investor lost the case on evidentiary grounds: for not proving discriminatory intent or effect (for reasons of German nationality), which would override the presumption of legality. In the holding of the Mixed Claims Commission, had the investor been singled out for being German in paying the taxes, the Commission would

IV, 593-8; available at http://legal.un.org/riaa/cases/vol_IV/547-716.pdf [hereinafter *Cook*]. Not to be confused with the 1927 decision involving the same petitioner over a successful recovery of unpaid money orders and interest thereof despite a long period for raising the claim. *See* George Cook v. United Mexican States, June 3, 1927, concurring opinion by Presiding Commissioner and Mexican Commissioner, June 3, 1927, pages 318-24, in UN Rep. Int'l Arb. (General Claims Commission (Agreement of Sept. 8, 1923, as extended by the convention signed Sept. 2, 1929)(Mex. US.), IV, 213-17; The American-Mexico Claims Commission was set up to provide redress for claims arising out of the Mexican Revolution that occurred between 1910 and 1920. General Claims Commission (Convention of Sept. 8, 1923) (Mex., US.), Sept. 8, 1923, Reports of International Arbitral Awards, v. IV pp. 11-14; http://legal.un.org/riaa/cases/vol_IV/1-769.pdf.

341. Kügele v. Polish State (1932), 6 ILR 69, Case No. 34 (Upper Silesian Claims tribunal) [hereinafter *"Kügele"*].
342. Revere Copper and Brass, Incorporated-Overseas Private Investment Corporation, Award, American Arbitration Association Case No. 16 10 0137 76, Aug. 24, 1978 [hereinafter *"Revere Copper"*]. *See also* Revere Copper and Brass Incorporated, v. Overseas Private Investment Corporation, 628 F.2d 81 (D.C. Cir. 1980), *aff'd*, Misc. No. 78-0296 (D.D.C. 1978) [hereinafter "Revere Copper US court proceedings"].
343. Emanuel Too v. Greater Modesto Insurance Associates and the United States, Award No. 460-880-2, Iran-US Tribunal Case No. 880, Dec. 29, 1989 [hereinafter ""*Too*"].
344. *Brewer* at 423.
345. *Id.*
346. *Id.*

have reviewed the validity of the municipal taxes. The holding does not address whether discriminatory intent or effect suffices in refuting the presumption of general validity of a tax. However, the consequence of a showing that the tax "specially levied" indicates that discriminatory effect would suffice in refuting the general presumption of validity.

[C] *George W. Cook v. United Mexican States*

In *Cook,* the petitioner raised a claim for the recovery of property taxes paid in an alleged breach of an exemption granted by a high official.[347] The American-Mexico General Claims Commission dismissed the claim for lack of a clear commitment by the state.[348]

Prior to the Mexican Revolution, the American citizen George Cook owned a parcel in the City of Guadalajara. In 1905, Mr. Cook received an offer from the governor of the respective state that in the event he erected a building then the governor would recommend to the legislature that the property be exempted from the payment of "the corresponding property tax" (Sp. *la contributión predial correspondiente*).[349] Between 1906 and 1907, Mr. Cook erected the building. In April 1909, the State Congress enacted a bill that exempted the property from paying real estate taxes for twenty years. In 1910, the Mexican Revolution broke out to continue until 1920. By 1917, the state legislature applied a blanket 0.2% tax on all urban real estate property for the first semester of the year that was deemed to encompass Mr. Cook's property. Mr. Cook challenged the tax on the grounds that it allegedly contravened the offer granted by the governor and the existing legislation.[350]

The tribunal disagreed with Mr. Cook. The majority followed a two-prong analysis. It first held that the urban tax ("special tax") did not violate the exemption as other taxpayers were obligated to pay both taxes ("special tax" and "real estate tax").[351] It then reasoned that the state had the sovereignty to pass and amend tax legislation. Bar any contractual obligations to the contrary, an exemption to taxation may be freely repealed; furthermore, any ambiguity should be interpreted in the interest of the state, as per the following:

> [...] The right of the State to levy taxes constitutes an inherent part of its sovereignty; it is a function necessary to its very existence and it has often been alleged, not only in Mexico, but in the United States and other countries that legislatures, whether of states or of the Federation cannot legally create exemptions which restrict the free exercise of the sovereign power of the State in this regard. [...] And even in those cases in which the said majority of the Supreme Court of the United States has held that that right inherent to the sovereignty of a

347. *Cook* at 596.
348. *Id.*
349. The American Agency who supplied a third-party brief posited that the "edifice" would be "an improvement to the city." *Cook* at 594 (summarizing the arguments of the American Agency).
350. *Id.* 593-4.
351. *Id.* 595.

State might be the subject of a contract, it has also ruled that the exemptions should be strictly construed in favor of the State.

[...]

"In determining whether there is a valid contract and whether by its terms an exemption from taxation is granted, every presumption will be indulged in favor of the power of the State to tax and against the existence of the exemption" (Corpus Juris Vol. 12, par. 607).

[...]

"An exemption from taxation does not confer a vested right, and it may therefore be modified or repealed by the legislature unless it has been granted under such circumstances that its repeal would impair the obligation of a contract" (Corpus Juris, Vol. 12, Par. 536).[352]

The Concurring opinion, from the US Commissioner, did not follow the majority on the first prong of the analysis but it agreed on the issue of the dismissal. According to the US Commissioner, the Spanish wording of the exemption did not exclude the imposition of further taxes. Instead, the US Commissioner questioned whether the state legislature had the power to grant such a specific exemption in the first place and at a later stage to repeal it.[353]

[D] *Kügele v. Polish State*

In *Kügele*, the Upper Silesian Arbitral Tribunal, assembled under the rules of the Geneva Convention of May 15, 1922, dismissed the claims of indirect interference with private rights.[354] The case, which followed the transfer of Upper Silesia to Poland, saw a German brewer challenging the "license fees" that ultimately led to the closure of the brewery in Polish Upper Silesia.[355] With the tribunal treating the license fee as a tax, the case addressed direct claims of indirect expropriation against the state resulting from measures of taxation.[356]

352. *Cook* at 595-6.
353. *Id.* 597.
354. *Kügele* at 34. Convention concerning Upper Silesia concluded at Geneva on May 15, 1922 (Germany-Poland), *available at* Austrian National Library http://alex.onb.ac.at/ (Accessed: May 30, 2020). The 1922 Geneva Convention granted individuals the right to bring a claim against the state following the Upper Silesia plebiscite that lead to the partition of the region between Germany and Poland. For a general summary of the case, *see* Park, *supra* note 9, at 125-7. *See also* Thomas Wälde and Abba Kolo, *Investor-State Disputes: The Interface Between Treaty-Based International Investment Protection and Fiscal Sovereignty*, 35:8/9 Intertax 424 -49, at 444 (2007).
355. *Kügele* at 69 (discussing the "series of license fees successively imposed by the authorities"). Prior to World War I, Upper Silesia had been part of Germany. Following the end of World War I, the Treaty of Versailles provided for the holding of a plebiscite on whether Upper Silesia would remain part of Germany. Following the contested results of the plebiscite, the Allied Forces referred the matter to the League of Nations that led to the partition of the Upper Silesia, enactment of the Geneva Convention and the establishment of an arbitral tribunal to resolve the disputes. *See generally* G. Kaeckenbeeck, "The Character and Work of the Arbitral Tribunal of Upper Silesia," *Transactions of the Grotius Society*, Vol. 21, Problems of Peace and War, Papers Read before the Society in the Year 1935 (1935), pp. 27-44. *See also* Park, *supra* note 9, at 125-7.
356. *See, e.g.*, Encana v. Ecuador, Award, LCIA Case UN 3481, Feb. 3, 2006 at 51 [hereinafter "EnCana Award"]. *See also* Wälde and Kolo, *supra* note 354, at 444.

The local authorities imposed a "series of license fees" that led to a decreased profitability and the ultimate closure of the business.[357] In dismissing the claimant's request for compensation for losses caused by the imposition of the license fees, the full reasoning of the Upper Silesian Arbitral Tribunal is as below:

> The increase of the license fee was not in itself capable of taking away or impairing the rights of the plaintiff ... The increase of the tax cannot be regarded as a taking away or impairment of the right to engage in a trade, for such taxation presupposes the engaging in a trade. It is true that taxation may render the trade less remunerative or altogether unremunerative. However, there is an essential difference between the maintenance of a certain rate of profit in an undertaking and the legal and factual possibility of continuing the undertaking. The trader may feel compelled to close his business because of the new tax. ... But this does not mean that he has lost the right to engage in the trade. For had he paid the tax, he would be entitled to go on with his business.[358]

The tribunal focused on two findings. First, the impact of a tax is to be reviewed in connection to the effect that it has on an established right. In *Kügele*, the claimant focused exclusively on the series of license fees, and specifically on the effect of a license fee increase as the basis for infringement on his private rights. The license fees, which may or may not qualify as taxes, narrow the inquiry: the brewer paid for the right to engage in a trade. The fee increase alone did not take away or impair those rights. The focus of the illegality inquiry lay on the frustration of a right to engage in a trade but not on the incremental impact arising from the increase. Second, the assumption of profit is not a necessary requirement for deducing the legality/illegality of a tax. A tax may affect the profitability of the business. However, there is an "essential difference between the reduction of profits" and the inability to continue operations (legally and factually).

The rationale from Kügele is unlikely to prevail in full without criticism today.[359] The analysis in *Kügele* predates the formal inquiry into the possibility of "creeping expropriation" albeit instances of "creeping expropriation" appeared in one form or another before *Kügele*.[360] The distinction between maintenance of profit levels and continuation of the business is essential for purposes of determining whether a tax is expropriatory.

[E] *Revere Copper and Brass Inc. v. Overseas Private Investment Corporation*

The *Revere Copper* decision concerns the expropriation by Jamaica of the American investor's interest in bauxite mining, which converted bauxite into aluminum. Unlike subsequent investor-state disputes arising out of BITs, the dispute arose out of an insurance contract/guarantee. Although the dispute was purely commercial in nature,

357. *Kügele* at 69.
358. *Id.*
359. *See* Park, *supra* note 9, at 126-7.
360. *See generally* Weston, *supra* note 12, at 147-52 (1975-1976).

this early ruling had greater implications for the investment arbitration regime as a whole.[361]

In 1967, Revere Copper entered into an investment agreement for the construction of an aluminum plant. The investment agreement provided that it would remain in force for twenty-five years. It notably included a stabilization clause that ensured that no further taxes on bauxite would be imposed for the duration of the contract. By the end of 1974, the investor had invested ca. USD 100 million and the plant had the capacity of producing 220,000 tons of aluminum.[362]

In 1972, a new government took over and initiated a review of the bauxite and aluminum industry. After setting up a specialized Bauxite Commission, it began modifying the local legislation with the aim of increasing revenue from bauxite mining and aluminum production.[363] The negotiations for a compromise reached no results. In 1974, the government introduced a "bauxite levy" that imposed a "tax on bauxite at a rate to be determined from time to time, the initial rate being 7.5 percent."[364] Then, the government steadily increased the rate.[365] In 1975, the investor Revere Cooper incurred a substantial loss due to the increased costs of bauxite levy (Table 3.1). By 1976, it closed down its operations.[366]

Table 3.1 Cost of Bauxite Levy in Nominal Terms (USD/Ton)

1974	1975	1976	1977
11.16	12.65	15.62	17.86

Source: *Revere Copper* at 12.

Revere Copper launched a challenge with the local courts, which reached the Supreme Court of Jamaica. The Supreme Court then held that the tax stabilization clause violated constitutional norms and that the investment agreement did not grant any rights to the investor with regard to future taxes.[367] In 1976, Revere Copper then brought an action on the basis of the insurance agreement against the guarantor (OPIC who succeeded USAID as guarantor), arguing that an expropriation took place.

361. *Revere Copper*, at 2 (The US investor in Revere Copper initiated a commercial claim against the Overseas Private Investment Corporation (OPIC) in reliance on the insurance contract/guarantee entered by the United States Government Agency for International Development (USAID) and Revere, the US investor in Jamaica. OPIC, as the insurer, succeeded USAID as party to the dispute).
362. *Id.* 4-6 ("for 25 years from the earlier of the date of the commencement of commercial production of alumina from the plant to be constructed by RJA or from a date 2-1/2 years from the date of the Agreement"). The tax stabilization clause was incorporated in clauses 12 and 13. *Id* at 5 and 23.
363. *Id.* 7-8.
364. *Id.* 12.
365. *Id.* 13.
366. *Revere Copper* at 16.
367. *Id.* 46.

Over a dissenting opinion, the majority of the tribunal found in favor of the investor but awarded nominal damages.[368] The investor prevailed against the insurance company after the tribunal found that an expropriation occurred following Jamaica's implementation of a levy on the mining of bauxite.[369] Although the investor recovered damages, that amount was nominal.

In the majority's opinion, the commitments by the government were a "classic" example of the government providing "substantial long term commitments" from investors in exchange for "substantial inducements in the way of tax."[370] The majority concluded that the actions of the government terminated the provisions of the contract, including the stabilization clause.[371] It reasoned that the Jamaican government had repudiated the contract and that such repudiation directly prevented the local entity "from exercising effective control over the use or disposition of a substantial portion of its property or from operating the property."[372]

The majority held that the government remained bound by its international obligations and submitted to the authority of an investment tribunal by continuing to agree to arbitration in subsequent draft amendments.[373] In the opinion of the majority, the Supreme Court decision was limited in the finding that the stabilization clauses were invalidated on the basis of domestic law, not international law that was applicable in this case. The tribunal also rejected the arguments raised by the host state that UN Resolution 1803 enabled the state to invoke national sovereignty over its resources over its prior commitments. In the opinion of the majority, UN Resolution 1803 reflected a *lege ferenda* formulation of the norms and in any event they did not permit the state to invoke sovereignty for purposes of "disregard[ing] commitments freely undertaken through the exercise of this same sovereignty."[374]

The dissenting opinion focused on the distinction that although a breach has occurred, the facts did not establish that the government's levy "directly prevented" the investor to "exercis[e] effective control."[375] The dissent found that two factors: (1) "the reasonableness of the tax" and (2) "the magnitude of its impact" were two

368. The investor recovered USD 1.13 million against a claim of USD 64.13 million. Dissatisfied with the final award, the investor moved for the correction and vacation in part of the award. That petition was not successful in the district court and the Court of Appeals. *See generally* Revere Copper US court proceedings at 84 (discussing that Revere Copper brought the action in arbitration). For the dissenting opinion, *see Revere Copper* at 94 et al.
369. *Revere Copper* at 2. *See* Rosalyn Higgins, *The Taking of Property by the State: Recent Developments in International Law*, 176 Collected Courses of the Hague Academy of Int'l L. 332-8 (1982) (highlighting that the opinion is divided on whether "a government, in the exercise of police powers [may] terminate contract rights even though the private party is not at fault and even though the contract itself envisages termination only in other circumstances which have not arisen"). *See also* Manciaux, *supra* note 222, at 315-16 (discussing *Revere Copper*).
370. *Id.* 43.
371. *Id.* 18.
372. *Id.* 55.
373. *Id.* 44 and 46-7.
374. *Revere Copper* at 35-7 and 42-3 (referring to Texaco Overseas Petroleum Company v. Libya, 17 I.L.M. 1 (1978) at 50 and 54).
375. *Id.* 101.

determining factors warranting a finding of no expropriation.[376] It reasoned that the type of tax did not correlate to the confiscatory nature of a tax, regardless of the tax being on income, extraction or receipts.[377] The dissent referred to an Icelandic case where a 25% property tax was not deemed to be expropriatory.[378] It also referred to two US national cases where a 20% tax on gross receipts was deemed constitutional,[379] as well as a 19.5% tax on the market value of mined coal.[380]

In all, *Revere Copper* was one of the first instances where taxation matters materialized in the formal investment regime; albeit in a commercial not a treaty setting. It materialized in an instance where the host government repudiated the provisions of a tax stabilization clause through the introduction of a levy of less than 10%. The measure, which eventually led to the closing of an aluminum-producing plant, was deemed to deprive the investor of "effective control." The majority held that an expropriation took place despite the Supreme Court invalidating the stabilization clause under national constitutional norms and a minority opinion opining that the levy alone did not cause the loss of "effective control." The majority reasoned that the powers derived from national sovereignty over natural resources do not offset international commercial such as the prohibition of expropriating without payment of just compensation. The disagreement between the majority and the dissenting opinion revealed the importance of the individual review of each tax measure to assess whether the elements of expropriation were present.

[F] *Too*

In *Too*, an Iranian national, who was the owner of a motel, restaurant, and cold-storage van business, argued that the US individually and indirectly through the insurance company expropriated his property after the Iranian-United States Hostage Crisis. The motel, restaurant, and cold-storage vans were destroyed by arson on separate occasions. After the insurance company failed to pay the insurance claim, the US Internal Revenue Service (IRS) moved for auctioning his liquor license to pay off overdue employment taxes. As a result, Mr. Too's personal and commercial property was foreclosed. In his defense, he argued that the cancellation of his US visa prevented him from traveling back from Europe to tend to the dispute with the insurance company and the foreclosure proceedings. Mr. Too also argued that local authorities did not exercise sufficient care for the protection and security of the property.[381]

376. *Id.* 113.
377. *Id.* 114.
378. *Id.* 113 (discussing Gudmundsson v. Iceland, Application No. 511/59, 30 I.L.R. 253, Dec. 20, 1960 [Euro. Comm. Human Rights, 1960]). *See also* Higgins, *supra* note 369, at 363-6 (discussing on whether the holding in *Gudmundsson* is in decline).
379. *Revere Copper* at 115 (discussing Pittsburgh v. Alco Parking Corp., 417 U.S. 269 (1974); 453 Pa. 245, 307 A.2d 851, rev'd.). In *Alco Parking*, the US Supreme Court reversed the findings of the Pennsylvania Supreme Court that the tax on receipts was "unreasonably high" and "burdensome." *Id.* 372-3.
380. *Id.* 113 (discussing Sunshine Anthracite Coal Co. v. Adkins, 310 U.S. 381 (1940)).
381. *Too*, paras. 22-3.

In dismissing the claim, the Iran-US Tribunal held that Mr. Too did not prove that the US police and fire authorities failed to exercise "due diligence" in the protection of his property. Local authorities actively investigated the various complaints raised by Mr. Too.[382] In a similar manner, the tribunal deemed that the US tax authorities did not act improperly. By narrowing the review only to the sale of liquor license, the tribunal held that the US could not be held responsible for foreclosure proceedings such as the ones against private property initiated by commercial actors.[383]

In *Too*, the Iran-US Tribunal fine-tuned the *Kügele* test to develop a standard that focused on discrimination and coercion of the alien's property rights to rebut the presumption of bona fide taxes. In addressing the effect of the sale of the liquor license to offset unpaid employment taxes, the tribunal dismissed the claim and reasoned that:

> a State is not responsible for loss of property or for other economic disadvantage resulting from bona fide general taxation or any other action that is commonly accepted as within the police power of States, provided it is not discriminatory and is not designed to cause the alien to abandon the property to the State or to sell it at a distress price.[384]

The dissent, however, focused on the cancellation of Mr. Too's visa as the triggering point that led to the confiscatory effect. Starting with late 1979/early 1980, the US did not recognize visas issued in Tehran due to the increased risk of fraud; after the Embassy was seized by the Iranian authorities the Embassy's visa plates were used improperly by Iranian authorities.[385] In the dissent's opinion, the loss of property was the result of the US's overly restrictive and ungrounded visa practices.[386]

[G] Cross-Analysis of the Five Cases

This quintet of cases illustrates the foundational outer limits to the states' power to tax, arising out of investment protection (Table 3.2).

Table 3.2 Summary Presentation of the Five Tax Expropriation Arbitrations

Brewer	(1903) A presumption of validity applies to regular application of a tax by public officials; the presumption may be refuted upon a showing that the tax was "specifically levied" on a group of people based on their nationality or other unlawful classification
Cook	(1927) An exemption from taxation may be freely modified or repealed by the legislature unless the repeal of such exception would impair the obligation of a contract; any ambiguity should be construed in favor of the state

382. *Id.* para. 23.
383. *Id.* para. 25. The allegations around the freezing of Mr. Too's alleged bank account were also dismissed for failure to provide proof.
384. *Id.* para. 26.
385. *See generally id.* para. 7. *Cf. Too* (dissenting opinion of Seyed Khalil Khalilian), para. 5 at 390-1.
386. *See Too* (dissenting opinion of Seyed Khalil Khalilian), para. 7 at 392.

Kügele	(1932) The state has broad power to tax: taxes are by definition a taking, but loss of income does not qualify as expropriation
Revere Copper	(1978) In exercising the power to tax, the state may not breach earlier commitments such as a commitment not to expropriate. National sovereignty over natural resources was not recognized as an enforceable right under the investment agreement
Too	(1989) Any tax measure, including enforcement thereof, is not unlawful unless it is discriminatory or unduly burdensome (cause abandonment of the property or resale of the property)

Source: Author's Own.

All cases revealed a pattern by which the expropriatory effect of a tax is reviewed individually without sweeping generalizations being made based on the tax rate or another characteristic.

In *Brewer* and *Kügele*, the inherent presumption is that a tax is valid. In *Brewer*, the presumption of validity is subject to non-discrimination limitations, the required burden of proof being unclear. Based on *Kügele*, an individual does not have an expectation to profit and a state may impose such taxes as best as it deems fit.

In *Cook*, the tribunal made the direct connection between the sovereignty of a state and its ability to shape policy as it deems fit. The tribunal expressly set out the absence of vested rights in a tax exemption unless such exemption is expressly granted by contract. The tribunal textually interpreted the scope of the tax for purposes of assessing whether the new tax falls within the scope of the tax exemption thereby revoking the tax exemption.

Revere Copper stands to establish that the delicate line for when a tax is confiscatory is somewhat obscure and requires loss of control in line with the standard expropriation analysis. Drawing on the specific language in the treaty, the majority reasoned that a tax will be confiscatory when it "directly prevent[s]" the investor to "exercis[e] effective control" over the investment. In *Revere Copper*, the dissent and the majority opinion disagreed on the qualification of a breach as expropriation with the dissent finding that the investor retained property rights over its operations whereas the majority deemed that the investor lost "effective control" despite retaining "property rights." The nature of the tax appeared immaterial in the context of the effect on the property rights.

Too provides an additional clarification for when a tax/levy could be unlawful, especially when linked to enforcement proceedings. Enforcement of tax arrears was not deemed unlawful unless it singled out the foreign investor in a discriminatory manner. Visa delays imposed on Iranian nationals in the course of the Iranian Embassy crisis did not mean that the taxation measures imposed on him were discriminatory or confiscatory in nature. In the majority's opinion, Mr. Too was subject to "a lawful levy of overdue taxes."

These stark positions impact the determination of the effect of the tax *enforcement* measures. In examining the facts, the majority held that Mr. Too has not argued that the tax levy was somehow discriminatory against Iranian nationals per se. Neither did Mr. Too prove that the IRS coerced him to sell the property rights at a distressed price when he retained the right to repurchase the liquor license.[387] In *Too*, the majority associated bona fide general taxation with "any other action that is commonly accepted as within the police power of the States."[388] The tribunal did not go as far as to state that the taxation power is a form of police power. It simply likened the two acts of the state. This finding by the majority carries great weight. The power to exercise tax *enforcement* measures may in fact find support in the police power of the state. Enforcement of tax measures carries the important link to policing unlawful conduct. In such manner, the state's police power becomes of relevance when reviewing the *enforcement* elements of taxation measures.[389]

In addition, the *Too* majority focused on two requirements, discrimination and coercion/undue burden, to offset the presumption of bona fide taxes. In the opinion of the majority, both need to be present for a tax measure to be unlawful. The discrimination element is not controversial. The principle of non-discrimination finds support in customary international law.[390] It is the second element that raises some concern. The *Too* decision incorporates a disjunctive "or" without a comma referring to two acts: the act "to abandon the property to the State" or "to sell it at a distress price." Given the parallel form of the infinitive "to abandon" and to "to cause," the disjunctive form sets out a two-prong element of the same test when referring to *coercion*. Coercion by the state being defined as "caus[ing] the alien to [either] abandon the property to the State or to sell it at a distress price."

Overall, *Too* closely follows the outer limits prescribed by Albrecht's standards focusing on two criteria to offset a bona fide presumption prevailing over tax matters. However, the Albrecht article prescribes two outer limits, expropriation and discrimination, viewed independently of each other. According to Albrecht, either a discriminatory or expropriatory measure would offset the presumption of a bona fide tax. The finding of the *Too* tribunal dictates a different conclusion: both criteria should be met before a rebuttal of the presumption of validity of the tax measure may be identified. A tax must be discriminatory and reveal government coercion in order to invalidate bona fide taxation measures.

387. *Too*, para. 27 ("This claim is dismissed because the Claimant has failed to show that the IRS's action *was anything other than a lawful levy for overdue taxes,* for which there is no State responsibility") (emphasis added).

388. *Id.* para. 26.

389. *See* Jorge Viñuales, *Sovereignty in Foreign Investment Law, in The Foundations of International Investment Law: Bringing Theory into Practice* 317-62, 336 (Zachary Douglas, Joost Pauwelyn, and Jorge E. Viñuales eds., 2014) (pointing out that 'the better view is not that the police powers doctrine only applies to certain types of interference but, instead, that a valid exercise of the police powers doctrine is more likely to be upheld as such for some types of regulatory action (general regulations) than others (targeted measures)').

390. *See* A.R. Albrecht, *The Taxation of Aliens under International Law*, 29 Brit. Y.B. Int'l L. 145-85, at 171 (1952).

§3.05 CONCLUDING REMARKS

At the outset, the sub-inquiry focused on what the key *elements* of a tax are, and how they interplay with investment protections mechanisms as observed in the first international arbitrations. The key elements could be formulated by examining tax subjects, the subject matter of a tax, and the jurisdiction to tax. Several definitions emerge containing different *elements*, rather than fixed criteria. From a taxation point of view, the term "tax" contains the requirement of an unrequited payment to the government where the determinative factor is the mandatory payment for which no direct reward is expected.

Therefore, the definition of a tax, be it at a subnational, national, or international level, needs to capture certain limits inherent in the nature of the tax. Taxes affect growth and provide the fiscal means by which states may shape policy. At the same time, taxes are at their core a taking. A state may tax everyone who falls under its jurisdiction on two main principles: residency and source. Acts that seemingly pass the scrutiny of domestic constitutional law may still be in breach of public international law rules, including customary international law and treaty provisions. One shall not infer that states would somehow act reasonably without error. These elements yield themselves to four inherent limits, as found in: national law, administrative limitations, customary international law and treaty obligations. They have already materialized in four formative international arbitrations, *Kügele*, *Cook*, *Revere Copper*, and *Too*, where the power to tax has been recognized but subjected to limitations. The tax's unlawful effects need to be reviewed individually based on their particular characteristics, scope, and application.

To the question of *what taxes* should remain the focus of the inquiry, the answer is *all taxes and tax measures*. In many cases, different versions of the terms would be used: either strict synonyms (such as "tax measures" and "taxation measures") or near-synonyms ("tax measures" and "tax provisions") but the inquiry remains the same. Regardless of whether they are in fact taxes or being implemented under the guise of taxation, the exercise of the state's authority to tax shall be reviewed against the outer limits of such power. The early foundational arbitrations dealing with tax provisions set out an instructive look into the sovereignty of the state. The four cases underlined the state's broad power to tax. They serve as a testament to a gradual recognition of the outer limits of the power to tax. In comparing *Kügele* to *Too*, rendered some half a century apart, one notes at the core the broad power to tax subject to the outer shell of clear demarcation of such core power. *Cook* and *Revere Copper* reinforce this outer shell: Cook being closer to the core with its holding that states may freely modify a tax exemption, while *Revere Copper* adheres firmly to the outer shell in that it recognizes that the state may make commitments and such commitments may not be broken.

The core of the state's taxation power has rested on confidence in government measures. A tax subject's confidence sets out the rationale for passing, exercising, and reviewing tax measures on the domestic level. In the FDI regime, the confidence factor matches the investor's rationale for investing in a country with the reasonable measures that a state may take in exercising its authority. The next chapter addresses the structure of the ECT Taxation Article to determine through its various layers of complexity the degree of confidence that a tax subject may expect in the application of the Treaty.

CHAPTER 4

The Taxation Article in the ECT and Other Select BITs

§4.01 INTRODUCTION TO THE STRUCTURE OF THE TAXATION ARTICLE

With the background of the general features of a tax and the early investment arbitrations related to taxation, the next sub-inquiry focuses on the formal structure of the ECT Taxation Article and whether there are any means to systematize the various elements of the Taxation Article and the tax provisions of other investment treaties.

ECT Article 21 adopts a complex structure found in international treaties, particularly those pertaining to taxation, by which a matter is subject to:

- an *exclusion* from the application of the treaty,
- followed by *specified inclusion(s)* despite the initial exclusion,
- the inclusion being layered with *limitations* or *exceptions*,
- the exceptions themselves being subject to *restrictions*.[391]

The structure of Taxation Article extends to four levels. It does not stop, at the first level, the *Exclusion* ("carve-out"), or at the second level, the *Specified Inclusions* ("clawback"), but instead goes several layers deep into the third level, *limitations* and *exceptions*, and at the fourth level, *restrictions* to exceptions. The less formal term "carve-out" commonly refers to the exclusion of the tax issues ("Exclusion"). The "clawback" refers to an inclusion where several matters ("Inclusion" or "Specified

391. For the ECT "complex" structure, *see* Park, *supra* note 9, at 116-18 (referring to the effect as the Russian nested doll or "matryoshka"). *See also* EU-Canada Comprehensive Economic and Trade Agreement (CETA), Chapter 28 and specifically Art. 28(7); at http://trade.ec.europa.eu/. For BITs, *see* 2012 US Model BIT Art. 21; http://www.state.gov; 2004 Canada Agreement on Foreign Investment Protection and Promotion Agreement (FIPA), http://www.italaw.com. For double taxation treaties, *see* 2006 US Model Double Taxation Treaty; http://www.irs.gov (Accessed: May 30, 2020).

Inclusions") are deemed to fall within the scope of the treaty when certain conditions are met.

Figure 4.1 Treaty-Tax Exclusion and Relevant Inclusions

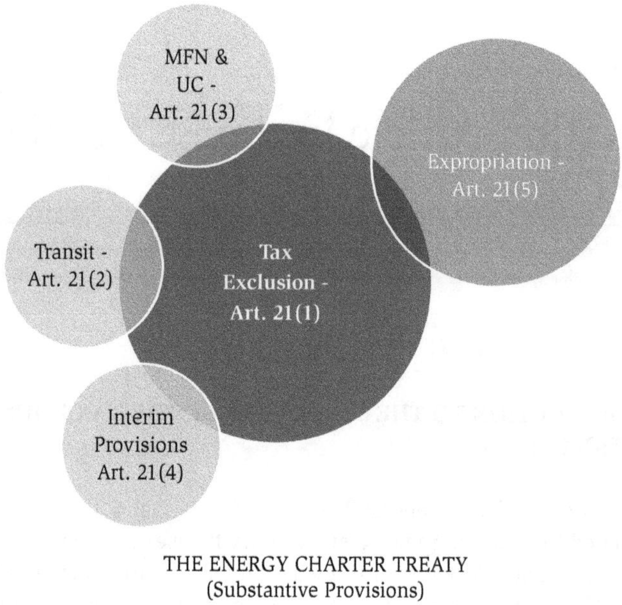

Source: Author's Own.

Due to the complexity of the Taxation Article, prior scholars have fittingly represented the multilayered dimensions of the Taxation Article in terms of Russian nested dolls/matryoshkas[392] or stacked diagrams.[393] Both of these perspectives represent the complexities of the Tax Article, except for one limitation. They do not capture fully the binary nature of ECT Article 21: that a matter is either covered by the substantive protections of the treaty or it is not. The binary nature of ECT Article 21 has yielded itself to the carve-out/clawback dichotomy because of the binary nature of the Taxation Article. However, putting aside the informal nature of these terms, the term "clawback" may inadvertently include a time element and further complicate the jurisdiction/merits inquiry. A formal "clawback" may be deemed to apply retrospectively (e.g., clawback in time) that may trigger issues with its validity.[394] Instead,

392. *See* William Park, *Arbitration and Tax, International and Comparative Perspectives* 179-205, paras. 10-30 (2009).
393. Ugur Erman Ozgur "Taxation of Foreign Investments under International Law: Article 21 of the Energy Charter Treaty in Context" (2015) at 52 (referring also to Park's description of the Russian nested doll); http://www.energycharter.org (Accessed: May 30, 2020).
394. Historically speaking *see* the UK statute aimed at refusing enforcement of foreign judgments rendering treble damages. UK Protection of Trading Interests Act, 1980 Section 6. *See also*

Figure 4.1 captures the binary nature of ECT Article 21 in the form of a multiple Venn diagram, namely that a measure is either subject to ECT coverage or not. In assessing the existing ambiguities,[395] the chapter begins with the definitions and interpretative rules in §4.02, proceeds to the limitations and exceptions in §4.03, then further presents the Exclusion and Specified Inclusion in §4.04, to conclude by answering the initial sub-inquiry in §4.05.

§4.02 DEFINITIONS AND INTERPRETATION RULES PERTAINING TO THE "TAXATION" ARTICLE

[A] Interpretative Rules

[1] Two Article-Specific Interpretation Rules Found in ECT Article 21(1) and 21(6)

Two specific rules for interpretation arise in the Taxation Article: one in ECT Article 21(1) and one in ECT Article 21(6). The analysis or interpretation of the terms, under this chapter, focuses on the *ordinary meaning* of such terms, as these materialize *in their context* and as they reflect *the object and purpose* of the ECT.[396] However, to understand these Inclusions and the function of the article, the reader requires an introduction into the various moving parts: the definitions and the interpretative rules that are article-specific.

Besides the carve-out/exclusion, ECT Article 21(1) contains an express rule for interpretation states:

> In the event of any inconsistency between this Article and any other provision of the Treaty, this Article shall prevail to the extent of the inconsistency.

In a similar relevant manner, ECT Article 21(6) sets out the following interpretative rule:

> (6) For the avoidance of doubt, Article 14 shall not limit the right of a Contracting Party to impose or collect a tax by withholding or other means.

[2] Priority in the Event of "Any" Inconsistency Focusing Toward a Self-Sustaining Mechanism

The second sentence in ECT Article 21(1) offers a degree of priority to the application of the Taxation Article over any provisions of the ECT. The priority afforded to this article has the limiting feature of being triggered only in the event of an inconsistency

---

Joseph E. Neuhaus, Power to Reverse Foreign Judgments: the British Clawback Statute under International Law, 81 Columbia L. Rev. 1097-133, 1097 n. 2 (quoting Lord Hacking "the clawback—to use that *unattractive* phrase") (emphasis added).

395. The relationship between ECT Article 21(1) and ECT Article 21(5) is the subject of further inquiry and will be discussed below. *See infra* Chapter 4.03 and 7.02.

396. *See, e.g.*, Vienna Convention on the Law of the Treaties, Art. 31(1).

between this article and other articles. In such case, the Taxation Article prevails and takes precedence over other articles.

This default rule reinforces the prevalence of these definitions over *any* other provisions in the treaty "in the event of *any* inconsistency."[397] It thus reinforces the self-sustaining mechanism inherent in the Taxation Article.

[3] Supremacy of a Contracting State's Power to Tax in ECT Article 21(6) over Freedom of Transfer Guarantees

A separate interpretative mechanism, found in ECT Article 21(6), reinforces the state's power to tax in relation to the ECT's provisions on the free transfer of moneys related to investment as found in ECT Article 14.

Article 14 refers to the duty of a Contracting State to ensure the freedom of transfer in and out of its Area for initial capital, returns, unspent earnings, etc.[398] It imposes a mechanism by which transfers of *inter alia* capital would be accomplished by reference to the market rate on the date of the transfer.[399] It ensures protection of creditors through securities regulations and other legal obligations.[400] The chapter also enables former Soviet Republics to agree on payments in a single currency subject to the limitation that other Contracting States are not treated less favorably.[401] It finally permits the state to restrict transfers of return under limited conditions provided that investment protection obligations are met.[402]

According to ECT Article 21(6), the guarantees of ECT Article 14 may not limit a Contracting Party in any meaningful manner with regard to taxation: meaning that the power to impose or collect taxes cannot be restricted. The reinforcement provisions of ECT Article 21(6) are in place on top of the interpretative rule in the second sentence in ECT Article 21(1) giving priority to the provisions of ECT Article 21 over all other treaties' texts "in the event of the ambiguity." ECT Article 21(6) lacks the restriction of a need of ambiguity for its provisions to apply. A reading of the ordinary meaning of the text suggests that, in relation to the transfer of capital, a state's power to tax should not be restricted regardless of whether an ambiguity exists or not. Article 21(6) reinforces the supremacy of the power to tax over ensuring freedom of transfers, as the state's power to tax may inadvertently conflict with the free transfer of capital, returns on income, contract payments or unspent earnings, etc. In such manner, the power to tax prevails.

397. ECT Art. 21(1) (emphasis added).
398. ECT Art. 14(1).
399. ECT Art. 14(3).
400. ECT Art. 14(5).
401. ECT Art. 14(5).
402. ECT Art. 14(6).

[B] Treaty Definitions

[1] Text of the Treaty

ECT Article 21(7) contains several provisions that may be seen as a definition or as a clarifying term. It does not define the term but ambiguously states:

> (7) For the purposes of this Article:
> (a) The term "Taxation Measure" includes:
> (i) any provision relating to taxes of the domestic law of the Contracting Party or of political subdivision thereof or a local authority therein; and
> [...]

Although the Treaty as a whole contains several definitions in ECT Article 1, the Taxation Article includes two sets of new definitions that are article-specific and are restricted only to this article. A similar approach is adopted in ECT Article 7 governing transit that adopts an integrated and self-sustaining approach, distinct from the remaining parts of the treaty. The two sets of tax-specific definitions pertain to: (1) CTA and (2) tax, taxation measures, and taxation provisions.

[2] Competent Tax Authority

The definition of the "Competent Tax Authority," in ECT Article 21(5)(c), focuses on *which authority* is meant with the term CTA. It does not, however, reveal *which country*'s authority is relevant. It only defines which authority should be consulted. Which country's authority is seized (that of the investor, respondent state or both) remains a critical issue for the specific review of expropriation triggering the consultation procedure, that is, ECT Article 21(5)(b).

In this context, the definition is helpful by specifying that the pertinent authority is either: (1) an authority specified in a double taxation that is in place between the Member States, or (2) bar the existence of such agreement, the ministry or the minister having the responsibility over tax matters. So in the context of an investment dispute between Spain and United Kingdom, as both countries being ECT Contracting States having signed and ratified the Treaty and a DTT is in place, the relevant tax authorities stipulated for the two countries are: for Spain, "the Minister of Economy and Finance or his authorised representative," and for UK, "the Commissioners for Her Majesty's Revenue and Customs or their authorised representative."[403]

In a case involving Spain and Germany where both countries are ECT Contracting States but no double taxation regime is in place, the respective authorities will be the minister or the ministry responsible for tax collection. In the example of Spain, it will be the Minister of Economy and Finance or his authorized representative, and in the

403. *See* Convention Between the United Kingdom and Northern Ireland and the Kingdom of Spain for the Avoidance of Double Taxation and the Prevention of Fiscal Evasion with Respect to Taxes on Income and on Capital, Spain-UK, Mar. 14, 2013, Art. 3(1)(i); https://assets.publishing.service.gov.uk/(Accessed: May 30, 2020).

example of Germany, it will likely be the Ministry of Finance or its authorized representative.[404]

[3] Tax, Taxation Matters, and Taxation Provisions

With regard to the first set of terms, ECT Article 21(7)(a), (b) and (d) deals with various tax terms. These three provisions refer to three terms: "tax," "taxation measures," and "tax provisions" yet only the term "taxation measure" is formally defined under the treaty.

ECT Article 21(7)(a) sets out a comprehensive definition of "taxation measures." It covers all matters pertaining to taxes arising out of a domestic law or international treaty. The main issue with this set of definitions is that the term "tax," which appears throughout the Tax Article, is not formally defined. Nor is it absolutely clear, the term's relationship to the term "taxation measure." This failure to clarify the relationship between "tax" and "taxation measures" gives rise to an inherent problem in the scope of application of the Exclusion and Specified Inclusions, especially when the term tax is used to define "taxation measures." This causes an uncertainty over interpretation. If the term "taxes" is used in a broader sense than "taxation measures," then the Specified Inclusion ("Clawback") using the term would conceptually apply in a broader sense than the Exclusion ("Carve-Out") that uses the term "taxation measures." An additional concern is whether any of these terms may be interpreted synonymously or interchangeably when the terms are used commonly throughout the article.

Moreover, the definition of tax in ECT Article 21(7)(b) sets out the scope of the tax on income or on capital to be broad to cover a large scope of direct taxes. Three of the four clawbacks refer to taxes on income and capital. ECT Article 21(7)(b) stipulates what taxes shall be considered in the context of taxes on income or capital. ECT Article 21(7)(b) contains several clarifications on what is meant by "tax" for purposes of taxes on income or capital and are linked directly to these three of the four clawbacks. All taxes directly borne by the affected entity and which stay with that legal entity are deemed as direct taxes. Other types of direct taxes are taxes on real estate and assets other than capital, and even sales tax by the investor. The definition in ECT Article 21(7)(b) expands the scope of the term to cover a broad scope of taxes, such as inheritance tax, estate tax, taxes on wages and salaries, including a catchall term "substantially similar taxes." Indirect taxes, unless otherwise restricted by the provisions of the clawback, would generally fall outside the scope of the definition.

ECT Article 21(7)(d) provides that the terms "tax provisions" and "taxes" do not include customs duties. The term "tax provisions" is used in the context of transit and MFN obligations stipulated in ECT Article 21(2)(a) and 21(3)(a). In this manner, the

404. *See, e.g.*, Convention between the United States of America and the Federal Republic of Germany for the Avoidance of Double Taxation and Prevention of Fiscal Evasion with Respect to Taxes on Income and Capital and to Certain Other Taxes, Ger.-U.S., Jan. 1, 1990, Art. 1(i); https://www.irs.gov/pub/irs-trty/germany.pdf (Accessed: May 30, 2020).

clarifying provision in ECT Article 21(7)(e) excludes customs duties from the scope of these terms (Table 4.1).

Table 4.1 Comparative Look into the ECT Terms "Taxes," "Taxation Measures," and "Tax Provisions"

Definition	*Defined*	*Use*
Taxes	Not formally defined except for a clarification appearing in ECT Article 21(7)(b) that the term does not cover customs duties.	- Expropriation-Specified Inclusion, as defined in ECT Article 21(5): "Article 13 shall apply to taxes." - Enforcement Exception in ECT Article 21(2) and 21(3): "... any Taxation Measure aimed at ensuring the effective collection of *taxes* ... ." - Definition in ECT Article 21(7) of Taxation Measures: "The term 'Taxation Measure' includes: (i) any provision relating to *taxes* of the domestic law ... and (ii) any provision relating to *taxes* of any convention for the avoidance of double taxation ... ."
Taxation Measures	Yes defined in Article 21(7): any provision 'relating to taxes' of domestic law, including from political subdivision, or from double taxation treaty or international agreement.	- Exclusion in ECT Article 21(1): "... nothing in this Treaty shall create rights or impose obligations with respect to Taxation Measures of the Contracting Parties." - Specified Inclusions in ECT Article 21(2): "Article 7(3) shall apply to Taxation Measures ... ." - Specified Inclusions in ECT Article 21(3): "Article 10(2) and (7) shall apply to Taxation Measures ... ." - Specified Inclusions in ECT Article 21(4): "Article 29(2) to (6) shall apply to Taxation Measures ... ."

Definition	*Defined*	*Use*
		- Enforcement Exception in ECT Article 21(2) and ECT Article 21(3): "... any *Taxation Measure* aimed at ensuring the effective collection of taxes ... ."
Tax Provisions	Not formally defined except that the definition does not cover customs duties, *see* ECT Article 21(7)(d).	Double Taxation Exception in Articles 21(2)(a) and 21(3)(a): "... with respect to advantages accorded by a Contracting Party pursuant to the *tax provisions* of any convention, agreement or arrangement ... ."

Source: Author's Own.

§4.03 THE FIRST TWO LEVELS: EXCLUSIONS AND SPECIFIED INCLUSIONS

[A] First Level: The Exclusion ("Carve-Out") in ECT Article 21(1)

[1] Structure

Certain tax matters are not subject to the protections of the ECT unless they fall under the application of a set of express provisions. Fundamentally, taxation matters are *excluded* from the application of the treaty (they are "carved out" from the treaty) unless there are *specific inclusions* indicating otherwise (a "clawback" brings them back from being "carved out").

[2] Treaty Provisions

ECT Article 21(1) contains the broad Exclusion ("Carve-Out") that states:

> Except as otherwise provided in this Article, nothing in this Treaty shall create rights or impose obligations with respect to Taxation Measures of the Contracting Parties.

The article begins with an overarching exclusion that contains two parts: (1) the actual exclusion and (2) an interpretative rule.

[3] The Tax Exclusion

The article sets out that matters pertaining to *taxation measures* fall outside the application of the ECT unless otherwise provided in this article. The exclusion specifically sets out that the ECT does not "create rights or impose obligations ... ." The

Exclusion notably uses the term "Taxation Measures" which, as seen above, cover a range of tax-related matters arising out of domestic law and international agreements.

The broad drafting referring to *creation of rights and imposition of obligations* allows for an evenhanded and unambiguous interpretation for both investors and other Contracting States. Investors may not derive rights, including building legitimate expectations, from taxation provisions. Contracting States are exempted from any commitments to investors or other Contracting States on tax-related matters. In other words, taxation measures do not generate rights or obligations unless otherwise specified in the article.

The Exclusion itself would not be complicated if it were not for two issues: the multilayered set of Inclusions, discussed below, and a definitional limitation. On the definitional limitation, the concern is with a state guising a measure as a taxation measure when it would otherwise not be tax-related. In the holding of the *Yukos* tribunal, the measures by the Russian Federation were deemed not to be bona fide taxation measures and thus fell outside the scope of the Exclusion in the first place.[405] Even though the Dutch courts continue to scrutinize the finding of the *Yukos* tribunal, there is support in favor of the argument that only genuine a.k.a. bona fide taxation measures are subject to the Exclusion.

[B] Second Level: The Four Specified Inclusions ("Clawbacks") of ECT Article 21(2), 21(3), 21(4), and 21(5)

[1] Four Rather Than One Specified Inclusions

There are four Inclusions that may be interpreted as *either* four different Inclusions ("clawbacks") *or* one Inclusion ("clawback") with four distinct parts. The distinction itself is inconsequential as the result is the same: matters are subject to the Inclusion ("clawback") despite a previous exclusion ("carve-out"). However, for purposes of this book, I rely on the concept of four distinct Specified Inclusions ("four clawbacks") as these are distinct in their scope and application.

The different Specified Inclusions that permit the inclusion of a tax-related claim are:

(1) MFN status arising in the transit context ("Transit-Specified Inclusion"), as per ECT Article 21 (2);
(2) the National Treatment (NT) and MFN clause arising in the investment protection context ("NT/MFN-Specified Inclusion"), as per ECT Article 21(3);
(3) interim trade-related matters ("Interim Trade-Specified Inclusion"), as per ECT Article 21(4); and
(4) expropriation ("Expropriation-Specified Inclusion"), as per ECT Article 21(5).

405. *Yukos* Award, paras. 1406, 1407 and 1447.

The next four paragraphs enable the reinstatement of a tax-related claim if these are related to matters pertaining to: (i) non-discrimination obligation in the transit chapter, (ii) MFN clause in the Investment Protection chapter, (iii) *interim* provisions on trade, and (iv) expropriation. For purposes of investment protection, the NT/MFN- and the Expropriation-Specified Inclusions are of the most interest, as these directly affect the treatment of investments.

[2] Non-discrimination-Specified Inclusion for Transit in ECT Article 21(2)

ECT Article 21(2) states:

> Article 7(3) shall apply to Taxation Measures other than those on income or on capital, except that such provision shall not apply to:
>
> (a) an advantage accorded by a Contracting Party pursuant to the tax provisions of any convention, agreement or arrangement described in subparagraph (7)(a)(ii); or
>
> (b) any Taxation Measure aimed at ensuring the effective collection of taxes, except where the measure of a Contracting Party arbitrarily discriminates against Energy Materials and Products originating in, or destined for the Area of another Contracting Party or arbitrarily restricts benefits accorded under Article 7(3).

ECT Article 21(2) links the Specified Inclusion to the provisions guaranteeing the facilitation and the freedom to transit for energy materials and products. In simple terms, energy materials and products, such as oil and gas, or energy distribution shall transit ECT Member States without distinction as to *inter alia* the origin of the product or material, or the destination of the said product or material.[406]

ECT Article 7(3) imposes a duty on ECT Member States to guarantee that energy materials and products in transit through a Member State shall not be treated in a manner less favorable than those originating or destined for the said Member State. Article 7(3) sets an exclusion for the application of the principle in instances where there is a contrary international agreement, much along the same lines as the exception in ECT Article 21(2)(a) and (b). This two-part obligation in ECT Article 7(3) frames the principle of non-discrimination in terms of both origin *and* destination for relevant materials and products. By means of example, gas shipped from Russia to Poland through Ukraine should not be treated any less favorably than gas shipped from Russia to Ukraine *or* gas produced in Ukraine shipped directly to Poland.

Cumulatively, ECT Article 7(3) may be summarized as incorporating the principle of non-discrimination to transit. The clawback allows for taxation matters pertaining to transit to be covered by the treaty, subject to a blanket exception pertaining to income and capital. In addition, a two-part individual exception applies to

406. *See* ECT Art. 7(1).

matters relating to a double taxation treaty or effective collection of taxes unless there is an indication of arbitrary discrimination by the Member State.

[3] National Treatment and MFN Clawback for Promotion of Investment in ECT Article 21(3)

[i] *Treaty Provisions*

ECT Article 21(3) links the Taxation Article to ECT Article 10(2) and 10(7). Article 10(2) refers to ECT Article 10(3), even in the latter.

ECT Article 10(2) states as follows:

> Each Contracting Party shall endeavour to accord to Investors of other Contracting Parties, as regards the Making of Investments in its Area, the Treatment described in paragraph (3).[407]

As ECT Article 10(2) refers to ECT Article 10(3), the latter states as follows:

> For the purposes of this Article, "Treatment" means treatment accorded by a Contracting Party which is no less favourable than that which it accords to its own Investors or to Investors of any other Contracting Party or any third state, whichever is the most favourable.[408]

ECT Article 10(7) states as follows:

> Each Contracting Party shall accord to Investments in its Area of Investors of other Contracting Parties, and their related activities including management, maintenance, use, enjoyment or disposal, treatment no less favourable than that which it accords to Investments of its own Investors or of the Investors of any other Contracting Party or any third state and their related activities including management, maintenance, use, enjoyment or disposal, whichever is the most favourable.[409]

Although convoluted, ECT Article 21(3) includes in the application of the treaty state measures related to taxation where these measures are linked to "national treatment" and "MFN" treatment. ECT Article 21(3) does not import the umbrella clause provisions of ECT Article 10(1). It also further subjects it to two main exceptions as found in ECT Article 21(3)(a) and (b) explored below.

[ii] *NT and MFN and Non-Discrimination Claims Pertaining to Taxation*

There are two distinct provisions that are triggered by the clawback/inclusion: those found in ECT Article 10(2) and 10(7). Whereas both Article 10(2) (by virtues of the definition in 10(3)) and ECT Article 10(7) combine the "national treatment" and

407. ECT Art. 10(2).
408. ECT Art. 10(3).
409. ECT Art. 10(7).

"MFN" treatment,[410] the provisions of ECT Article 10(7) may also commonly be referred to as incorporating a standard of "non-discrimination."

A critical distinction emerges between the two terms: ECT Article 10(2) refers to "investors," while ECT Article 10(7) refers to "investment." The differentiation in the two terms has given rise to the argument that: "the obligations set out in Articles 10(2) and 10(7) ECT apply to two distinct phases of the investment cycle: Article 10(2) ECT applies to the Making of Investments phase, whereas Article 10(7) ECT applies to post-investment phase."[411] Such a reading of the terms applying to distinct phases of investments may be reasonable, but it may be an extension of the treaty provisions beyond the actual text of the treaty.

Based on the ordinary meaning of ECT Article 10(2)/10(3), it cannot be excluded that investors retain the protections of the national treatment and MFN protection even in the post-investment phase. Similarly, there are no express limitations for extending the protections of ECT Article 10(7) to the making of the investment stage. In any event, the two provisions appearing in parallel in the clawback of ECT Article 21(3) speak for a broader scope of protection, without any limitation on either investments or investors for purposes of national treatment and MFN. ECT provisions emerge as consolidated measures of protections, distinct from those found in NAFTA, other model treaties or WTO.

The definition of the term "treatment" found in ECT Article 10(3) and the actual standard of protection, found in ECT Article 10(7), combine MFN and national treatment into one, constituting a common variation of the MFN clause.[412] Both provisions refer to treatment no less favorable than: (1) those afforded to local investors, which triggers the national treatment; and (2) investors of "any" other Contracting States, which triggers the MFN clause. The scope of such clause covers not only protection of investments per se but also investment-related activities, including broadly "management, use, enjoyment [and] disposal."[413]

The overarching subject matter of "national treatment" addresses the obligations made by a host state to provide treatment no less than favorable than it would to its own domestic investors. The "national treatment" obliges the host state "to make no negative differentiation between foreign and national investors when enacting and applying its rules and regulations and thus to promote the position of the foreign investor to the level accorded to nationals."[414] The review focuses on the substance and not the "formal" side of the measures.[415] This obligation is not limited to "like

410. In some instances, the provisions of ECT Art. 10(7) are referred to as "the standard for non-discrimination." *See* ECT Secretariat, *Blue Book: Making Investments in Energy Charter Member Countries Exceptions to the Principle of non-discriminatory Treatment* 7 (2016).
411. *See* MENA Chambers, Making Sense of the Taxation Provisions of the Energy Charter Treaty, July 22, 2015.
412. *See generally* Dolzer and Schreuer, *supra* note 54, at 208 (discussing German Model Treaty, Art. 3).
413. *See* ECT Art. 10(7).
414. Dolzer and Schreuer, *supra* note 54, at 198 (or in other words, "they are meant to provide a level playing field between the foreign investor and the local competitiory").
415. *Id.*

circumstances" or "like situations," as it may be the case with NAFTA or previous US Model Treaties or WTO jurisprudence.[416]

[4] Clawback for Interim Provisions on Trade in ECT Article 21(4)

ECT Article 21(4) states:

> (4) Article 29(2) to (6) shall apply to Taxation Measures other than those on income or on capital.

This Specified Inclusion ("clawback") provision seeks to harmonize the applicable standards for the review of trade matters when one of the countries is not a member of the WTO or other trade-related instruments but is unlikely to be used unless the application of specific transitional instruments is called into question.[417] ECT Article 29 and the clawback in ECT Article 21(4) serve as an important transitional harmonization mechanism for many ECT Member States. The ECT's history traced closely the parallel course of integration of Russia and former Soviet Bloc into the WTO. Many of the countries were not members of the GATT/WTO regime at the time of the ECT signing and some remain outside of the regime.[418]

In such fashion, the ECT contains critical harmonization mechanisms for the integration of Member States into the WTO regime without frustrating the protections afforded by both regimes. At its core, the Specified Inclusion provision in ECT Article 21(4) provides for the application of the interim trade-related measures to tax matters except for taxes on income or capital. By referring to ECT Article 29, the Specified Inclusion in ECT Article 21(4) allows for the application of a larger body of trade law found in the GATT/WTO case law. The harmonization provisions of ECT Article 29 remain an important mechanism for trade matters considering that the ECT principles are fundamentally aligned with the GATT/WTO practice.

The Specified Inclusion also reflects the complex, rich, and lengthy process for the negotiation of the ECT. ECT Article 29, whose application to taxes is reinstated pursuant to the clawback in ECT Article 21(4), refers to GATT and not the WTO. But considering that the Uruguay round in 1994 marked the final and largest GATT round of negotiations, the application of the WTO agreements appears reasonable. At the conclusion of the Uruguay rounds, the WTO was revitalized to include free trade in goods and services thus expanding the scope of application of the WTO trade process.

416. *Cf.* NAFTA Art. 1102. *See also* 1994 US Model Treaty, Art. II.1. *See generally* Dolzer and Schreuer, *supra* note 54, at 198 and 204-05 (discussing three early NAFTA decisions: SD Myers v. Canada, First Partial Award, Nov. 13, 2000, paras. 244-7; Pope & Talbot v. Canada, Award on Merits, Apr. 10, 2001, paras. 45-63, 68-9; and Feldman v. Mexico, Award, Dec. 16, 2002, para. 165).
417. *See, e.g.*, ECT Art. 29(5) introducing limitations for tariff increases, which could be challenged regardless of the application of the Tax Exclusion in ECT Art. 21(1).
418. Tadjikistan (2013), Kazakhstan (2015), Moldova (2001), and Ukraine 2008, which are ECT Contracting States, joined WTO after the ratification of ECT. Russia joined WTO in 2012, signed but never ratified the ECT. It formally rejected the ECT's application and formally withdrew from the Treaty. For example, Uzbekistan, Turkmenistan, Belarus, and Azerbaijan still remain outside the WTO regime despite being ECT Contracting States.

As the negotiations for the ECT commenced with the Charter of Europe in 1990 then proceeded to the signing of an energy charter for Europe, these negotiations developed into a sector-specific regime for energy.[419] While it was not feasible for the ECT negotiators to anticipate that the WTO would replace in full the GATT mechanisms, the parallel developments in the ECT and the WTO negotiation process explain the continuous alignment between the two regimes.

[5] The Expropriation Specified Inclusion in ECT Article 21(5)(a)

Perhaps the most important Specified Inclusion for investment protection appears in ECT Article 21(5)(a) and covers the provisions relating to expropriation. While the Specified Inclusion is short and refers to Article 13, ECT Article 13 covering investment protection against expropriation is lengthy and is not referred to directly in this book.

The Expropriation-Specified Inclusion, as it appears in ECT Article 21(5)(a), states:

> (5) (a) Article 13 shall apply to taxes.

It enables the reinstatement of all tax-related claims pertaining to expropriation. The provision does not contain any restrictions, as those found in ECT Article 21(2)-(4) excluding direct taxes on income and capital. It notably uses the term "taxes" as opposed to "Taxation Measures." In such manner, any claims for expropriation relating to "taxes" shall be covered by the Specified Inclusion.

The four Specified Inclusions all contain additional layers of complexity as discussed below.

§4.04 THIRD AND FOURTH LAYERS

[A] About Limitations and Exceptions

Every Specified Inclusion ("clawback") in ECT Article 21 either has a limitation or exception, or has both. The distinction between the terms should ordinarily be of little practical consequence as the result should be the same. Both the limitations and exceptions refer to matters being left out from the application of the Specified Inclusion ("clawback"). The *limitation versus exception* distinction raises critical questions pertaining to the outer limits of the obligation to refer disputes to competent national authorities, when the Specified Inclusion relating to Expropriation is triggered, as per ECT Article 21(5)(b); these issues are addressed below.[420]

In principle, there may be a procedural difference in how these matters are reviewed. A *limitation* confines a term to an inner limit.[421] An *exception*, however,

419. ECT Preamble.
420. *See infra* §4.04[B].
421. *See Limitation, Black's Law Dictionary* (11th ed. 2019) ("the act of limiting; the quality, state, or condition of being limited").

refers to matters being "excluded from a rule's operation."[422] A limitation would require an examination of the relationship of the items being restricted to the main term. The exception would presuppose that the matters subject to the exception would not be linked to the main term. At what level such review shall be performed requires a clear review of submission of the parties; however, it may be conceivable that the review of a limitation be restricted to a review of jurisdiction, and the review of an exception be ripe for a hearing on the merits. My position builds on existing case law to argue for a front-loaded approach where the review of limitations may be accomplished at a jurisdictional stage and such position is requested by the parties.

At the third level, reviewing the limitation and exception dichotomies, there are:

- one unambiguous limitation: the Direct Tax Limitation;
- two unambiguous exceptions: the Tax Treaty Exception and the Enforcement Exception;
- the obligation to refer a matter to a competent authority that may be perceived as an exception, limitation or even a procedural requirement.

The Effective Enforcement Exception is subject to a further Restriction Against Arbitrary Discrimination.

[B] Limitations: The Direct Tax Limitation

[1] The Direct Tax Limitation in Context

Three of the four Specified Inclusions ("clawbacks") contain a limitation concerning *certain* direct taxes ("the Direct Tax Limitation"). This limitation states that the Specified Inclusions shall apply to "Taxation Measures *other* than those on income or on capital."[423] In such manner, the Specified Inclusion is confined to an outer limit: it shall apply to taxation measures but not to *certain* taxation measures, namely those relating to income and capital. Three important considerations arise in the context of this limitation: (1) pertaining to the label "Direct Tax Limitation"; (2) the definitional issues of tax/taxation measures; and (3) the fourth specified inclusion not using this limitation.

[2] The Direct Tax Limitation Could Be about More Than Just Direct Taxes but the Focus Is on Direct Taxes

The use of the term "Direct Tax Limitation," chosen by me, is helpful but comes with drawbacks. Taxation measures on income and capital are *primarily*, but not exclusively, direct taxes. Personal income tax is what traditionally is envisioned by taxation measures on income. In a similar manner, capital gains taxes are what would ordinarily be envisioned under a tax on capital.

422. *Id.* ("Exception").
423. ECT Art. 21(2), 21(3) and 21(4) (emphasis added).

The definition in ECT Article 21(7)(b) provides support in favor of both that the Limitation could cover indirect taxes and that the bulk of the measures to which the Limitation applies is of direct nature: "taxes imposed on total income, on total capital or on elements of income or of capital, including taxes on gains from the alienation of property, taxes on estates, inheritances and gifts, or substantially similar taxes, taxes on the total amounts of wages or salaries paid by enterprises, as well as taxes on capital appreciation."[424]

It is conceivable that taxation of capital transfer through indirect taxation measures, such as administrative fees and stamp duties, may also be caught by the broader definition of taxation measures "on capital" and thus falls outside of the Specified Inclusion. Such indirect taxes although conceivable are rare or non-significant. However, a state may introduce such measures under the pretext of its administrative powers but these may be successfully challenged for being arbitrary when aggregated.[425]

An important concern about the Direct Tax Limitation is not only in what context it appears but also where and in what context it does *not* appear. The fourth Specified Inclusion relating to expropriation does not incorporate the Direct Tax Limitation, thereby leaving it open that direct taxes that are expropriatory in nature may be subject to the protection of the ECT.

[C] Two Exceptions: The Taxation Treaty Exception and the Enforcement Exception

[1] The Language for the Exceptions

Two of the four Specified Inclusions, those pertaining to *transit* and the *National Treatment/MFN*, contain exceptions. The exceptions are marked by:

> "except that such provisions shall not apply to ... ."[426]

There are two main sets of exceptions, referring to: (1) tax benefits arising out of double taxation and similar treaties ("Tax Treaties Exception") and (2) effective collection of taxes ("Enforcement Exception").

[2] Taxation Treaties Exception

The Taxation Treaty Exception appears in both the Transit- and NT/MFN-Specified Inclusions. Although similar in their wording, they contain some important variations.

On Transit (Article 21(2)(a)), the Tax Treaties Exception appears as follows:

424. ECT Art. 21(7)(b).
425. *See* Bogdanov v. Moldova, Arbitration No. V (114/2009), Final Award, Mar. 30, 2010, paras. 85-91.
426. ECT Arts. 21(2) and 21(3).

> *an advantage* accorded by a Contracting Party pursuant to the tax provisions of any convention, agreement or arrangement described in subparagraph (7)(a)(ii).

On NT/MFN (Article 21(3)(a)), the Tax Treaties Exception appears as follows:

> impose most favoured nation obligations with respect to advantages accorded by a Contracting Party pursuant to the tax provisions of any convention, agreement or arrangement described in subparagraph (7)(a)(ii) or resulting from membership of any Regional Economic Integration Organization[.]

The Taxation Treaty Exception effectively states that the *tax advantages* arising out of DTTs or similar international agreements that contain tax provisions remain unaffected by the provisions of the ECT. Subparagraph 7(a)(ii) includes the definition for Taxation Measures, which is defined as "any provision relating to taxes of any convention for the avoidance of double taxation or of any other international agreement or arrangement by which the Contracting Party is bound." The operative part for purposes of the Taxation Treaties exception concerns the type of international agreements, namely all types of international treatments: those relating to double taxation and otherwise.

The language adopted in the transit context and in the NT/MFN context generates two distinct measures of protections. Under the Transit-Specified Inclusion, where a tax benefit is granted pursuant to a double taxation or any other international agreement, the relevant benefit is not affected by the ECT.

Under the NT/MFN-Specified Inclusion, the focus shifts to the MFN clause as applied to taxation provisions too. The double MFN clause (in the Specified Inclusion and in the Exception) may appear confusing. However, at its core, the tax advantages from other DTTs and related agreements may not be introduced for purposes of the ECT. This provision also applies to membership in REIO that are meant to cover EU Members.[427] For example, where Country X extends tax benefits to Country Y, an investor from Country Z (where X, Y and Z are all members of ECT) may not invoke the tax advantages afforded by Country X to Country Y. In a similar manner, the investor from Country Z may not invoke the benefits arising out of Country X being part of REIO, like the EU. Tax Provisions would generally be subject to the general exclusion in ECT Article 21(1) and they would be subject to the exception for NT/MFN-Specified Inclusion pursuant to the Tax Treaty Exception.

The natural question that follows is whether the exception contains a temporal restriction with the use of the term "accorded by." Are the tax benefits from an international agreement restricted to the agreements entered by the Contracting State at the time when the obligations from the ECT arose? Or, may the Contracting States enter

427. *See* ECT Art. 1(3):

> "Regional Economic Integration Organization" means an organization constituted by states to which they have transferred competence over certain matters a number of which are governed by this Treaty, including the authority to take decisions binding on them in respect of those matters.

into new international agreements that would accord new tax advantages to Contracting States thereby restricting the application of the ECT-Specified Inclusion of NT/MFN and transit to subsequent tax matters?

A plain reading of the Limitation would militate for limiting the benefits provided by the treaties to the time when the ECT went into effect. However, a credible argument may also be made that, given the broad text of the Exception permitting the review of other treaties, the subsequent agreements and practice arising out of the application of the new international agreement may be relevant for purposes of interpreting the provision. In accordance with VCLT Article 31(3), both subsequent agreements and subsequent practice shall be taken into account together with the context of the treaty.[428]

[3] The Enforcement Exception

The Enforcement Exception focuses on the effective collection of taxes. In a similar manner as the Tax Treaties Exception, the Enforcement Exception is included in the two Specific Inclusions, those pertaining to transit and NT/MFN.

It states that:

> any Taxation Measure aimed at ensuring the effective collection of taxes ...

is excepted from the respective Specified Inclusions.

[D] The Fourth Layer: the Restriction Against Arbitrary Discrimination to the Enforcement Exception

The Enforcement Exception contains a further *restriction* which effectively confines the application of the exception to certain scenarios with some degree of variation.

Limitations and exceptions are essentially similar instruments curtailing the application of a Specified Inclusion. Restrictions to both limitations and exceptions are theoretically possible, but, as drafted, there is only an express limitation to an exception. The key restriction refers to the Restriction Against Arbitrary Discrimination as found in ECT Article 21(2)(b) and 21(3)(b), thereby subjecting measures that are arbitrarily discriminatory to be the subject of the Specified Inclusion and hence the protection of the treaty.

On Transit (Article 21(2)(b)), the Restriction Against Arbitrary Discrimination states:

> except where the measure of a Contracting Party arbitrarily discriminates against Energy Materials and Products originating in, or destined for the Area of another Contracting Party or arbitrarily restricts benefits accorded under Article 7(3).

On NT/MFN (Article 21(3)(b)), the Enforcement Exception appears as follows:

428. VCLT Art. 31(3).

except where the measure arbitrarily discriminates against an Investor of another Contracting Party or arbitrarily restricts benefits accorded under the Investment provisions of this Treaty.

The Enforcement Exception, supplemented by the Restriction Against Arbitrary Discrimination, states that taxation measures relating to the *effective* collection of taxes are excepted from the Specified Inclusion; that is, they are excluded from the provisions of the treaty, unless they are somehow arbitrarily discriminatory. The key distinction is the item used for the purpose of determining discrimination.

The Transit-Specified Inclusion focuses on the measure by a Contracting Party used against the energy materials of another Contracting Party (whether originating or destined). The NT/MFN focuses solely on the treatment of the investors of another Contracting State, namely on whether there is an arbitrary restriction of the investment benefits afforded by the ECT.

[E] Mandatory Requirements for Referral to CTAs as an Exception (Not Limitation) Referring to the Merits

ECT Article 21(5)(b) sets out the procedural provisions pertaining to the expropriation-related Specified Inclusion. It contains two gaps: whether the inquiry is taken as a procedural issue or a matter for the merits and which CTA, if not both, is called to rule on this issue. The use of the term "shall" in the chapeau of ECT Article 21(5)(b) indicates the existence of a referral requirement to the CTAs. Its provisions are straightforward. Whenever a tax-related claim arises pertaining to expropriation *or discriminatory treatment*, the investor or, absent such move by the investor, the arbitral tribunal shall refer the matter to the "relevant" CTA. The CTA shall be seized not only in the context of the Specified Inclusion of ECT Article 21(5)(a), when the Expropriation-Specified Inclusion is triggered, but also in other instances where discriminatory treatment is invoked.

The authority would be called to resolve the issue within six months. The findings are not binding on the tribunal. They *shall* be considered if the relevant authorities issue a final ruling within six months. If the relevant authorities arrive at a decision after the required six months, the arbitral tribunal *may* consider such findings. In any event, the referral to the competent authorities shall not delay the procedure by more than six months.

The referral to the "relevant CTA" is a mechanism inspired by the dispute mechanism in DTTs.[429] This procedural instrument is intended to filter out non-meritorious claims.[430] Referral to tax authorities is an increasingly common mechanism in DTT, where the regime is built on comity between Member States on tax matters. In the DTT-context, two states rely on direct collaboration between their tax authorities to ascertain accurately the tax information and reconcile it. By relying on

429. *See, e.g.*, ECT Art. 21(7)(c).
430. William Park, *supra* note 9, at 115 and 131 (quoted and discussed in *Yukos* Award, para. 1423).

comity, states may ensure accurate gathering of information on avoidance of double payment and alignment on the responsibility for payments.

A problematic issue in the Taxation Article is the use of the plural "competent authorities" when referring to the joint decision. In the DTT regime, there is an assumption of a joint decision reached by the two respective authorities. In terms of investment protection, the scope of the inquiry differs from that in the DTT-context. In the investment regime, the focus is less on what the taxpayer has paid (e.g. did the taxpayer pay taxes twice) and more on the legitimacy of the tax power (e.g., whether a tax is expropriatory). The investment protection regime differs from the double taxation regime *specifically* in that the collaboration between states is not a critical feature of the investment protection regime. In the absence of an express reference to a joint decision by both of the countries' CTAs, which state's tax authority has been seized first may lead to different results depending on whether the host or the investor's tax authorities would be seized to review whether a tax measure is expropriatory.

What value should be then attributed to this mechanism in the context of the Specified Inclusion on Expropriation? A CTA referral would ordinarily be viewed as a *procedural* requirement akin to the cooling-off period requirement found in various international agreements. However, the actual language in ECT Article 21(5)(b), most notably the absence of a joint decision-making and the distinction between "shall" and "may," indicates that the provisions are not a full-fledged limitation to the tribunal's jurisdiction and do not preclude the tribunal to hear the dispute. The language in ECT Article 21(5)(b), the absence of clarity of the rules that need to be applied by the CTAs on the interpretation of the non-discriminatory provisions, and the ambiguousness in the duty on the arbitral tribunals to consider the findings of such authorities if rendered within six months all speak to a constraint to observe such obligation for the duration of the referral period than the mere procedural requirement to wait for the submission of a claim. In the framework of the "Taxation" Article, the requirement to submit a claim to CTAs may be viewed as an exception. It does not prevent the tribunal from proceeding with the review, even during the review of the taxation claim until the CTAs have had a chance to review the issue within the six-month referral period.

§4.05 OTHER INVESTMENT TREATIES: BITs

[A] Taxation Articles in BITs

In addition to the ECT, there are several thousand BITs, some of which contain relevant tax-related provisions. The structure of the ECT's Taxation Article analysis may be extended to other treaties.

The United Nations Conference on Trade and Development (UNCTAD) has identified 2,897 BIT treaties out of which 2,338 were deemed to be in force and 2,577 were mapped.[431] The UNCTAD project has mapped the tax provisions in three key categories (Exclusion, Exception, and Specific Provisions); the extrapolated figures are presented in Table 4.2. Notably, 276 or 10.73% treaties contain a tax-specific exclusion linked to taxation.

Table 4.2 Tax Provisions in Numbers out of 2,577 UNCTAD-Mapped Treaties

Provisions	*Yes*		*No*		*Inconclusive and Non-applicable*	
	Number	*%*	*Number*	*%*	*Number*	*%*
Taxes are excluded from the substantive scope of the treaties ("Exclusion")	274	10.63%	2,301	89.29%	2	0.08%
Tax treaties not included in MFN ("Exception")	2142	83.12%	400	15.52%	35	1.36%
BITs with MFN clause	2533	98.29%	37	1.44%	7	0.27%
Special mechanisms	79	3.07%	2359	91.54%	139	5.39%

Source: Author's Own.

Although the vast majority of the BITs do not exclude tax provisions from the substantive scope of the treaty, when it comes to the MFN exception the picture looks drastically different. Nearly all the BITs (98.29%) contained an MFN clause. Of all the treaties surveyed, in a large majority of the cases (83.12%), DTT tax provisions were expressly excluded from the scope of the MFNs. These numbers speak heavily for the proposition that the primary concern with the tax provisions in BITs is to avoid any conflicting interpretations with DTTs. A small number of treaties (79 or 3.07%) or more specifically 28.83% of BITs with a tax exclusion also incorporate some special mechanisms relating to tax. Canada and the US constitute the lion's share of these BITs (53 or 67.09%) that incorporate a referral mechanism into CTAs.

[B] Tax Exclusions in Some Critical BITs

Considerable variations between the BITs arise in respect to the exclusion, specified inclusion and respective limitations. In the energy context, two specific treaties (the US-Ecuador and the Canada-Ecuador BITs) served as the precursors to the *Yukos* and Spanish disputes amounting to over twenty-eight contractual and treaty arbitrations

431. *See generally* UNCTAD, Investment Policy Hub, International Investment Agreement Navigator; https://investmentpolicy.unctad.org/international-investment-agreements/ (Accessed: May 30, 2020).

against Ecuador, but they essentially led Ecuador to terminate these and all other bilateral treaties.[432]

The US-Ecuador BIT Article X states as follows:

> 1. With respect to its tax policies, each Party should strive to accord fairness and equity in the treatment of investment of nationals and companies of the other Party.
> 2. Nevertheless, the provisions of this Treaty, and in particular Article VI and VII, *shall apply to matters of taxation only with respect to the following*:
>   (a) expropriation, pursuant to Article III;
>   (b) transfers, pursuant to Article IV; or
>   (c) the observance and enforcement of terms of an investment Agreement or authorization as referred to in Article VI (1) (a) or (b), to the extent they are not subject to the dispute settlement provisions of a Convention for the avoidance of double taxation between the two Parties, or have been raised under such settlement provisions and are not resolved within a reasonable period of time.[433]

The Canada-Ecuador BIT Article XII states as follows:

> 1. Except as set out in this Article, nothing in this Agreement shall apply to taxation measures.
> 2. Nothing in this Agreement shall affect the rights and obligations of the Contracting Parties under any tax convention. In the event of any inconsistency between the provisions of this Agreement and any such convention, the provisions of that convention apply to the extent of the inconsistency.
> 3. Subject to paragraph (2), a claim by an investor that a tax measure of a Contracting Party is in breach of an agreement between the central government authorities of a Contracting Party and the investor concerning an investment shall be considered a claim for breach of this Agreement unless the taxation authorities of the Contracting Parties, no later than six months after being notified of the claim by the investor, jointly determine that the measure does not contravene such agreement.
> 4. Article VIII [concerning expropriation] may be applied to a taxation measure unless the taxation authorities of the Contracting Parties, no later than six months after being notified by an investor that he disputes a taxation, jointly determine that the measure is not an expropriation.[434]

432. Transnational Institute (2017) "Ecuador Terminates 16 Investment Treaties"; https://www.tni.org/en/article/ecuador-terminates-16-investment-treaties (Accessed: May 30, 2020).
433. Treaty between the United States of America and the Republic of Ecuador concerning the Encouragement and Reciprocal Protection of Investment, signed on Aug. 27, 1993, in effect from May 11, 1997, terminated on May 18, 2018 (continues to apply for another ten years) [hereinafter "US-Ecuador BIT"]. *See* Department of State Office of the United States Trade Representative, Notice of Termination of United States-Ecuador Bilateral Investment Treaty, Public Notice 10418, Federal Register vol. 83 no. 97, May 18, 2018. Available at: https://www.gpo.gov/fdsys/pkg/FR-2018-05-18/pdf/2018-10659.pdf.
434. Agreement between the Government of Canada and the Government of the Republic of Ecuador for the Promotion and Reciprocal Protection of Investments E101522—CTS 1997 No. 25, signed on Apr. 29, 1996, entered into force on June 6, 1997, terminated on May 19, 2018 (continues to apply for another ten years) [hereinafter "Canada-Ecuador BIT"].

In a stark departure from these detailed provisions, the Danish-Russian BIT[435] contains a distinct structure whereby it contains a blanket exclusion for all tax-related matters. Article 11(3) contains the following text: "The provisions of this Agreement shall not apply to taxation ('Bestemmelserne i denne overenskomst skat ikke grelde for beskatning.')." The article is not followed by any other inclusion; it does not include any specified inclusions of any sort.

The US-Ecuador BIT adopts a permissive approach. Unlike the ECT, the US-Ecuador BIT does not have an express exclusionary rule ("carve-out"). Instead of express exclusionary language as "... nothing in this article shall apply to taxation measures"[436] or "this Agreement does not create rights or obligations with regard to taxation measures,"[437] the US-Ecuador BIT Article X(2) states that the Agreement shall apply to taxes only if certain conditions for the inclusions are met ("indirect exclusion/carve-out"). The US-Ecuador BIT provides for three inclusions relating to: (1) expropriation, (2) transfers, and (3) a broad inclusion for *investment agreements* subject to the limitation that the dispute arising out of the investment agreement was not subject to dispute resolution provisions of a DTT. Here, the tax exclusion ("carve-out") is implicit: the treaty does not apply to taxation unless it meets broad specific inclusionary condition subject to specific limitations. The implicit exclusionary rule is supported by the language, namely that the treaty's investment protection provision "... shall apply to matters of taxation only with respect to the following." The presence of "only" reveals the ordinary meaning that the treaty does not apply in other circumstances. This is supported by the second factor, namely that the application of the rule is prefaced with the word "nevertheless" that follows a broad and undefined obligation for the Contracting Parties to "strive to accord fairness and equity" in the treatment of foreign investment.[438] The exclusionary rule is implicit because although an exclusionary rule is not expressly stated, it is inherent in the construction of the respective paragraph that introduces three specified inclusions with predefined limitations.

The Canada-Ecuador BIT adopts a traditional pattern for tax treaties, as previously encountered in the ECT. It provides for an exclusion in Article XII(1): "nothing shall apply to taxation." It also contains an interpretation rule as that found in ECT Article 21(1) second sentence. In Article XII(2), the Canada-Ecuador BIT specifies that it shall not conflict with any tax agreement; if such conflict exists, the treaty convention prevails. This rule may serve as both an interpretation rule and a *limitation* pertaining to double taxation ("Double Taxation Treaty Limitation"), as the application of the Taxation Article may be limited in the event of any conflict with double taxation rule. The next two paragraphs cover the specified inclusions ("clawbacks") by which matters pertaining to taxation may still be applicable despite the exclusions.

435. Agreement between the Government of Denmark and the Government of the Russian Federation concerning the Promotion and Reciprocal Protection of Investments, Nov. 4, 1993 [hereinafter "Denmark-Russia BIT"].
436. *See, e.g.*, ECT Art. 21(1).
437. NAFTA Art. 2103(1).
438. US-Ecuador BIT, X(1).

[C] Exceptions and Special Provisions

The UNCTAD has identified that a majority of the tax provisions expressly state that the DTT provisions are expressly excluded from the MFN clause. So far, these provisions have rarely been subject to scrutiny and rarely cause any confusion as they seek to avoid a situation of a conflict of treaties between DTTs and BITs.

Regarding special provisions, the majority of the US and Canada BITs include a reference to the submission to tax authorities. The Canada-Ecuador BIT introduces a vague limitation relating to CTAs where the specified inclusion does not apply when the competent authorities of both Contracting States *jointly* decide, within six months, that the taxation measure does not contravene the respective provision (e.g., does not contravene the investment agreement or is not an expropriation). In such manner, this limitation contains three requirements: (1) joint decision by the competent authorities, (2) the time period for the decision, and (3) the requirement of such action. The *joint* decision has to be made within six months to avoid delaying the claim. Most BITs with special referral provisions envision a joint decision by CTAs on expropriation. Even in treaties specifying that the referral needs to be made to the host state, some mechanism for a joint referral is envisioned.[439] The investor would retain the right to seek a remedy from an investment tribunal in the event that the host state's CTA has not consulted with the investor's host state.[440]

§4.06 SUMMARY FINDINGS ON ECT ARTICLE 21

As to the sub-inquiry on whether there are any means to systematize the various elements of the ECT Taxation Article and the taxation articles of other investment treaties, the answer is a categorical yes. The Taxation Article contains several moving parts including rules of interpretation that set out article-specific definitions, rules of resolving interpretation conflict in favor of recognizing the state's power to tax, and avoidance of confusion as to the free transfer of capital.

The multilayered structure, best suited to address the complexity of the Taxation Article and taxation articles in other investment treaties, contains: (1) one general *exclusion* from the application of the treaty; (2) followed by four *specified inclusion(s)* to the initial exclusion; (3) where the inclusion(s) may be layered with either a

---

439. *See, e.g.*, Bilateral Agreement for the Promotion and Protection of Investments between the Government of the Republic of Colombia and the Government of the People's Republic of China, Colom.-China, Nov. 22, 2008; available at: https://investmentpolicy.unctad.org/ (Accessed: May 30, 2020):

> The investor must first refer to the competent tax authorities of the host Party the issue of whether the tax measure concerned involves an expropriation. In case of such referral, the competent tax authority of both Contracting Parties shall consult. Only if, within six months of the referral, they do not reach an agreement that the measure does not involve an expropriation, or in case the competent tax authorities of the Contracting Parties fail to consult with each other, the investor may submit its claim to arbitration under Article 9.

440. *Id.*

limitation or *exception*: in total one limitation, two exceptions, and one additional contentious limitation or exception or procedural requirement; and (4) finally the exceptions themselves being subject to one *restriction* covering protection against arbitrary discrimination as it concerns the Enforcement Exception.

In pure structural form, "the measure [that] arbitrarily discriminates" in the context of the effective collection of taxes is included in the protection of the treaty because:

- (level 1) all taxes are excluded, while
- (level 2) matters pertaining to transit and NT/MFN are subject to the inclusion under the Treaty, whereas
- (level 3) measures aimed at the effective collection of taxes are excepted from the Specified Inclusion, however
- (level 4) these measures are not excepted if they arbitrarily discriminate.

When organizing these moving interlocking parts, the limitations and exceptions apply to the individual inclusions of the Taxation Article and Table 4.3 emerges.

Table 4.3 Comprehensive Look at the Four Layers of Complexity in the Taxation Article (Exclusion, Specified Inclusion, Limitations and Exceptions, and Restrictions)

<table>
<tr><td colspan="5">Exclusion/Carve-Out, Article 21(1): Except as otherwise provided in this Article, nothing in this Treaty shall create rights or impose obligations with respect to Taxation Measures of the Contracting Parties</td></tr>
<tr><td rowspan="3">Specified Inclusion</td><td colspan="2">Limitations</td><td colspan="2">Exceptions</td></tr>
<tr><td>Direct Tax</td><td>Comp. Authority</td><td>Tax Treaty</td><td>Enforcement</td></tr>
<tr><td colspan="4">Restriction: e.g., Restriction Against Arbitrary Discrimination to Enforcement Exception</td></tr>
<tr><td rowspan="2">Transit: Article 21(2)</td><td rowspan="2">X</td><td rowspan="2">-</td><td rowspan="2">X</td><td>X</td></tr>
<tr><td>X</td></tr>
<tr><td rowspan="2">NT/MFN: Article 21(3)</td><td rowspan="2">X</td><td rowspan="2">-</td><td rowspan="2">X</td><td>X</td></tr>
<tr><td>X</td></tr>
<tr><td>Interim trade-related matters: Article 21(4)</td><td>X</td><td>-</td><td>-</td><td>-</td></tr>
<tr><td>Expropriation: Article 21(5)</td><td>-</td><td>X*</td><td>-</td><td>-</td></tr>
</table>

Source: Author's Own.

NB: * Referral to the competent authority may be required if the claim concerns not only expropriation but also *discriminatory* taxation treatment as per ECT Article 21(5)(b).

In all, the ECT article on "Taxation" is an extensively complex article containing a number of interlocking parts. As it concerns investment provisions, four issues remain unresolved and may yield themselves to friction that would materialize in case law on the following issues:

- In what manner do the limitations to the power to tax are incorporated in the respective treaties and the findings of the tribunals.
- The different meanings of the terms "taxes" and "taxation measures," and what is the precise relationship between these terms.
- What is the scope of the Exclusion ("Carve-Out") in ECT Article 21(1)?
- What is the scope of the two Specified Inclusions ("Clawbacks") referring to expropriation and MFN and the respective limitations and exceptions?
- What purpose does a CTA serve in the investment protection context, and what country's tax authority is relevant?
- How do tax issues materialize in the valuation phase and does the Tax Exclusion prevent tribunals from reviewing tax matters in the computation of damages?

These inquiries are reviewed below in the case law by drawing on the previously examined literature, the *travaux préparatoires* and foundational tax cases for a conclusion on the points of contention and the likely resolution. In all, the ECT Taxation Article can and should be systematized. It lends itself to a tiered review of several interlocking parts at various levels. With the categorization of exclusion, inclusion, and limitations and exceptions framework, the ECT systematization efforts offer a helpful insight into other treaties.

Chapter 5
Case Law Review

§5.01 GENERAL CONCERNS

The ECT and non-ECT case law has revealed certain patterns in the application of the tax provisions in investment treaties to past occurred events. The sub-inquiry examines the specific set of circumstances arising out of the ECT and non-ECT cases, further exploring whether the ECT and non-ECT (BIT) case law allows for any points of tension, resulting from the broad power to tax, to be reconciled in the context of the tax exclusion, inclusion, merits and valuation review available in the treaty. The two sets of cases need to be compared with care, as treaty specifics may determine the scope of the individual review and the means of interpretation for the specific text. Whenever there is deviation or a treaty-specific inquiry, this analysis addresses the case analysis in the context of the applicable treaty.

§5.02 RELEVANT BIT ENERGY CASES SETTING THE SCOPE OF THE INQUIRY

[A] General Presentation

The Ecuadorian cases and the *Yukos* BIT tax cases have preceded the ECT cases, in essence shaping and influencing much of the ECT jurisprudence. The BIT cases unveil the original points of tension arising out of taxation matters leading to the inquiry of whether the taxation issues are ECT-specific or as part of a particular pattern linked to taxation. Eleven cases are discussed below. Under the Russian BIT cases, the focus remains on *RosInvest* and *Renta4*.[441] The Ecuadorian cases cover nine cases in three

441. Rosinvest v. Russian Federation, Award on Jurisdiction, SCC Case No V(079/2005), Oct. 5, 2007 [hereinafter "*RosInvest*, Jurisdictional Award"] and Rosinvest v. Russian Federation, Final Award, SCC Case No V(079/2005), Sep. 12, 2010 [hereinafter "*RosInvest* Final Award"].

categories: (1) the VAT cases: *Occidental I*[442] and *EnCana*[443]; (2) the production-sharing contract (PSC) cases: *Occidental II*[444] as well as *Burlington*,[445] *Murphy I*[446] and *II*[447] and *Perenco*[448]; and (3) the energy and product distribution cases: *Duke Energy*[449] and *MCI Power*.[450] Although the Chevron cases against Ecuador fall outside this

Renta4 et al v. Russian Federation, Award on Preliminary Objections, SCC Case No V (024/2007), Mar. 20, 2009 [hereinafter "*Renta4* Preliminary Award"] and Renta4 et al v. Russian Federation, Award, SCC Case No V (024/2007), July 20, 2012 [hereinafter "*Renta4* Award"].

442. Occidental Exploration and Production Company ("OEPC") v. Ecuador, Award, LCIA Case No. UN 3467, July 1, 2004 [hereinafter "*Occidental I*"].
443. EnCana Corporation v. Republic of Ecuador, Partial Award on Jurisdiction, LCIA UN3481, Feb. 27, 2004 [hereinafter "*EnCana* Partial Award on Jurisdiction"]; *EnCana* Award (Horacio A. Grigera Naó dissenting) [hereinafter "*EnCana* Dissenting Opinion"].
444. Occidental Petroleum Corporation and Occidental Exploration and Production Company v. Republic of Ecuador, Decision on Jurisdiction, ICSID ARB/06/11, Sep. 9, 2008 [hereinafter "*Occidental II* Decision on Jurisdiction"]; Occidental Petroleum Corporation and Occidental Exploration and Production Company v. Republic of Ecuador, Award, ICSID ARB/06/11, Oct. 5, 2012 [hereinafter "*Occidental II* Award"]; and Occidental Petroleum Corporation and Occidental Exploration and Production Company v. Republic of Ecuador, Decision on Annulment of the Award, ICSID ARB/06/11, Nov. 2, 2015 [hereinafter "*Occidental II* Annulment Decision"].
445. Burlington Resources, Inc. v. Republic of Ecuador, Decision on Jurisdiction, ICSID Case No. ARB/08/5, June 2, 2010 [hereinafter "*Burlington* Decision on Jurisdiction"]; Burlington Resources, Inc. v. Republic of Ecuador, Decision on Liability, ICSID Case No. ARB/08/5, Dec. 14, 2012 [hereinafter "*Burlington* Decision on Liability"]; Burlington Resources, Inc. v. Republic of Ecuador, Decision on the Proposal for Disqualification of Professor Francisco Orrego Vicuna, ICSID Case No. ARB/08/5, Dec. 13, 2013 [hereinafter "*Burlington* Decision on Disqualification"]; Burlington Resources, Inc. v. Republic of Ecuador, Decision on Counter-claims, ICSID Case No. ARB/08/5, Feb. 7, 2017 [hereinafter "*Burlington* Decision on Counter-claims"], and Burlington Resources, Inc. v. Republic of Ecuador, Decision on Reconsideration and Award, ICSID Case No. ARB/08/5, Feb. 7, 2017 [hereinafter "*Burlington* Award"].
446. Murphy Exploration and Production Company International v. Republic of Ecuador, Award on Jurisdiction, ICSID Case No. ARB/08/3, Dec. 15, 2010 [hereinafter "*Murphy I*"].
447. Murphy Exploration & Production Company—International v. Republic of Ecuador, Partial Award on Jurisdiction, PCA Case No. 2012-16, Nov. 13, 2013 [hereinafter "*Murphy II* Partial Award on Jurisdiction"]; Murphy Exploration & Production Company—International v. Republic of Ecuador, Partial Final Award, PCA Case No. 2012-16, May 6, 2016 [hereinafter "*Murphy II* Partial Final Award"], and Murphy Exploration & Production Company—International v. Republic of Ecuador, Final Award, PCA Case No. 2012-16, Feb. 10, 2017[hereinafter "*Murphy II* Final Award"].
448. Perenco Ecuador Ltd v. the Republic of Ecuador and Petroecuador, Decision on Jurisdiction, ICSID Case No. ARB/08/6, June 30, 2011 [hereinafter "*Perenco* Decision on Jurisdiction"]; Perenco Ecuador Ltd v. the Republic of Ecuador and Petroecuador, Decision on Remaining Issues of Jurisdiction and Liability, ICSID Case No. ARB/08/6, Sep. 12, 2014 [hereinafter "*Perenco* Decision on Remaining Issues of Jurisdiction and Liability"] and Perenco Ecuador Ltd v. the Republic of Ecuador and Petroecuador, Decision on Reconsideration, ICSID Case No. ARB/08/6, Apr. 10, 2015 [hereinafter "*Perenco* Decision on Reconsideration"] and Perenco Ecuador Ltd v. the Republic of Ecuador and Petroecuador, Award, ICSID Case No. ARB/08/6, Sep. 27, 2019 [hereinafter "*Perenco* Award"].
449. Duke Energy Electroquil Partners and Electroquil S.A. v. the Republic of Ecuador, Award, ICSID Case No. ARB/04/19, Aug. 18, 2008 [hereinafter "*Duke Energy*"].
450. M.C.I. Power Group L.C. and New Turbine, Inc. v. the Republic of Ecuador, Award, ICSID ARB/03/6, July 31, 2007 [hereinafter "*MCI Power* Award"] and M.C.I. Power Group L.C. and New Turbine, Inc. v. the Republic of Ecuador, Decision on Annulment, ICSID ARB/03/6, Oct. 19, 2009 [hereinafter "*MCI Power* Annulment Decision"].

inquiry, some limited analysis is attributed to *Chevron I* where the tax issue was important for valuation purposes.[451]

[B] *Yukos* BIT Cases: Cases Get Set Aside after Prevailing Incrementally on the Merits

[1] Historical Context to the Yukos Dispute in Russia

In several parallel arbitrations, the investors alleged that the Russian Federation engaged *inter alia* in unlawful criminal prosecutions, massive tax reassessments that led to the bankruptcy of Yukos.[452] According to the investors in the Yukos group of companies, the ulterior motive for the cumulative actions undertaken by the Russian Federation was to gain control over the valuable company and eliminating Mikhail Khodorkovsky as a political opponent. With this purpose, the three shareholders alleged that the Russian Federation fabricated a mass tax claim that generated a substantial uncollectable debt that ultimately led Yukos into bankruptcy.[453] The Russian Federation responded that it properly assessed taxes and fines against the company after Yukos fraudulently evaded Russian corporate tax and abused the government-sponsored program to foster economic growth in designated economically underdeveloped areas.[454]

Little remains undisputed between the parties; Appendix I captures the overlap in undisputed facts. The timeline to the dispute may be divided into two parts: pre-2003 and post-2003 up to the bankruptcy of Yukos. Post-privatization and prior to 2003, Yukos rose to become one of the world's energy giants and the largest oil company based on "daily crude oil production."[455] Starting in 2003,[456] the Russian Federation assessed profit taxes and revenue-based taxes, VAT, and fines that led to the sale of Yukos' most valuable asset in an auction and ultimately to the bankruptcy of the company.[457] Besides the two BIT cases below, Russia was found to have breached the European Convention on Human Rights Article 6 and Additional Protocol Number 1 Article, thereby EUR 1,866 billion being awarded to former shareholders.[458]

---

451. Chevron Corporation and Texaco Petroleum Company v. The Republic of Ecuador (I), Partial Award on the Merits, PCA Case No. 2007-02/AA277, Mar. 30, 2010, paras. 551-53 [hereinafter "*Chevron I* Partial Award"]; Chevron Corporation and Texaco Petroleum Company v. The Republic of Ecuador (I), Final Award, PCA Case No. 2007-02/AA277, Aug. 31, 2011, paras. 309-14 [hereinafter "*Chevron I* Final Award"].
452. *Yukos* Award, para. 63.
453. *See generally Yukos* Award, para. 108 (directly reproducing investor's skeleton arguments).
454. *See generally Yukos* Award, para. 109 (directly reproducing the skeleton arguments of the Russian Federation).
455. *Yukos* Award, para. 72.
456. On Dec. 29, 2003, the Russian tax authorities issued a tax assessment for tax years 2000-2004 in the amount of USD 24.18 billion. *Yukos* Award, para. 517.
457. *Yukos* Award, paras. 1047-99 ("Yukos was struck off the register of companies and its shares were legally extinguished on Nov. 21, 2007"). *See also id.* 1099 (discussing Ruling of the Moscow Arbitrazh Court, Nov. 12, 2007).
458. OAO Neftyanaya Kompaniya Yukos v Russia App no 14902/04, Judgment (Just Satisfaction) (ECtHR, July 31, 2014), para. 756 (dismissing the allegation of indirect expropriation); OAO

[2] *The Two BIT Cases:* **RosInvest** *and* **Renta4**

Two separate arbitrations arising out of the Yukos affair were brought under BITs, which preceded the ECT case: *RosInvest* and *Renta4*. Both arbitrations were seated in Stockholm under two separate BITs. *RosInvest* was conducted under the UK-Soviet Union BIT (by extension Denmark-Russia BIT), whereas *Renta4* was conducted under the Spanish-USSR BIT (with arguments extending *inter alia* to the Denmark-Russia BIT as well). In both awards, the investor(s) prevailed but was not able to recover its legal fees, the fees far exceeding the amount recovered. Both arbitration awards were eventually set aside, but as the set-aside grounds were on different terms than tax matters, the final awards retain importance for tax analysis purposes.[459]

[i] RosInvest: *Tax Exclusion in MFN-Importing Treaty Does Not Preclude Jurisdiction and the Alleged Taxes Were Not Bona Fide*

In *RosInvest*, the arbitral tribunal held that expropriation of Yukos assets took place and that the actions of the Russian state breached the UK-USSR BIT. However, the amount of damages was low due to what the tribunal characterized a speculative investment in the acquisition of the Yukos shares as the adverse events in Russia were unfolding.[460] The investor had successfully defended a challenge on jurisdiction in a manner that went to the Supreme Court and even corrected previously problematic matters in Swedish law.[461] Once the arbitral tribunal issued the final award, the Russian Federation challenged the final award and obtained a default judgment that effectively set

---

Neftyanaya Kompaniya Yukos v Russia App no 14902/04, Judgment (ECtHR, Sept. 20, 2011). For general commentary *see* Andrew Newcombe, *Yukos Universal Limited (Isle of Man) v The Russian Federation: An Introduction to the Agora*, 30(2) ICSID Review—Foreign Inv. L. J., 283-92, 291 (2015) and Eric De Brabandere, *Yukos Universal Limited (Isle of Man) v The Russian Federation: Complementarity or Conflict? Contrasting the* Yukos *Case before the European Court of Human Rights and Investment Tribunals*, 30(2) ICSID Rev.—Foreign Inv. L. J. 345-55, 351 (2015) (discussing the ECtHR rejecting the finding of indirect expropriation).

459. In *RosInvest*, the award was set aside by means of a default judgment at the district court level, affirmed by the Court of Appeal. The dissenting opinion that was in fact a concurring opinion agreed to the result and had found that Russia's offer to arbitrate did not extend to purchasing of shares. Rosinvest v. Russian Federation, Svea Court of Appeal (T10060-10), Sep. 5, 2013. In *Renta4*, the Court of Appeal ruled that the BIT's main provision granting the investor the right to arbitrate under the treaty extended only to "mode of payments" once expropriation was undisputed. In addition, the Court of Appeal reasoned that the MFN clause did not apply to the importation of arbitration matters. *See* Svea Court of Appeal, T 9128-14, 2016-01-18, concurring opinion Patrik Schöldström, at 12-13.

460. *RosInvest* Final Award, para. 668. *See also id.* para. 666 ("The Tribunal finds it can accept Claimant's assertion that it made an investment at such a point in time when the market had in fact overreacted to transient events and the price of the shares was unjustifiably low, but that it cannot simply accept Claimant's alleged optimistic expectations regarding the future development of the value of the investment").

461. There were two issues that were corrected by this decision. The first issue was the adverse ruling in *Titan* that limited the Swedish court review of awards seated in Sweden. *See generally* Dan Engstrom and Cornel Marian, *The Swedish Yukos Saga: Rosinvest's pyrrhic victory over Russia and the fortunate correction of previous Swedish case law under which Swedish courts lacked jurisdiction over challenges against awards in the absence of any connection to Sweden*, IBA Arb. Newsletter 79-82 (2011).

aside the award. For purposes of taxation, *RosInvest* raises two main issues: (1) whether in the application of the MFN clause, the tax exclusion from the Comparator Treaty should be applied; and (2) the allegation of the *male fide*/non-bona fide tax measures.

On the MFN clause, the basis of the tribunal's jurisdiction was the UK-Soviet BIT ("Basic Treaty"), which did not contain an ISDS mechanism; the provisions of the Danish-Russian BIT ("Comparator Treaty") were successfully applied to uphold the jurisdiction of the tribunal. The issue was that the Comparator Treaty contained a sweeping exclusion of tax matters, so the inquiry focused on the *negative preclusion* effect of importing the tax exclusion from the Danish-Russian BIT.[462] The tribunal was reluctant to give a "shallow" treatment to the MFN so that the provisions of the Comparator Treaty would apply in their entirety.[463] It held that the tax exclusion in the Danish-Russian BIT was relevant only to the extent that the cumulative effect resulted in a breach of the UK-Soviet BIT.[464] In the tribunal's view, the tax exclusion in the Danish-Russian BIT did not exclude taking tax measures into account when reviewing "the cumulative effect of a general pattern."[465] The tribunal resolved this issue by examining the "cumulative combination of measures ... of which taxation [wa]s only one [issue]" while acknowledging the conflict resulting from importing provisions from the treaty that would otherwise not allow for the claim to be imported under that treaty in the first place.[466]

The *RosInvest* tribunal was also the first Yukos tribunal to adopt the non-bona fide nature of the alleged taxes adopted by Russia albeit for a substantive (not jurisdictional) review of whether expropriation has occurred.[467] Once it found that there was not a jurisdictional hurdle to review the taxation measures, the tribunal held that a state might expropriate by means of taxation and taxation-related measures.[468] The *RosInvest* tribunal confronted five sets of taxation and taxation-related measures: the VAT taxes, the profit taxes, repeat offender fines, the YNG auction, and the

The second issue was the multiple review of awards at multiple levels. In the 1999 version, the Swedish Arbitration Act (SAA) offered the opportunity to challenge the jurisdiction of the tribunal separately from the challenge to the final award. The challenge to jurisdiction could be launched before the district court. With the 2019 amendments, any challenges to jurisdictions would be launched before the Court of Appeal. *See* SAA § 2 in the pre-March 2019 amendments and post amendments. The amendments were implemented pursuant to Law 2018:1954.

462. *See* Denmark-Russia BIT, Art. 11(3). *See also RosInvest* Final Award, para. 271.
463. *RosInvest* Final Award, paras. 270-1. For claimant's arguments, *see RosInvest* Final Award, para. 260 (claimant argued that: (1) in using the MFN, the tribunal is not obligated to apply less favorable provisions and (2) it was the auctioned sale of Yukos' assets, not the adverse tax assessment, which caused the substantial deprivation).
464. *RosInvest* Final Award, para. 455.
465. *Id.* para. 618.
466. *Id.* para. 271. *But see id.* para. 270 ("were a Danish investor to make a claim under the Denmark-Russia BIT for an expropriation by way of taxation, the *treatment* afforded to the Danish investor under the Denmark-Russia BIT would mean that the investor was precluded from making a claim").
467. *RosInvest* Final Award, para. 620.
468. *Id.* para. 626 (referring to several sources, as invoked by claimant, including *inter alia* Restatement (Third) of Foreign Relations Law of the United States para. 712; *Occidental I* at para. 85 and *Too* at 387).

bankruptcy auction.[469] The tribunal clarified that it does not stand as an appeal body on Russian law; it further held that "the application of Russian tax law on Yukos must be seen as a discriminatory and as not a bona fide treatment of Yukos."[470] In fact, the tax assessment and tax enforcement measures ("the application of the tax law, the tax assessments on Yukos and the conduct of the auctions") were deemed by the tribunal to be non-bona fide.[471] The tribunal did not endorse respondent's arguments that the tax measures were justified due to the enforcement of the "bad faith doctrine," by which Russia alleged the trading companies in the low-tax regions were a sham and the proportionality principle by which tax benefits in the low-tax regions would otherwise require some link to the investment made.[472] Nor did the argument that the Russian authorities enjoyed a great degree of discretion gain any traction.[473] The tribunal hesitated to uphold such discretion, even after recognizing the "wide latitude" that the states have "in imposing and enforcing tax laws," when the state used such discretion extensively and against only one taxpayer.[474] In all, the "cumulative treatment" of *Yukos* amounted to unlawful expropriation where several measures (VAT and profit taxes) were expressly deemed not bona fide.[475]

[ii] Renta4: *No Jurisdiction under MFN but Tax Exclusion from Comparator Treaty Not Applied: Measures Adopted by Russia Are Not Bona Fide*

In *Renta4*, the investors were based in Spain (rather than the UK), thereby invoking the Spanish-Russian BIT ("Basic Treaty"). Claimants invoked the MFN as an alternative ground for the tribunal's jurisdiction. The tribunal held that it had jurisdiction over the dispute on the basis of the Spanish-Russian BIT, but such jurisdiction did not extend on the basis of the MFN provisions to the provisions of the Danish-Russian BIT ("Comparator Treaty").

Despite the finding of lack of jurisdiction on the basis of the MFN clause, the tribunal dismissed Russia's arguments for automatic exclusion of all tax matters in the presence of a tax exclusion in the Comparator Treaty.[476] In *Renta4*, the tribunal focused on the allegations of "abuse of the power to tax," which did not preclude the tribunal exercising jurisdiction, resembling a bona fide argument.[477] The tribunal distinguished between two types of complaints: complaints about 'types and levels of taxation' and, those about "abuse of the power to tax."[478] In the tribunal's opinion, a sweeping governmental decree instructing "all tax inspectors ... to collect everything that they can get their hands on from Danish investors" would be invalidated as to be an abuse

469. *Id.* para. 620.
470. *Id.* para. 454.
471. *Id.* para. 567.
472. *RosInvest* Final Award, paras. 449-50.
473. *Id.* paras. 496.
474. *Id.* para. 580.
475. *Id.* paras. 620 ff.
476. *Renta4* Preliminary Award, para. 74.
477. *Id.* para. 74.
478. *Id.* para. 74.

of the host state's power to tax.[479] According to the *Renta4* tribunal, complaints about the abuse of the power to tax could not be automatically excluded by the invocation of the tax exclusion clause under the BIT. However, in *Renta4*, the tribunal reasoned that the MFN clause in the Basic Treaty did not contain language permitting the tribunal "to enlarge" its competencies.[480] The tribunal found support in the presence of the language in the tax exception in the subsequent paragraph, which excepted the extension of any privileges to tax matters arising from DTTs.[481]

In *Renta4*, the tribunal similarly reviewed whether the imposition of the tax measures and the enforcement of the tax measures were bona fide for purposes of finding whether an expropriation has occurred. Consistent with *RosInvest*, the *Renta4* tribunal found that certain measures were not bona fide.[482] The *Renta4* tribunal deemed that the asset freeze and that the auction took place revealed a pattern of wrongdoing; in addition, "failure to even respond to settlement offers by Yukos" raised "significant doubts" that the Russian Federation acted in good faith during the process.[483]

Renta4 reinforced the proposition that a mere labeling of a measure as tax does not deprive the tribunal of carefully scrutinizing the nature of the measure.[484] The tribunal introduced a definition for a tax: defined as "the payment of a debt established by law in favour of the public treasury,"[485] further clarifying that a tax is by definition is a taking but such taking is not necessarily compensable.[486] Some latitude was acknowledged to be afforded to the states on matters of taxation, but the tribunal quickly distinguished between, on the one hand, the discretion in enacting and enforcing tax law and, on the other hand, the discretion to comply with an international treaty.[487] It held that there is a "presumption" that taxes adopted by the states are bona fide "unless there is convincing evidence that, upon a true characterization, they constitute a taking."[488] Everything that followed from the conduct of the state: the sale, the amount that the company was worth, and the failure to grant an extension indicated that the Yukos' tax delinquency was a pretext for seizing assets.[489] By closely following the findings of *RosInvest*, *Renta4* reached a similar conclusion: the YNG auction to one sole bidder together with all the actions preceding the auction indicated an intent to expropriate.[490]

479. *See id.*
480. *Renta4* Preliminary Award, para. 74.
481. *Id.* para. 113. *See also* Spanish-Russian BIT Art. 5(3) ("The treatment granted under this article shall not include tax exemptions or other comparable privileges granted by either Party to the investors of a third State by virtue of a double taxation agreement or any other agreement concerning matters of taxation"). *But cf. Renta 4* Dissenting opinion, para. 12 (disagreeing with the majority's interpretation of the term "treatment").
482. *Renta4* Award, para. 127.
483. *Id.*
484. *Id.* para. 179.
485. *Id.* para. 48.
486. *Renta4* Award, para. 48.
487. *Id.* para. 179.
488. *Id.* para. 180.
489. *Id.* paras. 129 ff.
490. *See even id.* para. 128.

[C] The Ecuadorian Cases

[1] Historical Context to the Ecuadorian Cases

In the case of Ecuador, several factors have created the auspices for a perfect storm of investment energy disputes with an unreasonably high number of tax-related issues, summarized in Appendix II.

The initial foreign investments in the hydrocarbon sector in the 1980s and 1990s relied on *services contracts* where the investors operated on offering "services" but recouped the costs of their investments on the basis of the service fees.[491] Under the "services contracts model," foreign investors were "service providers." The right to natural resources remained with the Ecuadorian state-owned entity, Petroecuador.[492] Foreign investors paid VAT on local acquisitions that were eligible for reimbursement as they were not formally exporting oil.[493] As the price of oil remained low,[494] Ecuador's revenues were also low. In 1993, Ecuador transitioned from services contracts to PSC (or "*participation contracts*"). The state or its state entity no longer absorbed the initial costs. Instead, the investor assumed the initial costs to be shared with the state when oil exploration would be viable in exchange for exclusive rights and the ability to sell oil abroad.[495] But the Bank Crisis of 1998 devastated any initial successes, with the state taking drastic tax measures as the oil prices started to rise.[496] By 2001, disagreements appeared to emerge about the VATs on oil exports. Under the existing tax regime at the time, VAT paid could be offset against other VAT; in the event of net overpayment, the paid VAT was reimbursable.[497] However, beginning with 2001, the Ecuadorian tax authority, *Servicio de Rentas Internas* (SRI), refused reimbursement of the VAT on the basis that the VAT was already incorporated in the cost-sharing formula. Several challenges followed before local authorities and investment tribunals that may be classified as the first wave of investment disputes.

In the aftermath of the VAT cases, several cases tackled the adverse effects on investments emerging from Law 2006-42 (commonly referred to as "Law 42").[498] Law

491. Law of Hydrocarbons (Ecuad.), Supreme Decree 1459, passed on Sep. 27, 1971, published in Official Registry No. 322, Oct. 1, 1971. Law 44 Amending the Hydrocarbons Law (Ecuad.), Official Registry No. 326, Nov. 29, 1993. *See also Occidental I*, para. 27. *Cf.* Law 44 Amending the Hydrocarbons Law (Ecuad.), Official Registry No. 326 of Nov. 29, 1993. Law No. 2006-42 Amending the Hydrocarbons Law (Ecuad.), Decree No. 1672 Implementing Law 42-2006 of July 13, 2006. Decree No. 662 (Ecuad.), Oct. 18, 2007 modifying Decree No. 1672.
492. *See Occidental I* Award, para. 26.
493. *Id.*
494. *See generally* Cameron, *supra* note 221, at para. 6-21 (referring to an USD 15/barrel presumably nominal price). For prices adjusted for inflation with 2017 as the base, *see infra* text accompanying Figure 5.1.
495. Cameron, *supra* note 221, at para. 6-21.
496. *Id.* 6-7 and 19-20. During the same time, Ecuador introduced a 1% tax on all financial transactions that "was devastating for the financial system as it was imposed in the middle of a liquidity crunch, thereby accelerating the collapse of various financial institutions, including Banco del Progreso, the largest bank of the system measured by deposits." *Id.* 19.
497. *Occidental I*, paras. 120-2 (discussing Articles 65 and 68, 69A of the Tax Law. Art. 65 was in effect until 1999).
498. *See generally* Peter Cameron, *supra* note 221, at para. 6-111.

42 amended the Hydrocarbon Law of 1993 enabling Ecuador to claim a participation share of at least 50% in the event of "windfall profits" defined as any "non agreed or unforeseen surpluses from the sale of oil."[499] Further amended in 2007, Law 42 increased Ecuador's claim to 70% for all contracts entered into after August 1, 2008, and at least 99% on all extraordinary income. The extraordinary income was measured as the difference between the current market price of oil and the inflation-adjusted price of oil at the time the PSCs were signed.[500] By 2006, the inflation-adjusted prices of crude oil had doubled relative to 1993, when the Hydrocarbon Law was amended to allow for PSCs.[501] By 2009, the inflation-adjusted prices had tripled. Figure 5.1 tracks the increase in inflated-adjusted prices of crude oil from when the Hydrocarbon Law was passed, further highlighting the financial incentive for Ecuador to pass legislation on the basis of the increase in sale price alone.

Figure 5.1 Price of Crude Oil (1989-2017) and Timeline of Ecuadorian PSC Legislation

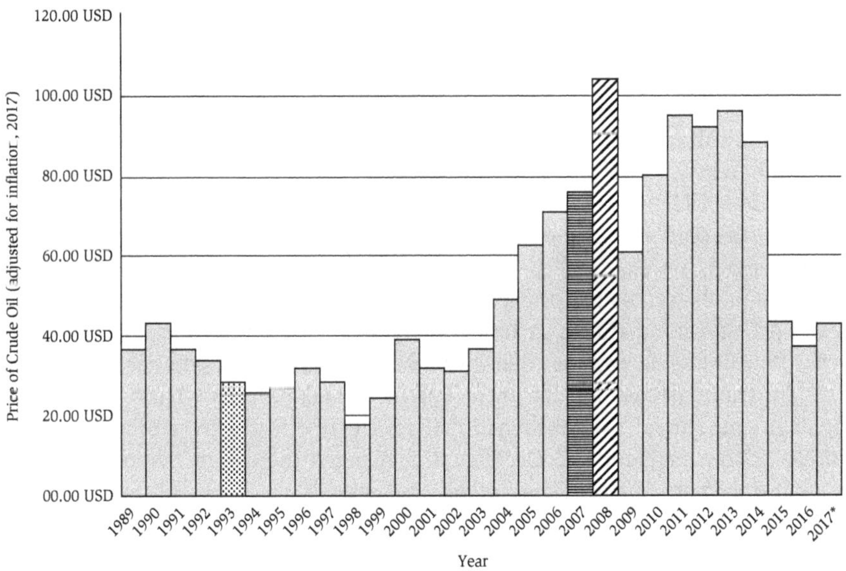

Source: Author's Own.

499. *See* Law No. 2006-42 Amending the Hydrocarbons Law (Ecuad.), Decree No. 1672 Implementing Law 42-2006 of July 13, 2006 Art. 2. Decree No. 662 of Oct. 18, 2007 modifying Decree No. 1672. *See also* Peter Cameron, *supra* note 221, at para. 6-111 and Julie Bedard et al., *The "Law 42" Arbitrations Against Ecuador and the Importance of BIT Language*, Skadden 2015 Insights -Global Litigation.
500. *See generally Burlington* Decision on Liability, para. 32.
501. *See generally* Tim McMahon, Historical Crude Oil Prices (Table); http://www.inflationdata.com (Accessed: May 30, 2020). Historical data corresponds to other sources such as oilprice.com or Bloomberg.com.

*Inflation-adjusted prices of crude oil with 2017 prices as the base.

Several types of cases arose out of the regulatory changes in Ecuador. They concern: (1) VAT, (2) production-sharing contracts, (3) power distribution, and (4) otherwise contract claims.[502] As the first two sets of cases arise directly out of taxation measures undertaken by the state and are specifically covered by the BITs, the analysis will focus on these two sets of cases, and group category three and four in one.

[2] Cases

[i] VAT Cases: Oxy I *and* EnCana

The VAT cases serve as a *prelude* to the subsequent disputes. The two VAT cases, *Occidental I* and *EnCana*, were subject to two separate BITs reaching different results on matters of taxation. Both *EnCana* and *Occidental I* tribunals held that there was no expropriation. Whereas in *Occidental I* (under the US-Ecuador BIT) the tribunal upheld that adverse VAT legislation may breach the other provisions of an investment treaty, in *EnCana* (under the Canadian-Ecuador BIT), the tribunal denied the investor's claims over a set of similar circumstances. In *EnCana*, the specified inclusions of the Canada-Ecuador BIT materialized to be far narrower than those in the US-Canada BIT where taxation matters arising from an investment agreement were included in the scope of the treaty.

In *Occidental I*, under the US-Ecuador BIT, the tribunal ordered Ecuador to refund the investor the paid VAT: not on the basis of expropriation (those claims determined as inadmissible) but on other standards (protection against arbitrariness and non-discrimination, as well as the provisions of NT and FET).[503] The tribunal disposed of the expropriation arguments as an admissibility issue.[504] After conducting a prima facie review, the tribunal determined that there was no "substantial deprivation" of property.[505] The tribunal reasoned that "taxes can result in expropriation as can other types of regulatory measures"[506] and that a formal transfer of title to a given property was not required.[507] Both Ecuador and Occidental challenged the award before the English courts but they were unsuccessful in their challenge.[508]

502. *See generally* Cameron, *supra* note 221, at para. 6-109.
503. *See Occidental I*, paras. 80, 89-92. *See also id.* para. 158.
504. *Occidental I*, para. 80.
505. *Occidental I*, at para. 89 (citing to Pope Talbot Inc. v. Canada, Interim Award, June 26, 2000 paras. 96, 102).
506. *Occidental I*, para. 85.
507. *Id.* para. 85.
508. Occidental's challenge appears to be an objection to Ecuador's set-aside proceedings, whereby Occidental argued that the dispute is not justiciable at all. *See* Republic of Ecuador v. Occidental Exploration and Production Co., [2006] EWHC 345 (Comm), Mar. 2, 2006; affirmed Republic of Ecuador v. Occidental Exploration and Production Co., [2007] EWCA Civ. 656, July 4, 2007. On Occidental's claims of non-justiciability, *see* Republic of Ecuador v. Occidental Exploration and Production Co., [2005] EWHC 774 (Comm), Apr. 29, 2005; affirmed Republic of Ecuador v. Occidental Exploration and Production Co., [2005] EWCA Civ. 1116, Sep. 9, 2005.

The tribunal ultimately found that a partial violation of the protection against arbitrariness, a full violation of the national treatment (NT) and FET had occurred. On the protection against arbitrariness, the tribunal reasoned that a violation may occur if the action "depend[s] on individual discretion; ... founded on prejudice and preference rather than on reason or fact."[509] The tribunal held that although not intentional, the conduct of the state tax agency, SRI, built on confusion in order to bring "some resemblance of order."[510] Such conduct was also built on a false assumption that VAT refund had already taken place.[511] The tribunal held that the conduct was also discriminatory.[512] The inconsistent conduct of local authorities affected the tribunal's conclusion of a breach of the FET standard, where the tribunal applying the objective criteria held that the tribunal drew on the Preamble and the case law to derive a binding standard of the state "to act in a consistent manner, free from ambiguity and totally transparently in its relations with the foreign investor."[513] Ecuador's intentions, namely whether it acted in good faith or not, did not affect the final determination of a breach.[514]

On NT treatment, the parties disagreed over the control group for purposes of comparing "no less favorable treatment ... *in like situations*" found in the BIT (Table 5.1).[515] Although Ecuador argued that all companies in the same sector should be used for purposes of the comparison, the tribunal agreed with the investor.[516] The relevant group for the comparison was all companies "engaged in exports," to be distinguished from the GATT/WTO standard.[517] Under GATT/WTO, the focus of "like situations" is on the treatment of *products* on the local market in terms of "being affected by a distortion to competition with similar products because of taxes and other regulations in the *country of destination*."[518] In terms of BIT protection, "like situations" focus on the *exporters* in the foreign markets. The analysis requires the review of whether the exporters are not placed "at a disadvantage in foreign markets because of the indirect taxes paid in the *country of origin*."[519]

509. *Occidental I*, at para. 162 (citing to the use in *Lauder* of the *Black's Law Dictionary* definition of arbitrariness). *See also* Ronald S. Lauder v. Czech Republic, UNCITRAL Final Award, Sep. 3, 2001, para. 221 (citing to *Black's Law Dictionary* 100 (7th ed., 1999)).
510. *Occidental I*, at para. 163.
511. *Id.* para. 164. The authorities had reasoned that a compensation has already taken place under the Contract. *Id.*
512. *Id.* para. 165.
513. *Id.* para. 185 (quoting Tecnicas Medioambientales Tecmed S. A. v. Mexico, Award of May 29, 2003, 43 ILM 133 para. 154 (2004)).
514. *Id.* para. 185 ("[t]his is an objective requirement that does not depend on whether the Respondent has proceeded in good faith or not").
515. *See Occidental I*, at para. 167 (referring to BIT Art. II(1) (emphasis added)).
516. *Id.* para. 173.
517. *Id.* paras. 168 & 173. *See also* Dolzer & Schreuer, *supra* note 54, at para. 205 (stating that *Occidental I* struck "an initial blow" to the approach of interpreting NT standard by relying on GATT/WTO standards).
518. *Occidental I*, at para. 175.
519. *Id.* (emphasis added).

Table 5.1 NT Treatment in Investment GATT/WTO Context after Occidental I

Regime	*Emphasis*	*Basis*
GATT/WTO	*Products*	Country of Destination
BITs	*Exporters*	Country of Origin

Source: Author's Own.

Two other matters remain of relevance to the tribunal's treatment of taxes: (1) the applicable law and (2) the submission of the dispute to local authorities for review. Regarding the applicable law, the tribunal held that, under Ecuadorian law, the investor was entitled to the VAT refund.[520] In reaching the said conclusion, the tribunal's analysis heavily relied on the interpretation of Ecuadorian tax law while deeming the rulings from the Ecuadorian Supreme Court not to be binding.[521] Based on two Ecuadorian cases, the tribunal found persuasive that the VAT reimbursement provisions in the local tax law extended to oil exporters.[522] Despite Ecuador's position to the contrary, the tribunal had little doubt that the Andean law was binding on the parties.[523] The Andean law contained two distinct decisions arguing for harmonization of intra-regional incentives and elimination of subsidies.[524] The tribunal found these to be binding on the Ecuadorian legal order. The tribunal did not find the application of trade law (WTO/GATT) relevant, as it only set out accepted principles and did not constitute binding customary law: the destination-principle VAT where reimbursement of VAT is attributable to export goods paid in the country of origin was deemed a best practice, not binding on the parties.[525]

Regarding submission of the dispute to local authorities, the tribunal found that the fork-in-the-road clause of the treaty was not triggered when the investor challenged SRI Resolution before local authorities. Although the issue was complicated by the investor's submission of the dispute to local authorities, the tribunal reasoned that the investor did not have a "real choice" as the period for the challenge was very short (twenty-one days) before the ruling would become final and binding.[526]

In *EnCana*, the tribunal found no breach of the Canada-Ecuador BIT as it deemed that the tax exclusion applied broadly and the expropriation inclusion/clawback applied narrowly. *EnCana* was seized under the Canada-Ecuador BIT. The tribunal dismissed all claims: those not related to expropriation for lack of jurisdiction and those

520. *Id.* para. 143.
521. *Id.* para. 137.
522. *Id.* paras. 140-1 (discussing *YPF Ecuador S.A. v. SRI* and *Bellwether* before the Ecuadorian Supreme Court). As discussed by the tribunal, the Tax Court held in *YPF Ecuador S.A.* that oil companies could not be beneficiaries of VAT reimbursement, but the decision from the Ecuadorian Supreme Court, Special Taxation Chamber reached a different result. *Id.* para. 141.
523. *Occidental I*, paras. 148-9.
524. *Id.* paras. 146-7 (discussing Commission Decision Nr. 330 of 1992 and Decision Nr. 388 of 1996; further reference is also made to the preparatory work of the Commission Decision Nr. 370).
525. Ecuador became a member of WTO in 1996, covering at least part of the relevant period.
526. *Occidental I*, para. 61.

related to expropriation on the merits.[527] In the partial award on jurisdiction, the tribunal joined the jurisdictional objections on taxation measures to the merits of the case.[528] In the final award, the tribunal held, first, that it did not have jurisdiction over the non-expropriation issues. By reviewing the claim in the context of the Canada-Ecuador BIT, the tribunal found that the claim did not concern an investment agreement; thus, it dismissed all the issues not related to expropriation for lack of jurisdiction.[529]

In the final award, the tribunal interpreted the tax exclusion by addressing the scope of the underlying taxation exception and the lack of the definition for the term "taxation measures."[530] Lacking a coherent definition, the tribunal focused on the link between "taxation measure" and 'tax[ation]' deriving a definition of essential elements inherent in the tax. The BIT defined only the term 'measure' so the scope of the 'taxation' element remained subject for interpretation. For purposes of defining "taxation," the *EnCana* tribunal set out two inquiries: (1) effect-driven, driven by what the tribunal would characterize as "its legal operation, not its economic effect" of a tax[531] and purely definitional, by which a tax law was defined as "one[:] which *imposes a liability*(I) *on classes of persons*(II) *to pay money to the State*(III) *for public purposes.*(IV)"[532] By reviewing the aim of a tax/taxation for "its legal operation, not its economic effect," the *EnCana* tribunal introduced the inquiry into the 'true purpose' of a tax.[533] Combined, 'taxation measures' were deemed to refer to aspects of the tax regime that determine how much tax is to be paid *or refunded.*[534] According to the tribunal, "a measure providing relief from taxation is a taxation measure just as much as a measure imposing the tax in the first place."[535] After pointing out that the claimant failed to contain the scope of the term,[536] the tribunal concluded that the term 'taxation' refers to both direct and indirect taxation,[537] both types being subject to the exclusion.

In *EnCana*, the tribunal found, over a strong dissent, that no breach of expropriation occurred: in either direct or indirect form.[538] The tribunal opined on the relationship between taxation and indirect expropriation, by highlighting that taxes: (a) are a form of lawful taking and (b) ordinarily do not create legitimate expectations in the regime being static:

527. *EnCana* Award, paras. 166-8, 179 & 199.
528. *Id.* paras. 37-9.
529. *Id.* paras. 149 (in the tribunal's conclusion, "EnCana's claim so far as it relates to the entitlement of the subsidiaries to VAT refunds is excluded from the scope of the BIT by Art. XII as a 'taxation measure', subject to the exception for expropriation").
530. *Id.* paras. 141-2.
531. *Id.* para. 141(4).
532. *EnCana* Award, para. 141(4) (emphasis and categorization added).
533. *Id.* para. 141(4).
534. *Id.* para. 141(3).
535. *Id.* para. 141(4).
536. The tribunal specifically pointed out that claimant did not raise the argument that the scope of the taxation exception should be somehow limited, i.e. applied only to direct taxes. *See id.* para. 141(2) ("[t]here is no reason to limit the term 'taxation' to direct taxation, nor did the Claimant suggest it should be so limited").
537. *EnCana* Award, para. 141(2).
538. *Id.* paras. 168, 172-200 & 200, n. 138.

> [i]n the absence of a specific commitment from the host State, the foreign investor has neither the right nor any legitimate expectation that the tax regime will not change, perhaps to its disadvantage, during the period of investment. Of its nature all taxation reduces the economic benefits an enterprise would otherwise derive from the investment; it will only be in an extreme case that a tax which is general in its incidence could be judged as equivalent in its effect to an expropriation of the enterprise which is taxed.[539]

The tribunal concluded that the investor did not experience such an extreme case of a taking to justify indirect expropriation. Although the investor had experienced losses due to the changes in the VAT legislation, it continued to operate and engage in "the normal range of activities" determined to include extraction and exportation of oil.[540] The tax was not deemed to constitute an "unreasonable interference" to make use and benefit of its investments, a contested standard from *Metalclad* for indirect expropriation.[541] The tribunal distinguished *Metalclad* as not being a taxation case, further holding that:

> Moreover Metalclad had nothing to do with taxation. From the perspective of expropriation, taxation is in a special category. In principle a tax law creates a new legal liability on a class of persons to pay money to the State in respect of some defined class of transactions, the money to be used for public purposes. In itself such a law is not a taking of property; if it were, a universal State prerogative would be denied by a guarantee against expropriation, which cannot be the case. Only if a tax law is extraordinary, punitive in amount or arbitrary in its incidence would issues of indirect expropriation be raised.[542]

Neither did the conduct amount to a direct expropriation. In the direct expropriation context, the tribunal was called to review the impact of the Ecuadorian actions on a "claim of money" and specifically of the VAT "returns" which under the Canada-Ecuador BIT fell under the definition of investment.[543] The tribunal reasoned that a law cancelling a liability could amount to expropriation because a VAT refund constituted a "material benefit" for an investor and a right to VAT refunds could be inferred.[544] The critical consideration was whether such right had already *accrued* or whether it was yet to materialize, a distinction being made between a law applying retrospectively to past transactions and one that applied prospectively to future transactions. The determination of whether such rights had accrued was to be determined in the context of the applicable law, namely the law of the host state.[545]

Regarding accrual, the analysis mirrored a denial of rights rationale. By drawing on the *Waste Management* standard for expropriation of intangible property by executive action, the *EnCana* tribunal reasoned that "[t]here are differences between alleged governmental nonperformance of contractual obligations and governmental

539. *Id.* para. 173.
540. *Id.* para. 174.
541. *Id.* para. 177.
542. *EnCana* Award, para. 177.
543. *Id.* paras. 181-2.
544. *Id.* paras. 183 and 189.
545. *Id.* paras. 184-5 (in this case, it was the law of Ecuador: "the rights affected must exist under the law which creates them, in this case, the law of Ecuador").

refusal to make payments allegedly required by statute, in particular tax refunds."[546] Thus, a good faith and defensible action by an executive body would not constitute a treaty breach, particularly on a questionable issue of law. However, a position taken by the executive branch contrary to the applicable law could possibly constitute a treaty breach, especially if such action were not defensible and done in good faith.[547]

According to the dissent, an expropriation took place and the majority overrelied on the *Waste Management* standard and domestic law.[548] The dissent viewed the deference afforded by the majority as overreaching; constituting a renvoi from international law to Ecuadorian law (domestic law).[549] Crucially, the dissenting opinion cautioned against reviewing subsequent tax legislation, which may legitimize unlawful conduct. The dissent viewed the aims of Law No. 2004-41 (2004) ("Interpretative Law") rectify the negative impacts of Section 69-A of the Tax Code (providing for the VAT refund), once it became applicable before national courts and imposed a renegotiation requirement of the sharing arrangement before a VAT refund could be issued:[550]

> [...] what is at stake is not whether a State may impose or not specific obligations—including tax obligations—for the future through the enactment of new laws or the modification of the existing ones or the sovereign rights of the State to do so under its own laws or international law, *but whether such legislation may have the effect of cleansing for the future wrongful State conduct according to the Treaty that has already taken place and started to have harmful consequences before the enactment of such legislation, and that remains unremedied from the international law perspective.*[551]

In this context, the dissenting opinion viewed the Interpretative Law as discriminatory and symbolic of non-public use of the tax measures,[552] whereas the majority deemed the same law as immaterial when the claims falling after the passing of said law were withdrawn.[553]

[ii] *Windfall Cases:* Burlington, Oxy II, Perenco, *and* Murphy I and II

The VAT cases were the prelude to the subsequent cases arising out of Law 42 as amended by Decree 662 effectively. The investors did not willingly concede to the new

546. *Id.* para. 192 (citing to Waste Management Inc. v United Mexican States (2004) 43 ILM 967, para. 174). *Waste Management* concerned non-performance of contractual obligations and the finding that a mere contract breach does not amount to a breach under the treaty (NAFTA); the determining factor is whether access to a challenge is "practically or legally foreclosed'. *See also EnCana* Award, para. 193 (referring to *Revere Copper*).
547. *EnCana* Award, paras. 194-5.
548. *EnCana* Dissenting Opinion, paras. 4 and 34-6.
549. *Id.* paras. 6 and 9-14 (the dissenting opinion also deemed the majority's opinion imposing a requirement for the investor to exhaust local remedies).
550. *Id.* para. 53.
551. *Id.* para. 12.
552. *Id.* paras. 40 and 43.
553. *EnCana* Award, para. 196.

terms increasing the state claim to 99% of the "unforeseen" income.[554] By Ecuador's accounts, twenty-three PSCs became the subject of the Law 42-related measures but fifteen of the twenty-three PSCs migrated to a service contract.[555] This record, however, is disputed. It is more likely that of the twenty-three contracts only four were fully transformed into service contracts. The remaining contracts either were of transitory nature or were ultimately settled.[556] Most of the cases emerge as a result of disputes linked to the same blocks with the consortium members led by Repsol YPF Ecuador, see Appendix II.[557]

The *Burlington* tribunal, seized under the US-Ecuador BIT, held that it had jurisdiction over the expropriation claims pertaining to taxation. At least for the jurisdictional phase, the tribunal determined that whether something is a tax for purposes of investment protection should be determined from a perspective of international law, not domestic law.[558] By relying on the four-prong standard from *EnCana*,[559] the tribunal found that Law 42 was a tax. It was: (1) an obligation as a law; (2) imposing liability on a "class of persons"; (3) to pay money to the state; and (4) to be used for public purposes.

In finding that Law 42 is a tax and determining jurisdiction over all expropriation claims and some non-expropriation claims, the *Burlington* jurisdictional award upheld that whether something is an investment for purposes of a BIT should be determined according to international law.[560] As Law 42 was a tax, any claims pertaining to Law 42 would fall under the tax exclusion unless otherwise provided by the treaty. Not all claims pertaining to Law 42 concerned matters of taxation.[561] Some claims, pertaining to indemnification obligations, did not raise matters of taxation.[562] The tribunal reasoned that a state's indemnification obligation arising out of a contract (e.g., PSC) is unrelated to the taxing power of the state.[563] Two private powers may enter into an indemnification clause without any control over the taxation levels.[564] Other umbrella clause claims challenging the validity of Law 42 as a tax failed once the tribunal held that Law 42 was a tax.[565] The tribunal then dismissed jurisdiction over all non-expropriation claims, as there was no investment agreement for purposes of catching the other claims within the coverage of the inclusion/clawback.[566]

554. *See generally* US Embassy Quito (Ambassador Linda Jewell), "Government of Ecuador Whipsaws Oil Companies," Wikileaks Cable: 08QUITO351_a, Apr. 18, 2008.
555. *Burlington* Decision on Liability, para. 51.
556. *Id.*
557. *See Murphy I*, para. 31.
558. *Burlington* Decision on Jurisdiction, paras. 162-3 ("*for purposes of jurisdiction*, the Tribunal needs *only* to decide whether Law 42 is a tax for purposes of Art. X of the Treaty under international law") (emphasis added).
559. *Id.* paras. 164-5. *See also EnCana* Award, para. 142(4).
560. *Burlington* Decision on Jurisdiction paras. 162-4 (referring also to *Duke Energy and EnCana*).
561. *Id.* para. 177.
562. *Burlington* Decision on Jurisdiction, para. 181 (umbrella clause 1 claim and first prong of the umbrella clause 3 claim).
563. *Id.* para. 182.
564. *Id.* para. 183.
565. *Id.* para. 181 (umbrella clause 2 claim and second prong of umbrella clause 3 claim).
566. *Id.* paras. 245-6.

When finding that Law 42 was not a confiscatory tax, the *Burlington* decision on liability concluded that a state has broad authority to tax; the limits are only those found in international treaties to which the state has entered into and customary law.[567] Under customary law, two limits to the state's power to tax exist: the prohibition against confiscatory taxation and the prohibition against discriminatory taxation.[568] The dispositive factor is the "effect of the tax" and it is similar to the finding of indirect expropriation.[569] Unlawful intent behind the measure does not replace the need to show substantial deprivation for purposes of a finding of a confiscatory tax. Confiscatory tax requires a showing that the investment is not commercially viable. Positive cash flows are likely to reveal the absence of confiscatory tax measures. Breach at the tax enforcement stage needs to show permanence and substantial deprivation of the investment (not the property owned by the investor).[570] In principle, the enforcement proceedings should have an economically neutral effect by which any debt would be extinguished by the measure enacted (e.g., property seized).[571] The deprivation has to be permanent: it needs to affect the investment or permanently affect the earning capacity of the investor. Creeping expropriation, not found in the case, could be found only when "'none' of the challenged measures separately constitutes expropriation."[572]

The majority recognized the broad taxation power subject to defined limits. According to the majority, the limits to a state's power to tax are those found in customary international law and international treaties to which the country has acceded.[573] In the majority's opinion, customary international law dictates two limits to a state's power to tax: the principle against non-discrimination and non-confiscation.[574] Confiscatory and expropriatory taxation are deemed to be used interchangeably, and it denotes a fact-based analysis of assessing when the taxation "takes too much."[575] The effect of the tax is essential.[576] A state's intention to confiscate may be indicative of the adverse effect but the intent per se is not definitive, according to the majority.[577] According to the majority (1) failure to adhere to the tax stabilization clauses; (2) the effects of Law 42 to increase taxation on windfall to 50% and (3) later to 99% did not amount to expropriation. Nor did the mechanisms to enforce ("coactiva") the payment of the alleged delinquent payments pursuant to Law 42 constitute expropriation.

On the tax per se, the majority found that the measure was not confiscatory at either 50% or 99%. As a tax on windfalls, the majority determined that the measure reduced the investor's "take on the total oil revenues" but it did not constitute a

567. *Burlington* Decision on Liability, paras. 391-3.
568. *Id.* para. 393.
569. *Id.* para. 395.
570. *Id.* para. 395.
571. *Id.* para. 468.
572. *Burlington* Decision on Liability, paras. 538-9 (discussing also *Revere Copper*).
573. *Id.* paras. 391-2.
574. *Id.* para. 393.
575. *Id.* para. 393.
576. *Id.* para. 401.
577. *Burlington* Decision on Liability, para. 401.

substantial deprivation.[578] The tribunal held that even at the 99% rate, the investment "preserved its capacity to generate a commercial return."[579] According to the majority, Burlington retained a positive cash flow, both annual and cumulative for each of the two blocks despite high amortization rates recorded in the critical period after the enactment of Law 42.[580] In addition, the majority found it credible that the intent behind Law 42 is to force investors to abdicate their rights under PSCs. However, as held above, intent alone does not replace the requirement of substantial deprivation.[581]

On the enforcement measures ("coactiva"), the majority also found that there was no expropriation as there was no substantial deprivation of the investment.[582] The "coactiva" measures involved the seizure of oil shipments and their assessment on the Ecuadorian market.[583] According to the majority, the relevant standard for determining the expropriatory effect of the tax enforcement measures is to assess the impact of the measures on the investor's investment, not on the property. For a lawful tax enforcement measure, the impact of the tax enforcement measure would be "economically neutral."[584] For every dollar collected through the sale of the property on an auction, the equal amount of the debt should be extinguished. In the majority's opinion, Ecuador's *coactiva* measures were not "economically neutral": they aggravated the economic impact. As noted by the majority, there were no bidders for the seized oil reserves besides Petroecuador; however, in the tribunal's opinion, that fact was not attributable to Ecuador.[585] In addition, the majority could not conclude that the investor's "right to earn revenue ceased to exist or that the investment was completely lost," thereby, finding that the tax enforcement measures did not amount to expropriation. In the opinion of the majority, the expropriation took place when Ecuador took over the blocks. Ecuador argued that it had been justified to enter the blocks after it had unilaterally terminated the PSC in accordance with the Ecuadorian law (so-called caducidad).[586]

As to the treatment of taxation, Professor Vicuna dissented with the majority's interpretation, which he perceived to be ruling in equity. According to the Vicuna dissent, the act of expropriation could not be limited to only taking possession of the property: the effects of Law 42, the enforcement measures ("coactiva") and the unilateral termination of the PSC ("caducidad") all justify a finding of expropriation, namely:

> It would appear that an investor, or for that matter any individual, might be squeezed by means of taxation or other measures until its income is largely or entirely diverted to the State. It would also appear that its remaining assets could be attached and auctioned so as to collect the taxes due. Finally, there would be termination of all its rights. None of such measures would entail liability. But do

578. *Id.* paras. 429-30.
579. *Id.* paras. 450 and 456.
580. *Id.* paras. 446 and 443-5 (on the dispute on amortization).
581. *Id.* para. 455.
582. *Burlington* Decision on Liability, para. 485.
583. *Id.* para. 472.
584. *Id.* para. 474.
585. *Id.* para. 476.
586. *Id.* paras. 512-13 (quoting Art. 74 of the Hydrocarbon Law).

> not send in the police or the army to take possession, this being the only measure resulting in unlawful expropriation. Because of the above reasons I respectfully believe differently.[587]

As its preceding case (*Occidental I*), *Occidental II* was brought under the US-Ecuador BIT. In majority it was found that Law 42 was not a tax over a strong dissent (in conflict with the *Burlington* findings), possibly shaped by the lateness of Ecuador's objection, which it raised only in its final submissions.

The *Occidental II* dismissed Ecuador's tax objection and found that Law 42 was not a tax.[588] The tribunal held that even if the measure were a tax, it would fall under the specified inclusion of the treaty ("exception to the exception") related to "an investment agreement."[589] In the opinion of the majority, Law 42 was a unilateral declaration by Ecuadorian authorities to increase their participation share.[590] According to the majority, Law 42 was "neither a royalty ... levy [n]or any other measure of taxation under the Participation Contract."[591] It was not a royalty because it did not constitute "payment for access to natural resources."[592] It was not deemed a levy because it did not concern with "the imposition of a fine or tax; the fine or tax so imposed."[593] The dissent viewed the unilateral decision by the Ecuadorian state to allocate a defined percentage of revenue earned by the contractor companies "exactly what a tax or levy does."[594] In addition, the dissent referred to both *Burlington* jurisdictional award that found that the matter was a tax and the *EnCana* and *Duke Energy* awards dealing with taxation matters.[595] In the annulment proceedings, the Annulment Committee concluded that the tribunal did not exceed its mandate when it found that it had jurisdiction and the measure was deemed not a tax. In the Annulment Committee's view, the taxation objection was moot, as it would have qualified under the "exception to the exception."[596]

In *Perenco*, the tribunal resolved the issue of Ecuador's total amount of damages and upheld Ecuador's counterclaim. Already in 2014, the tribunal found in part in favor of the investor in a decision on liability and outstanding issues to jurisdiction being issued. A decision of reconsideration followed in 2015 affirmed the partial decision on liability.[597]

587. *Burlington* Dissenting Opinion, para. 35. Note, however, that Professor Vicuña was ultimately removed on the basis of his response to comment where he made a remark, which the World Bank Chairman of the Administrative Council perceived to reveal his bias. *See Burlington* Decision on Disqualification, paras. 79-80.
588. *Occidental II* Award, para. 495.
589. *Id.* para. 499.
590. *Id.*, paras. 508 and 510.
591. *Id.*, para. 509.
592. *Id.*, para. 494.
593. *Occidental II* Award, para. 507.
594. *Occidental II* Award (B. Stern, dissenting), para. 10.
595. *Id.* para. 12 n. 3.
596. *Occidental II* Annulment Decision, para. 492.
597. *See generally Perenco* Award, para. 45 (after acknowledging that the arbitration has taken "a very long time," the delay with quantum was attributed to the adjustment of quantum models and issues surrounding the counterclaim).

Brought under the French-Ecuador BIT, the case confronted the Law 42 characterization as a tax in the context of a contract breach. The French-Ecuador BIT did not include a provision on tax matters, so the finding of a tax did not preclude the claims. The tax discussion focused on the breach of the contract terms, including its tax modification clauses, and how they related to a breach of treaty. The *Perenco* tribunal held that Law 42 was a tax and that a breach of the tax stabilization clause had occurred.[598] On whether Law 42 was a tax, the *Perenco* tribunal adopted the *EnCana* definition for a tax and focused on the "substantive effect" of the measure.[599] It noted that a tax may be designated differently at the "municipal" (national) level and international level.[600] According to the tribunal, what was decisive was Ecuador's inconsistency in characterizing Law 42. The tribunal agreed with the investor, namely that Ecuador sought to have it "both ways." Ecuador sought to characterize Law 42 as a tax to benefit from "special deference" when exercising its powers of taxation, and then to avoid its contractual obligations by characterizing Law 42 as not a tax.[601] For the tribunal, that the investor characterized Law 42 as a tax, throughout its challenges, became conclusive.[602]

The tribunal found that the contract breach of the tax stabilization clauses amounted also to a treaty breach albeit on a narrow basis.[603] According to the tribunal, Ecuador did not breach the treaty in enacting and applying Law 42.[604] Neither did Ecuador breach the treaty in terms of Law 42 impeding the investment at 50%.[605] Even in respect to the 99% tax on windfalls, the tribunal hesitated to find a breach as the tax effectively "transformed" the participation contracts into service contracts.[606] Although Ecuador did not affect the "management, preservation and use" by virtue of Law 42, it did breach the treaty's provision when "[the] enjoyment of the investment was impeded."[607] *Perenco* tied investment agreements to the state legislative framework by finding that a state's change in legislation "must still be mindful of the State's contractual commitments."[608] By referring to *Paushok v. Mongolia*, the tribunal held that a State "retain[s] flexibility to respond to changing circumstances unless they have stabilised their relationship with the investor."[609] Absent an agreement, an investor "should not be surprised to be hit with tax increases in subsequent years and such an

598. *Perenco* Decision on Remaining Jurisdictional Issues and Liability, paras. 375 and 377.
599. *Id.* para. 584.
600. *Id.* para. 585.
601. *Id.* paras. 584-5.
602. *Id.* para. 585.
603. *Perenco* Decision on Remaining Jurisdictional Issues and Liability, para. 590.
604. *Id.* para. 593.
605. *Id.* paras. 596 and 600.
606. *Id.* para. 606.
607. *Id.* para. 626.
608. *Perenco* Decision on Remaining Jurisdictional Issues and Liability, paras. 562 and 563 (highlighting that the PSCs were "anchored" in a legislative framework and that the investor could "reasonably expect" that the contracts would not be unilaterally altered or terminated "except in accordance with their [the contract] terms and state law").
609. *Id.* para. 586.

event could not be considered unpredictable."[610] Albeit referring to the legitimate expectations of the investor, the *Perenco* tribunal nonetheless noted that industry practices and expectations should be consulted in the examination of "whether there was a chance that the State would wish to revisit the economic bargain underlying the contracts."[611] The factual analysis then revealed that the breach of contract and by extension the treaty breach (Article 4 containing the FET) at 50% tax rate was rejected but upheld at 99%.

The *Murphy* disputes arise out of the adverse effects of Law 42 complicated by a set of procedural hurdles. They arose out of the US-Ecuador BIT. At the core of the disputes stood the 20% interest held by Murphy Oil in the consortium of firms, originally led by Conoco Ecuador, that won a 1985 bid that led to the signing of the service agreement.[612] In 1996, the Conoco-led consortium entered into a participation contract that was later affected by the adverse modifications carried by Law 42. In *Murphy I*, the state succeeded to secure a dismissal on the basis that the investor did not observe the six-month waiting period, which the *Murphy I* deemed as a "grave non-compliance," warranting the dismissal of the claim.[613] After the waiting period did not render any results, the investor then resubmitted the claim in *Murphy II*.[614]

In *Murphy II*, the tribunal dismissed Ecuador's initial jurisdictional objections that the investor was precluded from submitting the dispute to a different forum (UNCITRAL) rather than the original forum (ICSID).[615] At the merits phase, the investor succeeded in *Murphy II* to recover around USD 20 million plus compound interest on a claim of USD 355 million.[616] In the aftermath of *Burlington*, *Occidental I* and *II* and *EnCana* decisions, the question turned on whether Law 42 was in fact a tax; in which case, it would be excluded from the BIT's treaty protections. This was handled as a jurisdictional issue despite a partial award on jurisdiction being already rendered.[617] The *Murphy II* tribunal held that Law 42 was *not* a tax.

By relying on VCLT Article 31(1), the tribunal interpreted what is deemed "matters of taxation" for determining the outer limits of the BIT protections.[618] On ordinary meaning, the definitions of "tax law" and "taxation" from *EnCana* were

610. *Id.* para. 586 (quoting Sergei Paushok, CSJC Golden East Company and CSLC Vostokneftegaz Company v. Republic of Mongolia, UNCITRAL, Award on Jurisdiction and Liability, Apr. 28, 2011, para. 305).
611. *Id.* para. 588.
612. *Murphy I*, Dec. 15, 2010, paras. 6-7.
613. *Id.* para. 157.
614. *Murphy II* was submitted under UNCITRAL Rules, since on July 6, 2009, Ecuador formally denounced the ICSID Convention. Per Art. 71 of the Convention, the denunciation took effect receipt (Jan. 7, 2010). *See generally* ICSID, Contracting States and Measures Taken by them for the Purpose of the Convention, ICSID/8C/ p. 1 n. 4 (2018). *See also Murphy I*, Dec. 15, 2010, para. 164.
615. *Murphy II* Partial Award on Jurisdiction, Nov. 13, 2013, para. 200.
616. *Murphy II* Partial Final Award, paras. 121, 452 and 522. *See also Murphy II*, Final Award, Feb. 10, 2017 (dismissing claimant's request for modification and also inserting some corrections to the award but leaving the partial award in all material facts untouched).
617. *Compare Murphy II* Partial Final Award, paras. 156-92 *with Murphy II* Partial Award on Jurisdiction, paras. 159-204.
618. *See* US-EC BIT, Art. X(2) and *Murphy II*, Partial Final Award, para. 157.

generally accepted by both parties.[619] For purposes of the context, the tribunal deemed that the reference to "bilateral tax treaty" was inconclusive. The US and Ecuador had not signed a bilateral tax treaty, and in any event, expropriatory taxation measures would not ordinarily be addressed by bilateral tax treaties.[620] Those treaties have a different scope: they concern double taxation and tax evasion.[621]

The focus of the tribunal's analysis turned on the object and purpose of the treaty as relevant for purposes of the disputed term. The *Murphy II* tribunal placed a notable but not dispositive importance on the characterization of the measure under the state's domestic regime as emanating from the sovereign power to tax.[622] More to the point, the tribunal reasoned that:

> Most governments view these powers as a central element of sovereignty. Therefore, while they may be willing to accept international discipline over State conduct, they are reluctant to accept such oversight as regards their powers of taxation. This has led most State parties to modern investment treaties to omit taxation from a treaty's ambit, or restrict the treaty's application to certain types of taxes.[623]

By referring to several high-level officials' characterization of Law 42 as not a tax, the tribunal held that Law 42 was not a taxation law. The tribunal also promptly distinguished the VAT cases by pointing out that Law 42 was enacted outside of the tax regime and that the analysis from these cases had "limited" use.[624] It then carefully examined the existing cases that handled this matter.[625] It distinguished *Perenco* on the basis that the respondent, Perenco Ecuador Limited, characterized Law 42 as a tax.[626] It also distinguished *Burlington* on the basis that the tribunal reviewed the meaning of the law, according to international law, by focusing on the parties' agreement that a dispute "raises 'matters of taxation' whenever an investor challenges the validity or enforcement of a tax," thereby excluding some but not all of the investor's claims.[627]

By relying on *EnCana*, the tribunal also turned to the "legal operation" of the tax.[628] Despite meeting the criteria for a tax stipulated *inter alia* in *EnCana*, the measure was not a tax under national or international law as the "stated purpose of the law" was to amend certain oil contracts. A required payment by a group is not necessarily a tax.[629] The tribunal found it dispositive that the revenue obtained after the introduction of Law 42 "was classified as non-tax revenue."[630] As determined by the tribunal, the

619. *Murphy II* Partial Final Award, para. 159.
620. *Id.* paras. 161 and 163.
621. *Id.* para. 163.
622. *Id.* paras. 165-6.
623. *Id.*, paras. 165-6 (referring to Abba Kolo, *Tax "Veto" as a Special Jurisdictional and Substantive Issue in Investor-State Arbitration: Need for Reassessment?*, 32 Suffolk Transnat'l L. Rev. 475-92, 475 (2009)).
624. *Murphy II* Partial Final Award, para. 176.
625. *Id.* paras. 177-92 (discussing *Burlington*, *Occidental II*, and *Perenco*).
626. *Id.* para. 184 (citing to *Perenco* Decision on Jurisdiction and Liability, paras. 376-7).
627. *Id.* para. 178 (citing to *Burlington* Decision on Jurisdiction, paras. 165-6, 168, 177, 178-216).
628. *Id.* paras. 188 and 189-92.
629. *Murphy II* Partial Final Award, paras. 191.
630. *Id.* paras. 190 (referring to the two expert reports). *Id.* n. 287.

fact that non-tax revenue had increased for Ecuador where for the contractors it decreased was indicative of an alteration of the production-sharing agreement (PSA). As a whole, the *Murphy II* tribunal adopted the *EnCana* focus on examining the "legal operation" (not just economic effect) of a measure into a two-step approach. First, it would look at the domestic characterization of the measure. Second, it would examine the legal operation of the measure, presumably in the context of international law. Based on this two-prong approach, the *Murphy II* tribunal determined that Law 42 was not a tax.

[iii] Electricity Distribution Cases: Duke Energy *and* MCI Power

In parallel with the hydrocarbon crisis, Ecuador confronted massive shortages of electricity prompting several emergency measures, including as applicable to hydroelectric power, the country's second largest energy source.[631] The state allocated funds to the state-owned entity responsible for electricity Instituto Ecuatoriano de Electrificación (INECEL) to purchase energy.[632] In 1995, a state of emergency was instated and INECEL was authorized to enter into power purchase agreements (PPAs) with private parties. Two sets of cases emerge from the PPAs entered by INECEL: *Duke Energy* and *MCI Power*, both brought under the US-Ecuador BIT.

In *Duke Energy*, the tribunal extended the *EnCana* definition to cover even customs duties as taxes, hence falling within the scope of the tax exclusion. The investment agreement inclusion of the BIT was not deemed to apply. In *Duke Energy*, the tribunal reviewed the claims of violations of the payment obligations arising out of the PPA. The claimant invoked both the provisions of the PPA and the US-Ecuador BIT. The tribunal found that Ecuador breached both the PPA and the BIT's cumulative provisions for FET, FPS and NT. However, the *Duke Energy* tribunal held that it did not have jurisdiction over the dispute pertaining to customs duties.[633] In dismissing jurisdiction over customs duties, the tribunal relied on VCLT Article 31(1) to interpret the meaning of the term "matters of taxation." As the term was not defined under the BIT, the tribunal relied on the *EnCana* four-part definition[634] even though the *EnCana* definition is used for a different BIT.[635] According to the tribunal, the law governing the exemptions constituted taxation legislation. It was introduced to address matters of "national priority" and it covered "goods imported for the needs of an industry."[636] Echoing *EnCana*, the tribunal reasoned that relief from tax was deemed to be a taxation measure similarly as the measure imposing the tax would be.[637]

---

631. *See generally* US Energy Information Administration, Country Analysis Brief: Ecuador, Last updated Oct. 5, 2017.
632. *Duke Energy*, paras. 10-12.
633. *Id.* para. 188.
634. *Id.* para. 174 (citing to *EnCana* Award, para. 142, "a taxation law is one which imposes a liability on classes of persons to pay money to the State for public purposes").
635. *EnCana* was decided under the Canada-Ecuador BIT, whereas *Duke Energy* was decided under the US-Ecuador BIT.
636. *Duke Energy*, paras. 175.
637. *Id.*, para. 175 (quoting *EnCana* Award, para. 142).

Once the customs charges were deemed to fall under the BIT's tax exclusion, the analysis focused on whether the tribunal still had jurisdiction on the basis that the matter fell under any specified inclusions, most notably the inclusion pertaining to an investment agreement of the US-Ecuador BIT. For purposes of this determination, the tribunal adopted a two-step inquiry into: (1) existence of an investment agreement and (2) whether the claims fall within the scope of the investment contract.[638] The tribunal ruled that the dispute did not fall under a specified inclusion as the PPA was not an investment agreement.[639] As reasoned by the tribunal, PPAs cover installation of equipment, sale, and purchase of electricity. PPAs are distinct from, for example, concession agreements where the right to investment is expressly granted by the state.[640] It found that the PPA was actually between a state entity (not the Ecuadorian state) and a local Ecuadorian company, in which Duke Energy would later acquire an interest.[641] But even if the matters related to an investment agreement, the tribunal reasoned that claimant's allegations focused on the modifications of the customs regime but not on the observance and enforcement of the investment agreement.[642]

In *MCI Power*, all allegations of substantive treaty breach were dismissed. Notably, the tax audit was deemed not a breach of FET. In *MCI Power*, the dispute arose out of the non-payment by the Ecuadorian state entity for the energy under the "take-or-pay" model that led to the suspension of the operation of the two power plants and the termination of the private contract. The investor alleged a breach of the FET standard under the US-Ecuador BIT on the basis of the threat of a tax audit conducted by the Ecuadorian authorities. The tribunal held that no tax audit was conducted and that the claim of treaty breach was unsubstantiated. Claimants invoked a letter from the Ecuador's attorney general where it requested the Ecuadorian tax authorities (SRI) to notify the SRI Director General of the findings of the audit to be conducted for three years.[643] The tribunal interpreted the letter as "routine procedure" for revocation of permits. The tribunal could not deduce a breach of unfair or arbitrary treatment. In all, the threat of an audit did not amount to a breach of the FET.

[D] Other BIT Cases

The *Yukos* BIT cases and the Ecuadorian cases heavily influenced the ECT tax case law, as described below, in part due to what appears conflicting conclusions on key tax issues: whether a matter is a tax or whether it falls within the ambit of the treaty. A large number of other BIT cases touch upon taxation measures; some are linked to energy issues and some are not. Although the intersection of energy, tax, and investment law provides their unique set of challenges, several non-energy cases also offer helpful insights. These cases are:

638. *Id.*, para. 186.
639. *Id.* para. 181.
640. *Id.* para. 45.
641. *Duke Energy*, para. 186.
642. *Id.*, para. 187.
643. *MCI Power* Award, para. 365.

Energy:	*Total v. Argentina,*[644] *El Paso v. Argentina,*[645] *Nations Energy v. Panama,*[646] *Ampal v. Egypt,*[647] and *Conoco v. Venezuela.*[648]
NAFTA:	*Feldman v. Mexico,*[649] *Gottlieb v. Canada (energy case).*[650]
Non-Energy:	*Link-Trading v. Moldova,*[651] *Phoenix v. Czech Republic,*[652] *Paushok v. Mongolia,*[653] *Alghanim v. Jordan,*[654] *Goetz v. Burundi I,*[655] *Bogdanov v. Moldova III*[656] and *Bogdanov v. Moldova IV,*[657] *Ryan Schooner v. Poland,*[658] *Tza Yap Shum v. Peru*[659] and *UP and C.D Holding Internationale v. Hungary.*[660]

644. Total S.A. v. Argentine Republic, Decision on Liability, Dec. 27, 2010.
645. El Paso Energy International Company v. the Argentine Republic, Award, ICSID Case No. ARB/03/15, Oct. 31, 2011 [hereinafter "*El Paso* Award"], paras. 290-1. *See also* El Paso Energy International Company v. the Argentine Republic, Decision on Jurisdiction, ICSID Case No. ARB/03/15, Apr. 27, 2006. El Paso Energy International Company v. the Argentine Republic, Decision of the Ad hoc Committee, ICSID Case No. ARB/03/15, Sept. 22, 2014.
646. Nations Energy v. Panama, Award/Laudo, ICSID Case No. ARB/06/19, Nov. 24, 2010 [hereinafter "*Nations Energy*"].
647. Ampal v. Egypt, Decision on Jurisdiction, ICSID Case No. ARB/12/11, Feb. 1, 2016 [hereinafter "*Ampal* Decision on Jurisdiction"]. Ampal v. Egypt, Decision on Liability and Heads of Loss, ICSID Case No. ARB/12/11, Feb. 21, 2017 [hereinafter "*Ampal* Decision on Liability"].
648. Conoco v. Venezuela, Decision on Jurisdiction and Merits, ICSID Case No. ARB/07/30, Sept. 3, 2013 [hereinafter "*Conoco* Partial Decision"] *See also* Conoco v. Venezuela, Award, ICSID Case No. ARB/07/30, Mar. 8, 2019 [hereinafter "*Conoco* Award"].
649. Marvin Roy Feldman Karpa v. United Mexican States, Award, ICSID Case No. ARB(AF)/99/1, Dec. 16, 2002 [hereinafter "*Feldman*"]. For other cases arising out of the fructose syrup tax legislation, *see* Cargill v. Mexico, Award, Award, ICSID Case No. ARB(AF)/05/2, Sept. 18, 2009; Archer Daniels Midland and Tate & Lyle Ingredients Americas, Inc. v. United Mexican States, Award, ICSID Case No. ARB(AF)/04/5, Nov. 21, 2007; Corn Products Int'l v. United Mexican States, Decision on Responsibility, Jan. 15, 2008; Corn Products Int'l v. United Mexican States, Award, Aug. 18, 2009 (not public) (concurring opinion of Andreas Lowenfeld). *See also* NAFTA Arts. 1105 and 2103 and USMCA Art. 32.3.
650. *See generally* Letter Bob Hamilton, Canada Department of Finance, Policy Branch to Eric Solomon, Assistant Secretary Office of Tax Policy, US Department of Treasury, Apr. 22, 2008.
651. Link-Trading v. Moldova, Final Award, UNCITRAL, Apr. 18, 2002 [hereinafter "*Link-Trading*"].
652. Phoenix v. The Czech Republic, Award, ICSID Case No. ARB/06/05, Apr. 15, 2009 [hereinafter "*Phoenix*"].
653. Paushok v. Mongolia, Award on Jurisdiction and Liability, UNCITRAL, Apr. 28, 2011, para. 617 [hereinafter "*Paushok*"].
654. Alghanim v. Jordan, Order on Application for the Grant of Provisional Measures, ICSID Case No. ARB/13/38, Nov. 24, 2014 [hereinafter "*Alghanim*"]. *See also id.* Alghanim v. Jordan, Award, ICSID Case No. ARB/13/38, Dec. 14, 2017.
655. Goetz v. Burundi, Award/Sentence, ICSID Case No ARB/95/3, Feb. 10, 1999 [hereinafter "*Goetz I*"].
656. Bogdanov v. Moldova, Award, SCC Arbitration V (No. 114/2009), Mar. 30, 2010[hereinafter "*Bogdanov III*"].
657. Yuri Bogdanov and Yulia Bogdanova, Award, SCC Arbitration V (No. 091/2012), Apr. 16, 2013 [hereinafter "*Bogdanov IV*"].
658. Vincent J. Ryan, Schooner Capital LLC, and Atlantic Investment Partners LLC v. Republic of Poland, Award, ICSID Case No. ARB(AF)/11/3, Nov. 24, 2015 [hereinafter "*Schooner*"].
659. Tza Yap Shum v. Peru, Laudo/Award, ICSID Case No. ARB/07/6, July 7, 2011 [hereinafter "*Tza Yap Schum* Award"]. *See also* Tza Yap Shum v. Peru, Decision on Annulment, ICSID Case No. ARB/07/6, Feb. 12, 2015 [hereinafter "*Tza Yap Schum* Annulment Decision"].
660. UP and C.D Holding Internationale v. Hungary, Award, ICSID Case No. ARB/13/35, Oct. 9, 2019 [hereinafter "*UP and CD Holding*"]. *See generally* Edenred v. Hungary, Award, ICSID Case

[E] Sub-conclusion to the BIT Cases

The BIT case law unveils a set of issues that that are treaty-specific with broad patterns specific to taxation matters. Taxation schemes differ dramatically, as they materialize at different stages of the energy production process. As seen in the BIT cases, states tax heavily the energy sector at every stage of the supply chain.[661] Upstream, taxation involves rent-sharing by which the investor pays rent for the depletion of a finite natural resource.[662] Downstream taxation may focus on the treatment of the final products. Often downstream taxation would be limited to indirect taxes such as excises and VAT, which inadvertently would overlap with customs and import duties.[663] The BIT case law also reveals an effort to preserve the *jurisprudence constante* in that: (1) the cases themselves are aligned between each other and (2) they do not deviate significantly from the previous case law.

The two *Yukos* BIT awards hardly differ from each other on the treatment of bona fide taxation. They draw heavily on the *EnCana* and other Ecuadorian cases. What becomes discernable is a pattern of important cases agreeing that the standard for bona fide breach is high to meet and that, in the case surrounding Russia's actions against the Yukos, the standard was met. Both *RosInvest* and *Renta4* have been set aside, thus calling into question their binding effect and their role to the *jurisprudence constante,* but as both cases were set aside on matters unrelated to taxation, the probative value of these decisions on matters of taxation remains important.[664] Table 5.2 compares the findings of *RosInvest* and *Renta4* on tax matters.

Table 5.2 The Yukos BIT Decisions Compared on Matters of Taxation

Matter	RosInvest	Renta4
Jurisdiction on the basis of MFN	Yes	No
Tax Exclusion in Comparatory Treaty Applied	No	No
Rationale/Limitation	Tax exclusion from Comparator Treaty applicable only if it prevents "cumulative effect" of the Basic Treaty	Tax exclusion from Comparator Treaty not applicable to allegations of abuse of tax law
Definition of Tax	N/A	Yes
Bona Fide Applied	Yes for purposes of expropriation	Yes for purposes of expropriation

No. ARB/21, Dec. 13, 2016 (not public) and Sodexo Pass International SAS v. Hungary, Award, ICSID Case No. ARB/14/20, Jan. 28, 2019 (not public).

661. *See generally* Energy Charter Secretariat, *Taxation along the Oil and Gas Supply Chain* 8 (2008).
662. *Id.* 8, 12 and 13.
663. *Id.* 9 and 42-5.
664. *See Renta4* Award, para. 24 n. 1 (the tribunal notes "the possible persuasiveness of *Rosinvest* with respect to the merits, not its status as a matter of jurisdiction" after the default judgment).

Matter	RosInvest	Renta4
Discretion	No, but "wide latitude" recognized	No, but presumption of validity

Source: Author's Own.

Although the tribunals differed in their conclusion on the application of the MFN, they both agreed that tax exclusion from the Comparator Treaty did not apply. The tribunals differed in their reasoning. In *RosInvest*, the tribunal concluded that the tax exclusion from the Comparator Treaty would not apply unless it would somehow prevent the cumulative effect of the Basic Treaty, thus entering some doubt as to the extent an investor would be able to assert a "cherry picking" approach as to the provisions that would apply by virtue of the MFN. In *Renta4*, the tribunal directly stated that the tax exclusion did not apply to allegations of abuse of power. In any event, the language of the MFN clause would be highly relevant in guiding the scope of the exclusionary language found in the treaty and matching its relation to the scope of the treaty.

Both *RosInvest* and *Renta4* adopted the bona fide inquiry for purposes of a finding of a substantive breach of the treaty. In *RosInvest*, the analysis centered on the "cumulative effect" deemed to be *male fide* and two specific measures (the VAT tax and the profit taxes) were deemed not to be passed in good faith. The *Renta4* tribunal set out a definition for what a tax is, finding that if the tax measure is designed to be expropriatory, it shall be reviewed for the expropriatory effect. Neither of the two tribunals upheld the discretion afforded to tax on tax matters to apply to the Yukos facts; however, *RosInvest* referred to the "wide" discretion and *Renta4* discussed a refutable presumption of validity of taxes "unless there is convincing evidence that, upon a true characterisation, they constitute a taking."[665]

There are notable differences between the *Yukos* and the Ecuadorian BIT cases. The Ecuadorian cases do not deal with the bona fide inquiry; even if post-*Yukos*, this was invoked with the conduct of the Spanish authorities that appear to resemble, even if not being as extreme, those of the Ecuadorian authorities. Perhaps, the glue that holds the *Yukos* and the Ecuadorian BIT cases is the treaty-specific inquiry and the definitional conundrum of "what is a tax." The other Ecuadorian cases dealing with the same Law 42 had reached contradictory results on whether the law is a tax revealing different tensions in the definition linked to *inter alia* the elements of a tax, importance of the domestic law and ex parte review by the tribunal.

The Ecuadorian cases, though, take the discussion much further. Notably, *Burlington* has upheld a very clear demarcation of the power to tax that is closely followed in the ECT case and is central to this book. According to *Burlington*, the power to tax is subject to clear limitations from treaties and customary international law; for purposes of customary international law, the two limitations are against confiscatory and discriminatory taxation. These lessons from the Ecuadorian case materialize again

665. *Renta4* Award, para. 181.

in the *Yukos* BIT cases with a clear determination that *male fide* measures would not fall under the treaty.

The Ecuadorian cases explored three sets of distinct circumstances relating to tax. The three types of cases (VAT, PSC, and distribution cases), summarized in Table 5.3, contain different measures adopted by the state against foreign investors that reveal the treaty-specific protections afforded to investors. On VAT cases, *Occidental I* and *EnCana* reached different results explained in part due to the nature of the different BITs. *Occidental I* delved into the possible effects of a tax measure in relation to three substantive standards: arbitrariness, NT, and FET. *EnCana* had a broader reach. It introduced an actual definition for taxation that repeats in the ECT case law. It also distinguished taxation issues from other types of matters such as contractual obligations. *EnCana* correctly pointed out that the state is in an authority-wielding position when it exercises its taxation power. Under both *Occidental I* and *EnCana*, the role afforded to national law plays a crucial law in the findings of a breach, with the *EnCana* dissent heavily criticizing the referral to national law. Out of the PSC cases, *Burlington* sets out distinct limitations to the power to tax. Such limitations are found in treaties to which the state has acceded and customary international law. For purposes of customary international law, two limits exist. The state may not exercise its power in a confiscatory or discriminatory manner. This language has clearly guided further ECT decisions and is dispositive for purposes of this book. For purposes of confiscation, it is not the tax rate that is dispositive but whether it preserves the capacity to generate a commercial return. So even a 99% tax would not be confiscatory if the company still retains the possibility for generating a commercial return such as in the case of a windfall tax. But what *Burlington* reveals, although not directly addressed in the case, is that the confiscation happens upon collection.

The VAT cases and PSC cases are quite different, even when they are linked to the same entity. In *Occidental II*, the tribunal found that the contentious Law 42 was not a tax, in part due to the late submission of the parties. Whether Law 42 was not a tax was further reinforced in the other cases, most notably *Murphy II*, but in any event, some uncertainty remains particularly with regard to *Perenco* decision where the tribunal found it dispositive that the Law was a tax when Ecuador argued in other forums that it is a tax. The Ecuadorian cases underline that tax matters remain heavily influenced by procedural issues, which may affect the tribunal's findings. Finally, the distribution contracts continue the important inquiry into the effects of the taxation matters relative to the treaty obligations. *Duke Energy*'s contribution to the case law highlights that relief from taxation is linked to taxation and that the treaty provisions of the respective inclusions are outcome-determinative. *MCI Power* revealed the fact-intensive inquiry and specifically that the threat of a tax audit does not amount to a treaty breach.

Table 5.3 Deep Dive into the Ecuadorian Energy Arbitrations Pertaining to Taxation

No.	*Case*	*BIT*	*Type*	*Law 42*	*Decision*
1.	*Oxy I*	US-Ecu.	VAT	No	Investor partly wins. Breach of arbitrariness & discrimination, NT and FET. No breach of expropriation.
2.	*EnCana*	Can-Ecu	VAT	No	State prevails. Claims dismissed at jurisdiction: no claim related to investment agreement. No finding of expropriation: direct or indirect. Strong dissent over no expropriation.
3.	*Murphy I*	US-Ecu.	PSC	N/A	Case dismissed at jurisdiction.
4.	*Oxy II*	US-Ecu.	PSC	Not a tax	Investor prevails. Law 42 is deemed not a tax. Law 42 divides the tribunal on whether it is a tax or not, but leads to no annulment of the case after the tribunal holds that it would have been subject to the specified inclusion.
5.	*Burlington*	US-Ecu.	PSC	A tax	Investor prevails. Law 42 is a tax. Whether something is a tax should be reviewed under international law (at least for purposes of jurisdiction). Power to tax is subject to two limitations: treaty-based and customary international law. Expropriation took place when Ecuador entered the property (not by taxation measures or when it sought to enforce). Intent alone does not replace the need to show substantial deprivation.
6.	*Perenco*	Fra-Ecu.	PSC	A tax	Investor prevails. Law 42 is deemed a tax. Finding relevant for the contract breach: 1) Variation of Tax at national and international level. 2) States retain discretion unless they include a tax stabilization clause.
7.	*Murphy II*	US-Ecu.	PSC	Not a tax	Investor prevails. Law 42 is deemed not a tax. Not characterized as a tax and by operation not a tax.
8.	*Duke Energy*	US-Ecu.	Cust. Duties	N/A	On the BIT, the tribunal rules that the customs duties fall under the scope of the exclusion. No investment agreement was found. Investment agreement inclusion not applied.

No.	Case	BIT	Type	Law 42	Decision
9.	*MCI*	US-Ecu.	Tax Audit	N/A	The tribunal rules that it has jurisdiction but dismisses the claim on merits. Upheld in annulment. Tax audit alone or together with other measurements not deemed to constitute a breach of FET or expropriation.

Source: Author's Own.

§5.03 ECT CASES

[A] General Presentation

The focus of this subsection is to streamline the existing case law pertaining to the Taxation Article. As of March 15, 2020, taxation issues have emerged in forty ECT cases. These may be divided into two categories, as presented in Figure 5.2: (1) non-renewable energy cases and (2) renewable energy cases. In the first category fall the cases that are unrelated to the challenges of the solar incentive measures; given the importance of the Yukos proceedings, the non-renewable energy cases may be divided further into two categories: (a) the non-Yukos cases (*Amto v. Ukraine*,[666] *Nykomb v. Latvia*,[667] *Plama v. Bulgaria*,[668] *Mamidoil v. Albania*[669] and *Stati v. Kazakhstan*[670]) and (b) the *Yukos* cases where the three cases are grouped together.[671] The *Yukos* awards have been set aside by the Dutch courts of the first instance but reversed on appeal; the cases remain for review in the Dutch courts.[672] However, since the grounds for

666. Amto v. Ukraine, Award, SCC Arb. Nr. 080/2005, Mar. 26, 2008 [hereinafter "*Amto*"].
667. Nykomb Synergetics Technology Holding AB v. Latvia, Award, SCC, Dec. 16, 2003 [hereinafter "*Nykomb*"].
668. Plama Consortium Ltd. v. Bulgaria, Decision on Jurisdiction, ICSID Case No. ARB/03/24, Feb. 8, 2005 [hereinafter "*Plama* Decision on Jurisdiction"]. *See also* Plama Consortium Ltd. v. Bulgaria, Award, ICSID Case No. ARB/03/24, Aug. 27, 2008 [hereinafter "*Plama* Award"]. Plama Consortium Ltd. v. Bulgaria, Order, ICSID Case No. ARB/03/24, Sep. 6, 2005 [hereinafter "*Plama* Order"].
669. Mamidoil Jetoil Greek Petroleum Products Societe S.A. v. the Republic of Albania, Award, ICSID Case No. ARB/11/24, Mar. 30, 2015 (Steven Hammond dissenting) [hereinafter "*Mamidoil*"].
670. Stati et al v. Kazakhstan, Award, SCC Arbitration V (116/2010), Dec. 19, 2013 [hereinafter "*Stati* Award"]. *See also* Kazakhstan v. Stati, Judgment, Svea Court of Appeal Case Nr. T 2675-14, Dec. 9, 2016 [hereinafter "*Stati* Set Aside Decision"].
671. The *Yukos* arbitral proceedings involve three cases that were joined and for which the award was issued on the same day. The three awards are, for the most part, identical with the exception of some variations in paragraphs and the facts pertaining to the three corporate claimants. In this book, the primary reference is made to Yukos Universal Limited (YUL) v. the Russian Federation, PCA Case No. AA 227. The other two cases are: Hulley Enterprises Limited v. the Russian Federation, PCA Case No. AA 226, and Veteran Petroleum Limited v. the Russian Federation, PCA Case No. AA 228. Where there is a substantial deviation from *YUL*, a reference to the specific award is made.
672. *See supra* note 29.

set-aside did not relate to taxation matters and the Dutch courts are still reviewing the cases in appellate proceedings, the *Yukos* arbitration awards remain of considerable value for purposes of the ECT analysis.

Figure 5.2 Categorization of ECT Cases

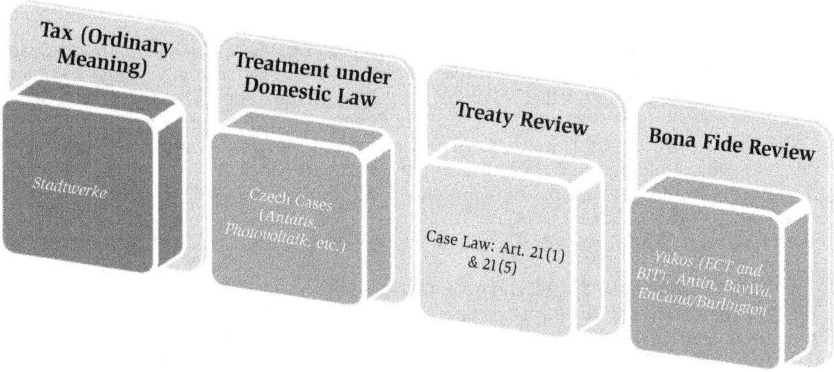

Source: Author's Own.

In the second category fall the renewable energy cases that were initiated against three European countries: Spain, the Czech Republic, and Italy. In terms of the cases against Spain, twenty cases have led to a final award or a decision on liability: *Charanne*,[673] *Eiser*,[674] *Isolux*,[675] *Masdar*,[676] *Antin*,[677] *Novenergia*,[678] *Greentech et al. v.*

673. Charanne B.V. & Construction Investments S.A.R.L. v. Spain, Award, SCC Arbitration 062/2012, Jan. 21, 2016 [hereinafter "*Charanne*"] (Art. 21 was not invoked in *Charanne*).
674. Eiser Infrastructure Limited, Energía Solar Luxembourg S.à.r.l. v Spain, Award, ICSID Case No. ARB/13/36, May 4, 2017 [hereinafter "Eiser"]. *See* Eiser Infrastructure Limited, Energía Solar Luxembourg S.à.r.l. v Spain, No. 17-CV-3808 (S.D.N.Y. June 27, 2017). *See also* Eiser Infrastructure Ltd v Kingdom of Spain [2020] FCA 157 (Austl. Fed. Ct. Feb. 24, 2020).
675. Isolux Infrastructure Netherlands, B.V. v. Spain, Award, SCC Arbitration V2013/153, July 12, 2016 [hereinafter "*Isolux*"].
676. Masdar Solar & Wind Cooperatief U.A.v. Spain, Award, ICSID Case No. ARB/14/1, May 16, 2018 [hereinafter "*Masdar*"].
677. Antin Infrastructure Services Luxembourg S.à.r.l. and Antin Energia Termosolar B.V. v. Kingdom of Spain, Award, ICSID Case No. ARB/13/31, June 15, 2018 [hereinafter "*Antin*"].
678. Novenergia II -Energy & Environment (SCA), SICAR v. Spain, Final Arbitral Award, SCC Arbitration 2015/063, Feb. 15, 2018 [hereinafter "*Novenergia* Award"]. *See also* Novenergia II -Energy & Environment (SCA), SICAR v. Spain, Procedural Order Nr. 17, SCC Arbitration 2015/063, Feb. 15, 2018 [hereinafter "*Novenergia* Rectification"]. Spain v. Novenergia II -Energy & Environment (SCA), SICAR, Order on Stay of Enforcement, Case Nr. T 4658-18, Svea Court of Appeal, May 15, 2018 [hereinafter "*Novenergia* Svea Order to Stay"].

Spain,[679] *NextEra*,[680] *9REN*,[681] *Cube Infrastructure*,[682] *RREEF Infrastructure*,[683] *SolEs*,[684] *Infra Red*,[685] *OperaFund*,[686] *RWE*,[687] *PV Investors*[688], *Stadtwerke*,[689] *BayWa*,[690] *Watkins*[691], and *Hydro Energy*.[692] One other public case, *SolarPark*, has been confirmed to have been discontinued.[693]

The Czech Republic has defended six cases under the ECT, in five of which a final award has been rendered: *Antaris*[694] and four other cases with the same arbitrators on

679. Foresight Luxembourg Solar 1 Sarl, Foresight Luxembourg 2 Sarl, Greentech Energy Systems A/S, GWM Renewable Energy I S.p.a, GWM Renewable Energy II S.p.a, v. Kingdom of Spain, Final Award, SCC Arbitration 2015/150, Nov. 14, 2018 [hereinafter "*Greentech et al. v. Spain*"].
680. NextEra Energy Global Holdings B.V., NextEra Energy Spain Holdings B.V. v. Spain, Award, ICSID Case No. ARB/14/11, May 31, 2019 [hereinafter "*NextEra* Award"]. *See also* NextEra Energy Global Holdings B.V., NextEra Energy Spain Holdings B.V. v. Spain, Decision on Jurisdiction, Liability and Quantum Principles, ICSID Case No. ARB/14/11, May 31, 2019 [hereinafter "*NextEra* Partial Decision"].
681. 9Ren Holding v. Spain, Award, ICSID Case No. ARB/15/5, May 31, 2019 [hereinafter "*9Ren Award*"].
682. Cube Infrastructure Fund SICAV and others v. Spain, Award, ICSID Case No. ARB/15/20, July 15, 2019 [hereinafter "*Cube Infrastructure* Award"]. *See also* Cube Infrastructure Fund SICAV and others v. Spain, Decision on Jurisdiction, Liability and Partial Decision on Quantum, ICSID Case No. ARB/15/20, Feb. 19, 2019 [hereinafter "*Cube Infrastructure* Partial Decision"].
683. RREEF Infrastructure (G.P.) Limited and RREEF Pan-European Infrastructure Two Lux S.à.r.l v. Spain, Decision on Jurisdiction, ICSID Case No. ARB/13/30, June 6, 2016, paras. 161-92 [hereinafter "*RREEF Infrastructure* Decision on Jurisdiction"]. RREEF Infrastructure (G.P.) Limited and RREEF Pan-European Infrastructure Two Lux S.à.r.l v. Spain, Decision on Responsibility and on the Principles of Quantum, ICSID Case No. ARB/13/30, Nov. 30, 2018 [hereinafter "*RREEF Infrastructure* Decision on Merits"].
684. SolEs Badajoz Gmbh v. Spain, Award, ICSID Case No. ARB/15/38, July 31, 2019 [hereinafter "*SolEs*"]. The tribunal issued a decision on rectification of the award on Dec. 5, 2019 but the decision is not publicly available. *See generally* ICSID Case Details at http://icsid.worldbank.org (Accessed: May 30, 2020).
685. Infra Red Environmental Infrastructure GP Limited et al v. Spain, Award, ICSID Case No. ARB/14/12, Aug. 2, 2019 [hereinafter "*Infra Red*"].
686. OperaFund Eco-Invest SICAV PLC and Schwab Holding AG v. Spain, Award, ICSID Case No. ARB/15/36, Sep. 6, 2019 [hereinafter "*OperaFund*"]. *See also id.* (Philippe Sands, dissenting) [hereinafter "*OperaFund*, Sands dissenting opinion"].
687. RWE Innogy GmbH and RWE Innogy Aersa S.A.U. v. Spain, Decision on Jurisdiction, Liability, and Certain Issues of Quantum, ICSID Case No. ARB/14/34, Dec. 30, 2019 [hereinafter "*RWE*"].
688. The PV Investors v. Spain, Final Award, PCA Case No. 2012-14, Feb. 28, 2020 [hereinafter "*PV Investors* Award"]. *See also* The PV Investors v. Spain, Decision on Jurisdiction, PCA Case No. 2012-14, Oct. 13, 2014 [hereinafter "*PV Investors* Decision on Jurisdiction"].
689. Stadtwerke München GmbH et al. v. Spain, Award, ICSID Case No. ARB/15/1, Dec. 2, 2019 [hereinafter "*Stadtwerke*"].
690. BayWa r.e. Renewable Energy GmbH, BayWare r.e. Asset Holding GmbH v. Spain, Decision on Jurisdiction, Liability and Directions on Quantum, ICSID Case No. ARB/15/16, Dec. 9, 2019 [hereinafter "*BayWa*"].
691. Watkins Holdings S.à r.l., et al v. Spain, Award, ICSID Case No. ARB/15/44, Jan. 21, 2020 [hereinafter "*Watkins*"].
692. Hydro Energy 1 S.à r.l., Hydroxana Sweden AB v. Spain, Decision on Jurisdiction, Liability and Directions on Quantum, ICSID Case No. ARB/15/42, Mar. 9, 2020 [hereinafter "*Hydro Energy*"].
693. Solarpark Management GmbH & Co. Atum I KG v. Kingdom of Spain, SCC Case No. 2015/163.
694. Antaris Solar GmbH and Dr. Michael Göde v. Czech Republic, PCA Case No. 2014-01, Award, May 2, 2018 (Gary Born, dissenting) (J. Tomka, declaration/partial dissent)[hereinafter "Antaris"].

the tribunal[695]—*Voltaic,*[696] *ICW,*[697] *Photovoltaik,*[698] and *WA Investments.*[699] A partial award has been rendered in *Natland*[700] that includes the finding on the merits. Although the *Natland* decision is not public, there is some indication that the award follows the same pattern as *Antaris* and the other four cases.[701] Due to its complexity and dissent specifically on tax issues, *Antaris* is attributed particular attention. For purposes of thoroughness, another decision involving the Czech Republic, *JCW Solar,*[702] is also examined where ECT was not invoked. Despite being rendered under the Czech Republic-German BIT, the *JCW Solar* award is relevant because Born's dissent is of direct relevance for other ECT awards.

Italy has witnessed six cases where decisions have been rendered: *Blusun,*[703] *Greentech,*[704] *CEF,*[705] *Eskosol,*[706] *Belenergia,*[707] and *Sun Reserve.*[708] At the time of writing this book, *Eskosol* remains pending but given its close link to *Blusun* and the

695. In *Voltaic Network, ICW, Photovoltaik* and *WA Investments,* the arbitral tribunal was formed of the same three arbitrators: Hans van Houtte, Mr. John Beechey, and Toby Landau.
696. Voltaic Network GmbH v. Czech Republic, Award, PCA Case No. 2014-20, May 19, 2019 [hereinafter "*Voltaic*"].
697. I.C.W. Europe Investments Limited, Award, PCA Case No. 2014-22, May 19, 2019 [hereinafter "*ICW*"].
698. Photovoltaik Knopf Betriebs-GmbH, Award, PCA Case No. 2014-21, May 19, 2019 [hereinafter "*Photovoltaik*"].
699. WA Investments-Europa Nova Limited, Award, PCA Case No. 2014-19, May 19, 2019 [hereinafter "*WA Investments*"].
700. Natland et al v. Czech Republic, Partial Award, PCA Case No. 2013-35, Dec. 20, 2017 [hereinafter "*Natland*"].
701. Damien Charlotin, *Natland v. Czech Republic (Part 1 of 2): Tribunal jurisdiction over claimants under three out of four treaties and declines to apply ECT's Tax Carveout to Contested Measure,* Investment Arbitration Reporter, July 26, 2018. *See also* Damien Charlotin, *Natland v. Czech Republic (Part 2 of 2): On the merits, Tribunal finds stabilization commitment in Czech legislation and breach of that commitment with introduction of the solar levy,* Inv. Arb. Rep., July 26, 2018.
702. Mr. Jürgen Wirtgen, Mr. Stefan Wirtgen, Mrs. Gisela Wirtgen and JSW Solar (zwei) GmbH & Co. KG v. Czech Republic, Final Award, PCA Case No. 2014-03, Oct. 11, 2017 [hereinafter "*JSW Solar*"].
703. Blusun S.A., Jean-Pierre Lecorcier and Michael Stein v. the Italian Republic, Award, ICSID Case No. ARB/14/3, Dec. 27, 2017 [hereinafter "*Blusun*"].
704. Greentech Energy Systems and Novenergia v. the Italian Republic, Award, SCC Case No. 095/2015, Dec. 23, 2018 [hereinafter "*Greentech et al. v. Italy*"]; The Italian Republic v. Greentech Energy Systems and Novenergia, Svea Court of Appeal, T 4236-19, Decision on Stay, Apr. 23, 2019.
705. CEF Energia BV v. the Italian Republic, Award, SCC Arbitration V 2015/158, Jan. 16, 2019 [hereinafter "*CEF*"]; The Italian Republic v. CEF, Decision on Stay, Svea Court of Appeal, T 3229-19, Mar. 28, 2019.
706. Eskosol S.p.A. in liquidazione v. the Italian Republic, Decision on Respondent's Application under Rule 41(5), ICSID Case No. ARB/15/50, Mar. 20, 2017 [hereinafter "*Eskosol* Partial Decision"]; *see also* Eskosol S.p.A. in liquidazione v. the Italian Republic, Decision on Respondent's Request for Provisional Measures, ICSID Case No. ARB/15/50, Apr. 17, 2017 [hereinafter "*Eskosol* Decision on Provisional Measures"]; *see also* Eskosol S.p.A. in liquidazione v. the Italian Republic, Decision on Italy's Request for Immediate Termination, ICSID Case No. ARB/15/50, May 7, 2019 [hereinafter "*Eskosol* Decision on Termination"].
707. Belenergia S.A. v. the Italian Republic, Award, ICSID Case No, ARB/15/40, Aug. 6, 2019 [hereinafter "*Belenergia*"].
708. Sun Reserve et al. v. the Italian Republic, Award, SCC Case No. V(2016/32), Mar. 25, 2020 [hereinafter "*Sun Reserve*"].

fact that several orders have already been rendered demands that *Eskosol* be reviewed at this early stage; the tribunal also ruled on the EU objection in *RockHopper* but has not taken up the taxation objection.[709] In such manner, *Eskosol* is included in the analysis below but *RockHopper* is not. *Greentech* and *CEF* arbitrations have been concluded; however, both awards are subject to set-aside proceedings before Swedish courts as the seat of the arbitration was in Stockholm. The Spanish, Czech, and Italian cases are addressed in the context of the non-renewable energy cases but on an individual basis.

On a preliminary basis, the case law reveals the gradual trajectory of the increased complexity of the tax claims that are closely tied to the factual developments in relevant legislation: where the early cases (*Amto, Plama, Nykomb, Mamidoil, Kardassopoulos,* and *Stati*) narrowly addressed the taxation matters, the tax review having changed with the *Yukos* awards. For this reason, the analysis of the post-*Yukos* cases follows analogously: it first starts with a background that includes the measures in question, it then proceeds to a discussion of the relevant matters, usually divided between jurisdictional issues and matters on the merits.

[B] Non-Renewable Energy Cases: Non-Yukos

[1] Spotlight on **Plama** *Where ECT Article 21 Was Invoked and Upheld*

The non-Yukos, non-renewable energy cases are traditionally the early cases where tax matters materialized. It involves five cases in the order of the awards being rendered: *Amto, Nykomb, Plama, Mamidoil,* and *Stati.* Besides *Plama,* none of the non-renewable energy cases delved deep into the Tax Exclusion of the ECT pre-*Yukos.*

In *Plama,* the tribunal dismissed the taxation issue on ECT Article 21 grounds but still conducted a detailed review of the nature of the tax. In passing, the tribunal noted the obligation to refer the matter to a CTA without specifying the outcome of not submitting the matter.[710] The arbitral tribunal examined the treatment of discounted debt under Bulgarian law resulting from the negotiation of a discount to the debt of the Bulgarian state-owned company that owned an oil refinery, which the investor characterized as "paper profits."[711] After succeeding on jurisdiction, the *Plama* tribunal dismissed all the investor's claims for substantive protection under the ECT, including those arising from the taxation of the discounted debt. According to the tribunal's reasoning, ECT Article 21 constituted an exclusion.[712] The *Plama* tribunal held that ECT Article 21 imposed on the investor an obligation to submit the claims to the CTA, which the investor failed to do.[713] After finding that ECT Article 21 applied as an exclusion, the tribunal reviewed the tax itself in detail to find that "no action by [Bulgaria] comes anywhere near to being unfair or inequitable treatment or amounting

709. *See RockHopper*, paras. 152-75.
710. *Plama* Award, para. 266.
711. *Id.* paras. 148, 149, 157, 256-64.
712. *Id.*, para. 266.
713. *Id.*, para. 266.

to expropriation."[714] The tribunal reasoned that upon the purchase of the shares in the state-owned company and upon negotiation of the debt, the investor knew or should have known that the reduced debt will be taxed.[715]

[2] The Other Non-renewable Cases Touching on Taxes but ECT Article 21 Not Invoked: **Amto, Nykomb, Mamidoil,** ***and*** **Stati**

It is not as if taxation matters did not materialize in the other non-renewable energy cases. Rather the opposite. In *Amto*, *Mamidoil*, and *Stati*, tax-related issues remained relevant for the dispute and to a certain extent serve as a precursor to the avalanche of cases that followed. In *Nykomb*, tariff reductions did not adopt any tax measures. In the early ECT arbitrations, neither the measures adopted by the states nor the positions of the parties incorporate tax provisions and tax-related defenses under ECT Article 21.

Amto was one of the initial cases to confront taxation matters without a formal invocation of ECT Article 21. The case focused on the Ukrainian tax authorities' aggressive enforcement procedures that the investor argued breached the FET and non-discriminatory provisions of ECT Article 10(1).[716] The *Amto* tribunal ultimately dismissed the Latvian investor's substantive claims, including those arising out of taxation matters. Despite the matter being substantially related to taxation, Ukraine did not invoke ECT Article 21 as a formal defense.[717]

In *Nykomb*, the investor established jurisdiction and prevailed on the merits when the tribunal found that Latvia's reduction of the tariff did not amount to expropriation but it violated the treaty provisions on non-discrimination and FET.[718] The case did not see any complex tax schemes. The reduction in tariff was accomplished solely on the basis of an interim payment arrangement between two companies, completed after the Latvian constitutional court decisions; hence, no formal tax objections were raised.[719] The tribunal did not see the reduction to meet the high threshold of indirect/regulatory/creeping expropriation deemed to include the "decisive factor" of "the degree of possession taking or control over the enterprise the disputed measures entail."[720] However, it found that when reviewing comparable entities, the reduction was discriminatory when the Latvian state did not meet its burden of proof to show that the conduct was not discriminatory.[721]

Similar to *Amto* awards, in *Mamidoil* the state did not raise an ECT Article 21(1) objection despite taxation matters materializing in the case. *Mamidoil* concerned an alleged illegal investment in the construction and operation of an oil container terminal

714. *Id.*, para. 267.
715. *Plama* Award, para. 267.
716. *Amto*, paras. 96-7.
717. The record in *Amto*, as emerging from the award, does not reveal that Ukraine has made such an objection. *See also* Nappert, *supra* note 184, at 12 (highlighting that the tribunal rejected the allegations over the Ukrainian tax authorities' actions in bankruptcy proceedings "without addressing [ECT] Art. 21").
718. *Nykomb* at 33, 34 and 38.
719. *See id.* 1, 28-9.
720. *Id.* 33.
721. *Id.* 34.

in the Durres port area in Albania.[722] The investor's main taxation-related argument focused on Albania's taxation of the import of petroleum products based on fictitious quantities assessed on the bill of lading, rather than shore outturn quantities.[723] The tribunal upheld its jurisdiction even over taxation matters: excises and VATs allegedly imposed on wrongful amounts.[724] It denied the substantive claims of the investor over a dissenting opinion.[725] According to the tribunal, the investor's allegations of discrimination were unsubstantiated, as the tax measures applied evenly to all importers.[726] The tribunal ruled that Albania could use "fictitious amounts."[727] Generally, the *Mamidoil* decision offered great deference to local authorities in shaping tax policy without any trace of ECT Article 21 being invoked.

In *Stati*, the investors prevailed on jurisdiction and merits in a dispute involving the cancellation of contracts for subsoil exploration. Among the measures complained by the investors were tax assessments with retroactive effects but Kazakhstan did not object on ECT Article 21(1) grounds.[728] The tax assessment involved corporate income taxes and specific export taxes that appeared to be raised rather late in the proceedings, mostly in relation to valuation issues.[729] In denying Kazakhstan's motion to exclude the tax from calculations, the tribunal ruled that the damages would include the adverse tax findings.[730] The investor had the duty to pay local taxes, but not for tax assessments made in breach of the ECT.[731] The tribunal held that the taxes were "created" by Kazakhstan after a change of attitude against the investor took place. With the tax assessments being retroactive, the tribunal deemed that the state bore the burden of proof that the disputed taxes were lawful. In the opinion of the tribunal, the decision of the Kazakhstan Supreme Court, which overruled prior decisions, did not meet the burden of proof for a fair and independent assessment. In the opinion of the *Stati* tribunal, the tax assessments breached the ECT.[732] The ECT provisions on taxation

722. *Mamidoil*, paras. 55-137.
723. *Id.* para. 779.
724. *Id.*, paras. 786-98.
725. *Id.*, paras. 496-9, 536-80, 581-5, 598-675, 691-735, 742-9, 764-71, 772-5, 786-98, 799-802 and 819-29. *See generally Mamidoil* Dissenting opinion of Steven Hammond.
726. *Mamidoil*, paras. 787-90.
727. *Id.* paras. 786-8. The tribunal likely meant "hypothetical" not "fictitious" amounts. "Hypothetical amounts" are commonly adopted across the taxation spectrum (from computing prospective deductions to complete equalization calculations).
728. *Stati* Award, paras. 1791-7. Claimants alleged: "the USD 62 million tax claim was manufactured and, as Scott Horten and PwC confirm, is part of a well-recognized strategy that Kazakhstan uses to pursue investors who have fallen out of favor with the President. *Id.* paras. 1789. Respondent alleged that the cumulative amount of the tax debt was USD 81.2 million. *Id.* 1793.
729. *Stati* Award, paras. 297, 298, 303, 306 and 314. *See generally* claimants' and respondent's arguments on lateness. *Id.* paras. 1790-1. The Kazakh legislation contained provisions that no export tax would be applied to exported crude oil. *Id.* para. 269.
730. *Id.* para. 1801 ("no deduction for Claimants' tax obligations are to be made from the damages found to be due for the ECT breaches").
731. *Stati* Award, para. 1799.
732. *Id.* paras. 1799-800. The tribunal has in at least one other non-renewable energy case taken into consideration taxation matters for purposes of valuation, where "windfall" tax and corporate income tax were not deemed to be adjusted downwards. *See generally* Ioannis Kardassopoulos v. The Republic of Georgia, Award, ICSID Case No. ARB/05/18, Mar. 3, 2010, paras. 617 & 623 [hereinafter "*Kardassopoulos*"].

were, however, not formally raised or addressed. In *Stati*, the language of the tribunal indicated that damages linked to alleged tax matters "abusively made in breach of the ECT" are recoverable. According to the *Stati* tribunal, the state bears the burden of proof to show that the disputed tax matters are not part of conduct already established to be unlawful by claimants.[733]

[C] Non-Renewable Energy Cases: *Yukos*

In *Yukos*, the investors prevailed on the jurisdiction and the merits. Despite a brief setback in having the award set aside in the first sentence, the Hague appellate court reversed the set-aside decision, breathing new air into this critical arbitration award that invalidated the Russian alleged tax measures as being confiscatory and not being bona fide.[734]

The tribunal was seized with the question to rule on the exclusion of all tax-related matters (the bulk of the claims) from the jurisdiction of the tribunal already at the jurisdictional phase.[735] The tribunal decided to defer the decision on whether the objections refer to jurisdiction or admissibility to later in the dispute "the next phase of the arbitration." It reasoned that the background and the motivation behind Russia's actions "go to the heart of the dispute." The tribunal held that "[it] will not rule on this crucial issue in a vacuum."[736]

In the final award, the *Yukos* tribunal divided its analysis into *direct* and *indirect* jurisdiction. The *Yukos* tribunal began its inquiry with *indirect* jurisdiction by which a claim that falls within the scope of the ECT Article 21(1) exclusion could still fall within the tribunal's jurisdiction on the basis of the ECT Article 21(5) inclusion/"clawback." In distinguishing between "tax" and "taxation measures," the tribunal dismissed the respondent's argument that "taxation measures" should be interpreted broadly and be deemed broader than a "tax."[737] While noting that "tax" is not defined in the treaty, the *Yukos* tribunal applied VCLT Article 31 to interpret the use of the term "tax" in the ECT Article 21(5) inclusion/"clawback." The tribunal did not find the *travaux préparatoires* particularly helpful. With regard to the June 1993 draft that replaced the term "taxation measure" with "tax," the tribunal found that for it to extrapolate a motivation by the drafters to limit the scope of the "clawback," it would have expected for "a motivation [for such restriction] to have found some additional support in the record."[738] In all, the tribunal concluded:

> the ordinary meaning of "tax" used in Article 21(5) cannot be narrower than the meaning of "Taxation Measure" used in Article 21(1).[739]

733. *Stati* Award, para. 1799.
734. *See* Yukos Court of Appeal Judgment, paras. 5.2.8–5.3.
735. *Yukos* Decision on Jurisdiction, paras. 579-82 (comparing ECT Art. 21(1) with ECT Art. 21(5)).
736. *Id.* paras. 584-6.
737. *Yukos* Award, para. 1410.
738. *Id.* para. 1415.
739. *Id.* paras. 1411-13.

It reasoned that a narrower interpretation of the term "tax" in relation to the term "taxation measures" would mean that a number of claims would be left out so as to create "a gaping hole in the ECT where investors would stand completely unprotected from expropriatory taxation."[740] Such a finding did not lead, in the opinion of the tribunal, to a conclusion that is "ambiguous or obscure" to lend itself to additional rules of interpretation under VCLT.

On the issue of the impact of the failure to submit the claim to CTAs, the tribunal held such requirement as futile.[741] In applying the provisions of ECT Article 21(5)(b)(i), the standard of futility was determined as:

> a referral must be regarded as *clearly futile* if there is no possibility that the relevant authorities would in fact be able to come to some timely and meaningful conclusion about the dispute or make any timely determinations that could potentially serve to assist the Tribunal's decision-making.[742]

The tribunal then found that the referral would be futile on two grounds: practical and doctrinal. On a practical level, the *Yukos* tribunal reasoned that the case record was enormous and it was inconceivable that the parties could reduce the record for a meaningful submission to the local authorities, particularly in light of the different analysis being conducted by tax authorities.[743] On a doctrinal level, the *Yukos* tribunal noted that the provisions imposing the obligation to submit the claim to CTAs should be interpreted in good faith. On the basis of such good faith interpretation, the tribunal reasoned that a referral is not required "if following the referral procedure would clearly be futile under the circumstances of a specific case."[744] In support of this proposition, the *Yukos* tribunal relied on the principle in diplomatic protection that exhaustion of local remedies is not necessary when doing so would offer no reasonable redress.[745] On the merits, the *Yukos* tribunal held that the Russian Federation breached ECT Article 13. It did not find that Russia expropriated the assets, instead that it had taken measures that had an effect "equivalent to nationalization or expropriation."[746] The tribunal reasoned that "the true objective" was not "tax collection."[747] The tribunal reiterated its doubts about the feasibility of the low-tax areas on which the Yukos conducted its tax optimization schemes involving "trade companies."[748] However, the fact that the Russian Federation applied VAT on oil that has been imported and the auction of the company's prime assets to far below its true value indicated a conclusive breach of ECT Article 13.[749]

740. *Id.* para. 1413.
741. *Id.* para. 1421.
742. *Yukos* Award, para. 1426 (emphasis added).
743. *Id.* para. 1423.
744. *Id.*, paras. 1423-4.
745. *Id.* paras. 1423 and 1425 (referring to 2006 ILC Draft Articles on Diplomatic Protection Art. 15(a)).
746. *Id.* para. 1580.
747. *Yukos* Award, para. 1580.
748. *Id.* para. 277. The low-tax areas provided for exemptions from "federal corporate profit tax" on the basis that the legal entities met certain criteria. *Id.* para. 280. The federal corporate profit tax amounted to up to 19%. *Id.* para. 282.
749. *Yukos* Award, para. 1579.

A finding of *indirect* jurisdiction on the basis that expropriation was found would suffice for the tribunal's conclusions; however, the tribunal went further and held that it has *direct* jurisdiction over the claims because the alleged tax measures were not bona fide. The operative standard emerges from the notable paragraph 1407 that states:

> 1407 [....] the Tribunal finds that, in any event, the carve-out of Article 21(1) can apply only to bona fide taxation actions, i.e., actions that are motivated by *the purpose of raising general revenue for the State*. By contrast, actions that are taken only *under the guise of taxation*, but *in reality aim to achieve an entirely unrelated purpose* (such as the destruction of a company or the elimination of a political opponent) cannot qualify for exemption from the protection standards of the ECT under the taxation carve-out in Article 21(1).[750]

The *Yukos* tribunal incorporated the previous BIT decisions to find that the tribunal may look behind the alleged tax measures to examine *inter alia* whether the tax is actually a tax, or is being passed under "the guise of taxation" without any purpose of raising general revenue for the state. The tribunal reasoned that it needed to conduct such added scrutiny; otherwise states could avoid their substantive obligations under the ECT by "mere labeling of" a measure as a taxation measure.[751]

The tribunal relied on prior decisions to find such added scrutiny. The *Yukos* tribunal held that its findings were in line with prior decisions, including those against Ecuador.[752] According to the *Yukos* tribunal, the *EnCana* tribunal deemed that for a measure to fall under the tax exclusion of a treaty, it must be "'sufficiently clearly connected to' or connected to a tax law or regulation" in such manner that "an arbitrary demand" would not qualify to fall under the tax exclusion.[753] The tribunal further distinguished *Burlington* in that allegations of measures enacted in bad faith could still fall under the scope of the tax exemption (e.g., be deemed bona fide) provided that they were not entirely unrelated to the raising of public revenue.[754] The operative part is that a tax must be enacted for purpose of "raising of general revenue." As the measures carried the ultimate aim of destroying the investors, the *Yukos* tribunal held that the taxation-related claims did not become subject to the ECT Article 21(1) exclusion.[755] Moreover, the *Yukos* tribunal did not agree that the bona fide review would somehow prejudge the determination of the tax measures as expropriatory and would somehow

750. *Id.* para. 1407 (emphasis added).
751. *Id.* para. 1433.
752. *Id.* paras. 1437-8 (citing to *RosInvest* Final Award, para. 628 and *Renta4* Award, para. 179). *See also Yukos* Award, paras. 1439-40 (discussing EnCana v. Ecuador, LCIA UN3481, UNCITRAL, Award, Feb. 3, 2006 and Burlington Resources v. Ecuador, ICSID Case ARB/08/5, Decision on Jurisdiction, June 2, 2010). Professor Crawford who was the presiding arbitrator in *EnCana* appeared as a witness in *Yukos* testifying that "the [*Encana*] decision was not meant to imply 'that anything labelled as a taxation measure is excluded' by a taxation carve-out." *Id.*
753. *Yukos* Award, paras. 1440-1 (discussing *EnCana* Award, para. 142(1)).
754. *Id.*, para. 1443 (distinguishing *Burlington* Decision on Jurisdiction, paras. 175 and 207). In *Burlington*, claimants argued that Ecuador used its '"sovereign taxation power" in bad faith' to renegotiate the investment agreement. *Burlington* Decision on Jurisdiction, para. 175.
755. *Yukos* Award, paras. 1443-4 ("[t]he tax assessments levied against Yukos [...] were essentially aimed at paralyzing Yukos rather than collecting taxes [...]").

conflate the application of the Tax Exclusion with the protection standards themselves.[756] By giving full credence to ECT Article 21(1) arguments as a formal objection to the jurisdiction of the tribunal, the *Yukos* tribunal changed the landscape of ECT cases on matters of taxation.

[D] Renewable Energy Cases: The Czech Republic

[1] General Conditions

The timelines of the renewable energy cases mirror each other. The Czech Republic, much like Spain and Italy, adopted incentives to increase investment in the energy sector so as to meet the EU targets for renewable energy. The sole difference is that the Czech Republic joined the European Union in 2004 immediately before the ambitious targets were rolled out.[757]

In 2005, the Czech Republic implemented ambitious mechanisms to incentivize investment in the renewable energy sources (RES).[758] In all, the incentive schemes extended on the established tax incentive mechanisms for RES producers from the 1990s that included: (1) exemption from income tax in the year of the plant being in operation and five years thereafter (Tax Holiday) and (2) accelerated depreciation rates.[759] The 2005 incentive mechanisms established: (1) a preferential treatment for RES producers; (2) a feed-in-tariff (FiT) and (3) green bonuses.[760] The most critical component of the incentive mechanisms was establishing a stable FiT ensured by a guarantee that the FiT would not drop by more than 5% from the previous year.[761]

In a similar manner as in Spain and Italy, the Czech Republic's incentive schemes became so popular that they created a boom in investment with suppliers creating a surplus of energy leading to at times a negative price at peak production times.[762] In 2010, the Czech Republic introduced a levy ("Solar Levy") that was applied on revenues generated by the photovoltaic power plants.[763] The Solar Levy applied for payments to solar energy producers at two different rates based on the system incentive

756. *Yukos* Award, para. 1434.
757. The Treaty of Accession fixed a national target of 8% for the Czech Republic, where 8% of the gross consumption of energy would be generated from renewable sources. *See Antaris* Award, para. 107 (discussing Annex II of the 2003 Treaty of Accession). In 2009, the target was later increased to 13% by 2020. *See id.* para. 118 (discussing Directive 2009/28/EC).
758. Act 180/2005 adopted on Mar. 31, 2005; in force, Aug. 1, 2005.
759. Act 586/1992. *See generally ICW*, para. 130.
760. Act No. 180/2005.
761. *ICW*, para. 142 (quoting an article of Marting Bursik, former Minister of the Environment, referred to by the claimant).
762. *See generally ICW*, para. 176.
763. *Antaris* Award, para. 217 (the tribunal held that the investor withdrew the claims surrounding the repeal of the income tax exemption, which reinforced the tribunal's decision that it does not have jurisdiction over such disputes). *See* Act on Promotion, 180/2005; *see also Antaris* Award, para. 82 (The levy *followed* the implementation of legislation granting preferential access to the grid and guaranteeing fifteen years of recovery of investment by means of feed-in tariffs).

implemented in 2005: under the feed-in tariff system at a rate of 26% and for the green bonuses system at a rate of 28%.[764]

In 2012, the state went further and scaled back on the incentives and implemented a packet of amendments, which included the termination of contracts with the grid suppliers (preferential treatment), it imposed an obligation for producers to pay the negative price in the event of surplus, and it even introduced recycling fees for photovoltaic equipment.[765] The Solar Levy was later extended to apply beyond the three-year period, and it ultimately led to the cancellation of the RES incentive schemes. The detailed timeline is provided in Appendix III.

[2] Case Overview

Four sets of cases are discussed below: *Antaris*, the *Voltaic* cases, *Natland* and *JSW Solar*. In *Antaris*, the tribunal was called to interpret the scope of the tax exclusion ("carve-out") in relation to the definition of taxation measures. The majority applied the VCLT for purposes of interpreting the ECT and its definition on taxation measures, but it also introduced a two-step review particularly with regard to matters deemed as taxation measures under domestic law. The Tomka concurrent opinion deemed that the Solar Levy was a tax under domestic law, but because it was introduced as means to avoid legal scrutiny, it was not bona fide.

Four cases, grouped together and known as the *Voltaic* cases, follow the same pattern as *Antaris* with several distinctions. The *Voltaic* cases incorporated a similar two-step inquiry as *Antaris*: (1) under domestic law and (2) under general public international law, where the two inquiries are independent of each other, namely that both criteria need to be met for a measure to qualify as a tax measure for purposes of the ECT exclusion/carve-out.[766]

The Solar Levy was deemed not to be a tax within the domestic law definition of ECT Article 21(7) and the inherent limits of ECT Article 21(1).[767] Under the first prong (domestic law), the four *Voltaic* cases define the issue in terms of burden of proof. According to the *Voltaic* tribunals, ECT Article 21(7)(a)(i) imposes on the respondent the burden of proof to establish that the measure is a tax under domestic law. The tribunals reasoned that such interpretation is consistent with the express text of the treaty and "with the character of Taxation Measures as an exception to the more general terms of the ECT."[768] The tribunals viewed ECT Article 21(7)(a)(i) as a renvoi

764. *See generally ICW*, para. 176. Act 346/2010. *See also Antaris* Award, para. 152-9.
765. Act No. 165/2012.
766. *See, e.g.*, the use of the term "second and independently." *Voltaic*, para. 260; *ICW*, para. 308; *Photovoltaik*, para. 249; and *WA Investments*, para. 327.
767. The Income Tax Measures and the Shortened Depreciation Fall were deemed to fall within the ECT Carve-Out. Although the tribunal did not use the same strong language as in *Antaris* on the abandonment or the concession of the claim by claimants, the conclusion was that there was "little doubt" that the two fell within the ECT Carve-Out. *Voltaic*, para. 243; *ICW*, para. 291; *Photovoltaik*, para. 232; and *WA Investments*, para. 310. Note that Income Tax Measures and Tax Holiday are used interchangeably. *Voltaic*, para. 130; *ICW*, para. 130; *Photovoltaik*, para. 129; and *WA Investments*, para. 130.
768. *Voltaic*, para. 245; *ICW*, para. 293; *Photovoltaik*, para. 234; and *WA Investments*, para. 312.

to domestic authorities,[769] where only measures that qualify as tax measures under local law qualify as tax measures under the treaty.[770] The tribunals further recognized that ECT Article 21 imposes "international limits," but these were not triggered in the Czech cases as the matter did not qualify as a tax measure under domestic law.[771] By observing that the measure was defined as a "levy" and not a "tax" and by referring to the Czech Supreme Administrative Court decision,[772] the *Voltaic* tribunals reasoned that the Czech Republic did not meet its burden of proof.[773]

Although the *Natland* award has not been made public, it appears to follow the same pattern as the *Antaris* decision on jurisdictional issues. The Solar Levy was determined to fall within the scope of the Article 21(1) exclusion in part due to the inconsistency in the Czech Supreme Administrative Court interpretation of the matter as a tax.[774] The remaining measures, the tax holiday and the depreciation rules, were found to fall squarely within the scope of the tax exclusion.

Natland is significant in that it is the sole Czech case where the tribunal held in favor of the investors for the breach of the substantive provisions of the ECT. Indirect references to the confidential award reveal that the tribunal accepted the argument that states may bind themselves by means of legislation and that the Czech Republic has committed to certain stabilization measures by introducing the fifteen-year commitments in the Act of Promotion.[775] Given that the award is not public, the analysis below exercises caution in not overly relying on the records from secondary sources.

JSW Solar did not invoke the ECT and was brought exclusively under the intra-EU BIT between the Czech Republic and Germany. A possible explanation for not invoking the ECT by the investors, pre-*Achmea*, could be found in the limitations prescribed by ECT Article 21, previously untested before the *JSW Solar* award was rendered in 2017, otherwise, not found in the Czech-Germany BIT.[776] According to the majority, the

769. *Voltaic*, para. 248; *ICW*, para. 296; *Photovoltaik*, para. 237; and *WA Investments*, para. 315.
770. *Voltaic*, para. 249; *ICW*, para. 297; *Photovoltaik*, para. 238; and *WA Investments*, para. 316.
771. *Voltaic*, para. 249; *ICW*, para. 297; *Photovoltaik*, para. 238; and *WA Investments*, para. 316.
772. *Voltaic*, para. 251; *ICW*, para. 299; *Photovoltaik*, para. 240; and *WA Investments*, para. 318.
773. *Voltaic*, para. 252; *ICW*, para. 300; *Photovoltaik*, para. 241; and *WA Investments*, para. 319. The Czech Republic attempted to argue that the decisions of its highest administrative court did not have legal precedence and binding effect. *Voltaic*, para. 254; *ICW*, para. 302; *Photovoltaik*, para. 243; and *WA Investments*, para. 321. This argument was found unpersuasive, particularly given the subsequent proceedings in Czech constitutional court where the Ministry of Finance took the opposite opposition, *Voltaic*, paras. 255-6; *ICW*, paras. 303-4; *Photovoltaik*, paras. 244-5; and *WA Investments*, paras. 322-3.
774. Damien Charlotin, *Natland v. Czech Republic (Part 1 of 2): Tribunal jurisdiction over claimants under three out of four treaties and declines to apply ECT's Tax Carveout to Contested Measure*, Inv. Arb. Rep., July 26, 2018.
775. Damien Charlotin, *Natland v. Czech Republic (Part 2 of 2): On the Merits, Tribunal finds stabilisation commitment in Czech legislation and breach of that commitment with introduction of solar levy*, Inv. Arb. Rep., July 26, 2018. There is also indication that the *Natland* award referred to the Mr. Tawil's dissent in Charanne v. Spain for the proposal that the FET standard requires "regulatory stability." *Id.*
776. Luke Eric Peterson, *In shadow of mass solar claims, another UNCITRAL BIT arbitration quietly moves forward against Czech republic*, Inv. Arb. Rep., Jan. 10, 2014 ("no invocation of ECT, perhaps for reasons of ECT's tax exception"). *See also* Agreement between the Czech and

statutory guarantees did not amount to "absolute guarantees of revenues."[777] Instead, the only reasonable link was to "buy-out" prices at which level payback of capital expenses was linked to 7% over fifteen years.[778] In what the majority saw ambiguity, the dissent of Gary Born saw certainty.[779] The language in the Czech legislation provided, in the opinion of the dissent, two distinct sets of guarantees that were later retracted by the Solar Levy. *JSW Solar*, despite being issued under the Czech-Germany BIT, reached the same analysis as the *Antaris* decision.

[3] Cumulative Findings

The contribution of the Czech cases is threefold: two pertaining to jurisdiction and one to the merits. First, the Czech cases clarified the "two-prong" test, inherent in the ECT, but by extension theoretically applicable to similarly drafted treaties. In order for a state to use a measure as a tax measure for purposes of excluding it from the tribunal's jurisdiction, the state shall establish: (1) that the alleged measure is a tax under domestic law and (2) falls within the ambit of the treaty. Inherent in this analysis is that the state carries the burden of proof; at least for the first prong that an alleged exclusionary measure is actually a tax.

In terms of domestic law, the Czech cases set relatively clear criteria. The *Antaris* majority refers to the VCLT Article 31(3) and the nonsensical approach of leaving it up for the states to decide whether a matter is a tax under domestic law, in which case all matters would fall outside the protection of the treaty if the state wishes to draft the legislation as such. Although the tribunal did not specify which specific provision of VCLT Article 31(3) was most appropriate, it could be derived from VCLT Article 31(3)(c) that when interpreting a treaty, tribunals shall review together with the context of the treaty "any relevant rules of international law applicable to the relations between the parties."[780]

Antaris and the *Voltaic* tribunals equally recognized the importance of treaty limits even when none are expressly mentioned in ECT. Both sets of cases embraced the standard from *Yukos* that for a tax to fall under the scope of ECT Article 21(1) it needs to have the aim of "raising the general revenue for the State." In this manner, the *Voltaic* tribunals contributed to fine-tuning the *Yukos* standard and state that the *main* objective of the measure needs to be raising the general revenue, whereas *Antaris* dismissed any possibility of revenue generation. The *Voltaic* tribunals also deduced the limits in many respects from the *Yukos* analysis that the inherent limit found in the treaty derives from abuse of rights principles, thereby setting the outer limits of ECT Article 21 even when the treaty lacks any express provisions.

Slovak Federal Republic and the Federal Republic of Germany on the promotion and reciprocal protection of investments, Compilation of Laws 573/1992, at 3435-8 [hereinafter "Czech-Germany BIT"].

777. *JSW Solar* Award, para. 367.
778. *Id.* paras. 367-8.
779. *Id.* (dissent), paras. 27.
780. VCLT Art. 31(3)(c).

Second, still pertaining to jurisdiction, the Czech cases elucidate the requirement of the qualification under domestic law for purposes of determining investment protection under the treaty. What emerged from *Antaris* and was later reinforced further in subsequent cases is that any material ambiguity about the tax nature of the measures under domestic law may have a detrimental effect on the state.

In basic terms, a measure needs to be convincingly a tax under domestic law to enjoy treaty protection. Material ambiguity over the alleged tax nature of the regulatory measure would preclude the state to invoke the tax exclusion of ECT Article 21. To assess whether a measure is deemed a tax, a cumulative review would be adopted including the actual name,[781] the basis for the administering authority,[782] scholarly works,[783] and with considerable weight to be attributed to case law from national courts.[784]

In addition, *Antaris* revealed another commonly held feature of a tax measure incorporated in domestic law. For a tax measure to be valid, there cannot be any reciprocity or benefit as a result of the payment, at least under domestic law. What the *Antaris* tribunal outlined in the heated dispute among the experts was that "non-equivalence" is an important characteristic of a tax. This approach was followed by experts in the subsequent cases.[785] The requirement of non-equivalence brings the definition of a tax in line with the OECD/IBFD definitions.

The Czech cases presented a consistent pattern, as observed in Table 5.4. With the exception of the Tomka dissent in *Antaris*, the ambiguity in the treatment of the Solar Levy under domestic law prevented the state to assert the objection that the issue be excluded from the tribunals' jurisdiction. The Tomka concurrence was the sole decision in the series of awards where the opinion was expressed that the host state conduct breached the tax treaty provisions on the basis of structuring the measure with the "aim" of reducing the previous commitments provided by the state.[786]

781. *See, e.g., Antaris* Award, para. 229.
782. *See, e.g., id.* para. 230(the Solar Levy was being administered by the Tax Administration Law).
783. *See, e.g., id.* para. 231.
784. *See, e.g., id.* para. 232 ff. Judge Tomka cautions on overreliance on determination by national law when contradictory decisions emerge on the same issue. *See Antaris,* Concurring decision, paras. 7-8.
785. *Voltaic*, para. 252; *ICW*, para. 300; *Photovoltaik*, para. 241; and *WA Investments*, para. 319.
786. *See* Tomka concurring opinion, para. 12.

Table 5.4 Detailed Jurisdictional Review of the Czech ECT Cases

Case	*Outside of the Exclusion Article 21(1)*	*Within the Exclusion of Article 21(1)*	*First Prong: Under Domestic Law*	*Second Prong: Under International Law*	*Reference to Yukos*
				Only for Solar Levy	
Antaris	Solar levy	None: (1) Income tax Exemption and (2) depreciation rules abandoned or not contested by claimants	Not a tax under domestic law	Not a tax under international limits	Yes
Antaris (Tomka concurrence)	Not addressed, so like the majority	Not addressed, so like the majority	**Yes, a tax under domestic law**	Falls outside the international limits	Indirect reference (some link)
Antaris (Born dissent)	Not addressed, so like the majority	Not addressed, so like the majority	Not addressed	Not addressed	Not addressed
*Natland**	Solar levy	(1) Tax Holiday for new plants, and (2) depreciation rules	Not a tax under domestic law	Not available	Not available
ICW	Solar levy	(1) Tax Holiday for new plants and (2) depreciation rules	Not a tax under domestic law	Not a tax under international limits	Yes, does not rise to same conduct
Voltaic	Solar levy	(1) Tax Holiday for new plants and (2) depreciation rules	Not a tax under domestic law	Not a tax under international limits	Yes, does not rise to same conduct

Case	*Outside of the Exclusion Article 21(1)*	*Within the Exclusion of Article 21(1)*	*First Prong: Under Domestic Law*	*Second Prong: Under International Law*	*Reference to* Yukos
				Only for Solar Levy	
Photovoltaik	Solar levy	(1) Tax Holiday for new plants and (2) depreciation rules	Not a tax under domestic law	Not a tax under international limits	Yes, does not rise to same conduct
WA Investments	Solar levy	(1) Tax Holiday for new plants and (2) depreciation rules	Not a tax under domestic law	Not a tax under international limits	Yes, does not rise to same conduct

Source: Author's Own.

* Not public.

Third, on merits, the Czech cases reveal a degree of hesitation by tribunals when giving weight to any commitments in legislative instruments. The *Antaris* majority award and the *Voltaic* cases equally take the position that the Czech legislation did not establish any clear commitments by the state in the Act of Promotion, despite the long commitment for the recovery of assets. These decisions speak firmly that the commitments made, if any, were linked to buy out prices and not to specific revenue generation to warrant any legitimate expectations. Behind these decisions stands the strong Born dissent in *Antaris*, who noted that the commitments in the Czech legislation were express and "crystal clear."[787] The same analysis was followed in *JSW Solar*, a non-ECT case, in which Gary Born also dissented. In all, the Czech cases add an important contribution to the non-renewable legislation post-*Yukos* (Table 5.5).

Table 5.5 Comparative Review of the Czech Cases

Case	*Jurisd. Found*	*Success on Merits*	*Article 21 Invoked*	*Exclusion/ Carve-Out Applies*	*Clawback Upheld*	*Jurisd. over Tax Measure*
*JSW Solar**	Yes	No	N/A	N/A	N/A	N/A
JSW Solar (Born dissent)	Yes	**Yes**	N/A	N/A	N/A	N/A
Antaris	Yes	No	Yes	Yes**	N/A	No

787. *Antaris* dissent, para. 12.

Case	*Jurisd. Found*	*Success on Merits*	*Article 21 Invoked*	*Exclusion/ Carve-Out Applies*	*Clawback Upheld*	*Jurisd. over Tax Measure*
Antaris (Tomka concurrence)	Yes	No	Yes	Yes **	N/A	No
Antaris (Born dissent)	Yes	**Yes**	Yes	Yes **	N/A	No
*Natland****	Yes	**Yes**	Yes	Yes **	N/A	No
ICW	Yes	No	Yes	Yes **	N/A	No
Voltaic	Yes	No	Yes	Yes **	N/A	No
Photovoltaik	Yes	No	Yes	Yes **	N/A	No
WA Investments	Yes	No	Yes	Yes **	N/A	No

Source: Author's Own.

* Not an ECT case per se. Although very similar to the other Czech cases, *JSW Solar* was brought under Czech-Germany BIT in *pre-Achmea*, likely, to avoid the ECT exclusion.
** Exclusion does not apply to the Solar Levy: the essential measure invoked by the claimants; it does apply to other measures.
*** Not public. Partial award found success on the merits but damages phase has not been completed. Final award is still pending.

[E] Renewable Energy Cases: Italy

[1] General Conditions

Six Italian cases, *Blusun, Greentech, CEF, Eskosol, Belenergia,* and *Sun Reserve,* reviewed the scaling back of FiTs regime by means of four types of allegedly tax-related matters: windfall/Robin Hood Tax, administrative charges, imbalance costs, and municipal property taxes. In addition, Italy formally withdrew from the ECT on December 31, 2014, with the binding effect on January 1, 2016.[788] The Italian government's explanation linked the decision to withdraw to financial contributions, when, in fact, it may have been due to concerns over emerging litigations.[789]

788. *See* ECT Art. 47(2) where the notice becomes effective one year after its receipt. Energy Charter Secretary has confirmed that notice of withdrawal has been received on Dec. 31, 2014; https://energycharter.org/who-we-are/members-observers/countries/italy/ (Accessed: May 30, 2020). MENA Chambers opine that Italy planned to withdraw already with the passing of Law Nr. 190 of Dec. 23, 2014. *See generally* MENA Chambers, Note 12—Italy's Withdrawal from the Energy Charter Treaty, May 5, 2015; http://www.menachambers.com/ (Accessed: May 30, 2020).
789. Kyriaki Karadelis, *Italy to Quit Energy Charter Treaty*, Global Arb. Rev., Apr. 23, 2015.

Italian commitments are, as in the case of Spain and the Czech Republic, triggered by the EU-wide initiatives aimed at increasing RES energy production and energy/electricity consumption from RES.[790] In the Italian context, the scaleback occurred in a series of measures enacted by several administrations. These involved, as described in detail in Appendix IV:

(1) the extension of the windfall tax ("Robin Hood Tax") to RES producers during the Berlusconi administration;
(2) new administrative measures introduced with Canto V in Summer 2012, during the Monti government;
(3) the administrative approach was reinforced in 2013 with the Law Decree Destinazione Italia during the Letta administration;
(4) *Spalma-incentivi* introduced the major rebalancing measure in Summer 2014, during the Renzi administration.
(5) Cumulatively, the Italian cases centered on the treatment of four distinct measures: (1) administrative charges introduced by Conto V; (2) imbalance costs; (3) Robin Hood Tax; and (4) Italian municipal property taxes/charges: property tax (IMU) and service tax (TASI).

[2] Case Overview

The Italian cases involved six cases grouped in five groups: *Blusun* and *Eskosol* (arising from the set of facts), *Greentech, CEF, Belenergia, and Sun Reserve. Blusun* and *Eskosol* focused primarily on the scaling back of the FiT regime in the form of the decrees prior to 2012 that did not involve any specific taxation measures. *Blusun* and *Eskosol* are grouped together. In *Blusun*, Italy did not raise any tax-related objections whereas the *Eskosol* remains still pending and the *Eskosol* claimants unsuccessfully sought to intervene in the *Blusun* proceedings.[791]

In *Greentech*, the "Robin Hood Tax" and municipal property tax were deemed to be a tax and fall expressly within the meaning of ECT Article 21, thereby being excluded from the scope of the tribunal's jurisdiction. The *Spalma-incentivi* decree and all other measures were not deemed as taxes. The tribunal held that, by introducing the tariff reduction scheme of the *Spalma incentivi* decree, Italy had breached the FET standard. The other claims of modifications to the price scheme, tariff payment term, administrative fees, and other measures were dismissed.[792]

In a departure from *Greentech*, the *CEF* tribunal attributed great weight to the findings of the Italian Supreme Court and upheld all four mechanisms as taxes. Where the *Greentech* and *CEF* tribunals differed is on the treatment of the administrative fee and imbalance costs. On the administrative fee, the *CEF* tribunal held that there was no

790. Leg. Decree 387/2003 (implementing EU Directive 2001/77/EC of Sept. 27, 2001 ("First Renewable Directive")).
791. *Eskosol* Partial Decision, para. 31.
792. *Greentech* Award, para. 594. Investors recovered EUR 11.9 million on a claim of EUR 25.06 million. *Id.* 12.

denying that these fees were "consideration for a given service rendered by a public body."[793] The Conto V administrative fee was applied only to PV operators for purposes of funding "a service in support of such photovoltaic operators." However, in the opinion of the CEF tribunal, the consideration did not absolve the fee to be a tax. As reasoned by the tribunal, the Conto V administrative fee resembled municipal garbage taxes that under Italian law are treated as taxes.[794] Even though there are fees for services rendered, they are charged on all homeowners regardless of whether one benefits from the service or not. The reasoning of the *CEF* tribunal appears to put substantial weight on the mandatory nature of the measure, as prescribed by Italian law. The *CEF* tribunal held that even the imbalance costs were a tax. It applied its analysis for the administrative fee *mutatis mutandis* to the imbalance costs.[795]

In *Belenergia*, the focus was only on the imbalance costs where the tribunal held that the imbalance costs qualified as "Taxation Measures." According to the *Belenergia* tribunal, the definitional provisions of ECT Article 21(7)(a)(i) should not be interpreted restrictively.[796] The tribunal relied on the term 'include' to deduce that the definitional provisions were "not exhaustive," thus being subject to a broad interpretation.[797] In the opinion of the *Belenergia* tribunal, the domestic law requirements were met. The measure was established by law, as required by Article 23 of the Italian Constitution.[798] According to the tribunal, the name of the particular measure ('imbalance costs') was not dispositive. The tribunal incorporated the reasoning of the Italian Constitutional Court decision by which taxation measures have three characteristics: (1) mandatory contribution, (2) absence of reciprocity, and (3) "contribution is linked to public spending with a relevant economic purpose."[799] As held by the tribunal, "substance prevails over form."[800]

In *Sun Reserve*, the investor did not succeed on the merits. On matters of taxation, the tribunal relied heavily on the Italian domestic law to uphold whether a measure was a tax. As in *Greentech* but unlike *CEF*, it upheld that the Robin Hood Tax and the classification of the immovable property qualified as a tax. While the investor relied on the "autonomous international law" standard that materialized in the Ecuadorian cases, the respondent emphasized the use of the domestic standard for what a tax shall be. The tribunal reconciled the two and noted that the standards overlap; it used for the most part the overlapping standards ("mandatory" and "absence of reciprocity") and would come to rely on the other two ("reliance on redistribution" and "expression of sovereignty") only if necessary.[801] The tribunal reasoned that even the Italian version

793. *Id.*
794. CEF Award, para. 199.
795. *Id.* paras. 201-2.
796. *Belenergia*, paras. 370 & 373 ("ECT Article 21(7)(a)(i) cannot be restrictively interpreted").
797. *Id.*
798. *Id.* para. 374 (discussing Italian Constitution Article 23 that states 'no obligation of a personal or financial nature may be imposed on any person except by law').
799. *Id.* 375.
800. *Id.*
801. *Sun Reserve*, para. 522.

of the treaty resolved that the term "tax" or fiscal measures as it appears in Italian ("tributi") is broader than the term "taxation measures" ("imposte").[802]

[3] Cumulative Findings

Both *Blusun* and *Eskosol* expose that the FiT scalebacks do not necessarily trigger tax issues. *Greentech* and *CEF* confronted tax-related measures that followed the Eskosol bankruptcy, which gave rise to the *Blusun* and *Eskosol* cases as observed in Table 5.6. While the *Eskosol* arbitration is still pending, *Greentech* and *CEF* awards are currently under review in set-aside proceedings before the Swedish courts.

Greentech, CEF, Belenergia and *Sun Reserve* offer a mismatch of results and findings on taxation matters. In *Greentech* and *CEF*, the investors succeeded on the merits arising out of the same legislative mechanism (*Spalma-incentivi* decree), albeit taxation matters being treated differently. *Sun Reserve* and *Greentech* witnessed the same treatment of taxation measures but in *Sun Reserve*, the investor did not succeed on the merits.

Table 5.6 ECT Cases Against Italy Where an Award Has Been Rendered

Case	*Gen'l Jurisd.*	*Success on Merits*	*Article 21 Invoked*	*Carve-Out Applies*	*Clawback Upheld*	*Jurisdiction over Tax Matters*
Blusun	Yes	No	No	N/A	N/A	N/A
*Greentech***	Yes*	Yes	Yes	Yes	Not discussed	No
*CEF***	Yes*	Yes	Yes	Yes	Not discussed	No
*Eskosol****	Yes	N/A***	N/A	N/A	N/A	N/A
*Belenergia****	Yes	No	Yes	Yes	No	No
Sun Reserve	Yes	No	Yes	Yes	Not discussed	No

Source: Author's Own.

* Except for the tax matters excluded under Article 21(1).
** in set-aside before Swedish courts (Svea Court of Appeal) due to the use of the arbitration rules of the Stockholm Chamber of Commerce (SCC) and the seat of the arbitration being Stockholm.
*** Final award is still pending, or period for the request of annulment has not expired.

Greentech and *CEF* tribunals tackled four types of measures with different conclusions: *on the windfall tax/Robin Hood Tax* and *the municipal property tax* (IMU

802. *Id.* para. 518.

and TASI). Belenergia addressed only the imbalance costs. On the Conto V *administrative charge* and *the imbalance cost*, the *Greentech* and *Sun Reserve* reached one result, while the *CEF* tribunal reached a different result, see Table 5.7.

Table 5.7 The Categorization of the Measures Within the Meaning of ECT Article 21 (Greentech, CEF and Belenergia)

Case	*Robin Hood*	*Canto V Admin Charges*	*Imbalance Costs*	*Municipal Property Taxes: IMU/TASI Charges*
Greentech	Yes	No	No	Not contested, but tribunal issues sua sponte review that it falls within Art. 21
CEF	Yes	Yes	Yes	Yes
Belenergia	N/A	N/A	Yes	N/A
Sun Reserve	Yes	No	No	Yes
	Alignment	Misalignment	Misalignment	Alignment

Source: Author's Own.

The *Greentech* tribunal reached different conclusions on whether the four taxes fall within the scope of Article 21. On the Robin Hood Tax, it held that it was a tax measure falling within the scope of ECT Article 21.[803] Although not contested as a tax by the investors, the municipal property charges on immovable property (IMU and TASI) were deemed to fall within the scope of Article 21. The other two measures (administrative charges and imbalance costs) were deemed not to be "taxation measures" within the scope of ECT Article 21. In *Greentech*, the tribunal has reviewed its jurisdiction over the right to compensation over the municipal property tax sua sponte. It interpreted ECT Article 21 broadly as to prevent reviewing the right compensation *even* when one of the parties has not contested the nature of the alleged measure.

Despite its succinctness, the *CEF* tribunal's conclusions on the Robin Hood Tax and the municipal property charges do not come as a surprise. On the next two measures, the succinctness begs for clarity. The *CEF* tribunal relied on the standard proposed by the respondent on the use of domestic law. Under this standard, all measures appear to fall under the definition of a tax despite potential questionable issues linked to the non-reciprocity element. The *CEF* tribunal did not engage in a discussion of any inherent limits arising out of ECT Article 21. The analysis of the *CEF* tribunal did not reveal any need to go beyond the domestic law standard.

803. *Greentech* Award, paras. 175, 226-7.

Finally, in all four cases, *Greentech, CEF, Belenergia*, and *Sun Reserve*, the ambiguity from the Italian version of the ECT treaty comes to light. In *Greentech*, the tribunal did not address the distinction. In *CEF*, the tribunal dismisses the objection as nonsensical and relies on the domestic interpretation. Only in *Sun Reserve*, the use of the terms in the Italian version is ultimately reconciled to be in line with other versions of the treaty.[804] In all, the Italian cases did not alter the landscape of the ECT with regard to interpreting the different translated versions of authenticated texts. However, the *Belenergia* and *Sun Reserve* tribunals did engage in treaty interpretation.

[F] Renewable Energy Cases: Spain

[1] Historical Context to the Spanish Cases

The history of the tumultuous Spanish RES legislative regime is grouped in three stages: (1) investment promotion (pre-2010); (2) reduction (2010-2013); and (3) overhaul by abandoning previous regime and adoption of new regulatory regime (2013-2014).[805] Notably, Law 15/2012 introduced the tax on the value of the production of electric energy (TVPEE)[806] that involved a 7% levy on the gross income on all electricity produced.

During the first stage (*Incentive*), Spain allocated considerable resources to increase production of energy by solar and wind sources in part due to initiatives from the European Union to increase energy production from RES.[807] The first regime of feed-in-tariffs in 1998[808] later adjusted to the consumer price index (CPI).[809] However, prior to 2007, Spain's success to generate RES production has been lackluster.[810] This changed in 2007 with Royal Decree 661/2007 when Spain introduced an overly generous FiT system. Spain introduced a fixed value for FiTs for a specific period of time. The formula applied for the first twenty-five years for solar energy, but provided for a regulated tariff even beyond twenty-five years.[811] A less onerous system than Royal Decree 661/2007 followed in 2008 that still allowed for generous FiTs.[812] In 2008, Spain retained a generous system but intended consequently to address the issues through several issues, including *inter alia*: registration of facilities, introduction of quarterly tenders for quotas, adjustment of the formulas, and correction of the duration of facilities.

---

804. *See Sun Reserve*, para. 518 (by interpreting Art. 21(7), the tribunal found the term "tax"/"fiscal measures" to include "taxation measures," thus bringing the interpretation of the term in line with the *Yukos* decision and the English version of the treaty).
805. *See generally 9Ren* Award, paras. 76-115 and *Greentech* Award, paras. 58-150.
806. TVPEE or in Spanish impuesto sobre el valor de la producción de la energía eléctrica (IVPEE).
807. *RREEF Infrastructure* Partial Decision, para. 88.
808. Royal Decree (Spain) 2818/1998.
809. Royal Decree (Spain) 436/2004.
810. *See generally 9Ren* Award, paras. 78-81 (Spain reached only 25% of its target by 2007 at 84 MW on a target of 371 MW).
811. *Id.*
812. Royal Decree (Spain) 1578/2008.

In the second step (*Reduction*), the incentives from 2007 initiatives generated considerable investment and attracted considerable positive attention.[813] This rapid rise came at a cost. By the end of 2008, the tariff deficit that computed the money payable under the tariff regime reduced by the regulated energy prices amounted to EUR 6 billion.[814] This financial imbalance led to the reduction or scaling back of the generous schemes. With the Spanish solar industry, it was soon noted that the incentive schemes created a large and unsustainable tariff deficit.[815] The 2008 reduction was intensified in 2010 with the introduction of two initiatives, Royal Decree 1565/2010 and Royal Decree 14/2010, that introduced: the elimination of the second part of the tariff that was not activated (all tariffs after twenty-five years),[816] the introduction of additional technical requirements to protect the systems in the event of power failure,[817] a limitation of operating hours for the facilities to be eligible for the reduced tariff based on "climatic zones" where the facility is located (the impact of this provision was mitigated with the option for operators to sell on the open market if they were deemed not to meet the operating hours' requirement),[818] and charges of EUR 0.5 / MW for access to transport and distribution networks ("access toll fee").[819] These initiatives were further strengthened in 2012 with the introduction of Royal Decree Law[820] 15/2012 that introduced the TVPEE. It also introduced the Water Levy, a similar levy on hydroplants. Royal Decree Law 2/2013 also made changes to the method by which the CPI was used that involved the introduction of constant taxes by excluding certain tax effects from the calculation of inflation.[821]

In the third stage (*New Regulatory Regime*), it became clear by late 2013 that the reduction initiatives did not adequately address the large financial deficit. The Spanish

813. Royal Decree (Spain) 661/2007 led to Spain meeting 85% of its PV target. *Greentech* Award, para. 56. The "success" of the Spanish regime prompted President Obama to state that the US ought to take a cue from Spain. *See generally* Institute for Energy Research, *Spain's Green Energy Experiment: a cautionary tale* at 1; available at: http://instituteforenergyresearch.org/ (Accessed: May 30, 2020), at 2-3.
814. *Greentech* Award, para. 116. Institute for Energy Research estimated that the deficit was EUR 5 billion. Institute for Energy Research, *Spain's Green Energy Experiment: a cautionary tale* at 1; available at: http://instituteforenergyresearch.org/ (Accessed: May 30, 2020), at 6.
815. *See generally Eiser* Award, para. 124. *See also Charanne* Award, para. 134 ("the growth of the working capacity experienced by solar photovoltaic technology is being much higher than expected [...] in May 2008, it had already reached the 1,000 MW of working capacity").
816. Royal Decree (Spain) 1565/2010 Art. 1.10.
817. Royal Decree 1565/2010 Art. 1.5 and 18.
818. Royal Decree (Spain) 14/2010, First Additional Provision.
819. Charanne v. Spain, Award, paras. 158, 167-8 (discussing Royal Decree 14/2010, First Additional Provision).
820. In the hierarchy of Spanish norms, the Royal Decree law stands above the royal decree as in addition to being able to change the law, it may be enacted in "extraordinary need or urgency." *9Ren* Award, para. 66. *Greentech* Award, para. 61.
821. Royal Decree (Spain) 14/2010, Art. 1 (replacing the current CPI with "el Índice de Precios de Consumo a *impuestos constantes* sin alimentos no elaborados ni productos energéticos"; Eng. "the Consumer Price Index *with constant taxes* without unprocessed food or energy products") (emphasis added).

trade deficit had reached EUR 40 billion or 4% of the GDP.[822] Royal Decree Law 9/2013 repealed Royal Decree 661/2007 and Royal Decree 1578/2008, together with the accompanying schemes. The legislative measures that followed introduced a new regulatory regime that fine-tuned the remuneration and departed from a fixed FiT setup. Royal Decree Law 24/2013 introduced remuneration-based on the wholesale market with remuneration parameters defined separately based on a detailed list of factors. In addition, Royal Decree 413/2014 introduced "reasonable rate of return" for a specific installation based on: investment incentives and operating incentives. Although there are a number of other legislative measures involved, Appendix V summarizes the main legislative initiatives involved in the eleven cases described below.[823]

Forty-six ECT cases have been filed against Spain under the ECT arising out of the tariff schemes set up to promote investment in solar energy and other forms of renewable energy. Twenty cases have resulted in a final or a partial award where the issue of liability was decided, arranged in the following chronological order: *Charanne, Eiser, Isolux, Masdar, Antin, Novenergia, Greentech, 9Ren, Cube Infrastructure, NextEra, RREEF Infrastructure, SolEs, Infra Red, OperaFund, RWE, PV Investors, Stadtwerke, BayWa, Watkins,* and *Hydro Energy*.[824] The focus of the cases has been almost exclusively the solar energy sector. In three cases, *Cube Infrastructure, RREEF Infrastructure,* and *Hydro Energy,* issues pertaining to hydroelectric and wind plants were triggered, respectively. Of the solar cases, five cases involved disputes linked to concentrated solar power (CSP); the rest linked to photovoltaic power and the difference between the two is that the CSP plants resemble traditional thermal energy plants. The early cases (*Charanne, Eiser,* and *Isolux*) set out the scope of the inquiry. The later cases crystalized the relevant criteria.

822. *See generally* Greentech Award, para. 117. *See also* Institute for Energy Research, *Spain's Green Energy Experiment: a cautionary tale* at 1; available at: http://instituteforenergyresearch.org/ (Accessed: May 30, 2020). *Cf* five years earlier, the budget deficit stood slightly over EUR 10 billion.

823. For a full list of ECT cases, please *see* the International Energy Charter, Energy Charter Treaty; https://www.energychartertreaty.org/ (Accessed: May 30, 2020). For a general list of relevant legislation, *see* London School of Economics, Grantham Research Institute on Climate Change and the Environment, Collection of Legislation; available at: http://www.lse.ac.uk/GranthamInstitute/ (Accessed: May 30, 2020).

824. The final awards are organized based on the date of the award, except for *RREEF Infrastructure* given that the award on jurisdiction was rendered earlier: *Charanne* (Jan. 21, 2016), *Eiser* (May 4, 2017), *Isolux* (July 6, 2016), *Masdar* (May 16, 2018), *Antin* (June 15, 2018), *Novenergia* (Feb. 15, 2018), *Greentech* (Nov. 14, 2018), *Cube Infrastructure* (Partial Decision, Feb. 19, 2019; Award, July 15, 2019), *NextEra* (May 31, 2019), *9Ren* (May 31, 2019) and *RREEF Infrastructure* (Partial Decision, Nov. 30, 2018), *SolEs* (July 31, 2019), *Infra Red* (Aug. 2, 2019), *OperaFund* (Sep. 6, 2019), *RWE* (Dec. 30, 2019), *PV Investors* (Feb. 28, 2020), *Stadtwerke* (Dec. 2, 2019), *BayWa* (Dec. 9, 2019), *Watkins* (Jan. 21, 2020), *Hydro Energy* (Mar. 9, 2020).

[2] Case Overview

[i] Early Cases Set the Scope of the Inquiry: Charanne, Eiser, Isolux, and RREEF Infrastructure

With the initial round of cases, there remained a high degree of uncertainty on the treatment of the measures instituted by Spain. In *Charanne*, tax objections over the TVPEE did not materialize under ECT Article 21(1) in part because the claimant requested a review of the legality of the 2010 measures excluding subsequent measures adopted in 2013.[825]

With *Eiser*, a full onslaught on the TVPEE commenced on its treatment as a *male fide* measure. In *Eiser*, the tribunal upheld that the TVPEE fell within the tax exclusion of ECT Article 21(1), namely by determining *inter alia* that a press release did not establish bad faith. The *Eiser* tribunal reasoned that for a measure not to be bona fide, it would require that "Spain knew or should have known that the RD 661/2007 tariffs cannot be substantially altered, and so knowingly violated its obligations under the ECT by adopting Law 15/2012." In *Eiser*, the tribunal also did not find that failure to refer the matter to a competent authority prevented its review. While the *Eiser* tribunal upheld the inadmissibility of the expropriation nature of the TVPEE on the basis of ECT Article 21(5)(b), it deemed that it was not obligated to refer the matter to CTAs as the expropriation claim did not "figure in the [...] final award."[826]

In *Isolux*, the investors prevailed on jurisdiction but *not* on merits, with a dissenting opinion being entered on the merits.[827] Although *Isolux* arises closely out of similar circumstances as *Charanne*, the tribunal had in fact ruled on the lawfulness of the post-2010 measures, including the TVPEE. The *Isolux* tribunal held that the TVPEE fell within the scope of ECT Article 21(1) exclusion.[828] Its impact is relevant for assessing: (1) the link between good faith and bona fide tax measures where obscurity in the law did not amount to *male fide* taxes and (2) impact of the failure to refer a matter to CTAs did not make the claim inadmissible.

In *RREEF Infrastructure*, the investors prevailed on jurisdiction and succeeded on the merits. In the decision on jurisdiction, the *RREEF Infrastructure* tribunal deferred the review of the tax issues on the merits. Although the *RREEF Infrastructure* Decision on Jurisdiction was one of the first decisions, the final award emerged late. In the final award, the tribunal upheld unanimously that the TVPEE fell within the scope of ECT Article 21(1), the burden of proof that claimants must disprove that the tax is not bona fide, and the value of the levy as a cost is relevant for the damages calculation.[829]

825. These arguments were raised specifically in the *Isolux* proceedings that arise out of a similar set of circumstances. *See generally Charanne* Award, para. 395 ("[...]the claims have been limited to the consequences of the 2010 norms, while complaints regarding the subsequent norms have been submitted by different companies of their group to another arbitral tribunal").
826. *Eiser* Award, paras. 266, 269 and 297.
827. *See Isolux* Award, paras. 478 and 619. *Isolux* Tawil Dissenting opinion.
828. *Isolux* Award, para. 741.
829. *RREEF Infrastructure* Decision on Merits, para. 191. *See also RREEF* Decision on Jurisdiction, para. 21.

[ii] The Crystallization of Case Law following Masdar, Antin, Novenergia, 9Ren, *etc.*

The next wave witnessed sixteen cases emerge in the last three years. The cases crystalized the treatment of the TVPEE as a bona fide taxation measure with few invocations of the inclusions of ECT Article 21(2)-(6). A select number of cases are briefly discussed below.

In *Masdar*, the investors prevailed on jurisdiction and succeeded on the merits.[830] The tribunal reviewed the ECT Article 21(1) objection in the context of *ratione voluntatis*.[831] In reaching the conclusion that TVPEE was a tax within the scope of ECT Article 21(1), the tribunal heavily incorporated existing case law. In line with the previous cases, the *Masdar* tribunal relied on *Yukos* but distinguished the facts in *Yukos* as being "extreme" and "egregious."[832] The tribunal held that the circumstances arising out of the TVPEE did not meet the "high bar" set out by *Yukos*.[833] Otherwise, the *Masdar* tribunal acknowledged the tension with the direct connections between TVPEE and the stated aims of "environmental protection and sustainability"; however, these tensions did not amount to the measures being non-bona fide. In essence, *Masdar* incorporated the rationale from *Isolux* that reduction of deficit rather than misstated aim of protection of the environment does not establish bad faith,[834] and from *Eiser* on the broad power of the state to exercise its taxation powers.[835]

Antin, in which the investors prevailed on jurisdiction and succeeded on the merits, contributed to the existing jurisprudence threefold: (1) it clarified the three-prong test first seen in *Eiser* for the definition of a tax under international law; (2) following the facts meeting such definition, it linked the bona fide review to abuse of rights and lack of good faith; and (3) adopted this high standard to statements made by the government official. The *Antin* tribunal accepted the parties' submissions of the EnCana test first seen in *Eiser*. The tribunal acknowledged that ECT Article 21(1) would not apply in "exceptional circumstances" or "extraordinary circumstances," where there is a showing that the host state implemented the measure in "lack of good faith."[836]

Novenergia contributed to the tax-related case law with the introduction of the high threshold of the validity of a taxation measure. After finding that the tax measures met the domestic law definition of ECT Article 21(7)(a)(i),[837] the tribunal adopted the

830. Claimants recovered, excluding interest and legal/arbitration costs, EUR 64.5 million on a claim of 250 or alternatively EUR 184 million. *Masdar* Award, paras. 592, 655 and 697.
831. *Masdar* Award, paras. 257 ff. There were two objections on *ratione voluntatis*: the other being linked to the denial of benefits inquiry arising out of ECT Art. 17(1) that was also dismissed. *See generally id.* para. 231 ff.
832. *Id.* para. 288 (citing and discussing *Yukos* Award, para. 1407).
833. *Id.* para. 291.
834. *Id.* para. 293(citing to *Isolux* Award, para. 740).
835. *Masdar* Award, para. 294 (citing to *Eiser* Award, paras. 266, 270-1).
836. *Antin* Award, para. 322 (referring to *Yukos* Award, paras. 1404 and 1407; *see also id* para. 314).
837. *Novenergia* Award, para. 521 ("[F]or the Tribunal there is no doubt that the provisions of Law 15/2012 are provisions relating to a tax of the domestic law of a Contracting Party as set out by Art. 21, section (7)(a)(i) of the ECT").

"assumption" or "the starting point" that "the taxation measure was in fact adopted in good faith" with the claimant bearing the burden of proof of establishing invalidity.[838] The *Novenergia* tribunal distinguished the measures implemented by Spain against those addressed in the *Yukos* awards where the measures were found to be taken "for the purpose of destroying a party or political adversary."[839] No allegations of the TVPEE falling under any inclusions/clawbacks of ECT Article 21(2)-(5) appear to have been made despite expropriations being alleged but dismissed.

In *Greentech*, the claimants prevailed on jurisdiction and succeeded on the merits with a dissenting opinion on the issue of liability and application of EU law.[840] When called to evaluate the nature of the TVPEE, the *Greentech* tribunal found that the TVPEE constitutes a tax for purposes of ECT Article 21(1) and that no inclusions/clawbacks were applicable.[841] In *Greentech*, claimants sought to move away from the bad faith argument and focus on the economic effect of the law. In applying the EnCana test adopted by the parties, the tribunal reasoned that "the economic measure should not displace a finding that a measure is a tax as a matter of law."[842] In the *Greentech* tribunal's holding, all these elements were present with regard to TVPEE. The tribunal went further and reinforced the requirement of a showing of bad faith in order to deem a measure not being bona fide.[843] According to the *Greentech* tribunal, the investors did not prove such high standard and thus TVPEE falls outside the scope of the inquiry of the tribunal. On the merits, the tribunal has touched upon several matters that in other cases were argued to be taxes, including "access toll charges."[844] In any event, the *Greentech* tribunal did not find that the investor had legitimate expectations that the regulatory regime would not change specifically with regard to the introduction of such charges.

In *Cube Infrastructure*, the allegations of ECT breach focus not only on the PV plants but also on hydro investments. On the issue of the jurisdiction over the TVPEE and the Water Levy, the *Cube Infrastructure* tribunal held that both of those measures fell within the scope of ECT Article 21(1).[845] After concluding that both measures have "the appearance of a tax," *Cube Infrastructure* tribunal underlined the application of the rules of treaty interpretation rules under international law, not domestic law for

838. *Id.* paras. 759-63.
839. *Id.* para. 522 (referring to *Yukos* Award, para. 1407 and *RosInvest* Final Award [no pincite in the original]).
840. Claimants recovered, excluding interest and legal/arbitration costs, EUR 39 million on a claim of EUR 58.2 million. *Greentech* Award, paras. 540 and 562. *See also Greentech* Award 39 ff (Dissenting Opinion of Raul Vinuesa) (dissenting on the application of due diligence, which concerns the issue of liability).
841. *Greentech* Award, para. 251 ("none of these clawbacks are relevant to this jurisdictional objection").
842. *See id.* paras. 257-8 (claimants insisted that the tribunal needs to go beyond the "Respondent's subjective intent" and instead examine "[the] legal and economic effect" of the measure). *See also Cube Infrastructure*, para. 229 (same test was advanced there but it was not accepted by both parties and generally dismissed by the tribunal).
843. *Greentech* Award, para. 259 (discussing *Yukos*).
844. *See infra* §5.06[C]-[D] (discussing the treatment of imbalance costs in *Greentech v. Italy* and *CEF v. Italy*).
845. *Cube Infrastructure* Partial Decision, para. 233.

purposes of determining whether the taxation measure is actually a bona fide measure within the meaning of ECT Article 21(1).[846] Instead, the tribunal focused on the factual allegations, which it determined to be "flimsy" for a finding of a tax not being bona fide.

NextEra is the largest award to date against Spain with damages in the amount of EUR 290 million.[847] In *NextEra*, the tribunal held that the TVPEE fell within the scope of ECT Article 21(1) by formulating the review in terms of *ratione voluntatis*.[848] In a very short ruling on the issue, the *NextEra* tribunal accepted the *EnCana* test and ruled that the TVPEE was a tax. It held that it was irrelevant that the "economic effect" had been that of a "tariff cut."[849] It further clarified that the TVPEE was not relevant for purposes of damages. Perhaps, the most valuable contribution of the *NextEra* decision is its short and rare interpretation of the ECT Article 21(3) inclusion/clawback. Claimants argued that TVPEE was *not* a tax on income but "rather on gross revenue for the production and transmission of electricity." The tribunal reasoned that TVPEE is a tax on revenue "derived from the supply of electricity into the Spanish grid." The tribunal further clarified that "[t]here is no basis for assuming that the reference to income in Article 21(3) of the ECT contains a reference to net income."[850] Other measures such as access tolls and the CPI index had not been objected to for having tax-related impacts.[851]

In *9Ren*, the tribunal held that in the absence of a demonstration of bad faith, the TVPEE fell within the scope of the ECT Article 21(1) exception.[852] The tribunal found that even based on the four-prong standard proposed by the claimant, the TVPEE was a tax. In the opinion of tribunal, the TVPEE (1) was established by law; (2) imposed obligations "on a defined group of people"; (3) the revenues went to the Spanish state; and (4) was used for a public purpose.[853] For purposes of the obligation being established by law, the tribunal held it sufficient to examine the practice of the Spanish courts. The tribunal determined that the public purpose requirement is sufficiently met with the reduction of a public deficit. In this context, the tribunal incorporated the unrequited element of a tax as part of the "public purpose."[854]

In the *SolEs*, the tribunal deemed the TVPEE "generate[d] revenue for the State"; its provisions were consistent with a tax measure, as passed in accordance with

846. *Cube Infrastructure* Partial Decision, para. 221 ("[t]hat is a question to be approached on the basis of the principles of international law concerning the interpretation of the treaties, and not, for example, upon the basis of an interpretation of EU or any other domestic law").
847. Claimants recovered, excluding interest and legal/arbitration costs, EUR 290 million on a claim of EUR 720.6 million. *NextEra Partial Decision*, paras. 14, 16-17. Investors started with a claim of EUR 393.6 million (later amended to EUR 521.4 million) *NextEra* Partial Decision, para. 552. *AES et al v. Spain*, PCA Case No. 2012-14, where the claims rise to EUR 1.9 billion, remains pending (at least based on the public records).
848. *NextEra Partial Decision*, para. 187. There were two objections on *ratione voluntatis*: the other being linked to the denial of benefits inquiry arising out of ECT Art. 17(1) that was dismissed for reasons that Spain invoked it in a "timely fashion." *See id.* paras. 245 ff.
849. *Id.* para. 372.
850. *Id.* para. 383. *See also id.* paras. 373 and 380-1.
851. *NextEra* Partial Decision, para. 14.
852. *9Ren* Award, para. 207 (quoting *Eiser*, para. 270 "The power to tax is a core sovereign power that should not be questioned lightly").
853. *9Ren* Award, paras. 198, 199, 202 and 203.
854. *9Ren* Award, paras. 198 and 203.

Spanish law.[855] For these reasons, the tribunal did not find it difficult that the TVPEE was a tax. The tribunal was not convinced that the TVPEE was a tariff cut.[856] Evidence that the legislature had knowledge of treaty obligations is not sufficient for a finding of a treaty breach. The tribunal reasoned that despite several measures being introduced (including adjustment to the CPI index), Spain has held a consistent approach that only the TVPEE was a taxation measure, subject to the Tax Exclusion.[857]

In *OperaFund*, the tribunal held that the MFN-Specified Inclusion did not apply because TVPEE was a tax on capital or income.[858] According to the tribunal, it held that the TVPEE was a "tax on income under the ECT" and by such finding the MFN Inclusion did not apply.[859] The tribunal paid tribute to the *jurisprudence constante* by referring to *Eiser* (including the dissenting opinion), *Isolux*, *Novenergia*, and *Masdar*, and agreeing that it does not have jurisdiction over the TVPEE.[860] What is notable about *OperaFund* is that it concluded that the TVPEE was a "tax under international law."[861] The last twelve months have seen the completion of *PV Investors* which completed the longest arbitration, arising from the time before some of the measures were adopted. The recent conclusion of other Spanish cases such as *Infra Red* and *BayWa* has seen the investors attempt to shift the focus of the arguments away from the bona fide inquiry to the additional argument that the TVPEE falls under the MFN inclusion/clawback.[862]

[3] Cumulative Findings

In all, the Spanish cases offer a cornucopia of arguments by investors that the TVPEE was not a bona fide, against a unanimous conclusion that TVPEE was bona fide tax within the scope of the ECT Article 21(1) exclusion. Of the twenty cases rendered against Spain, the tribunal found that it had jurisdiction in all cases. In eleven of the thirteen cases, it found for the investors; only in three of the initial cases, *Charanne*, *Isolux* and *Stadtwerke*, did the investors not recover on the merits. In eighteen cases, the tribunal was called to rule on whether the TVPEE fell within the scope of the ECT Article 21(1) exclusion. In all of these eighteen cases, the tribunals held that the TVPEE fell within the scope of ECT Article 21(1). In *Charanne* and *PV Investors*, the legality of the TVPEE was not particularly addressed because the bulk of the dispute centered on the measures leading up to 2010, given that the TVPEE was introduced only in 2012. The high-level over overview is presented in Table 5.8.

855. *SolEs*, para. 272.
856. *SolEs*, paras. 273-4.
857. *SolEs*, para. 275.
858. *SolEs*, para. 276.
859. *See SolEs*, para. 415.
860. *SolEs*, para. 404.
861. *OperaFund*, para. 704.
862. *See Infra Red*, paras. 309-18 and *BayWa*, para. 310.

Table 5.8 RES Cases Involving Spain

Case	*Gen'l Jurisd.*	*Success on Merits*	*Article 21 Invoked*	*Excl. 21(1)*	*Incl. 21(2)-(5)*	*Cost Impact Dam.*	*Gross Up*
Charanne	Yes	No	N/A	N/A	N/A	-	
Eiser	Yes	Yes	Yes	Yes	No	-	
Isolux	Yes	No	Yes	Yes	No		
Masdar	Yes	Yes	Yes	Yes	-	-	
Antin	Yes	Yes	Yes	Yes	-	-	
Novenergia	Yes	Yes	Yes	Yes	-	-	
Greentech	Yes	Yes	Yes	Yes	No	-	
9Ren	Yes	Yes	Yes	Yes	-	-	
Cube Infrastructure	Yes	Yes	Yes	Yes	-	No	
NextEra	Yes	Yes	Yes	Yes	No	-	
RREEF Infrastructure	Yes	Yes	Yes	Yes (at the merits stage)	-	Yes	
SolEs	Yes	Yes	Yes	Yes	-	-	
Infra Red	Yes	Yes	Yes	Yes	No		No
OperaFund	Yes	Yes	Yes	Yes	No	Likely no	
RWE	Yes	Yes	Yes	Yes	-		
PV Investors	Yes	Yes	N/A	N/A	N/A	No	No
Stadtwerke	Yes	No	Yes	Yes	-		
BayWa	Yes	Yes	Yes	Yes	No		
Watkins	Yes	Yes	Yes	Yes	-		
Hydro Energy	Yes	Yes	Yes	Yes	No		

Source: Author's Own.

The twenty Spanish cases reveal a repeated review of similar circumstances. Besides the TVPEE, two other measures were reviewed: (1) the access tolls and (2) the CPI adjustment measures involved a recalibration of the CPI by excluding taxes. By adjusting the tax base for purposes of the tariffs, the CPI adjustment did involve a recalculation of the tariffs affecting the tax matters. In a similar manner, access toll fees may arguably be deemed a tax but they were not argued as such. In *NextEra*, the CPI adjustment was specifically listed as one of the measures that amounted to a breach. In *Greentech*, these measures were not deemed to trigger liability.[863] Appendix VI presents a deep dive into these reoccurring issues.

863. *Greentech et al v. Spain*, para. 411.

The holdings of all these cases align on the treatment of the TVPEE and other taxes that become relevant. Not all cases refer to *Yukos*, but all cases adhere to a high standard for determining whether a measure that meets the definition of a tax shall be invalidated as not being bona fide. The thirteen awards vary in how they reach this conclusion. They range from introducing an "assumption" of validity to a succinct dismissal of the jurisdictional objections.[864]

Two of the cases, *Eiser* and *9Ren* opined on the state's power to tax. When taxation matters were taken up during the jurisdictional stage as in *RREEF Infrastructure*, the tribunal deemed that jurisdictional issues linked to taxation matters need to be taken up in the context of liability, as the issues are closely intertwined.[865] Tribunals differed in their determination of the measure before embarking on a review of the bona fide standard, as well as on the treatment of domestic law; some required careful scrutiny of the domestic standards for purposes of ECT Article 21(7)(a).[866] Others focused on domestic standards and international standards, or as in *Cube Infrastructure* and later *OperaFund*, the tribunal ruled that the matter is solely for concern of treaty interpretation; domestic law and international law were not relevant for purposes of interpreting the definition in ECT. The *Cube Infrastructure* approach was also followed in *OperaFund* where the tribunal relied only on the definition of tax under international law to uphold that the TVPEE fell under the Tax Exclusion without regard to the "tax" versus "Taxation Measure" distinction.[867]

The involvement of the EnCana test that first emerged in *Eiser*, albeit not expressly being referred to as such, has rather complicated the review in relation to the definition under ECT.[868] The three-prong test sets out the inquiry into whether an alleged tax: (1) is established by law, (2) imposes obligations on a defined class of persons, (3) generates revenues going to the state, and these revenues are used for public purposes. What was important is to assess how the *EnCana* test fits within the ECT requirement. The theme of "revenue generation" permeates throughout the case law, as evidenced in *Eiser* and *SolEs*.[869] In *Cube*, the last prong was adjusted to include the requirement of non-reciprocity ("unrequited transfer").[870] From *9Ren*, there is some indication that the EnCana test would somehow qualify a taxation measure under ECT, or at least determine its legality. In *OperaFund*, *EnCana* was referenced together with *Burlington* and *Duke Energy* to incorporate a lighter version of the test formed of

864. *See, e.g.*, *9Ren* refers to *Masdar* and *Eiser*, *see 9Ren* Award, para. 207. The tribunal in *NextEra* does not refer to any cases at all. *See, e.g.*, NextEra, Partial Decision, paras. 372-3; 383-4. *Novenergia* Award, para. 521.
865. *RREEF Infrastructure* Decision on Merits, paras. 180 and 191.
866. *Antin* Award, para. 306 and *Novenergia* Award, para. 521.
867. *See Cube Infrastructure* Partial Decision, para. 221. *OperaFund*, para. 404.
868. *Eiser* Award, para. 266. *EnCana* Award, para. 142. *See also* Duke Energy Electroquil Partners & Electroquil S.A. v. Republic of Ecuador, ICSID Case No. ARB/04/19, Award, Aug. 18, 2008, para. 174; Burlington Resources v. Republic of Ecuador, ICSID Case No. ARB/08/5, Decision on Jurisdiction, June 2, 2010 ("Burlington"), paras. 164-5.
869. *SolEs*, para. 272. *See also Eiser* Award, para. 268 (citing to *Yukos* Award, para. 1407).
870. *Cube Infrastructure* Partial Decision, para. 229 ("to pay money to the State for public purposes and without any benefit to the taxpayer").

three criteria, where revenue generation was omitted from the criteria. These thresholds were deemed to have been met when the tribunals relied on them.[871] In essence, the impact of the EnCana test on the other decisions remains questionable. The early cases saw claimants argue that the tax was initiated in bad faith.[872] When this argument was dismissed in *Eiser*, claimants focused instead on the "economic effect" and that the tax measure needed to be made in good faith. The tribunals did not agree, often stating very explicitly that they would not second guess the Spanish fiscal policy.[873]

The Spanish cases address some inclusions/clawbacks: most notoriously in *NextEra* and *Infra Red*, the argument that the TVPEE was not a tax on income was dismissed for purposes of the Article 21(3) inclusion. In the tribunals' opinions, there was no basis to deduce that the ECT reference to taxes on income or capital would mean taxes on "net income."[874] In *OperaFund*, the MFN Inclusion was barely entertained when it was deemed that the TVPEE was a tax on income. The early cases saw also disagreements on the impact of referrals to the CTAs. *Eiser* noted the ambiguity in this requirement but did not go as far as to say that it was an unnecessary requirement. Although the *Eiser* tribunal deemed that the requirement was not complied with, it did not find necessary to have the matter submitted for review, as the claims failed on the merits.[875] In *Isolux*, the tribunal held that the requirement did not lead to inadmissibility but solely to an adverse award on costs in the event that the requirement was not met.[876] In *RREEF Infrastructure*, the tribunal expressly stated that the TVPEE might be considered for purposes of estimation of damages.[877] A large portion of cases including *Eiser*, *Masdar*, *Cube Infrastructure*, *9Ren*, and *NextEra* point in the other direction.[878] Issues of due diligence have commonly come up under scrutiny by the Spanish tribunals,[879] including on the requirement of examining the legal regime governing tax matters.[880]

[G] Sub-conclusion to the ECT Cases

The aim of this section has been to streamline the rapidly growing ECT jurisprudence. While forty ECT cases have triggered tax-related inquiries, only eight were resolved

871. *Eiser* Award, para. 266; *Cube Infrastructure* Partial Decision, para. 230. *NextEra* Partial Decision, para. 372. *9Ren* Award, paras. 198-202. *OperaFund*, paras. 404-5.
872. *See, e.g., Eiser* Award, para. 267.
873. *Greentech* Award, para. 258. *NextEra* Partial Decision, para. 372. *See also 9Ren* Award, para. 203 ("It is not the function of an ECT tribunal to micromanage Spain's tax policy").
874. *NextEra* Partial Decision, para. 383. *Infra Red*, para. 318.
875. *Eiser* Award, paras. 294 and 298.
876. *Isolux* Award, para. 758.
877. *RREEF Infrastructure* Decision on Merits, para. 191.
878. *Eiser* Award, para. 272; *Masdar* Award, para. 621; *Cube Infrastructure* Partial Decision, para. 362; *9Ren* Award, para. 416; and *NextEra Partial Decision*, para. 373.
879. *See, e.g., Eiser* Award, para. 119. *See also Antin* Award, para. 114-34.
880. *See Greentech* Award, para. 379. The requirement of due diligence was debatably set out in Parkerings v. Lithuania, ICSID Case No. ARB/05/8, Award, Sept. 11, 2007, para. 332. *See also Isolux* Award, para. 528.

pre-2016. The Tax Exclusion has been invoked in every renewable energy case but two, *Charanne* and *PV Investors*.

Two factors explain this phenomenon. The first explanation concerns the obscurity of the Taxation Article but also in the measures adopted by the states themselves. The first cases such as *Amto* and *Mamidoil* did not invoke the Tax Exclusion despite taxation matters being central to the case. In *Nykomb*, the reduction of the tariff was completed unilaterally without a tax component attributed to it (unlike the Spanish cases where the TVPEE was applied on all energy production). In *Plama*, one of the first ECT cases, taxation matters enjoyed but a cursory review. This soon changed in *Yukos* where taxation matters stood at the heart of the dispute. Due to its size and complexity, ECT Article 21(1) was no longer overlooked and repeatedly investors invoked the argument that the taxes were not passed in good faith (e.g., were not bona fide) to circumvent the Tax Exclusion

The second explanation lies in the explosion of the net number of ECT cases. The total number of ECT cases has been rapidly on the rise, particularly in the post-*Achmea* age when ECT remains one of the few remedies by which intra-EU investment disputes could be addressed. A large portion of the increased ECT caseload comes from renewable energy cases where tax-related issues have been at the core of the dispute. This trend causes the ECT cases to be divided into two broad categories: renewable energy cases and non-renewable energy cases.

Forty taxation-related cases are reviewed with a detailed breakdown of the numbers being presented in Appendix VII. Investors predominantly use the ICSID (twenty out of forty cases), where SCC and UNCITRAL are evenly split (ten each). Out of the forty cases, jurisdiction has been found in all cases. On the merits, claimants prevailed in twenty-five cases (62.5%), with the same rate for both renewable and non-renewable sectors: five out of eight (62.5%) in the non-renewable sector and twenty out of thirty-two (62.5%) in the renewable sector.

The biggest discrepancy occurs in the invocation of ECT Article 21 between the renewable and non-renewable cases. In the non-renewable energy cases where taxation matters materialized, Article 21(1) was invoked in four cases; three of which were the *Yukos* cases. In *Plama* and the *Yukos* cases, where the Tax Exclusion/Carve-Out was applied, the Tax/Exclusion was upheld. In the renewable energy cases, the Tax Exclusion and Article 21(1) took a more important role. Article 21 was invoked in twenty-eight out of thirty-two cases (87.5%). For most of the cases, the analysis stopped at the decision for the exclusion. Given the *Yukos* handling of the indirect jurisdiction and the triggering of the expropriation exception, the non-renewables fared better in addressing the inclusions/clawbacks in three out of eight cases (37.5%), while in the renewable sector the figure is five out of thirty-two cases (15.6%) where all the uses of the clawbacks were dismissed. Only the *Yukos* decisions prevailed on the use of an inclusion/clawback, but even in that case, the use of the inclusions was deemed not dispositive because the measures were found *male fide*.

What becomes apparent from the case law is that the *Yukos* arbitration has had a profound effect on the ECT case law, changing profoundly the treatment of taxation affecting both renewable and non-renewable energy cases alike. *Yukos* modified the ECT Article 21 landscape putting it in a category of its own due to the specific measures implemented in the case and the factual record involving the treatment of the VAT, profit taxes, and the ultimate auction of the company's most important assets. For the non-Yukos non-renewable energy cases, *Plama* was the only case delving into Article 21(1), but little weight could be attributed to the tribunal's finding on the exclusion since it explored in details the measures themselves. From the non-Yukos non-renewable energy cases, *Stati* stands out by reinforcing the position that abusive tax measures shall be subject for the review of the tribunal that contrasted to *Mamidoil* where the tribunal applied strong deference to local tax authorities. In neither *Mamidoil* nor *Stati* did the host state invoke ECT Article 21.

The legislative measures that gave rise to the renewable energy arbitrations may be traced to the European Union's initiatives to increase the production of energy from RES. The three jurisdictions confronting the bulk of the investment disputes are Spain, the Czech Republic, and Italy. The Spanish cases constitute, by far the largest portion of the non-renewable energy cases: twenty of the thirty-two renewable energy decided cases (62.5%). The key tax legislation, the 7% TVPEE was found to fall outside the review of the tribunals in the vast majority of the cases: eighteen of the twenty cases (90%). In *Charanne*, the TVPEE did not formally materialize. In *PV Investors*, the investors did not prevail on the FiT claim but succeeded on the alternative claim recovering the reasonable return on investment, which was not adjusted to the 7% levy.[881] In all other remaining ten cases, the tribunals found that the TVPEE issues fell within the scope of ECT Article 21(1) exclusion, thus outside of the court's jurisdiction. The paths of analysis differ slightly but they reach the same result: tribunals did not find that the TVPEE in itself was not a bona fide tax. An anomaly emerges out of the *RREEF Infrastructure* where the tribunal concluded that it may still review the impact of the tax for other purposes; the case is still pending on final quantum calculations.

The Czech cases paint a different picture. Even though tribunals held that they had jurisdiction in all cases, claimants prevailed only in one case, *Natland*, and the award remains confidential. In the remaining cases, the tribunal held that they had jurisdiction over tax matters as the record revealed that local courts casted doubt on the tax treatment of the alleged measures. Over a vehement dissent, the tribunal dismissed the arguments for liability on the basis that no firm commitments were made in the local regulations. According to the majority opinions in the cases where the Czech Republic prevailed, investors could not rely on the fact that the Czech legislation would not change.

What makes the Italian cases different is that Italy formally withdrew from the ECT.[882] Otherwise, the pattern of cases reveals a similarity to the Spanish cases. From five cases, tribunals have found jurisdiction in all cases. The claimants have succeeded in two of the five cases (40%): one was dismissed and one remains pending (*Eskosol*). Article 21(1) was invoked in three cases: in the third case (*Blusun*), together with the pending case, the focus centered on denial of permits. The critical feature of the Italian cases is the individual review of the different types of taxes with even opposite results.

---

881. *See* PV Investors Award, para. 792.
882. Italy remains bound to ECT for investments made prior to its withdrawal for a period of twenty years. *See* ECT Art. 47(3).

Ultimately, the treatment of the taxes did not have a final outcome on the dispute because the taxes in question were not deemed to constitute a breach on the merits. In all, the renewable energy cases reveal that prevailing on the Tax Exclusion for purposes of jurisdiction is not a guarantee of success on the merits.

§5.04 EXTRAPOLATION OF KEY FINDINGS

[A] Framework

This subsection explores the sub-inquiry: how does the ECT and non-ECT (BIT) case law allow for the observed points of tension to be reconciled in the context of the tax exclusion, inclusions, merits, and valuation review with regard to the various inquiries (ordinary meaning, domestic standard, treaty standard, and overriding inquiries) and considering procedural requirements (jurisdiction, merits, provisional measures, etc.)? Even though arbitral jurisprudence will occasionally depart from "complete doctrinal coherence" when real-world pragmatism is desirable, several unifying themes may nonetheless be extrapolated from both ECT and non-ECT case law.[883] From the outset, this section examines the impact of tax measures on the merits of the case in a limited manner: based on the assumption that the substantive review of a tax measure does not differ materially from other powers of the state. This section categorizes the aforementioned case law into six categories: (1) overarching issues linked to the power to tax, (2) applicable concerns regarding the Tax Exclusion (carve-out), (3) interpretation and definitional conundrums, (4) inclusions/clawback, (5) limitations and exceptions, and (6) valuation concerns.

[B] The Power to Tax and the Examination of Various Limits

[1] The Pattern from the Early Cases

The power to tax emerges in the holdings of arbitral tribunals as an essential sovereign power subject to certain limits. Derived from its fiscal authority to conduct economic activity, the state retains the sovereign power to impose taxes at its own discretion. Case law and commentary focus heavily on the negative implications of the taxation power, or, as in the holding of *McCulloch v. Maryland*, "the power to tax is the power to destroy."[884] However, the power to tax happens to be "the one great power upon which the whole national fabric is based."[885] As held in another US Supreme Court case, the power to tax "is not only the power to destroy, but it is also the power to keep

883. *See* Brenda Hale, President of the Supreme Court of the United Kingdom, Principle and Pragmatism in Developing Private Law at 44.10 (Mar. 7, 2019); http://www.law.cam.ac.uk (Accessed: May 30, 2020) ("The trouble is that real judges need to make judgments in real cases involving real people and it is unrealistic to expect complete doctrinal coherence from them ...").

884. McCulloch v. Maryland, 17 U.S. 316, 431 (1819).

885. Nicol v. Ames, 173 U.S. 509, 515 (1899).

alive."[886] In the domestic setting, the power to tax and by extension the limitations to such power will be ordinarily dictated by constitutional and public law.[887] The underlying principle entrusted in the power to tax builds on the *social contract* theory that relies, in turn, on *confidence*: confidence in the actions of the state.

The early foundational international law cases linked to investment and taxation, *Kügele, Brewer, Cook, Revere Copper,* and *Too*, speak of the state enjoying a broad power to tax. Whereas the earlier cases (*Kügele, Brewer* and *Cook*) focus on the power to tax and the presumption of validity, the later cases (*Revere Copper* and *Too*) concern themselves with the limitations to the power to tax. *Brewer* appears to be the first case to establish a presumption of validity. *Kügele* stands for the broadest justification of the power to tax. It assumes no expectation of profit and no expectation that the tax regime may not change. But even in *Brewer* and *Kügele,* there is an inherent limit. In *Brewer,* the limit is linked to non-discriminatory practices by the state. In *Kügele,* one may extrapolate a vague notion of expropriation, observed in the impact that a tax bears on a person's trade ("had the person paid the tax, he would be entitled to go on with his business").[888] In *Cook,* the Commission viewed the power to tax to be comparable to police powers or the right to eminent domain.[889] Where the Commission conceded that the power to tax could be limited by a subsequent agreement, such "surrender" of the power to tax need be "by clear, unambiguous language, which will admit of no reasonable construction consistent with the reservation of the power."[890] Cook stands for the proposition that in the absence of such unequivocal language, great deference should be given to the state.

Unlike *Kügele, Brewer* and *Cook, Revere Copper* and *Too* materialized after World War II where international instruments and subsequent case law began to crystallize the limits to the state exercising its power to tax. In *Revere Copper,* the government of Jamaica was found to have given specific commitments, by means of a stabilization clause restricting the change in law for the next twenty-five years. The stabilization clause was upheld even when alleged conduct by the state purportedly went against the proposition that the stabilization clause would be upheld.[891] When viewed against the holding in *Cook, Revere Copper* stands for the proposition that the stabilization clause constituted unambiguous language of a reservation to the power to tax.

In *Too,* the majority of the Iran-US Tribunal relied on the *Restatement* and the two earlier cases (*Kügele and Brewer*) to uphold the broad power to tax as being similar to other police powers of the state, "provided it is not discriminatory and is not designed to cause the alien to abandon the property to the State or to sell it at a distress price."[892] These two limits, articulated in the *Restatement,* capture the findings in *Brewer* that recognize discriminatory taxation as a limit of the state power to tax and those of *Kügele*

886. *See id.*
887. *See supra* Chapter 3.
888. *Kügele,* para. 69.
889. *Cook* at 595-6.
890. *Cook* at 596.
891. *Revere Copper,* at 37 (both Reynolds and Kaiser were told, however, that "the Government did not consider a 25-year income tax arrangement as a sensible arrangement").
892. *Too* at 387.

against specifically designated measures that may cause the abandonment of property (e.g., loss of a liquor license).

From these five foundational cases emerges a pattern that: (1) taxation measures are similar to other powers of the state; (2) such powers are inherent and broad; (3) they are subject to certain limits; (4) these limits may be derived from the state restricting its powers by means of a contract or the state is otherwise limited in exercising its broad powers to tax; and (5) when it comes to the latter, a state may be otherwise limited in passing expropriatory and discriminatory taxes.

The sources for the legal authorities justifying the power to tax and the accompanying limits, where relevant, in the early cases appear vague. In *Cook*, the state restricting its powers appear to be rooted in the domestic law of the espousing state bringing the claim (US), pointing to reliance on a waiver theory.[893] In *Revere Copper*, which in essence is a case arising out of an international contract (not a treaty) the legal authority was general contract law with some reference to "international law."[894] Finally, *Too* relied on existing precedent as captured in the Restatement, thus not relying on a binding instrument but rather a mere reiteration of the law.[895]

[2] Crystallization of the Pattern in the BIT and ECT Cases

The new wave of investment cases has essentially cemented the existence of limits and began to crystallize the outer limits of these limits. *Yukos* effectively formalized the limits of the power to tax; however, the path to *Yukos* passes through the early Ecuadorian BIT cases.[896]

An early conceptualization of an outer limit to the power to tax is recorded in *EnCana*. The case balances the limits of the tribunals (that it does not sit as an appellate court) with the requirement that a tax be rooted in and imposed by law ("Tax authorities are not robber barons writ large, and an arbitrary demand unsupported by any provision of the law of the host State would not qualify for exemption [...]").[897] The requirement that a tax be rooted in law (*nulla poena sine lege*) constitutes, to a large degree, a conceptualization of the protection against arbitrary actions and is itself a limit.

The firmest conceptualization of the outer limits to the power to tax emerges from *Burlington*. The tribunal upheld that "taxation is a prerogative of state sovereignty" but that it is subject to limits.[898] *Burlington* discusses three limits; in that taxes may not be (1) expropriatory, (2) discriminatory or (3) confiscatory. These limits derive from two

893. *See Cook* at 595 ("[...]even in those cases in which the said majority of the Supreme Court of the United States has held that that right inherent to the sovereignty of a State might be the subject of a contract [...]").
894. *Revere Copper*, at 39 (the tribunal upheld "the international law rule that a government is bound by its contracts with foreign parties notwithstanding the power of its legislature under municipal law to alter the contract").
895. *See generally Restatement*, *Black's Law Dictionary* (11th ed. 2019).
896. *Burlington* Decision on Liability, paras. 391-3. *Renta4* Award, para. 48. *See also Yukos* Award, para. 1443 (discussing *Burlington* Decision on Liability, para. 207).
897. *EnCana* Award, para. 142(1).
898. *Burlington* Decision on Liability, paras. 391-2.

sources: customary law and "protection granted under international law to foreign investments"; the latter conceivably captured by an investment treaty.[899] According to *Burlington,* customary international law imposes the two limitations of non-discriminatory and non-confiscatory taxes. The concept of expropriatory taxation finds its source in the instruments for the protection of foreign investment. Expropriatory taxation and confiscatory taxation are nearly interchangeable concepts, albeit the latter is rooted in customary law and may include protection against "abuse of powers." General taxation, though, would be viewed as "permissible exercise of regulatory powers [...] not an expropriation."[900]

In *Yukos,* the tribunal incorporated the *EnCana* and *Burlington* findings to hold that a tax demand motivated "by a purpose extraneous to taxation" would constitute an "arbitrary demand" and not fall within the protection of a treaty.[901] Not all measures will fall within the ambit of a treaty protection. For a measure to fall within a tax carve-out/exclusion, "it would have to be "sufficiently clearly connected to" or supported by some taxation law."[902] In such manner, arbitrary conduct by the state emerges as an outer limit to the power to tax and it is reviewed below in the context of a bona fide analysis. In any event, both *RosInvest* and *Renta4* have adopted a similar review.[903] In *RosInvest,* for example, the tribunal determined that the use by the Russian tax authorities and court of the principle of the sham corporation was "a novel application of the law, rather vague in content and limits, and expansively used against Yukos in a way not shown to have been used before or against other comparable tax payers."[904] In *Renta4,* the tribunal held that measures that are "designed to make a dispossession outside the normative constraints and practices of the taxing power" are expropriatory.[905] Other tribunals have analogously embraced the broad power for states to tax[906] and limitations derived therein.[907]

In the subsequent ECT law case law, the power to tax emerges consistently as being rooted in the sovereign authority. In *Eiser,* the tribunal held that the power to tax is a "core sovereign power that should not be questioned lightly."[908] In *9Ren,* the tribunal deemed that the power to tax also involved the determination of "who" may be taxed.[909] In *Hydro,* the tribunal referred to "the exercise of the sovereign power to tax" when reviewing whether such power was exercised in bad faith.[910] In *Stadtwerke,* the tribunal referred to the "fundamental sovereign right" to tax and the hesitation of states to accept any limits, as below:

899. *Id.* para. 392.
900. *Burlington* Decision on Liability, paras. 391, 392 and 394.
901. *Yukos,* para. 1440 (quoting *EnCana* Award, para. 142(1)).
902. *Id.*
903. *See RosInvest* Final Award, para. 449 and *Renta4* Award, para. 48.
904. *RosInvest* Final Award, para. 449.
905. *Renta4* Award, para. 48.
906. *See Conoco* Partial Decision, para. 312 (parties accepted the premise "the power to tax is in principle within the customary regulatory or sovereign powers of the State").
907. *See, e.g., Burlington* Decision on Liability, paras. 392-3.
908. *Eiser* Award, para. 270. *See also* Watkins, paras. 559-60 quoting Eiser's findings on "sovereign right" to tax/regulate.
909. *9Ren* Award, para. 200.
910. *Hydro* Decision, para. 518.

> [O]ne must bear in mind that the power to tax is a fundamental sovereign right that belongs to all governments; a sovereign right they have wide discretion in exercising. Moreover, the power to tax is fundamental to the power to govern since it provides governments with the necessary means to carry out their governmental functions. As a result, all governments jealously protect the power to tax and strongly resist any external limitations on it.[911]

These perennial references to sovereignty reinforce the proposition that the power to tax is a distinct power of the state, well rooted in its sovereignty. The negotiation history of the ECT particularly, where the text of the Taxation Article was nearly exclusively drafted and negotiated between finance ministers, reveals a restrictive or "defensive" drafting of limitations to the power to tax.[912] When called to interpret the application of the ECT Article, authorities have cited sovereignty as being "an important consideration" when determining the purpose of the ECT.[913]

So even if the power to tax is not controversial, what constitutes the power to tax and the limits to its respective elements remains unexplored. The power to tax centers on three main inquiries: *whom*, *what*, and *how*. As noted in *9Ren*, the first inquiry is into *whom*, namely *whom* may the state tax? The power to tax requires the assessment of the tax base or the tax subjects. In *9Ren*, the inquiry focused on taxing producers of energy, thereby transforming a tax from traditionally being a tax on profits into a tax on revenue. The *9Ren* tribunal dismissed such challenge on the basis that the state enjoys broad leeway in determining whom to tax[914] and that a tax on revenue is not only common but also increasingly desired. The tribunal referred, in passing, to the increased multinationals creating tax schemes for avoiding taxation.[915] Incidentally, it was the internal tax-minimization scheme that was called into question in *Yukos*, which the *Yukos* tribunal held that left much to be desired.[916] On the issue of tax subjects, the line of distinction between *9Ren* and *Yukos* was that, unlike in *9Ren* where the tax applied broadly to a large spectrum of tax suppliers, in *Yukos* the tax application singled out only one legal entity. Indeed, whereas the state has a broad power to decide over its tax subjects (*whom* it may tax), it may not exercise such power in a targeted or discriminatory manner.

The second inquiry is into *what*: what taxes may the state impose and on what specifically? In a similar manner to who may be taxed, the state has broad latitude to impose any type of tax applicable to any item or activity in the economic cycle. The state may apply to taxes on income, capital, sales, purchases, dividends, interest, consumption, etc. Several taxes may be applied to the same stream earmarked for

911. *Stadtwerke*, para. 169.
912. *Stadtwerke*, paras. 172-3 (discussing Craig Bamberger's statements on the negotiation history of the Taxation Article and opining "it seems that in the ECT negotiations, the Contracting Parties left the negotiation of that Article's provision to officials in their ministries of finance, a group of persons who by position and inclination would resist as far as possible any limitations on their countries' power to tax").
913. *Infra Red*, para. 317.
914. *9Ren* Award, para. 200.
915. *9Ren* Award, para. 201.
916. *Yukos* Award, para. 1404 ("[...]Yukos was vulnerable on some aspects of its tax optimization scheme, principally because of the sham-like nature of certain elements of its operations in at least some of the low-tax regions").

different purposes: social security contributions and income taxes are tied to earned income, a sales tax may include an excise and an additional regional-specific tax.

Despite the broad power to pass any tax, subjecting a wide range of activities and goods in the economic cycle, there remain inherent limitations to the state's powers to tax. A legitimate purpose of a tax is to generate revenue for the state, so a *reasonable* reason behind a tax may seldom be questioned. While a specific tax may not necessarily be the best means of achieving an objective, its failure to meet the objective does not invalidate the tax measure. A blanket sales tax need not have the purpose of reducing consumption to be valid. A tax benefit need not be self-sustaining to offer sufficient cost advantage to incentivize a particular tax behavior.[917] Certain taxes may carry specific desired regulatory aims (e.g., Pigouvian taxes). Even a bad tax need not be an invalid tax.

Inherent limits are found even in the domestic administrative processes that serve as a verifiable check. The nature of the domestic tax and its scope of application fall routinely under the review of the national bodies with authority over tax matters. The state may introduce taxes that would leave certain issues uncertain, such as which products are being taxed, the specific rate of taxation for a particular product, or whether a product is excluded from the application of the tax.[918] Unless states undertake commitments to the contrary in either treaty, contract, or legislative forms, the state has broad powers to decide on *what* type of taxes to pass and over *what* type of products or economic activities shall be taxed.

The final inquiry is into *how*: how does the state administer, place levies, and collect taxes? In principle, the state shall enjoy broad powers to conduct the administration of tax laws and the collection of taxes. There is a need to differentiate between, on the one hand, the administration of tax laws and, on the other hand, the pure enforcement of tax laws. As discussed in *RosInvest*, collection of taxes may inevitably trigger the police powers of a state when the state enforces its tax laws.[919] Some suggestion has been made that in the presence of "evidence of intent to expropriate," the state may not rely on its police powers.[920] Targeted action could be an indicia of increased scrutiny (Table 5.9).[921]

917. Sandra Wappelhorst, Peter Mock and Zifei Yang, *Using Vehicle Taxation Policy to Lower Transport Emissions*, Int'l Council on Clean Transp. Eur, Dec. 2018, at iii and 33-5; at http://www.theicct.org (Accessed: May 30, 2020).

918. *See, e.g.*, Case C-517/07 (Afton Chemical Ltd. v. the Commissioner of Her Majesty's Revenue & Customs), Judgment of the Court (Third Chamber), Dec. 18, 2018 (interpreting the series of EU directives on harmonization of excises to cover all extenders in motor fuels, including "mineral oils" that are not "energy specific").

919. *See generally RosInvest* Final Award, paras. 456 and 559 (discussing claimant's arguments and the respondent's response).

920. *RosInvest* Final Award, para. 4 (summarizing Professor Newcombe's expert testimony).

921. *See* Viñuales, *supra* note 389, at 336.

Table 5.9 Taxation Power and Its Limits

Question	*Formalization*	*Limits*
Who?	*Who* may be taxed?	Discrimination
What?	*What* taxes are involved?	Abuse, Expropriation
How?	*How* are the taxes implemented?	Arbitrariness/ abuse of power

Source: Author's Own.

The administration of tax laws differs in processes and jurisdiction but is generally rooted in administrative law and administered by tax agencies. For example, application of sales taxes will see consumers pay the tax to retailers at the point of purchase. Retailers may then have a reporting duty to regulatory administrative authorities. In the case of VATs, business consumers may have quarterly reporting and payment obligations. Property taxes may instead be subject to a lengthy process of appraisals, notification, equalization, application of tax rates, and assessments. For collection purposes, enforcement of tax law will require a notification, penalty process, seizure, and sale of assets to cover outstanding tax debts. In both administrative processes and enforcement of tax laws, procedural mechanisms are subject to domestic law that may incorporate distinct limits. Even the administrative processes may incorporate general limits such as excess of power, the collection of taxes may inevitably trigger issues related to police powers and proportionality.

In *Yukos*, the state singled out one taxpayer, it applied back taxes, and it seized the most valuable assets without due process. The recipient of the state actions was a political opponent. To the question as to whether the state may dispose of its political opponents by means of tax matters, the answer is no. Nothing prevents taxation matters from applying indiscriminately to everyone, including political opponents.

Simply being in political opposition does not absolve one from tax liability. The narrow focus is then into the factors that make the exercise of the power to tax unlawful. These fall in generally three main categories: illegal discriminatory treatment ("singling out"), abuse of rights or authority, and confiscation. *Yukos* is an extreme case where all elements of the state power to tax were breached. Other cases involving Spain, Italy, and the Czech Republic have seen investors allege, albeit unsuccessfully, that those state's conduct rose to the same level as Russia's conduct in *Yukos*.

The renewable energy case law developed in the context of the ambitious targets set by the European Union that some EU states (Spain and the Czech Republic) aimed to achieve with subsidies: schemes that were challenged by foreign investors. Many of these subsidy schemes were cost-based, rather than market-based, achieving the targets but at a considerable and devastating cost. In all, tribunals should not indulge into "microscopic examination as to the purely economic or theoretical nature of the tax."[922] What they need to guard against is a law that breaches any established standards, be they treaty-based or found in customary law, as observed in *Burlington.*

[3] Current Status of the Case Law on State Power to Tax and Its Limits

The existing case law reveals two unequivocal facts: (1) the state power to tax is rooted in the sovereign power of the state and it is perceived to be broad (presumption of validity); and (2) the power to tax is subject to limits. The following issues remain unclear, listed from the least to the most: (1) what those *limits* are, (2) what the *origins* of these limits are, and (3) how they are to be *conceptually incorporated* in the analysis.

As to the least unclear, three actual *limits* have emerged from the case law and appear to be crystallized. These three limits are: expropriation/confiscatory, non-discrimination, and arbitrariness/abuse of power, meaning that the state is prohibited in exercising the power to tax in any of these three manners. In addition, the state may validly restrict its power to tax by means of an agreement (that is, with a stabilization clause in a contractual contract). Due to the contractual nature of the latter limit, it is not discussed at length in this book as it deals with investment treaty matters; however, for purposes of this analysis, the contractual limitation is still noted as an express limitation to the power to tax to the extent that the state may contract on limiting the power to tax under domestic law.[923] Table 5.10 details the sources and the authorities for these limits.

Table 5.10 Sources for the Limits to the Power to Tax

Limit	*Sources*	*Means of Incorp.*	*Authorities*
Non-discrimination	Customary international law	- Gen'l principles (Brewer, Too) - Treaty (EnCana) - Bona fide inquiry (RosInvest/ Renta4)	*Brewer, Too, EnCana,* Restatement, *Renta4* and *RosInvest*
Confiscatory/Expropriatory Measures	Customary international law or Investment protection treaties	*Bona fide inquiry and treaty provisions*	*Burlington, Kügele,* Restatement, *Yukos, Renta4, RosInvest*

922. *See* Nicol v. Ames, 173 U.S. 509, 515-16 (1899) (Prior to XVI Amendment, US courts were called to review whether direct taxes were properly apportioned and whether indirect taxes were uniform in line with US Constitution, Article I, Section 8, Clause 1 and Section 9, subdivisions 4 and 5).

923. *See generally* Constantine Partasides and Lucy Martinez, *Of Taxes and Stabilisation, in The Guide to Energy Arbitrations* (J William Rowley, Doak Bishop and Gordon Kaiser eds., 2015), 46-62 at 62 ("in determining the legality and binding nature of such clauses, international tribunals will look beyond local legal standards").

Limit	*Sources*	*Means of Incorp.*	*Authorities*
Abuse of Rights/Arbitrariness	Customary international law	*Bona fide inquiry and inherent function of the term*	*EnCana, Burlington, Yukos, Renta4, RosInvest*
Contract/Stabilization Clauses	Contract law and conflict of law rules	*Direct in the interpretation of the agreement*	*Revere Copper*, etc.

Source: Author's Own.

The origins of these limits are found in three sources (from least precise to more specific): customary international law, treaties that the states consented to, and international contracts. Customary international law is by definition difficult to ascertain, and the specific criteria established by customary international law are difficult to pinpoint. Treaties and specifically investment protection obligations arising from such treaties are easier to identify. They are binding on the state in the framework of treaty applications. Investment agreements are by their structure contracts with entities that are either state-owned or an arm of the state. When validly entered into by the state apparatus, the sources of these obligations remain binding on the state.

The clearly evasive topic is how these limits are incorporated in the analysis of the application of said limits to real facts. For the most part, how the limits are incorporated is heavily dependent on the sources themselves. In international agreements, the analysis is straightforward. Where the consent of the state is expressed in a contract, it becomes binding and is incorporated in the contract analysis. In a similar fashion, when the expression of a limit is incorporated in a treaty, treaty interpretation rules prevail and the application of said limits is given value within the context of the treaty. But, as observed in *Burlington*, the confiscatory/expropriatory limit to the power to tax is both treaty-based and customary in nature. Where an expropriation inclusion/clawback exists in a treaty, the limit is already built into the treaty and would be subject to treaty interpretation and application.

The evasive nature of the issue of how the limits are incorporated leads to the concern of whether these limits, particularly those found in customary international law, could stand on their own. The *Yukos* cases, building on *EnCana* and *Burlington*, suggest that the application of customary law norms depends on state conduct.[924] If the state conduct is egregious in the fact that it lacks to be "sufficiently clearly connected" to a tax law or is otherwise patently abusive or arbitrary, a tribunal will not give effect to such provisions.[925] The basis for the tribunal not giving effect to such provisions may be found in the definition of the term itself or the direct application of the customary international law norms.[926] In *Burlington*, the tribunal adopted the *Saluka* approach by

924. *See Yukos* Award, paras. 1440-1. *Burlington* Decision, para. 392. *EnCana* Award, para. 142.
925. *Yukos* Award, para. 1440.
926. *See Yukos* Award, para. 1442-4; *Burlington* Decision, paras. 391-3.

which "relevant rules of general customary law" shall be incorporated in the interpretation of the treaty.[927]

In such manner, the inherent limits applicable to customary international law would be incorporated in the interpretation of the treaty, particularly on terms that would remain undefined such as "tax." The *Infra Red* award, for example, referred to "sovereignty being inherent in the purpose" of the ECT by virtue of the EEC.[928] While sovereignty is certainly an "important consideration" for the purpose of the ECT, the Charter itself refers to "the framework of State sovereignty and sovereign rights over energy resources and in a spirit of political and economic co-operation," the latter (political and economic cooperation) could only be achieved if certain limits are applied to the broad power to tax.[929] The tribunal would still be limited in not going too far, or as in the words of the *Stadtwerke* tribunal, "[the] Tribunal has no mandate to graft further limitations on the Contracting States' taxation powers that are not reflected in the text of the ECT itself."[930]

[C] Exclusions/Carve-Outs

[1] The Scope of the Tax Exclusion

A tax exclusion/carve-out excludes the application of the tax matters from the substantive or jurisdictional review of an arbitral tribunal. It internalizes the broad regulatory scope that states exercise over taxation matters. As a primary aim, the ECT Tax Exclusion excludes any contrary obligations arising from DTTs by means of MFN clauses. These provisions call into question several distinct inquiries: (1) what the general scope of the tax exclusion is; (2) procedural issues such as whether the matter is taken at the jurisdictional rather than the merits and whether provisional measures could be granted; (3) what constitutes the bona fide inquiry into the validity of the tax (as opposed to the validity of an investment); (4) to what extent the domestic law applies and how it interrelates to the terms of the treaty; and (5) what the burden of proof is and on whom it falls.

[2] Procedural Issues: Jurisdictional/Merits, Risk of Conflating and Provisional Relief

When confronted with taxation provisions, tribunals differ on their approach to bifurcate proceedings. Certain cases address taxation matters already at a jurisdictional stage.[931] It is not uncommon, however, that the tribunal takes the taxation issue in the decision on jurisdiction and liability, leaving the computation of damages for a separate

927. *Burlington* Decision, para. 392 (quoting Saluka Investments BV v. The Czech Republic (hereinafter "Saluka"), UNCITRAL, Partial Award of Mar. 17, 2006, para. 254).
928. *Infra Red*, para. 317.
929. *See* European Energy Charter, Preamble and Title I: Objectives.
930. *Stadtwerke*, para. 170.
931. *Charanne* Award, para. 32; *Eiser* Award, para. 20; *Masdar* Award, para. 32.

award.[932] Other cases have witnessed the denial of the request for bifurcation with the full scope of the inquiry reviewed in a final award.[933]

A handful of taxation cases have witnessed taxation matters early, already in connection to the decision to bifurcate at the jurisdictional stage: *Plama*, *Yukos*, and *RREEF*. Except for *Plama*, which ought to be reviewed against its facts and the absence of a tax objection at the jurisdictional phase, both the *Yukos* and *RREEF* decisions have deferred the jurisdictional objections to taxation matters until the discussion of liability. Such deferrals are not only reasonable but also in fact necessary when the tribunals are confronted with the allegations that the claims fall under a specified inclusion (e.g., expropriation).

Deferral to the merits does not mean that a tribunal is prevented from dividing its inquiry into jurisdiction and merits, nor does it mean that jurisdictional objections and decisions on liability are conflated, if a jurisdictional bifurcation were to occur. A common issue raised by the parties is the concern about "conflating the issues" or being subject to the "gateway theory." Both "conflation" and "gateway theory" assume that investors would present a broad range of taxation-related matters to the tribunal, under the guise of expropriation, even matters unrelated to expropriation which would ordinarily fall outside of the review of the tribunal.[934]

Both objections take issue with the tribunal not being able to separate the inquiry. In the Spanish cases, the risk of conflation was minimal, considering that the allegations over the illegality of the TVPEE did not preclude the review of all other measures adopted by Spain. The difficult issue concerns decision over allegations of expropriatory taxation measures in the presence of a tax exclusion to the tribunal's jurisdiction. The tax exclusion functions as a bar to the tribunal's jurisdiction. The existence of an expropriatory claim may, however, require the tribunal to find that it has *provisional* jurisdiction over the claims to the extent of the expropriation inclusion/clawback will be reviewed. The tribunals may thus set out the four corners of the inquiry already at the jurisdictional phase. A tribunal may use the *Oil Platforms*[935] test to assess whether the claims, if taken on their prima facie value, would prevent the tribunal from jurisdiction. When no inclusions/clawback-like claims are asserted, tribunals may still rule on their jurisdiction in a separate award.

Both *Yukos* and *RREEF Infrastructure* jurisdictional decisions did precisely that. In the jurisdictional awards, the tribunals have set out the four corners of the jurisdictional inquiry, which was then completed at the merits stage. In *Yukos*, there was a definite finding of expropriation that was addressed with the merits; the tribunal reserved its inquiry on jurisdiction upon the finding of expropriation by which it was

932. *See RWE* Decision on Jurisdiction, Liability and Certain Issues of Quantum; *Bay Wa* Decision on Jurisdiction, Liability and Directions on Quantum; *Hydro Energy* Decision on Jurisdiction, Liability and Directions on Quantum; *RREEF* Decision on Responsibility and the Principles of Quantum; *Cube Infrastructure* Decision on Jurisdiction, Liability and Partial Decision on Quantum; *NextEra* Decision on Jurisdiction, Liability and Quantum Principles.

933. *See, e.g.*, *Charanne*; *Eiser*; *Masdar*, *Antin*, *Novenergia*, *Greentech*, *9Ren*, *SolEs*, *Infra Red*, *Stadtwerke*, *OperaFund* and Watkins. For a detailed list, *see* Appendix VI.

934. *Yukos* Award, para. 1434. *See also Ampal* Decision on Liability, para. 187.

935. Oil Platforms (Islamic Republic of Iran v United States of America), Preliminary Objection, Separate Opinion Higgins, ICJ Reports 1996, at 832.

not prevented to examine expropriatory conduct. Even where "the risk of conflation" is highest in the context of the bona fide review of a tax, adherence to the *Oil Platforms* test would ensure the preservation of separate inquiries.

In procedural terms, tax matters also trigger the need for provisional measures or interim relief. Provisional relief may be multifaceted, but most commonly, it would be a stop of the enforcement of tax measures. It may also occur as a request for an injunction to suspend parallel proceedings such as review of tax measures before national courts (*lis pendis*). In ECT provisions, the only attempt to obtain provisional relief from enforcement of tax measures failed. In *Plama*, the investor moved before the investment tribunal to discontinue all court proceedings, including those related to the enforcement of tax measures, pending before Bulgarian courts. The tribunal rejected such claim in its entirety.[936] According to the *Plama* tribunal, neither the right to non-aggravation nor the right to maintain the status quo was sufficiently established by the investor.[937]

In *Plama*, much of the outcome on provisional measures was dependent on the nature of the relief sought by the investor. Nonetheless, provisional relief for suspension of tax enforcement proceedings has been granted in at least one recent BIT case. In *Alghanim v. Jordan*, the tribunal distinguished the *Plama* findings on the specific ground that unlike in *Plama*, the case against Jordan involved a challenge of the tax measures both in the investment proceedings and in the national courts. In such instance of overlap, the *Alghanim* tribunal issued an injunction order.[938] Two factors emerge from both *Plama* and *Alghanim* that would affect the outcome on provisional matters: first, how the main request for relief is formulated may affect the decision for provisional relief. Second is the nature of the overlapping proceedings in the national courts and investment arbitration. In the latter, when those overlap, provisional measures could be warranted. However, *Alghanim* did not confront any preclusion of the tribunal's jurisdiction by the existence of a tax exclusion, which was present in *Plama*.[939] In the presence of tax exclusion, the tribunal's ability to grant provisional measures may be further restricted.

[3] From Procedural Objections to Bona Fide Review

The tax exclusion is a powerful arrow in the quiver of the state. States retain broad powers to apply and enforce taxation measures against their nationals and foreign investors; particularly in instances when tax subjects aggressively aim to reduce their tax liability beyond lawful measures. For taxation matters as a whole, the presence and

936. *Plama* Order, para. 50. *See also Plama* Award, para. 26.
937. *Plama* Order, paras. 45-7.
938. *Alghanim* Order, para. 76.
939. In *Alghanim* Order, the relevant BIT did not retain a tax exclusion and the dissent criticized the low-standard granted by provisional relief. *See* Agreement Between the Government of The Hashemite Kingdom of Jordan and the Government of the State of Kuwait for the Encouragement and Protection of Investments, Kuwait-Jordan BIT, *signed* on May 21, 2001, *in force from* Mar. 19, 2004; at https://investmentpolicy.unctad.org/ (Accessed: May 30, 2020). *Cf. id.* Art. 4(3)(b) (a DTT limitation was included).

the actual extent of the state consent (*ratione voluntatis*) determines the scope of the review that may adopted by an international tribunal in reviewing the actual tax matters. In the absence of a tax exclusion, the language of the treaty covering the general resolve of investments disputes would be dispositive and cover tax matters. In the presence of a tax exclusion, the state does not consent to resolve taxation-related disputes unless it has limited that exclusion by other means (e.g., inclusion, limitations or exceptions). Any limitations to the state's consent will then have to be well rooted in other mechanisms such as prior commitments by the state, customary international law or other general principles of public international law.

Taxes retain the elements of a fiscal instruments implemented in a political climate. Excluding or carving out taxation measures from the jurisdiction of investment tribunals may inadvertently lead to reclassification of all adverse measures as taxation measures. Taxes retain the elements of fiscal instruments implemented in a political climate. If states may escape international liability by means of taxation measures, reclassifying any adverse measures as domestic tax measures would provide states with a carte blanche to expropriate or behave abusively without the consequence of liability.[940] In *Yukos* terms, it would create "a loophole in the protective scope of the ECT."[941] In the international context, sham taxes should not materialize beyond the domestic framework contained by the domestic courts. Yet, sham taxation is a painful reality when states use their taxation powers for reasons other than generating public revenue; such as retaliation against a state by targeting its nationals in a trade dispute or neutralization of political opposition.[942]

In assessing the legitimate exercise of the state's power to tax, two far extremes of the spectrum emerge: (1) collection and enforcement of lawfully applied taxes against non-payers (aka "tax dodgers") and (2) unlawful use of the state power to tax against the state's existing commitments. The latter gives rise to the inquiry on whether a tax may be bona fide: whether the purported tax is *actually* a tax. There are thus four specific inquiries, currently adopted by various tribunals: (1) ordinary meaning of the term "tax"; (2) review under domestic law, where relevant; (3) treaty-specific provisions; and (4) bona fide standard.

940. *Yukos* Award, para. 1433. *Antaris* Award, para. 218.
941. *Yukos* Award, para. 1413 and 1433 (incorporating claimant's characterization of "a gaping hole in the ECT").
942. *See Yukos* Award, para. 811. For trade-related matters, *see* Marvin Roy Feldman Karpa v. United Mexican States, Award, ICSID Case No. ARB(AF)/99/1, Dec. 16, 2002 paras. 101, 103 & 116; Cargill v. Mexico, Award, Award, ICSID Case No. ARB(AF)/05/2, Sept. 18, 2009, paras. 220 & 297; Archer Daniels Midland and Tate & Lyle Ingredients Americas, Inc. v. United Mexican States, Award, ICSID Case No. ARB(AF)/04/5, Nov. 21, 2007 paras. 142 & 209-12; Corn Products Int'l v. United Mexican States, Decision on Responsibility, Jan. 15, 2008, paras. 137-8; Corn Products Int'l v. United Mexican States, Award, Aug. 18, 2009 (not public) (concurring opinion of Andreas Lowenfeld) ("It follows that the host state cannot take out against the investor its disputes with the state of the investor's nationality, and that the investor cannot be held responsible for the actions of its host state").

Figure 5.3 The Four Distinct Inquiries

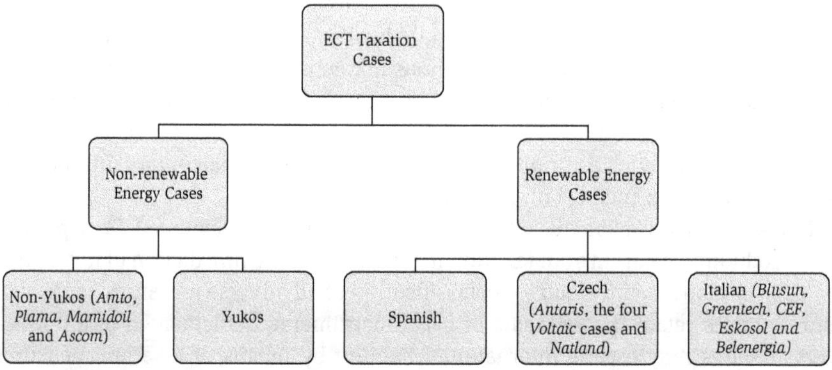

Source: Author's Own.

[4] *Bona Fide Standard as a Procedural/Evidentiary Standard and the Problem with the Pigouvian Taxes*

Of these four inquiries, the most contentious standard is the bona fide review. Bona fide stands for "in good faith."[943] According to *Yukos*, the bona fide inquiry is limited to the aim of the tax measure, or more accurately, it is concerned with its negative. The inquiry is into whether the "actions that are motivated by the purpose of raising general revenue for the State."[944] The Yukos inquiry is consistent with both the hermeneutic and teleological approaches of VCLT Article 31(1). Long-term cooperation and complementariness and mutual benefits would be rendered meaningless in cases of sham or abusive taxes.

Good faith represents a "well-established principle of international law":[945] it serves as "a general principle of law"[946] and "a principle of customary international law."[947] It aims "to fill legal gaps when no treaty or customary law has been

943. *See Bona fide, Black's Law Dictionary* (11th ed., 2019).
944. *Yukos* Award, para. 1407. *Cf. Voltaic*, para. 265; *ICW*, para. 313; *Photovoltaik*, para. 254; and *WA Investments*, para. 332 ("main objective of the measure was other than raising general revenue for the state").
945. Land and Maritime Boundary between Cameroon and Nigeria (Cameroon v Nigeria) (Preliminary Objections) [1988] ICJ Rep 275, para. 38.
946. ICJ Statute Art. 38(1)(c).
947. *See generally* Nuclear Tests Case (New Zealand v France) (Judgment) [1974] ICJ Rep 457, para. 49. Andrew Mitchell, *Good Faith in WTO Dispute Settlement*, 7 Melb. J. Intl. L. 339, 345 (2006). *See also* Stephan Schill and Heather L. Bray, *Good Faith Limitations on Protected Investments and Corporate Structuring, in Good Faith and International Economic Law*, in 88-116 at 89 (Andrew Mitchell, M. Sornarajah and Tania Voon eds., 2015).

developed."[948] Under the broad spectrum of good faith fall a number of principles of which "abuse of rights" is one of them.[949] According to the abuse of rights doctrine, the tribunal is not obliged to give effect to a right, such as the right derived from a taxation exclusion that is exercised abusively.[950] Both principles of public international law, abuse of rights and good faith, aim at the same. Any measures that are not passed in good faith are deemed to be abusive and, in any event, not given effect under international law.[951] Tribunals have extended the rule for the *interpretation* of a treaty in good faith, under VCLT Article 31(1), to *performance* of treaty obligation in good faith.[952]

A second and related basis for the bona fide review is found in the abuse of rights as upheld in the *Yukos* and *Antin* cases. In *Yukos* the tribunal's refusal to give effect to the alleged domestic measures relied on the abuse of rights doctrine.[953] Notably in *Antin*, the tribunal has offered the basis of the bona fide inquiry by reference to Hersch Lauterpacht's writing, by which "no right, however well established, which could not, in some circumstances be refused recognition on the ground that it has been abused."[954] Yet, this approach is not without criticism. The quote itself originated from *Phoenix v. Czech Republic* and was implemented against the investor for purposes of determining the lack of a qualified investment (bona fide investment). In *Phoenix*, the right of the investor to bring an investment claim was nullified for lack of an investment when such investment was not made in good faith (the investment was not bona fide).[955] *Antin* appears as an outlier where the standard for the existence of a bona fide investment was linked to the inquiry into the bona fide tax, for purposes of the tax exclusion.[956] However, given that both inquiries concern a jurisdictional review into the scope and application of the treaty, the bona fide inquiry for purposes of finding an investment is not that remote from the bona fide inquiry into the nature of the tax. If the investor may not avail itself from the protections of the treaty because its investment is

948. Land and Maritime Boundary between Cameroon and Nigeria (Cameroon v Nigeria)(Preliminary Objections) [1988] ICJ Rep 275, para. 39 (referring and quoting Border and Transborder Armed Actions (Nicaragua v Honduras) (Jurisdiction and Admissibility) [1988] ICJ Rep 69, para. 94); also referred to in *RREEF Infrastructure* Decision on Merits, para. 187.
949. Andreas Ziegler and Jorun Baumgartner, *Good Faith as a General Principle of (International) Law, in Good Faith and International Economic Law* 9-36 at 9 (Andrew D. Mitchell, M Sornarajah and Tania Voon eds., 2015) (describing the principle of good faith as "the Swiss army knife" among international principles). *See also id.* 12-13, 16, 35.
950. *Antin* Award, para. 316 (referring to *Phoenix v. Czech Republic*, para. 107 quoting Hersch Lauterpacht, *Development of International Law by the International Court* 164 (1958)). *See also Voltaic*, para. 266; *ICW*, para. 314; *Photovoltaik*, para. 255; and *WA Investments*, para. 333 (quoting *Phoenix v. Czech Republic*, para. 107).
951. *Renta4* Award, para. 181; *Masdar* Award, paras. 281-2, 292; *Antin* Award, para. 314 (equating bona fide directly with good faith). *See also Novenergia v. Spain* Award, para. 162.
952. *Voltaic*, para. 266; *ICW*, para. 314; *Photovoltaik*, para. 255; and *WA Investments*, para. 333.
953. *Yukos* Award, para. 1437 (quoting to *RosInvest* Award, para. 628). *See also Antin* Award, paras. 314 and 316.
954. *Antin* Award, para. 316 (referring to *Phoenix v. The Czech Republic*, Award, ICSID Case No. ARB/06/05, Apr. 15, 2009, para. 107 [hereinafter "*Phoenix*"], quoting Hersch Lauterpacht, Development of International Law by the International Court, London, 1958, p. 164).
955. *Phoenix*, paras. 107 & 112-13 (referring also to *Plama* Award adopting a dual review under the treaty and under domestic law).
956. *See Antin* Award, paras. 314 & 316.

not bona fide, is it not reasonable that the state may similarly not invoke a tax exclusion to exclude all tax matters from the protection of the treaty when such taxes are not bona fide?

From the existing ECT case law, there is a uniform consensus that establishing that a tax is not bona fide (or that the tax is *male fide*) is an elevated standard, likely difficult to establish.[957] In *Yukos*, the conduct of the state was deemed to be so extreme so as to find that the measures were patently confiscatory and had no relationship to fiscal policy. The operative standard for bona fide taxation was deemed as: "actions that are motivated by the purpose of *raising general revenue* for the State."[958] In *Yukos*, the tribunal found that the alleged tax measures of the state, even if validated by the domestic courts, had the purpose of "mainly to impose massive liabilities based on VAT and related fines, and were essentially aimed at paralyzing Yukos rather than collecting taxes."[959] Further cases determined that *Yukos* involved "extraordinary circumstances" or "extraordinary conduct" by the state.[960] To date, no other case outside of *Yukos* has found similar conduct in the acts of the state.

The ECT cases that followed the inquiry adopted the *Yukos* ECT award for purposes of jurisdiction, further finding that the high threshold for bona fide review was not met despite a wide variety of arguments: the funds did not flow into the public treasury but into the electricity system,[961] in the presence of public statements[962] and ambiguous public statements by high officials responsible for energy issues,[963] and even when local government challenged the constitutionality of the dispute supplemented by the EU Commission inquiry into the nature of the tax.[964]

The matter is further complicated by the fact that the *Yukos* ECT award delved into the bona fide inquiry for purposes of jurisdiction, namely whether the claims fell under the tax exclusion/carve-out.[965] However, the previous *Yukos* BIT cases addressed the bona fide inquiry for purposes of substantive review, namely whether the measures constituted expropriation.[966] Although the bona fide inquiry for purposes of indirect expropriation and jurisdiction may overlap, these inquiries remain as two different inquiries, especially considering that the jurisdictional inquiry would deprive the tribunal of its jurisdiction.

---

957. *See, e.g., Eiser* Award, para. 269. *Novenergia* Final Award, para. 522 ("the evidentiary threshold incumbent on the Claimant is high"). *SolEs*, para. 273 ("The Tribunal agrees with Respondent that this explicit tax carve-out could only be overridden in extraordinary circumstances.").
958. *Yukos* Award, para. 1407 (emphasis added).
959. *Yukos* Award, para. 1444.
960. *Compare Yukos* Award, para. 1407; *Renta4*, para. 179 and *RosInvest* Final Award, para. 628 *with Eiser* Award, paras. 268-9, 271, *Masdar* Award, paras. 284-5, *Antin* Award, para. 322. *See also SolEs*, para. 276.
961. *9Ren* Award, para. 202.
962. *Eiser* Award, para. 269 (tribunal defining the objections of claimants as to the public statement as "too slender a reed to sustain Claimant's case").
963. *Antin* Award, para. 319 (discussing the comments of José Manuel Soria, the Spanish Minister of Industry, Energy and Commerce as not being "even a close call" when he commented on "a series of general measures" but opted for TVPEE to address the budget deficit).
964. *RREEF Infrastructure* Decision on Merits, para. 189.
965. *Yukos* Award, para. 1407("the Tribunal finds that, in any event, the carve-out of Art. 21(1) can apply only to bona fide taxation actions").
966. *See RosInvest* Final Award, paras. 454-5, 497 & 567. *Renta 4* Award, paras. 45 and 48.

But, is "raising general revenue for the state" a sufficiently clear standard to characterize what a bona fide tax is? The inquiry centers on whether the tax measure has anything to do with the raising revenue. Under the *Yukos* standard, if the tax raises revenue, then the tax is bona fide. If not, then the tax is *male fide* and, based on the *Yukos* BIT cases, may amount to indirect expropriation or another breach of the treaty's substantive provisions. However, the focus on "revenue generation" may miss a number of seemingly valid taxes passed within the state's legitimate exercise of its regulatory powers and falling within its sovereignty over fiscal matters. For example, Pigouvian taxes will remain a difficult anomaly to account for in a legal standard. A Pigouvian tax is by definition a tax on negative externalities aimed to mitigate its effects.[967] A Pigouvian tax that brings less revenue than a sales tax will not have the purpose of "raising general revenue" but instead curb certain negative behavior.

So on the one hand, the state may properly adopt Pigouvian taxes. *Kügele* and *Cook* both point to the proposition that states may enact taxes without violating any guaranteed treaty obligations. As seen above, states are permitted to enact Pigouvian taxes and not lose the benefit of the tax being a bona fide tax. For example, tax measures on high-fructose corn syrup may be reasonable for combating high rates of diabetes, but not when these are implemented in a discriminatory fashion aimed at targeting investors.[968] On the other hand, a measure that is aimed to eliminate a public opponent may, in fact, be quite effective in generating "revenue" for the state, particularly since it would put private assets to the disposal of the state.

In *Antaris* and the *Voltaic* cases, the *Yukos* general standard was fine-tuned to inquire into the "main objective" of the measure.[969] In these cases, the ECT Article 21 Tax Exclusion/Carve-Out did not apply to "measures the main objective of which was *other than* that of the raising of general revenue for the State."[970] The discussion into the true nature of a tax incorporates the *EnCana* inquiry, where the dispositive inquiry focused on the "legal operation" not the "economic effect" of the tax.[971] An examination of the "legal operation" of a tax, as establishing the actual "intent" of a tax, requires heavy and conclusive evidence of wrongdoing from the state. Hence, inquiring into the "main objective" of a measure and the classification of the measures in terms of "other than raising general revenue" enable tribunals to account for the reality that taxes are not passed in a political vacuum.

Would a tax that misses its mark on its objectives (environmental purpose, curbing certain behavior, etc.) fail to be bona fide? The answer is: likely not. Although

967. *See generally Pigouvian Taxes, Externalities: What to Do When the Interests of Iindividuals and Society Do Not Coincide?*, The Economist, Aug. 19, 2017.
968. *See, e.g., Marvin Roy Feldman Karpa v. United Mexican States*, Award, ICSID Case No. ARB(AF)/99/1, Dec. 16, 2002 paras. 101, 103 & 116; Cargill v. Mexico, ICSID Case No. ARB(AF)/05/2, Sept. 18, 2009, paras. 220 & 297; *Archer Daniels Midland and Tate & Lyle Ingredients Americas, Inc. v. United Mexican States*, Award, ICSID Case No. ARB(AF)/04/5, Nov. 21, 2007 paras. 142 & 209-12; Corn Products Int'l v. United Mexican States, Decision on Responsibility, Jan. 15, 2008, paras. 137-8.
969. *Voltaic*, para. 265; *ICW*, para. 313; *Photovoltaik*, para. 254; and *WA Investments*, para. 332.
970. *Antaris* Award, para. 248. *Voltaic*, para. 265; *ICW*, para. 313; *Photovoltaik*, para. 254; and *WA Investments*, para. 332 (emphasis added).
971. *EnCana* Award, para. 142.

the standard of "raising general revenue for the State" remains to be developed, it is likely, based on the existing case law, that a tax aimed at generating revenue for the state would be found valid even if it falls short of its objectives and even if there are better means to achieve the aims.[972] In finding that a measure was not a tax, the split *Antaris* tribunal held that even if the alleged measures attempted to reduce the feed-in-tariffs, they would not be deemed to be enacted in bad faith.[973]

The approach emerging from the ECT case law appears most reasonable. States may freely pass tax measures even when the aim is expressly to curb certain behavior (e.g., Pigouvian taxes) or when the tax measures do not succeed in the purported aim. Tax income is necessary for the health and survival of a modern state, setting annual budgets and fiscal priorities being intermixed with rich political discourse reflecting countervailing policy objectives. As a complex machine, a modern state, regardless of being democratic or authoritarian, carries expenses and these expenses are met with government-raised revenue by means of taxation.[974] Shifting political objectives do not invalidate a tax, unless such shifting objectives are consolidated and patently passed with an ill intent as found in *Yukos*.

A degree of pragmatism is thus required. The bona fide inquiry is not into whether some unlawful or bad faith elements materialized during the complexity of implementation, administration or levying of a tax, but rather whether the tax per se is a tax in bad faith.[975] In *Yukos*, collection of taxes may be deemed a legitimate aim but the manner in which the state acted provided "compelling evidence" that the state was not interested in "good faith collection exercise but rather was intent on confiscating [...]."[976] The *Yukos* cases, both the ECT and BIT serve as outliers where the state conduct rose to such a high threshold that, in the opinion of the arbitral tribunals, the measures could not be deemed as a reasonable tax. None of the cases before *Yukos* confronted this inquiry. The renewable cases that followed unsuccessfully sought to fall within the same threshold, namely the reduction in subsidies by means of taxation measures was argued as *male fide*. Neither adverse comments by ministers nor contradictory statements, as argued in the Spanish cases, rise to the high threshold of conduct that was deemed unlawful in *Yukos*. Even where the set-aside of the *Yukos* cases may put in doubt the binding effect of these awards, the bona fide inquiry has gained traction.

---

972. *See generally Masdar* Award, para. 290 ("there are undoubtedly questions that might be raised by economic effects and the purpose of the Levy"). *See also Cube Infrastructure*, paras. 225-6. *9Ren* Award, paras. 202-3 (addressing claimant's objections that the connection between TVPEE to renewable energy was "laughable"). *RREEF Infrastructure* Decision on Merits, para. 190.
973. *Antaris* Award, para. 253.
974. Even in states with low fiscal deficits (e.g., Saudi Arabia), some taxation of corporations or application of excised taxation is mandatory even when direct tax on individuals is not used. *See generally* Deloitte LLC, International Tax Saudi Arabia Highlights 2019, Apr. 2019; http://www2.deloitte.com (Accessed: May 30, 2020).
975. *See Novenergia* Award, para. 524.
976. *Yukos* Award, para. 980 (refusal to entertain settlement proposals "raises doubts").

[5] Qualification under Domestic Law and Treaties

Referring to the four aforementioned inquiries (as presented in Figure 5.3), the next review is into the separate inquiries under the BIT and domestic law, namely the relationship between the two bodies of law. The determinative consideration is when a matter is deemed to be considered a tax under domestic law but its application is questionable in the larger international context, or vice versa.

A prerequisite for a tax exclusion to apply in the first place is that it needs to qualify as a tax under the domestic regime. ECT Article 21(7)(a) incorporates the rudimentary principle that in order for a measure to fall within the scope of the treaty (e.g., exclusion/carve-out), it needs to meet domestic law requirements. The section does not conclusively define what a "tax measure" is.[977] Although the section is not conclusive on what domestic law shall apply ("of the domestic law of the Contracting Party"), a reasonable interpretation is that it is the law of the host state.

Aside from the ambiguity in the term "tax" relative to "taxation measures" addressed below, the qualification of a measure under domestic law appears not only reasonable but also inherent in the scope of the application of the treaty. The inquiry invites a two-step analysis: first, the alleged measure needs to be reviewed for a prima facie standard, whether it qualifies as a taxation measure under the binding definition applicable to the parties (be it domestic law, treaty, or contract definition).[978] The second inquiry is into the *true nature* of the alleged taxation measure: is the measure what it is purported to be. In the Czech cases, this two-step principle was critical because the measures did not qualify even under the first leg of the inquiry.[979] In finding that the measure was not a tax under domestic law, the Czech tribunals did not have to proceed to an inquiry into the bona fide nature of the tax. For purposes of investment arbitration, the principle of bona fide taxation emerges from *Yukos*, where the application of the national taxation regime to investors came specifically into question.[980]

Any conflict or potential ambiguity in the treatment of such measures within the national legal regime would inadvertently bar the state from invoking the measure as an exclusion. The issue of how the tax was treated under domestic law came to a junction in the Czech cases where the decisions of the local courts (Supreme Administrative Court and Constitutional Court) contained ambiguities on the treatment of the alleged taxation measure (Solar Levy).[981] Even where the concurrent opinion disagreed on the extent of the binding precedential value of this misalignment in the domestic case law, the requirement of clarity in the domestic law on the alleged measure

977. *See BayWa*, para. 298. *See also Stadtwerke*, para. 161.
978. *Voltaic*, para. 249; *ICW*, para. 297; *Photovoltaik*, para. 238; and *WA Investments*, para. 316.
979. *See generally Antaris* Award, para. 224 ("a two-step analysis is required: a characterization under domestic law followed by an application of Article 21's inherent limits"); *Voltaic*, para. 260; *ICW*, para. 308; *Photovoltaik*, para. 249; and *WA Investments*, para. 327. *See also Antin* Award, para. 316 (referring to *Phoenix*, para. 112 adopting the two-step inquiry into the bona fide inquiry under domestic law and treaty law from *Plama*).
980. *See Yukos* Award, para. 1407. *See also RosInvest* Final Award, paras. 628 (referring *inter alia* to Restatement (Third) of Foreign Relations, *Occidental* Award, para. 85 and *Too*, para. 387).
981. *See, e.g., Antaris* Award, paras. 241-2.

becomes intuitive.[982] For a state to be able to invoke a measure as falling within its power to tax, the measure actually needs to be *unambiguously* a tax under domestic law, or otherwise qualify under the treaty. By means of otherwise qualifying under the treaty, the tax provisions may also be directly drawn or arising from an international agreement in which the host state is bound, commonly via a double taxation agreement.[983] In principle, any tax commitment binding on a state *ought to* be ratified or otherwise incorporated in the domestic regime so it forms a part of the domestic law of the host state. For this reason, meeting the domestic requirement is but the first step and a precondition, when such is specified in the treaty, for the measure to fall within the scope of the treaty.

[6] Burden of Proof

Given the ambiguity in the review of what it means to have a bona fide measure, the burden of proof in the application of the Tax Exclusion may be an outcome-determinative consideration. Does the state need to establish that a measure is devoid of any ambiguity as to its scope, purpose, and application? Or, does the investor need to establish an abuse of rights or some sort of bad faith to offset the presumption of validity?

The logical first step for the presentation of evidence sets the burden of proof on the party asserting a specific proposition.[984] This simplified rule, despite building on a logical assumption, balances contravening interests. In investment arbitration, the claimants have the obligation to establish the breach of a treaty. However, a tax exclusion is invoked exclusively in a defensive manner by states, thereby imposing on the state the onus of establishing that any given measure falls outside the scope of the treaty.

The starting point for the jurisdictional objection is that the respondent state retains the burden of establishing the legal and factual grounds for the application of the exclusion.[985] For the invocation of a defense, states shall at a minimum establish that the measure constitutes a valid taxation measure, under domestic law, triggering

982. *See id.* (concurrent opinion Tomka).

983. *See, e.g.*, ECT Art. 21(7)(a)(ii). So far no taxation measures have been invoked on the principle that they met a DTT or international agreement; those measures invoked by investors have been exclusively generated and levied by states on their own initiatives.

984. The Mavrommatis Jerusalem Concessions [1925] PCIJ (ser A) No 5 para. 65. *See* Swedish Arbitration Act, para. 25 line 1. *See also Foreign Investment Disputes: Cases, Materials and Commentary* (W. Michael Reisman et al. eds., 2d ed. 2014) Chap. 12.07.C (quoting and discussing Karl-Heinz Bockstiegel, *Presenting Evidence in International Arbitration*, Foreign Int'l L.J. 16(1), 2-3 (2001) and Charles N. Brower, *Evidence Before International Tribunals: The Need for Some Standard Rules*, 28 Int'l Law 47, 49 (1994)).

985. *See Yukos* Award, para. 1441 ("for a measure to come under the treaty's carve-out, it would have to be 'sufficiently clearly connected to' or supported by some taxation law, regulation or actual practice (the latter of which would in turn have to be based on a taxation law or regulation)").

the tax exclusion of a treaty such as the ECT.[986] As seen in the Czech cases, the state shall establish the validity of such measure under domestic law unequivocally. Any material ambiguity arising out of local practice would hinder the application of the court rules. The domestic standard may be met by *preponderance of evidence* in reference to local court rules, the definition of the measure, use of domestic statutory instruments, etc. Pending challenge proceedings ought not to be sufficient proof unless a court has ruled convincingly that a measure is not a tax.

Tribunals seized to determine the issue of bona fide taxation measures have reaffirmed that states enjoy great deference on the validity of a taxation issue.[987] These findings are reasonable, as taxes need to serve a public purpose. As later fine-tuned in *Masdar* and *RREEF Infrastructure* tribunals, a tax may miss the mark on promoting environmental matters and instead only reduce the budget deficit,[988] but this discrepancy does not need to bring a tax outside the scope of a tax exclusion.[989] The threshold is easily achieved when considering that reduction of budget deficit and combating tax evasion fall squarely within the public purpose.

The question turns on whether a respondent does still bear the burden of proof when a valid tax, under domestic law, is called into question for being passed under the "guise of taxation" and not being linked to revenue.[990] In *Yukos*, the host state implemented the disputed tax measures on the grounds of curbing abusive tax practices and punishing tax evasion.[991] These measures were upheld by local courts.[992] The logical conclusion is that the claimant has the interest and the ability to prove the contrary, namely to disprove that a domestically valid taxation measure shall not fall under the review of an investment tribunal.

The standard for such review shall be expressly argued by the investor: whether a showing of bad faith or abuse by the state is required, or a lower standard should be justified by being linked to raising "general revenue." In a similar manner, claimants will possess the factual background to cast doubt on the presumption of validity of domestic norms unless the treaties expressly contain an additional requirement. In the absence of an additional standard that the states need to meet in order to avail themselves of the treaty, the claimant bears the burden to disprove that a valid domestic measure shall not bear the benefits of a tax exclusion under the treaty.

986. *See Voltaic*, para. 244 ("it is clear that the Respondent bears the burden of proof of establishing that the Solar Levy may be characterized as a 'provision relating to taxes of the domestic law' within the meaning of Article 21(7)(a)(i) of the ECT").
987. *See RosInvest* Final Award, para. 580; *see also Novenergia* Award, paras. 522 and 524. *Masdar* Award, para. 285. *Isolux* Award, para. 739.
988. *See, e.g., Masdar* Award, paras. 290 and 291. *RREEF Infrastructure* Decision on Merits, para. 190 ("[i]t might be true that the Respondent could have used other means than a fixed tax levy to achieve its policy objective"). *See even Greentech et al v. Spain* Award, para. 258 ("the economic analysis of a measure should not displace a finding that a measure is a tax as a matter of law").
989. *Yukos* Award, para. 1407.
990. *Yukos* Award, para. 1407.
991. *See, e.g., Yukos* Award, paras. 73 and 109 ff. (Russian Federation alleged criminal fraud and tax evasion).
992. *See Yukos* Award, paras. 92 and 521.

In such manner, a *shifting burden of proof* is inescapable. A valid domestic tax measure may be presumed to be bona fide, unless proven otherwise. A large number of already-decided Spanish cases have clustered around a presumption of validity of tax measures once determined under domestic law, thereby shifting the burden to the claimants to invalidate the said rule or to refute the presumption altogether.[993] Figure 5.4 reveals the different steps by which the various layers for a taxation-related review, such as the one applicable for ECT, apply.

Figure 5.4 Shifting Burden of Proof in Multilayered Tax Provisions

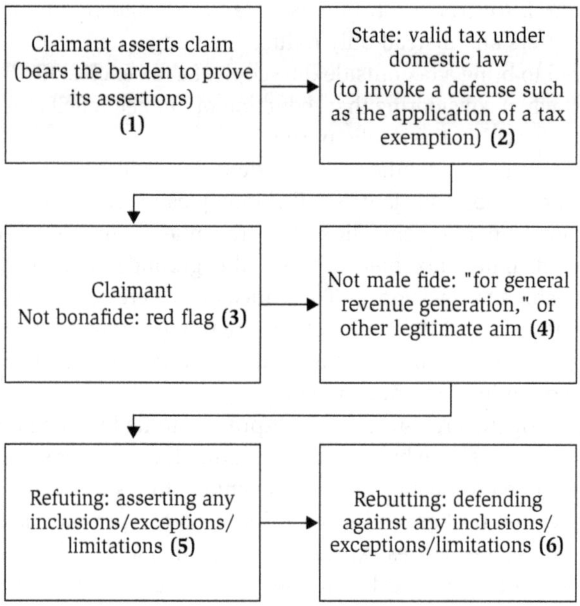

Source: Author's Own.

In Step 1, claimant bears the burden of establishing the basis for a valid arbitration (existence of the offer to arbitrate in a treaty). In Step 2, respondent bears the burden to establish that the matters linked to a *valid domestic tax measure* shall be excluded, consistent with the restrictive application of the principle of good faith in line with "a notion of good faith restrained."[994] Most of the cases support this proposition, except for *Stati*. In *Stati*, the tribunal held that the burden of proof remained on the

993. *See* Stephan Schill, *Ordering Paradigms in International Investment Law: Bilateralism-Multilateralism-Multilateralization*, *in The Foundations of International Investment Law: Bringing Theory into Practice* 109-141, 125 (Zachary Douglas, Joost Pauwelyn and Jorge E. Viñuales eds., 2014) ("While precedent, in this view, does not bind later tribunals, it shifts the burden of argumentation by demanding a reasoned justification for departing from established precedent [...]").

994. *See generally* Schill and Bray, *supra* note 947, at 89-90.

respondent. *Stati* is a distinguishable case since there the respondent did not invoke ECT Article 21(1) on alleged taxation matters. The tribunal was then correct in holding that the burden of proof for invoking the exclusionary properties of the taxation matters remained squarely with the respondent.

Steps 3 through 5 could be deemed as one step or several steps. Only after a prima facie case is made on the basis of the tax exclusion such as ECT Article 21(1) would the burden shift to claimant to prove that the claim is not bona fide or that should otherwise be included in the review of the tribunal. A tax measure need not be perfectly aligned on its purpose and scope, but it needs to be valid under domestic legislation. Claimant would receive back the proverbial "hockey puck" then to establish that the alleged domestic tax measure shall not enjoy the benefits of the treaty. In Step 3, the investor could point to the unreasonableness of the measures for the burden to shift back to the state to prove a level of legitimacy.[995] Step 4 would then have the state clarify the bona fide scope: whether the legitimate scope for general revenue or as seen above, for any other purpose that would be reasonable under the circumstances. Only after such argument could be made, in Step 5, as seen in the Spanish cases, the investor would have the burden to refute the assertions made by the state, or for establishing that the measure falls under the particular inclusion which would trigger the state to defend against the application of the limitation and inclusion/clawback in Step 6.

[D] Interpretation and Definitional Conundrums

[1] General

What is in a definition? When it comes to tax and taxation matters, the definitions may determine the outcome of the objection to tribunal's jurisdiction over taxation matters. In ECT and non-ECT tax-related cases alike, tribunals inquired into the term for purposes of determining the *scope* of the tax. While ECT Article 21(1) refers to "Taxation Measures," ECT Article 21(5) inclusion refers to "taxes." The issue is further accentuated by the fact that in the Italian and French translations of the treaty the translate terms for "taxes" and "taxation measures" are further intertwined[996] despite the different authenticated versions of the treaty having the same weight.[997]

[2] Ordinary Meaning

Whether the tax was passed "in good faith" is interlinked to the ordinary meaning of the term "tax." The term "taxes" is notably left undefined in the ECT;[998] hence, the inquiry focuses on the ordinary meaning of the term. VCLT Article 31(1) incorporates

995. *See infra* §6.02 for why a shifting burden of proof based on the existence of red flags should be applied.
996. *See infra* 5.03[D][5]. The Italian and French versions use the term for "taxation measures" for purposes of the specified inclusion in ECT Art. 21(5).
997. ECT Art. 50.
998. *See generally Yukos*, para. 1411; *Greentech v. Spain* Award, para. 253.

the teleological[999] and hermeneutic approaches[1000] by which the term shall be interpreted in "good faith" in accordance with the "ordinary meaning" of the term examined "in their context" and taking into account the "object and purpose" of the treaty.[1001]

The term "taxation measures" is not difficult to assess in the ECT context. It is well defined in ECT Article 21(7)(a) linking it to domestic and DTT definitions. But its relationship to a basic "tax" is harder to assess. In fact, the term "tax" has been evasive in public international law containing legal, fiscal and economic characteristics. In the ECT, the term tax is left undefined, left uncapitalized, pointing to a general textual definition. So the hermeneutic approach would require that the term be interpreted in its most authentic textual form.

The "purpose" of the ECT is found in ECT Article 2 linking the establishment of a legal framework to: (1) promotion of "long-term cooperation" in the energy field, (2) on the basis of "complimentaries and mutual benefits," and (3) by cross-referencing to "the objectives and principles of the Charter."[1002] The "objectives" of the Charter build on three pillars: (1) development of trade, (2) cooperation, and (3) energy efficiency and environmental protection. In such manner, the term should be interpreted in the context of promoting "long-term cooperation" on the principles of "complimentaries and mutual benefits" of the parties, while relying on the three pillars of the Charter.

In the Spanish cases, the tribunals were seized with the question of looking "behind the label" of a tax.[1003] Although tribunals commonly dismissed the allegation that it should look into the subjective intent of the tax,[1004] the definition of a tax became highly relevant and tribunals differed in their approach. In most of the Spanish cases, even claimants accepted that the TVPEE is a tax under the international standard.[1005] However, the Spanish cases differ dramatically on the use of the *EnCana* standard and the interrelationship of this standard with the bona fide standard. The approaches range from leaving open the application of the good faith inquiry altogether,[1006] to linking bona fide taxation to the general definition of the tax[1007] or often distinguishing the good faith inquiry and the general definition of a tax as two separate inquiries.[1008]

999. *See generally* ILC Draft Articles of the Law of the Treaties with commentaries, Yearbook of the Int'l L. Comm. Vol. II 218 (1966) (comment to the old Arts. 27 and 28; new VCLT Arts. 31 and 32).
1000. For the "hermeneutic sensibility" in jurisprudence, *see generally* JHH Weiler, *The Interpretation of Treaties—A Re-examination Preface,* The European J. Int'l L. 21: 3, 507 (2010).
1001. VCLT Art. 31(1).
1002. ECT Art. 2.
1003. *Greentech et al v. Spain* Award, para. 255. *See also Antin* Award, paras. 290, 303-4.
1004. *See, e.g., Greentech et al v. Spain* Award, para. 257. In *Greentech v. Spain,* the tribunal dismissed the argument that it should examine the "legal and economic effect" instead of respondent's "subjective intent."
1005. *See, e.g., Eiser* Award, para. 266.
1006. *See Greentech et al. v. Spain* Award, para. 259 ("Even if the Tribunal were to interpret Article 21(1) ECT as applying only to 'bona fide' tax measures (*which the Tribunal does not decide*)") (emphasis added).
1007. *9Ren* Award, para. 195 (incorporating the element of "raising general revenue" from *Yukos* into the definition of tax).
1008. *See, e.g., Antin* Award, para. 314 (holding that a matter that meets domestic and international law may still be excluded "in exceptional circumstances" where good faith is absent).

Among the Spanish cases at least, a consensus emerges on the definition of a tax binding claimants and the Spanish state.[1009] Drawn from the *EnCana* standard, the tax definition in the Spanish cases draws on three to four elements: (1) obligation settled in domestic law, (2) application on a class of people, (3) payment to the state, and (4) public purpose.[1010] In *Eiser* and *9Ren*, the tribunal distinguished the "payment of money" to include "generat[ing] revenue" bringing the inquiry closer to the *Yukos* standards.[1011] In *Cube Infrastructure*, the prong that the payment needs to be for a "public purpose" was adjusted to include the requirement of non-reciprocity ("unrequited transfer").[1012] In *OperaFund*, the three-prong standard is deemed to be the definition of "a tax under international law."[1013] This reciprocity element from *Cube* materializes in cases where the domestic standard is called into question: the Czech cases under domestic law where it is found to be lacking, and in two Italian cases, including in *Greentech* where it is also found to be lacking in the administrative charges.[1014]

[3] Toward a Definition

Examining the definition of a term through the teleological inquiry does not dispose of the requirement of examining the "ordinary meaning of the term," thus conducting a hermeneutic inquiry. The number of definitions of the ordinary meaning of the term "taxation" could extend in countless categories covering economic and religious definitions;[1015] for purposes of this inquiry six sets of definitions are categorized in three categories, as described in Table 5.11: fiscal, legal/textual, and investment-specific. The six relevant definitions for purposes of defining the "ordinary meaning" of the term are those discussed or defined in the following: OECD, IBFD, *Black's Law Dictionary*, *Renta4*, *EnCana*, and the Spanish Cases as below.

1009. *Eiser* Award, para. 266; *Greentech v. Spain* Award, para. 255 (noting that the parties "broadly agreed" on the application of the *EnCana* test).
1010. *Eiser* Award, para. 266; *Cube* Partial Decision, para. 230. *NextEra* Partial Decision, para. 372. *9Ren* Award, paras. 198-202.
1011. *Eiser* Award, para. 266. *9Ren* Award, para. 195.
1012. *Cube* Partial decision, para. 229 ("to pay money to the State for public purposes and without any benefit to the taxpayer").
1013. *OperaFund*, para. 404.
1014. *Greentech et al. v. Italy* Award, para. 244. *See also Belenergia* Award, para. 370. Note that the Italian cases differ on whether the administrative charge is a tax or not. *See supra* Chapter 5.05.
1015. *See supra* §3.02[A] (discussing the OECD, IBFD and the *Black's Law Dictionary*).

Table 5.11 Definitions of Tax

Origin	*Type*	*Definition*
OECD	*Tax-heavy*	*Compulsory unrequited payment to general government.*
IBFD	*Tax-heavy*	*A government levy that is not in return for a specific benefit and is not imposed by way of a fine or penalty (e.g., for non-compliance with the law), except in some cases where it corresponds to tax-related offences.*
Black's Law Dictionary	*Textual / Legal*	*A charge, usu. monetary, imposed by the government on persons, entities, transactions, or property to yield public revenue.[...] Although a tax is often thought of as being pecuniary in nature, it is not necessarily payable in money.*
Renta4	*ITA: Non-ECT*	*The tax is the payment of a debt established by law in favour of the public treasury [...].*
EnCana	*ITA: Non-ECT*	*Caxation law is one which imposes a liability on classes of persons to pay money to the State for public purposes.*
Spanish Cases	*ITA: ECT*	that the tax be laid-down by law; that such law imposes an obligation on a class of people; and that such obligation involves paying money to the State for public purposes. 9Ren distinguishes the "payment of money" to include "generates money that goes to the state." OperaFund: deemed to be the definition of a tax under international law.

Source: Author's Own.

Various definitions contain similar elements: they center on a mandatory payment obligation required by the state authorities for purposes of a legitimate purposes. The pure tax definition also contains a non-reciprocal element.[1016]

In the fiscal context as materialized in domestic definitions, there is an element of reciprocity, or at least absence thereof, that is fundamental in the tax-heavy definition of a "tax" found by the OECD and IBFD. According to the OECD/IBFD definition, a tax must be "unrequited," namely, the taxpayer may not derive a benefit from the tax. The "unrequited" manner thereby distinguishes a tax from access fees, union fees, or for a direct service received. For example, an excise remains a tax even though the revenue from excises on fuel taxes may be used to combat climate change.[1017] Such benefit from excises is widespread and is not specific to the taxpayer. Often, the benefit may be less evident for the subject paying the tax. With "grid fees," the power suppliers pay grid operators "grid fees" which are ultimately passed to the consumers. "Grid fees" may compensate for infrastructure costs as well as administrative costs, metering or

1016. *See, e.g.,* OECD and IBFD definitions.

1017. *See, e.g.,* in *9Ren,* the tribunal discusses a tax on cigarettes being used to combat the adverse effects of smoking. *9Ren* Award, para. 203.

surcharges.[1018] The consumers may likely draw a direct reciprocal benefit from metering or administrative support (e.g., phone line support), but less so from overarching infrastructure and maintenance support that is meant to be covered by public funds.

The element of non-reciprocity need not be controversial and it is certainly present in the existing case law. In *Yukos*, the investors did not derive a reciprocal element from the imposition of the alleged tax measures. Existing case law has incorporated this provision under the domestic review, as it is the case with the Italian and Czech cases. But the element of non-reciprocity would enable the definition to incorporate the Pigouvian tax scenario, as well as the grid fees without straining the "public purpose" requirement of a tax. In any event, the Spanish cases and the OECD/IBFD are not divergent from each other; an overarching definition would involve incorporating several elements, including the "unrequited/non-reciprocity requirement" along the following lines:

> a compulsory unrequited payment, as mandated by law, to general government for a public purpose.

[4] Tax and Taxation Matters: One Broader or Narrower Than the Other

The term "tax" adopts a general definition whereas "taxation measures" appear specific and assumes a formal qualified act. In principle, the ordinary meaning of the terms indicate that they could be used as synonyms, much like "drinks" and "beverages." The complexity is accentuated by the fact that whereas "taxation measures" is a defined term, "tax" is not.[1019] The ECT *travaux* do not provide clarity except for the determination that the change was done quickly in the ECT Tax Subgroup without much explanation.

Two competing interpretations came into conflict in *Yukos*: namely the position of the investors that a tax should not be interpreted to be more restrictive than that for "Taxation Measures," against that of the respondent where "Taxation Measure" is meant to include taxes.[1020]

Interpretation 1: (investor in Yukos*)*

"Tax" in ECT Article 21(5) is broader than the exclusion because it envisions a broader scope of coverage than the exclusion for purposes of resolving any alleged discriminatory measures under DTT by reference to CTAs.

1018. *See generally* Sören Amelang, *Power Grid Fees—Unfair and Opaque*, Clean Energy Wire, Jan. 26, 2017; https://www.cleanenergywire.org (Accessed: May 30, 2020).
1019. *Cf. BayWa*, para. 298 ("taxation measure" is deemed not defined under ECT but its definition includes certain activity).
1020. *See generally* MENA Note 13, *supra* note 199, paras. 52-8.

Interpretation 2: (respondent in Yukos*)*

"Taxation Measure" in ECT Article 21(5) is broader than the exclusion because it envisions a broader scope of application, as argued by the Russian Federation in *Yukos*.

In such context, the reasoning of the *Yukos* tribunal yields the possibility of a third interpretation; namely on how to treat defined and undefined terms under the treaty that could be interpreted as synonyms. In such instance, the two terms retain a distinct categorization, as delineated in Figure 5.5. The defined term under the treaty retains the definitional elements prescribed by the treaty: in the case of "Taxation Measure" the requirement that the measure qualifies as such under domestic law or DTT. The undefined term under the treaty retains the generic elements of the term, including those elements that are unqualified (e.g., not falling within the qualified definition). By having a generic and non-generic definition, the treaty permits the review of the domestic acts as expropriation without the tribunal ruling expressly on the validity of the domestic laws. Such holding would be precisely in line with ECT's object and purpose where the tribunal may review the expropriatory/confiscatory nature of a purportedly valid tax/taxation measure under domestic law without passing judgment on the validity of the domestic taxation measure. The *BayWa* decision appears to support such interpretation, namely by distancing the reasoning from the fact that one term is not broader or narrower than another but neither is properly defined.[1021] Hence, the third interpretation defined below may sufficiently reconcile the overlapping terms.

Interpretation 3: (Reconciled interpretation based on the Yukos *findings)*

"Taxation Measure" in ECT Art. 21(1) is used to cover "taxes" and vice versa "taxes" in ECT Art. 21(5) is meant to cover "Taxation Measures." However, the use of "Taxation Measure" is used as a qualified measure under domestic law or DT that would otherwise be limited to exclude specific measures linked to income or capital, whereas the definition of tax remains undefined and applicable to instances not covered by the "qualified" definition.

Figure 5.5 "Tax" and "Taxation Measures" under ECT

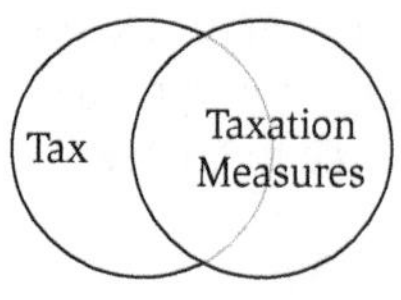

Source: Author's Own.

1021. *See BayWa*, paras. 298-300.

[5] On the Treaty in Different Languages

In accordance with ECT Article 50, the treaty was signed in six versions (English, Russian, French, German, Italian, and Spanish versions), each being "equally authentic."[1022] The English and Russian versions, which serve as the primary drafting and negotiation languages of the treaty, are consistent with each other. However, the other four versions of the treaty appearing in German,[1023] Spanish,[1024] French[1025] and Italian[1026] contain notable differences, of which the significant deviation is found in the Italian version. Given the different versions of the treaty, what is a tax and what is the relationship of a tax to taxation measures?

The six versions of the ECT reveal two deviations in the respective wordings of the chapter: (1) on the use of the word for "taxes" in expropriation inclusion/clawback and (2) the formulation of the direct taxation measures other than those on capital. Five versions of the treaty refer to the general term linked to ("taxes") for purposes of the expropriation to be distinguished from the defined term "Taxation Measures." The Italian version is the only one using taxation measures for both the tax exclusion and the expropriation inclusion/clawback. Both the French and the Italian versions use alternative wordings for defining the overarching "Taxation Measures." All versions of the treaty, save the French and the Italian versions, use the same term for the tax in the Article 21(7) definition as in Article 21(1) and 21(5). The French version refers to the "Taxation Measures" as "disposition fiscales" for purposes of the definition of Article 21(7) but "impots" for purposes of the expropriation exception in ECT Article 21(5). The Italian version introduces the term "imposte" for the definition but as seen above uses the term "misure fiscali" for both the tax exclusion and the expropriation exception. All four versions of the treaty, except for the English and the Russian versions, use various formulations for direct taxes. The French version refers specifically to "impots" when defining the Direct Tax Limitation, so as to describe taxation measures other than "taxes"/"income" on capital and income. The Spanish version does the same: it uses "impuestas" in the limitation. In both French and Spanish, the term used in the Direct Tax Limitation is the same as in the Tax Exclusion. The major deviation is in the German and the Italian versions where in German for the first two inclusions: where the pattern is the same as in French and Spanish; it uses "Stuern" in Direct Tax Limitation but "steuerliche Maßnahmen" for "Taxation Measures." In the final inclusion for interim provisions, the German version refers to the same pattern

---

1022. *See* ECT Art. 50; the treaty appears also in Japanese, Chinese, and Arabic translations. There is no indication that these versions are to be considered "authentic texts" as per VCLT Art. 33(2).

1023. The Russian version uses "**Налоговые Меры**" in ECT Article 21(1) and (7) whereas in ECT Article 21(5), it uses the generic term "**налоги**."

1024. The Spanish version uses "medida impositiva" in ECT Article 21(1) and (7) whereas in ECT Article 21(5), it uses the generic term "impuestos."

1025. The French version uses "mesures fiscales" in ECT Arts. 21(1) and 21(7) for taxation measures. While in ECT Art. 21(5), it refers to "impots" as taxes, in ECT Art. 21(7) it refers to "disposition fiscale" where the English version uses the term taxes.

1026. The Italian version uses "mesura fiscale" in ECT Article 21(1) and (5), whereas the definition of the taxation measure/"mesura fiscale" incorporates the term "imposte."

observed in the English and Russian terms "other than" without a reference to "taxes."[1027] Finally, the Italian version also contains a discrepancy in all three instances of the Direct Tax Limitation. Although the Italian version stays true to the English and Russian versions by not referring to taxes as a descriptive factor after "other than," the Italian version instead used two different terms for taxation measures in the context of the Direct Tax Limitation: "norme fiscale" and "misure fiscale" (Table 5.12).[1028]

1027. *See* ECT Art. 21(4), German version ("die nicht das Einkommen oder das Vermögen betreffen"). *Cf.* ECT Art. 21(2)-(3) where the term used is "*steuerliche Maßnahmen* mit Ausnahme der *Steuern* vom Einkommen oder vom Vermögen."
1028. ECT Art. 21(2)-(3) "misure fiscali diverse da quelle sul reddito o sul capitale." *Cf.* ECT Art. 21(4): "norme fiscali diverse da quelle del reddito o sul capitale."

Table 5.12 Comparison of the Various Versions of the ECT Taxation Chapter

	Article 21(1) Tax Exclusion	*Article 21(5) Expropriation Inclusion*	*Article 21(2)-(4) Direct Taxes*	*Article 21(7) Definition*	*Consistency Against English Version*
English	Taxation Measures	Taxes	– all three references use the same structure – Taxation Measures Other than those on income and capital	*Taxation Measures* in terms of *Taxes*	–
Russian	**"Налоговые Меры"**	**"Налоги"**	– all three references use the same structure – **"*налоговых мер* в отношении дохода или капитала"**	***Налоговая мера*** In terms of ***Налоги***	*Consistent*
French	"les mesures fiscales"	"Impôts"	– all three references use the same structure *But*: use of "impot" for purposes of defining the limitation – Mesures fiscales que les "*impots*" sur le revenu ou sur la fortune'	"Mesures fiscales" in terms of "*disposition fiscale*"	Not fully consistent: – definition uses a different term than in 21(5) – direct taxes adds reference to "taxes" (Art. 21(5))

	Article 21(1) Tax Exclusion	*Article 21(5) Expropriation Inclusion*	*Article 21(2)-(4) Direct Taxes*	*Article 21(7) Definition*	*Consistency Against English Version*
Spanish	"Medidas impositivas"	"Impuestos"	– all three references use the same structure *But*: use of "impuestas" for purposes of defining the limitation "Medidas distintas de los *impuestos* sobre la renta o el capital"	"Medida impositiva" in terms of "impuestos"	Not fully consistent: direct taxes adds reference to "taxes" (Art. 21(5))
German	steuerliche Maßnahmen	Steuern	"*steuerliche Maßnahmen* mit Ausnahme der *Steuern* vom Einkommen oder vom Vermögen" 21(2)-(3), but "*steuerliche Maßnahmen*, die nicht das Einkommen oder das Vermoögen betreffen"	steuerliche Maßnahme in terms of Steuer	Not fully consistent: direct taxes add reference to "taxes" for 21(2)-(3) but not 21(4)

Italian	"Misure fiscali"	"Misure fiscali"	21(2) and (3): "*misure fiscali* diverse da quelle sul reddito o sul capitale" 21(4): "*norme fiscali* diverse da quelle del reddito o sul capitale"	"Misure fiscali" in terms of "*imposte*"	*Not consistent*: major deviation in – 21(1) and 21(5) using the same term, instead as different terms – "misure fiscal and norme fiscali" used for the same term 21(4) cf. 21(2)-(3)

Source: Author's Own.

According to VCLT Article 33(1), each of these versions is authoritative given that the ECT lacks any clause giving some priority to one version in case of conflict. Although the terms are presumed to have the same meaning,[1029] in case of aberration, one is called to look again at the object and purpose of the treaty when reconciling the texts. Three cases used different approaches to dismiss the overreliance on the variations in the different versions, particularly with regard to the Italian version of the text: *Yukos*,[1030] *Greentech v. Italy*,[1031] and *Antaris*.[1032] The tribunals' findings of dismissing the discrepancies in the text support the position that the terms "tax" and "taxation measures" are in fact synonyms, subject to being substituted. Hence, it is reasonable to interpret the terms with the assistance of VCLT Article 33(4) to determine that the term used in the expropriation inclusion/clawback should be of a general unqualified nature whereas the one for the tax exclusion/carve-out to be of a qualified nature.

[E] Inclusions and Limitations

[1] Expropriation

The key inclusion in ECT Article 21 is the expropriation inclusion/clawback. The expropriation inclusions provide that the provisions on expropriation (ECT Article 13) shall apply to "taxes," as opposed to the term "Taxation Measures" used in the Taxation Exclusion.[1033] While the substantive scope of the expropriation inclusion in ECT Article 21(5) is succinct, the procedural mechanisms such as the referral mechanisms to the CTAs are more complex.

Since the 1990s, direct expropriations are rare as they require a formal transfer of title by an official act, which states are no longer brazen about to undertake.[1034] Besides *Yukos*, other ECT cases have not examined the nature of taxes as expropriatory measures. In *Yukos*, the tribunal deemed that the acts of the Russian state constituted an indirect expropriation ("measures having an effect 'equivalent to nationalization or expropriation'"), but as seen above, the alleged taxation measures were not bona fide.[1035] Regardless of the characterization of the measures, the actions of the state did

1029. *See* VCLT Art. 33(3).
1030. *Yukos* Award, para. 1415 (dismissing respondent's reliance of *travaux* pertaining to the different version of the drafts). For respondent's arguments, *see id.* paras. 1380 and 1389.
1031. *Greentech v. Italy* Award, para. 244 (the tribunal determines that it does not need to rule on the broad or narrow interpretations of the various versions of the treaty).
1032. *Antaris* Award, para. 246. Tribunal uses VCLT Art. 33(4).
1033. *See* ECT Art. 21(5).
1034. *See* Dolzer & Schreuer, *supra* note 54, at 101. *See also* Rudolf Dolzer, *ConocoPhillips v Venezuela and Gold Reserve v Venezuela: Expropriation: A New Focus on Old Issues*, 30(2) ICSID Review—Foreign Inv. L. J. 378-83, 378 (2015). *But cf. Kardassopoulos*, para. 408. Kardassopoulos is what has been described as a "classic" direct expropriation. *Id.* paras. 241, 386-408. *See also Conoco* Partial Decision, paras. 315-16, 359 (where direct expropriation is found).
1035. *Yukos* Award, para. 1580. *See also* Christopher S Gibson, *Yukos Universal Limited (Isle of Man) v The Russian Federation: A Classic Case of Indirect Expropriation*, 30(2) ICSID Rev.—Foreign Inv. L. J. 303-14, 304 (2015) (describing the "pragmatic approach" to indirect

not meet the requirements for a lawful expropriation: the public interest of the measure was questionable, the measures were deemed discriminatory, there was absence of due process of law and no compensation was granted.[1036] In *Yukos*, the tribunal's finding of an expropriation led to the tribunal not examining the allegations of the FET breach.[1037] The same set of circumstances did not amount to a finding of indirect expropriation in the ECHR proceedings, despite finding a breach of interference with property.[1038]

This book does not seek to embark on the impossible task to describe what constitutes an indirect expropriation for purposes of taxation; particularly since there are only a few ECT cases dealing with these issues. Nonetheless, some observations could still be made. As seen above, taxation issues materialize in the context of indirect or creeping expropriation, not direct expropriation.[1039] In the ECT case law, a finding of expropriation (irrespective of involving taxation or otherwise) remains rare.[1040] One explanation may be found in what Rudolf Dolzer has described a tendency by arbitral tribunals to find a breach of the FET standard rather than indirect expropriation.[1041] *Yukos* may very well stand as an outlier in the finding of indirect expropriation. The later ECT cases, such as the Spanish cases, reinforce the overreliance on the FET. This use of the FET standard, rather than indirect expropriation, means that taxation measures remain outside of the review of ECT tribunals while taxes would fall within the Tax Exclusion and not be covered by any other inclusions. Similarly, the BIT cases reveal a tendency to overly rely on the FET standard rather than indirect expropriation. For example, in *Occidental I*, the tribunal found a breach of the FET but could not

expropriation). For a general discussion of substantive protections in pre-Spanish cases, *see* Ali Lazem, The treatment of Tax in Investor State Arbitration of Expropriation and National Treatment Protection, PhD Dissertation, Brunel Law School at 106 (2014); http://www.bura.brunel.ac.uk (Accessed: May 30, 2020).

1036. *Yukos* Award, paras. 1581-5.

1037. Rarely would a tribunal be seized with "exceptional circumstances" as found in *Yukos*, where the entire mechanism set in motion would be motivated by taxation measures. Taxation would seldom be the investor's main claim. The cases (ECT and non-ECT cases alike) reveal the opposite pattern: where a finding of FET deemed a review of expropriation unnecessary. As observed in *Murphy II* and *Stati*, a finding of a breach of other standards would make the expropriation review often unnecessary. *See Murphy II* Award, paras. 29-32 and *Stati* Award, paras. 1095 and 1203-5.

1038. OAO Neftyanaya Kompaniya Yukos v Russia App no 14902/04, Judgment (Just Satisfaction) (ECtHR, July 31, 2014), para. 756 (dismissing the allegation of indirect expropriation). Eric De Brabandere, *supra* note 458, at 351 (discussing the ECtHR rejecting the finding of indirect expropriation).

1039. *See* Weston, *supra* note 11, at 153-4.

1040. Although indirect expropriation is commonly alleged by the parties, the only two decisions where expropriation was found under the ECT remain *Yukos* and *Kardassopoulos*. *Yukos*, para. 1580 and *Kardassopoulos*, para. 408. *Kardassopoulos* has been characterized as a "classic" direct expropriation. *Id.* paras. 241, 386-408. In *Nykomb*, the tribunal found that the measures were discriminatory. *See generally* Hobér, *supra* note 20, at 346.

1041. *See* Dolzer, *supra* note 1034, at 378 ("counsel and tribunals have tended to focus less on rules of expropriation and more on the scope of rules on fair and equitable treatment (FET) in cases of host State interference with foreign investment below the threshold of a formal taking").

identify a "deprivation of the use or reasonably expected economic benefit of the investment, let alone affecting a significant part of the investment."[1042]

Even where the power to tax stands out as a distinct power of the state, perhaps even among the most essential, there is little guidance pointing to any specific characteristics unique to tax powers as opposed to other regulatory powers for purposes of expropriation. A finding of unlawful expropriation whether by means of taxation or other regulatory powers requires a showing of the same standards: establishing the unlawfulness of the government taking. In principle, states may freely take property (much like they may freely amend taxes) so long as they do so for, for the reasons, as incorporated in ECT Article 13: (1) public purpose, (2) not discriminatorily, (3) under due process of law and (4) accompanied by the payment of "prompt, adequate and effective compensation."[1043]

In many respects, indirect expropriation by means of taxation is no different than other forms of expropriation requiring a finding of a "complete" or "substantial deprivation."[1044] Substantial deprivation needs to be linked to the state conduct relating to taxation: a tax increase alone cannot be regarded as a taking or an impairment.[1045] The deprivation need not occur as a one-time act. Transfer of property is not required for a finding of expropriation, which may occur through regulatory measures.[1046] A broad range of state acts could be deemed indirect expropriation. In *EnCana*, the tribunal upheld that the cancellation of the state liability (e.g., return of VAT paid) to the investor is capable of being deemed as expropriation.[1047]

Nonetheless, despite the broad state acts covered by expropriation, indirect expropriation remains a high standard to meet as evidence by the BIT cases that supplement the ECT jurisprudence on tax issues. In *Link-Trading*, abolishing the VAT exemptions was not deemed an indirect expropriation, and indirect expropriation particularly by means of taxation was linked to "abuse" as in "abusive taking." The tribunal clarified that "abuse arises where it is demonstrated that the State has acted unfairly or inequitably towards the investment, where it has adopted measures that are

1042. *Occidental I* Award, para. 89. *See also* Nations Energy v. Panama, Award/Laudo, ICSID Case No. ARB/06/19, Nov. 24, 2010 paras. 479, 480 (Sp. "La razón para ello es fácil de entender, dada la importancia de la política fiscal para la soberanía del Estado."). *But cf. id* (José María Medina Chillón dissenting) (holding that the tax exclusion could be reviewed for FET when the treaty used "only to").

1043. *See* ECT Art. 13(1). *See also* Anne K. Hoffmann, *Indirect Expropriation, in Standards of Investment Protection* 151-70, 152 (August Reinisch ed., 2008); August Reinisch, *Legality of Expropriations, in Standards of Investment Protection* 171-204, 176 (August Reinisch ed., 2008).

1044. *See Charanne*, paras. 461-7; *Mamidoil*, paras. 566-72; *Plama* Award, para. 191 and Liman Caspian Oil BV and NCL Dutch Investment BV v. Republic of Kazakhstan, Award, ICSID Case No. ARB/07/14, June 22, 2010, para. 293. For BIT cases, *see EnCana* Award, para. 177 and *Paushok*, para. 333 (referring to *EnCana* Award, para. 177).

1045. *Kügele* at 34. *See also* Link Trading v. Moldova, Final Award, UNCITRAL, Apr. 18, 2002, para. 91 (finding that the investor did not prove expropriation for reasons that it did not show "that the cause of the subsequent decline of its business was a direct result of the elimination of its customers' tax exemption as opposed to the devaluation of the Moldovan currency and the resulting decline in its customers' buying power").

1046. *Occidental I* Award, para. 85.

1047. *EnCana* Award, para. 183.

arbitrary or discriminatory in character or in their manner of implementation, or where the measures taken violate an obligation undertaken by the State in regard to the investment."[1048] Similarly, in *El Paso*, the Argentinian tax measures (withholding tax on crude oil and LPG of ca. 20%) did not amount to indirect expropriation as they did not result "in the neutralization of the property rights."[1049]

The evidence for a showing of indirect expropriation is often voluminous and requires careful scrutiny by the tribunal.[1050] In *UP and CD Holding*, the tribunal upheld, by drawing on *Burlington* and *RosInvest*, that "loss of the shares' economic value" may be a protected interest subject to expropriation. The inquiry is into whether the "measures taken together as a package resulted in dispossession"; the measures included changes in the tax regime for the meal vouchers and administrative decisions that followed. The introduction of a "tax differential" favoring the meal cards and vouchers introduced by Hungary amounted to dispossession when viewed as "a package of measures."[1051]

Perhaps one distinguishing factor of indirect expropriation by means of taxation is that the inquiry on the indirect expropriation by taxation will overlap with the definition of a bona fide taxation. The type of compensation determines the legality of expropriation: failure to provide applicable compensation determines the illegality of expropriation. The definition of compensation varies; it includes several criteria and variations of "just," "adequate," "prompt" or "effective" compensation or a combination of these terms. The ECT expropriation criteria match the "Hull formula" as they require payment of "prompt, adequate and effective compensation."[1052] As taxation is by definition a regulatory taking, it is unlikely to be followed by any sort of compensation from the state. Hence, a tax may raise a distinct inquiry, but otherwise it would not be different from other types of regulatory takings.[1053]

[2] MFN-Inclusion, Other Inclusions and Non-discrimination

As explored in the background section to the Taxation Article, the original purpose in introducing the article was to avoid any conflicts with DTTs.[1054] An investment tribunal's review of any breaches of MFN obligation MFN inclusion/clawback was nonetheless retained for indirect taxes (e.g., "taxes other than on income and capital"). Such approach is reasonable. Investment treaties are intended to provide substantive

1048. *Link-Trading*, para. 64.
1049. *El Paso* Award, para. 299.
1050. Gibson, *supra* note 1035, at 306 (when referring to *Yukos* "This detailed focus on the facts is a necessity in cases of indirect expropriation").
1051. UP and C.D Holding, paras. 305, 331 and 347. *See generally* Edenred v. Hungary, Award, ICSID Case No. ARB/21, Dec. 13, 2016 (not public) and Sodexo Pass International SAS v. Hungary, Award, ICSID Case No. ARB/14/20, Jan. 28, 2019 (not public).
1052. *See* ECT Art. 13(1)(d). For a discussion on the "Hull formula," *see* M. Sornarajah, *The International Law on Foreign Investment* 414 (3 ed., 2010). *See also* Dawson and Weston, *supra* note 11, at 734-5.
1053. *Cf.* Lazem, *supra* note 1035, at 268-9 ("*lex specialis* character [...] because arbitrators apply stricter rules to finding a state liable for tax expropriation").
1054. *See supra* §2.05.

protection for protecting investments, including from adverse taxation matters; however, they are not intended to import more favorable provisions from DTTs. The risk of conflict is greatest with direct taxes where DTTs may in fact provide extensive rules for how direct taxes shall be treated between competing jurisdictions. For indirect taxes (such as VATs and excise taxes), the DTTs may be silent or the protection of the investments may weigh heavier than in the case of direct taxes in the balancing act between taxation and investment protection.

In the ECT context, five decisions have confronted the application of the MFN inclusion/clawback. These five cases, all arising in the Spanish renewable energy context, rejected the investors' arguments that the TVPEE was not a direct tax (it found that it fell within the Direct Tax Limitation).[1055] Other inclusions, as arising from ECT Article 21(2), 21(4) and 21(6), have not materialized in any cases. In general, other inclusions appear rare in the investor-state arbitration regime.[1056] One possible distinction concerns the allegations of discriminatory treatment by the state. While the Direct Tax Limitation is reviewed in the next section, the provisions of non-discrimination overlap with the MFN and NT treatment, so they are examined in this section.[1057]

Non-discriminatory treatment triggers several substantive investment protections mechanisms, including expropriation, FET, NT, MFN and even the protection against discriminatory treatment when described as a separate treatment in the treaty.[1058] Discriminatory treatment traces back to the foundational cases such as *Brewer*, *Kügele* and *Too* where allegations of nationality were raised by the claimants but rejected by the tribunals.[1059] The principle of non-discriminatory treatment is engrained in the ECT context, including in the expropriatory context where a state's expropriatory conduct could not be deemed lawful if it is conducted in a discriminatory manner.[1060]

Perhaps the most far-reaching holdings on tax matters were found in *Alghanim*, a BIT case. In *Alghanim*, the majority of the ICSID tribunal suspended the enforcement of the tax assessment on the sale company (to be distinguished from *Plama*), against the dissent, who found that the standard for relief was very low.[1061] Arbitrariness was deemed to include an assault on "the rule of law," but not on "a rule of law." A politically motivated rule may be deemed arbitrary and fall under the definition of

1055. *Greentech et al. v. Spain*, para. 251, *NextEra* Partial Decision, paras. 383-4. *OperaFund*, para. 415. *Infra Red*, paras. 316-17. *Hydro Energy*, para. 519 and *BayWa*, para. 314.

1056. *See also* Marvin Roy Feldman Karpa v. United Mexican States, Award, ICSID Case No. ARB(AF)/99/1, Dec. 16, 2002 (upheld the breach of NT provisions under NAFTA on the refusal to reimburse excise taxes on tobacco products). For a discussion on NT and taxes, *see* Lazem, *supra* note 1035, at 244-64.

1057. *See infra* §5.04[E][3].

1058. *See* Dolzer & Schreuer, *supra* note 54, at 195 ("in fact, discrimination based on *nationality* is addressed in investment treaties by way of two specific standards: national treatment and MFN treatment") (emphasis added).

1059. *Brewer*, at 423 (arguing discrimination as a German national in Venezuela); *Kügele* at 69 (arguing discrimination as a German national in Upper Silesia under Polish control), and *Too*, paras. 22-3 (Mr. Too argued that the measures were discriminatory on him because he was an Iranian national post Iran hostage crisis of 1979).

1060. ECT Art. 13(1)(b).

1061. *Alghanim* Order, paras. 75 and 91. *See id.* (dissenting opinion Marcelo Kohen, paras. 4-5).

arbitrariness. The tribunal found no evidence that "tax measure" was politically motivated, the inquiry of whether a tax is politically motivated if evidentiarily heavy.[1062]

Otherwise, discriminatory conduct with regard to taxation is difficult to establish. Even in *Alghanim*, the tribunal held that protection against discrimination is intended to cover acts that are: "discriminatory and exposes the claimant to sectional or racial prejudice," keeping in mind that "[a] common feature of tax laws is to draw precise distinctions between different forms of corporate organisation and transactions in terms of their taxability. This does not in itself constitute discrimination."[1063] The application of a tax exemption only to publicly traded companies was deemed reasonable; it was not deemed to be discriminatory.[1064]

Discriminatory treatment and arbitrariness are commonly invoked side by side. In *Tza Yap Shum*, the tribunal held that "the seizure or confiscation of property for failure to pay taxes is a legitimate tool of tax administrations, as long as it is carried out in accordance with reasonable legal procedures and is not done in a confiscatory, abusive or discriminatory manner." However, the award noted that there is a "remarkable consensus" around the fact that taxation and the enforcement of tax measures can acquire an expropriatory nature if it is confiscatory, arbitrary, abusive or discriminatory.[1065] However, the broad regulatory power means that "generally excessive tax" is not deemed as an arbitrary tax.[1066] As held in *Paushok*, without an agreement to the contrary, which "limits or prohibits tax increases," changes in tax law should not be deemed "unpredictable." High levels of taxation, even the highest in the industry, do not mean a breach of FET/minimum standard. Taxation levels may even be high compared to other industries. They should be distinguished for the specific industry as opposed to general application.[1067]

In *Ryan Schooner*, bonus schemes for tax officials to incentivize collection of taxes did not reveal unlawful conduct as such schemes were deemed to be in line with tax collection practices across several jurisdictions.[1068] There was no expropriation as the measures did not amount to total loss or substantial impairment. Tax proceedings were not deemed to be arbitrary, biased, discriminatory or biased, or implemented as a "cover for expropriation," even when the investor was prevented from presenting evidence. The standard applied in investment arbitration is not of an appeal court but

1062. *Alghanim* Award, paras. 277, 79 and 283 (discussing Elettronica Sicula S.p.A. (ELSI) (United States of America v Italy) (Judgment) (1989) ICJ Rep 15.).

1063. *Id.* para. 426 (discussing Waste Management II, Award, ICSID Case No. ARB(AF)/00/3, Apr. 30, 2004 para. 98).

1064. *Alghanim* Award, paras. 391-6. *Cf. Id.* (dissenting opinion of Yves Fortier, paras. 7-16). *See also id.* paras. 432, 476-8.

1065. *Tza Yap Shum* Award, paras. 94-5, 148, 173, 181. *See also* a *Tza Yap Shum* Decision on Annulment, para. 157 (upholding the award and dismissing the argument that the tribunal overrelied on footnote 151 in *EnCana*).

1066. *Paushok*, para. 321.

1067. *Id.* paras. 303, 305, 310 and 314-15 (distinguishing *Occidental I*).

1068. *Schooner*, paras. 484-5, 490-1, 493.

that of a review under the BIT of whether the "abuse of tax law" amounted to a breach of the BIT provisions, which in this case did not occur.[1069]

In *Total,* application of export tax deemed to be valid and non-discriminatory when they did not "actually interfere[] or restrict[] existing or planned crude oil"; in the absence of an express exemption, negative effect on prices was not deemed sufficient to establish confiscatory effect and "windfall profit taxes" were deemed common.[1070] But separate elimination of a tax exemption was deemed to violate FET when applied retroactively and administrative authorities confirmed the opposite.[1071]

It is not uncommon for tax matters to arise specifically in specifically designated zones such as special economic zones (SEZ) and free economic zones (FEZs), set up by the states to provide preferential treatment to generate economic activity. Such zones permit traditionally closed economies to gradually open up to a competitive economic framework: although they are not specifically applicable to energy companies, the special treatment arising from these zones may extend to energy investments as well. Claims of discrimination would be more common in these zones, due to their special status. In *Goetz I*, discrimination was defined as "involv[ing] differential treatment of persons in similar situations but no discrimination was found."[1072] Revocation of the FEZ certificate was deemed to have deprived the investors of any usefulness of their investments amounting to indirect expropriation.[1073] In ICSID proceedings, both domestic law and international law shall apply, assuming "a complimentary relationship [be] allowed to prevail." So even when a measure was deemed to be legal under domestic law, adequate compensation was required to be paid under the substantive provisions of the BIT.[1074]

In two cases against Moldova, in the presence of a stabilization law applicable for FEZ, "administrative charges" were deemed to fall within the scope of the stabilization law for customs duties when charges were "obviously designed to fulfill the purposes typical for customs duties";[1075] however, environmental charges were not deemed cloaked or linked to customs duties subject to the stabilization law for customs duties. Discriminatory conduct was determined to be reviewed when compared to other producers operating in similar FEZs, not operating under the same law.[1076]

In all, a state's exercise of the power to tax, incorporated in the tax exclusions/carve-out, is rarely overridden by means of other inclusions/inclusions,

1069. *Id.* para. 495.
1070. Total, paras. 433 & 435.
1071. *Id.* paras. 441-2.
1072. *Goetz I*, para. 121(Fr. "Une discrimination suppose un traitement différencié appliqué à des personnes se trouvant dans des situations semblables").
1073. *Id.* para. 124. *See also* Dolzer & Schreuer, *supra* note 54, at 107. *See also* Convention between the Belgium and Luxembourg Economic Union and Burundi on the Encouragement and Reciprocal Protection of Investments, Belg & Lux. Econ. Union—Burundi BIT, Sept. 26, 1995 (not including any tax exclusion); at https://investmentpolicy.unctad.org/ (Accessed: May 30, 2020).
1074. *Goetz I*, para. 98 (referring to ICSID Convention Art. 42) (Fr. "il faut le rappeler, la première phrase de l'article 42 de la Convention du CIRDI—c'est un rapport de complémentarité qui doit prévaloir"). *See generally* Dolzer & Schreuer, *supra* note 54, at 290.
1075. *Bogdanov III*, para. 83.
1076. *Bogdanov IV*, paras. 192, 198 and 207.

even when these are expressly provided in the treaty. The only point of contention remains the claims of discriminatory treatment that touch upon several substantive treatments, which in all has been rarely upheld in the taxation context.

[3] Direct Tax Limitation

Five Spanish cases (*NextEra, Infra Red, OperaFund, BayWa* and *Hydro Energy*) have confronted the issue whether the TVPEE fell within the Direct Tax Limitation to the MFN-Specified Inclusion.[1077] How the tribunals reasoned may have differed, but the result is the same across these five decisions. The consensus from these decisions is that the TVPEE was a direct tax: a tax on gross income and hence excluded from the jurisdiction over the arbitral tribunal as it does not fall within the scope of the MFN-Specified Inclusion of ECT Article 21(3).

The five tribunals adopted one or several of the following three approaches in validating the TVPEE: (1) the text itself not referring to "net income," (2) analogies to other provisions of the treaty indicating a broader scope of the Tax Exclusion, and (3) reference to other secondary sources (ECT Secretariat/OECD). In *NextEra*, the tribunal dismissed the objection that the TVPEE was a "Taxation Measure other than on income or capital." It reasoned that the TVPEE was a tax on revenue, thus, a "tax on gross income." The tribunal held that there was "no basis" to deduce from the treaty that ECT Article 21(3) applied to "net income" and found that the TVPEE was not covered by the inclusion/clawback of ECT Article 21(3).[1078] A similar but more succinct argument followed in the *OperaFund* where the tribunal dismissed the arguments on the basis that the TVPEE was a tax on income.[1079]

The *Infra Red* tribunal went into details and applied the VCLT 31 to interpret the term "taxes on income and capital" in "excessively broad" terms. It did not find the OECD definition particularly helpful, nor the clarifications from the ECT Secretariat. Instead, it relied on the principle of "sovereignty" deemed to fall "in keeping" with the purpose of the ECT, by means of a reference to the EEC.[1080] The *Hydro Energy* tribunal reached the same result for substantially the same reasons (no express provision limiting the definition to net income, the language being broad to include "elements of income"), but also by endorsing the ECT Secretariat's findings that the MFN inclusion is meant to cover only "indirect taxes."[1081] Similarly, *BayWa* reached the same decision with the caveat that it held for an even broader proposition, namely that a tax on total income actually would mean a tax on gross revenue.[1082] All five tribunals focused their inquiries on the distinction between net income and gross income (perhaps less so in *OperaFund*), where the investors argued that the TVPEE is a tax on net income, which

1077. *NextEra* Partial Decision, paras. 383-4. *OperaFund*, para. 415. *Infra Red*, paras. 316-17. *Hydro Energy*, para. 519 and *BayWa*, para. 314.
1078. *NextEra* Partial Decision, paras. 383-4.
1079. *OperaFund*, para. 415.
1080. *Infra Red*, paras. 316-17. *See also id.* paras. 314-15 (rejecting the ECT Secretariat's and the OECD's definitions).
1081. *Hydro Energy*, para. 519.
1082. *BayWa*, para. 312.

is aimed to be covered by the ECT. They consistently held that the ECT Article 21(3) reference to direct taxation is not meant to cover "net income" but "gross income."

Another approach may be to question the TVPEE's characterization as a tax on gross income. Parties have unsuccessfully argued that the TVPEE is not a bona fide tax. Tribunals have consistently upheld that investors have not met the high burden of proof for holding that a tax is not bona fide. However, the high burden of proof for a bona fide tax does not exclude that a tax could be bona fide but still not be what it purports to be. In this case, the TVPEE could still be a bona fide tax but not "a tax on gross income." Gross income requires a deduction for the goods sold (COGS) from the gross revenue.[1083] The determinative factor is whether the TVPEE is a reduction of a FiT, or a standalone tax. Given the background of the TVPEE, it is not a stretch to reason that the TVPEE albeit being a bona fide tax has the effect of reducing gross revenue, effectively lowering the gross profit. Such a reading would meet even the broadest approach adopted by *BayWa*, namely that the terms of the Direct Tax Limitation are actually a tax on "total revenue."[1084] In addition, a tax on gross receipts like TVPEE would factor into COGS, because it remains directly proportional to gross revenue. Finally, it would not be a stretch to view the TVPEE not as a direct tax but an excise tax viewed as a per-unit tax, hence, falling outside the definition of a direct tax ("tax on capital and income").

[4] The DTT/Tax-Related Agreement and Collection of Taxes Exceptions

The DTT/tax-related exception has materialized only in the parties' arguments in *NextEra*. The tribunal did not go too far into treaty interpretation. It limited its analysis to the tax falling outside the scope of the inclusion on the grounds that the TVPEE was a tax on income. However, the parties' arguments went further and addressed the exceptions. Spain argued that even if TVPEE were not deemed a tax on income, it should still be excluded on the grounds that the Spain-Uruguay BIT invoked by claimants was a type of agreement falling within the exception of ECT Article 21(3). Claimants sought to introduce the FET from the Spain-Uruguay BIT, by means of the MFN clause, so as to apply to taxation matters. Neither the arguments made by Spain nor the investors gained much traction. Spain argued that Spain-Uruguay BIT should not apply because it was "any convention" despite the fact that the BIT did not include any tax provisions.[1085] In the ECT context, both the Transit and the MFN Inclusions introduced a limitation by which the MFN should not be extended to any benefits

1083. *See generally* Park, *supra* note 9, at 140 (discussing gross revenue taxation and long-term capitalization such as the one in Compania General de Tabaco de Filipinas v. Collector of Internal Revenue, 275 US 87 at 100 (1927)).
1084. *See BayWa*, para. 312. The proposition that "tax on income and capital" is meant to cover "tax on revenue" remains to be debated, as this expansive reading in *BayWa* appears primarily in dicta.
1085. *NextEra* Decision on Liability, paras. 377 and 380.

resulting from the DTTs. These exceptions are common[1086] and refer to the original purpose of the tax exclusion, as evidenced in the ECT *travaux*, namely to keep the investment treaties separate from the DTTs. By coming full circle, this book highlights the original purpose of the tax exclusions, which was to ensure that the investment protection mechanisms do not run into conflict with the DTT provisions.

[F] CTAs and the Requirement of a Joint Decision

The referral to the CTAs serves as a filter in DTTs where a joint decision on the issue would preclude a dispute being referred to a tribunal. In DTTs, mutual agreement procedures (MAPs) are mandatory before arbitration and permit a taxpayer to challenge the actual application or the imminent application of a tax in breach of double taxation principles.[1087] The taxpayer may subsequently bring an arbitration upon the CTAs not being able to resolve the issue within a specified period, ordinarily two years.[1088] The procedures have been in use in the taxation sense long before the 1990s with an increase use in the recent years.[1089]

In investment treaties, the referral to the CTAs also serves as some sort of a filtering mechanism due to the "inherent confiscatory nature of taxes," which may require the review by administrative agencies.[1090] The tax authorities' screen is common in the US and Canadian investment treaties.[1091] Drafted primarily by the US delegation, the CTA referral provisions in ECT Article 21(5)(b) resemble (but are not identical to) the provisions in NAFTA (by reference to a decision by the "competent authorities" in plural), which has now been revised in USMCA Treaty to specify exactly what authority should be seized.[1092] The primary distinction between the ECT and the

1086. *See, e.g.*, Agreement between the Government of the Republic of Finland and the Government of the Republic of Belarus on the Promotion and Protection of Investments, Fin.-Belr., signed on June 8, 2006, in force from Apr. 10, 2008 [hereinafter "Finland-Belarus BIT"].

1087. *See generally* OECD Model Tax Treaty on Income and Capital (2017), Art. 25(1) [hereinafter "OECD Model DTT"].

1088. *See* OECD Model DTT Art. 25(5).

1089. *See generally* John Avery Jones et al., *The Legal Nature of the Mutual Agreement Procedure under the OECD Model Convention—I.*, Brit. Tax Rev., 1979: 6, 333-53, 334-6 (1979) (comparing the 1963, 1974 and 1977 Model OECD treaties). *See also* Protocol 3 Amending the Convention between the United States of America and Canada with Respect to Taxes on Income and Capital, Apr. 24, 1995, Art. 14. *See generally* Jones et al., *supra* note 1089, at 338 (discussing the MAP as "neither judicial nor an arbitration procedure" and that EEC Commission initiative to introduce arbitration to DTT failed in 1976).

1090. Andrea Menaker and Heather van Slooten Walsh, *The Energy Charter Treaty and US Investment Treaties: an overview of key contrasts, in Investment Protection and the Energy Charter Treaty* (Graham Coop and Clarisse Ribeiro eds., 2008), 307-18 at 314. *See also* Park, *supra* note 9, at 131-2. To be distinguished from the "fork-in-the-road" provisions when challenging tax authorities' decisions within short period of times, *see generally Occidental I*, para. 61.

1091. *See generally* US Model BIT Art. 21(2)(2012). *See also* Menaker and van Slooten Walsh, *supra* note 1090, at 314.

1092. *Compare* ECT Art. 21(5)(b) *with* NAFTA Art. 2103(6). *See also* USMCA, Art. 32.3 ("An investor of the United States or Mexico that seeks to invoke Article 14.8 (Expropriation and Compensation) with respect to a taxation measure must first refer to the designated authorities of the Party of the investor and the respondent Party"). NAFTA and ECT were

US treaties is the binding nature of the requirement as a precondition for bringing a claim.[1093] For instance, in at least one case (*Gottlieb v. Canada)*, the claim for expropriation that Canada discriminated against US nationals in their treatment of energy income tax trusts was preempted to proceed when US and Canadian CTAs found that the treatment did not amount to expropriation. Investors did not proceed on other grounds.[1094]

The ECT cases have struggled to generate a consensus on the CTA provisions. Four ECT cases have addressed the CTA referral process: *Plama*, *Yukos*, *Isolux*, and *Eiser*. Five other cases (*Novenergia*, *Greentech v. Spain*, *Infra Red*, *Hydro Energy*, and *SolEs*) were seized with the objection without a conclusive decision by the tribunal on the requirement.[1095] In *Plama*, the tribunal acknowledged that the obligation to refer to "the competent authority" exists and that the investor failed to do so.[1096] The tribunal went on and decided the tax issue as not raising a prima facie case of expropriation or FET without delving into the impact of not referring the dispute to jurisdiction and the requirement that the tribunal does so, in the event the parties have not done it.[1097]

In *Yukos*, the tribunal determined that adhering to the referral requirement was futile.[1098] The review applied specifically to "indirect jurisdiction," namely when the expropriation inclusion/clawback was triggered. In the opinion of the *Yukos* tribunal, measures "under the guise of taxation" would be subject to the CTA referral requirement, provided that the expropriation inclusion is invoked.[1099] In *Yukos*, the tribunal incorporated the conclusions from the 2008 article of Professor William Park, invoked by respondent, that the referral requirement was designed "to assist tribunals "to distinguish normal and abusive taxes"' but it was held inapplicable to the case at hand.[1100] The tribunal reasoned that its inquiries and those of the tax authorities are distinct. Whereas the tax authorities examine "discrete taxes or discrete issues related to taxes," investment tribunals make their conclusions "on a consideration of the totality of the evidence."[1101] As the case record was "enormous," the standard for futility applied by the tribunal involved a determination that "there is no possibility

negotiated in close proximity to each other in the early 1990s with both coming into force in 1994. For NAFTA *travaux*, *see* Bernard D Reams and Jon S. Schultz, The North American Free Trade Agreement (NAFTA): Documents and Materials Including a Legislative History of the North American Free Trade Agreement Implementation Act: Public Law 103-82 (Oceana, 2003). For ECT *travaux*, *see supra* Chapter 2.

1093. *See* NAFTA Art. 2103(6) (the referral requirement must be exercised before bringing a claim and may be deemed to serve as a veto to the tribunal's jurisdiction). *See also* Menaker and van Slooten Walsh, *supra* note 1090, at 314 and Park, *supra* note 11, at 132.

1094. *See generally* Letter Bob Hamilton, Canada Department of Finance, Policy Branch to Eric Solomon, Assistant Secretary Office of Tax Policy, US Department of Treasury, Apr. 22, 2008.

1095. *Novenergia* Award, para. 753. *Greentech et al. v. Spain*, para. 234. *Infra Red*, paras. 199-200. *SolEs*, para. 173. *Hydro Energy*, paras. 304.

1096. *Plama* Award, para. 266.

1097. *Plama* Award, para. 267.

1098. *Yukos* Award, para. 1428.

1099. *Yukos* Award, para. 1420.

1100. *Yukos* Award, para. 1423 (discussing Park, *supra* note 9, at 131).

1101. *Yukos* Award, para. 1423. Professor Park's comments on the purpose of the referral requirement to distinguish between "normal and abusive taxes" applied mainly to NAFTA. Park, *supra* note 9, at 130.

that the relevant authorities would in fact be able to come to some timely and meaningful conclusion."[1102]

The early Spanish cases, *Eiser* and *Isolux*, stand in opposition on the responsibilities of the tribunal with regard to the CTA referral. In *Eiser*, the tribunal held that the referral requirement was not futile but that it was not necessary for the tribunal to make the referral once the investors failed to meet the requirement.[1103] It held that despite imperfections in the drafting of ECT Article 21(5), the referral requirement "envision[s] a process of interaction between national tax authorities regarding a vexed question of international law - when and whether a tax measure may be expropriatory."[1104] The *Eiser* tribunal identified the ambiguity in the referral requirement and specifically on whose state's CTA shall be involved: "Article 21(5) appears to envision a process of interaction between national tax authorities regarding a vexed question of international law - when and whether a tax measure may be expropriatory."[1105] The tribunal resolved this ambiguity by presuming that the CTAs of both the host state and of the investor shall be involved, at least for purposes of the referral made by the arbitration tribunal.[1106] In reaching its decision, the tribunal applied VCLT Article 33(4) and compared the Spanish, English, and French. The tribunal noted that unlike in French and English where the investor needs to make a referral to CTA (*singular*) and the tribunal to CTAs (*plural*), the Spanish version required the opposite (referral to CTAs by investor but singular for the tribunal). In what appears to be the safest possible interpretation, the *Eiser* tribunal held that the interpretation imposing on the tribunal the obligation to refer the matter to all relevant CTAs appears to be most in harmony with the treaty, in accordance with VCLT Article 33(4).[1107]

In *Isolux*, the tribunal clarified that the failure to meet the CTA requirement does not render a claim inadmissible. By applying VCLT Article 31, the *Isolux* tribunal reached the conclusion that the use of the term "shall" makes the requirement mandatory. Failure to meet the requirement by the parties carries the implication that the tribunal shall make the referral with the possible consequence of an *adverse cost implication* against the defendant. In the end, the *Isolux* tribunal held that claimant met the requirement despite the late submission.[1108] The *Isolux* decision, when read together with the *Yukos* decision reinforces the reading that the CTA requirement is not a limitation to the tribunal's jurisdiction, but an issue to be resolved on matters of costs (e.g., exclusion).

In five later Spanish cases (*Novenergia*, *Greentech v. Spain*, *Infra Red*, *Hydro Energy*, and *SolEs*) the parties invoked the limitation without a conclusive finding by

1102. *Yukos* Award, paras. 1422 and 1426.
1103. *Eiser* Award, paras. 294, 296-8.
1104. *Eiser* Award, para. 294.
1105. *Eiser* Award, para. 294.
1106. *Eiser* Award, para. 282 ("... it is not apparent whether the 'relevant' authority is that of the investor's State or that of the respondent state. (In a situation where an arbitral tribunal is to seek referral, according to the English text of the ECT, the tribunal 'shall make a referral to the relevant Competent Tax Authorities' –presumably both.)").
1107. *Eiser* Award, para. 282 n. 328.
1108. *Isolux* Award, para. 753 (claimant received the findings of the Spanish CTA on Apr. 21, 2016; the report was dated Mar. 29, 2016 and the Award was rendered on July 13, 2016).

the tribunals.[1109] In *Novenergia*, the tribunal reached the inadmissibility issue on other grounds and left the CTA issue unaddressed.[1110] In two of these (*Infra Red* and *Hydro Energy*), the record reveals that the Spanish authorities even issued an opinion that the alleged measures were not expropriatory.[1111] In all of these decisions, the tribunals dismissed the claims without delving into the express implications of failing to refer the matters to CTAs. Perhaps, only in *Hydro Energy*, was there a vague reference to the CTA where the tribunal upheld that there was no expropriation for purposes of the expropriation inclusion as applicable by virtue of ECT Article 21(5).[1112] Otherwise, the tribunals after *Eiser* did not address the implications of the CTA referral process.

The CTA limitation in the ECT contains three steps: submission, decision, and review, as per Table 5.13: ECT's CTAs Limitation in Three Steps. Under the first step, the parties are obligated to submit the dispute over expropriation and discriminatory measures to a CTA; absent such step by the parties, the tribunal shall make the referral with the possibility of rendering an advance cost decision. However, the rationale for an adverse cost decision is ambiguous considering that the duty to refer the discriminatory and expropriatory disputes to CTA falls on both parties. Under the second step, the CTAs would review and issue a decision. The period envisioned by the ECT is short, six months, and sets out the rules to be applied by CTAs. In this case, it is important to note that the use of the CTAs in plural indicates some sort of multilateral decision between several entities, consistent with the MAP process inherent in DTTs.

Under the third step, the investment tribunal would need to apply the CTAs' decision. A different treatment is envisaged for expropriation and discrimination cases: CTAs' findings on expropriation cases would be guiding but not binding, whereas CTAs' findings on discrimination would be binding if rendered within six months. The different treatment of the CTA decisions on expropriation and non-discrimination invites the inquiry into the effect of failing to refer the dispute to CTAs. Based on the treaty provisions, it would be reasonable to deduce a binding requirement for non-discrimination cases, but something less stringent for expropriation cases. This finding is consistent with the tribunal's decision in *Yukos*, which deemed that referral of the expropriation claims to the CTA would be futile.

1109. *Novenergia* Award, para. 753. *Greentech et al. v. Spain*, para. 234 (in *Greentech* the investor sent a "letter" to the Spanish tax authorities for a referral whether the tax is expropriatory). *Infra Red*, paras. 199-200. *SolEs*, para. 173. *Hydro Energy*, paras. 304, 526.

1110. *See, e.g.*, *Novenergia* Award, para. 753. In *Novenergia*, the respondent argued that the tribunal would "be able" to review the claim for alleged expropriation on the basis that the CTAs "will be have given the opportunity to state their opinion within six months." The tribunal has not addressed the implications of this requirement and whether it was met or not; instead, it held that the measure was a bona fide taxation measure subject to the tax exclusion.

1111. *Infra Red*, paras. 199-200 (objection for failure to refer was withdrawn after the tax authorities issued the conclusions; not clear what the conclusions were but presumably that the TVPEE was not exclusionary). *See also Hydro Energy* & paras. 304, 526 (claimants made the referral even though they argued that "it was not required"; the tax authorities confirmed that the TVPEE and the Water Levy was not an expropriation).

1112. *Hydro Energy*, para. 522.

Table 5.13 ECT's CTAs Limitation in Three Steps

Step	*Whom*	*Obligation*	*Implication*
1 Submission	Parties	"Shall" refer to CTA claims of "expropriation or discrimination."	None stipulated: but failure to do so may trigger costs (*Isolux*).
	Tribunal	If the parties do not do so, the tribunal "shall" refer such claims.	Failure to do so may render the award susceptible to attack for manifest disregard/excess of mandate/error in procedure.[1113]
2 Decision	CTAs (plural)	"strive to resolve" the dispute within 6 months.	Failure to do so does not prevent the tribunal from proceeding.
		For discrimination, apply the non-discrimination provisions of the relevant tax authority, otherwise, OECD Model Tax Convention.	
3 Review	Tribunal	Expropriation: "may take into account" any conclusions reached by CTAs.	Not bound.
		Discrimination: - "shall take into account' the decision rendered within the 6-month period. - "may take into account" the decision rendered after the 6-month period.	Bound by decisions rendered within 6 months.Not bound by decisions rendered after 6 months.

Source: Author's Own.

1113. *See* Convention on the Recognition and Enforcement of Foreign Arbitral Awards, Art. V(1)(c), June 10, 1958, 84 Stat. 692, 330 U.N.T.S. 3. *See also* International Centre for Settlement of Investment Disputes, Disputes, Convention, Regulations & Rules, 17 U.S.T. 1270 Art. 52(1)(b) and (d)(1965) (amended in 2006); http://icsid.worldbank.org/ (Accessed: May 30, 2020).

[G] Valuation

Taxation issues commonly arise in the computation of damages: the quantum section of the arbitration proceedings.[1114] Hence, there are two distinct inquiries: (1) the impact of the tax exclusion on the valuation of damages together with whether a pretax or after-tax rate of return should be evaluated to compute damages for the computation of damages, and (2) whether the award of damages should be net of taxes. Both inquiries are relevant for purposes of determining the scope of application of tax exclusions, if any, to the valuation of damages.

[1] A Tax Exclusion Does Not Cover Computation of Damages: Particularly When Pre-tax Issues Are Involved

An emerging consensus is that a tax exclusion, such as the one found in the ECT, does not preclude an arbitral tribunal from assessing the impact of taxes on damages. The language of the Tax Exclusion in ECT Article 21(1) is far-reaching; it states that "nothing in the Treaty shall create rights or impose obligations with respect to Taxation Measures [...]."[1115] Applying a broad reading, a tribunal would not have jurisdiction to assess the implication of any tax issues on damages as these would "create rights" for the investor and "impose obligations" on the Contracting States.[1116] However, such expansive interpretation was rejected. In *RREEF*, the tribunal held that even though the tribunal lacks jurisdiction over the matter, tax issues may remain relevant for other purposes, leaving open the inquiry into the possible implications of tax matters not only for purposes of substantive issues but also for valuation of damages. The tribunal reasoned that the measure was a levy, thereby a "cost" which may be reviewed for purposes of determining "the reasonable return."[1117] But the treatment of the tax as a cost does not sufficiently explain why tax matters at the valuation phase are not covered by the tax exclusion. A tax is always a cost.

In the ECT Spanish case, a critical concern was the tribunal's valuation of the Spain's replacement of the feed-in-tariff with a 7.398 pretax projected internal rate of return (IRR).[1118] When valuation methods adopt a discounted cash flow (DCF), the determination of whether a pretax or after-tax compensation method is used carries considerable impact on the monetary compensation.[1119] Posttax return is by definition lower than a pretax return, unless the tax rate is somehow zero, which in such

1114. *See generally Chevron I* Partial Award, para. 553.
1115. ECT Art. 21(1).
1116. *See, e.g.*, Spain's arguments in *PV Investors* Award, para. 858.
1117. *RREEF Infrastructure* Decision on Merits, para. 191.
1118. *See, e.g.*, *Stadtwerke*, para. 361; *BayWa*, para. 514. *RREEF Infrastructure* Decision on Merits, para. 567. *See also RWE*, para. 740 (upholding the RREEF approach) and *NextEra* Decision on Liability, paras. 667-8 (where the tribunal adopted "a nominal tax rate" of 30%).
1119. DCF being the most commonly used method for valuations, other methods such as Asset Present Value (APV), Capitalized Cash Flow (CCF) and Adjust Book Value (ABV) require a careful examination of a wide range of tax issues, including duration and permanency of tax rates, treatment of capital gains, difference in rates for dividends and interest, etc. Marc Kantor, *Valuation for Arbitration* 209-14, 217-19 and 25 (2008).

exceptional cases would be the same. By means of a practical example, a 26% pretax rate of return may be the equivalent of a 16% after-tax rate of return at a 40% income tax rate.[1120] Comparative lease transactions and third-party offers to assess market value may be treated as income and be subject to income and withholding tax for purposes of DCF.[1121] The treatment of taxation will hence have a direct impact on the evaluation of damages.

Regardless of the tax treatment of the measure (in the Spanish cases the pretax treatment of the IRR), the Tax Exclusion would yield itself to a good faith interpretation that it covers "[substantive] rights and obligations"; hence, a tribunal would retain jurisdiction to review tax matters relating to a breach of substantive rights and obligations falling within its jurisdiction. Such approach was upheld in *PV Investors*, where the tribunal deemed that the Tax Exclusion applies only to the inquiry of whether "[the] impugned measures" are subject to the exclusion.[1122] In such manner, tribunals would not be prevented to exercise jurisdiction over tax matters for purposes of computation of damages, provided that the tax matters themselves are not the "impugned measures" subject to the dispute.

[2] Tax Gross Up Is Generally Excluded as Being Overly Speculative

Any applicable tax rates are similarly relevant for valuation purposes. Appropriate compensation is deemed to include the amount, plus interest but net of taxes. The formula for compensation is meant to "make the Claimant whole" but not to overcompensate the investors by compensating the investors for taxes that would otherwise not be due. In *Chevron I*, where the inquiry under the domestic law dominated the case, the relevant inquiry was into whether "an honest, impartial, and independent Ecuadorian judge" would have awarded taxes on the recoverable amount.[1123]

Different source rules may also expose the award of damages to the taxation of the same award in two or more jurisdictions further reducing the amount of recovery.[1124] Awards of damages may be taxed in certain jurisdictions as income,[1125] prompting the inquiry whether the enforcing courts may decide to increase the damages ("gross up") to account for the adverse effect on taxes.[1126]

The consensus so far is that the award on damages will *not* be net of taxes. In *Eiser* and *Occidental*, the tribunals dismissed the request to award damages "net of tax," even when these were expressly computed on an after-tax basis.[1127] *Masdar* and

1120. *Id.* 191-2.
1121. *See generally Kardassopoulos* Award, paras. 613-17.
1122. *PV Investors* Award, para. 860.
1123. *Chevron I* Partial Award, paras. 551-2.
1124. *See generally* Eddie Tobis, *Avoiding Double Taxation on International Arbitration Awards*, J. Damages Int'l Arb. 4:2, 15-39 (2017).
1125. *See generally* IRC. § 61. *Cf.* IRC §§ 104, 105.
1126. Clemens v. Centurylink Inc and Qwest Corp., 874 F.3d 1113 (9th Cir. 2017). *See also* Eshelman v. Agere Sys., Inc., 554 F.3d 426, 440-3 (3d Cir. 2009); EEOC v. N. Star Hosp., Inc., 777 F.3d 898, 903-4 (7th Cir. 2015); Sears v. Atchison, Topeka & Santa Fe Ry., Co., 749 F.2d 1451, 1456-7 (10th Cir. 1984). *Cf.* Rann v. Chao, 346 F.3d 192, 197-8 (D.C. Cir. 2003).
1127. *Eiser* Award, para. 456. *See also Occidental* Award, para. 853.

Antin followed this approach.[1128] So did *OperaFund, PV Investors, Infra Red, RWE, SolEs, Watkins,* and *BayWa.*[1129] For the most part, the "gross up" argument commonly fails for lack of evidence, not for reasons that ECT Article 21(1) did not apply.[1130] In *Watkins*, for example, the claimant sought the decision of the Dutch tax authorities on the applicable tax rate but has not managed to submit the decision in the case. On that basis, the *Watkins* tribunal held that the investor failed to meet its burden of proof and dismissed the claim.[1131] According to the tribunals, the computation of damages "net of tax" was deemed either not to be proven or "speculative and pre-mature."[1132] To avoid the speculative discussion, a possible solution is to bifurcate the decision on quantum and, where appropriate, obtain relevant tax authorities' advisory opinion on the application of any taxes to an award of damages.

§5.05 EXTRAPOLATION OF KEY FINDINGS

In answering the initial sub-inquiry, both the ECT and non-ECT case law reveal specific points of tensions arising out of taxation matters (namely in terms of the review by arbitral tribunal); these cases also offer the means for reconciliating any such points of tension. Although perfect doctrinal coherence is far from being possible, there is a distinct pattern that would be easily understood if classified and grouped on the basis of the categorization: tax exclusion, inclusion, merits including the review of expropriation and breaches of other substantive provisions, and valuation review.

It is not a stretch to deduce that tax matters may contain some distinguishing characteristics such as the fact that taxes are, by definition, a taking subjecting them to creeping or indirect expropriation. However, such distinguishing characteristics do not make taxes particularly different than any other forms of regulatory takings. The tax inquiry is jurisdictional heavy due to the purpose of tax provisions such as the ECT's Tax Exclusion that exclude tax matters from the treaty. In the first ECT cases, for example, substantive review was nonetheless unavoidable when issues of expropriation materialized and their review was deferred to the merits. The line between jurisdiction and merits is not blurred, as the respondent argued in *Yukos*. As evidenced by the renewable case law, the split between jurisdiction and merits may easily be accomplished for a large portion of the cases, where the second leg of the analysis is often not warranted by the absence of exceptional circumstances. This carries the implication that the full inquiry into the multilayered ECT provisions does not

1128. *Masdar*, para. 660. *Antin* Award, para. 673.
1129. *OperaFund*, para. 704; *SolEs*, paras. 552-3; *PV Investors* Award, paras. 861-2, *Infra Red*, para. 598 (claimants deemed not to have discharged their burden of proof); *Watkins*, para. 758, and *BayWa*, paras. 621-6. *But cf. RWE*, paras. 745 & 747 (deferring the decision on the gross up to settlement between the parties and, failing such settlement, to a final award).
1130. *PV Investors* Award, para. 860, *See also Masdar*, paras. 658-60 (respondent raised the lack of jurisdiction by virtue of the tax exclusion but the issue was not addressed by the tribunal), and *OperaFund*, para. 704.
1131. *Watkins*, para. 758.
1132. *Eiser* Award, para. 456. *See Occidental II* Award, para. 853; *OperaFund*, para. 704; *SolEs*, paras. 552-3.

materialize for a large majority of cases. For purposes of a full review, the dissertation addresses a shifting burden of proof for each stage of these inquiries.

The bulk of the inquiry remains in the definitional requirements, particularly in the different use of the term "tax" and "taxation measure." In most cases, a tax undertaken by the state will be a bona fide tax. Granted, *Yukos* has opened the inquiry into the bona fide nature of the tax, which has been examined but not followed in other cases due to the high threshold of proof. However, the breach found in *Yukos* did not rely solely on the tax not being bona fide. In addition, in the BIT cases, the bona fide inquiry was not conducted for purposes of a jurisdictional inquiry but for a finding of the breach itself; in either case, these inquiries are likely to overlap and generate some confusion. This book takes the view that what may be deemed as a problematic error in treaty drafting is actually a useful means for tribunals to fully review the scope of the expropriation inclusion without running afoul of ruling on the domestic treatment of the alleged tax. In such manner, "tax" and "taxation measure" are synonyms taking different roles: the latter is a qualified definition and the former is a general term. With the undefined term of "tax," a set of elements may be relevant to deduce applicable characteristics of the term when interpreting the term in accordance with VCLT Article 31(1). These elements should be carefully scrutinized for whether an indirect expropriation has occurred.

In all, there is room for the case law to grow and provide further clarifications on the complexity of the ECT Taxation Article and other BITs' taxation provisions. The role of CTAs and the narrow as opposed to the broad interpretation of the "other than income or capital" limitation are all subject to further argumentation based on the circumstances confronted by parties in renewable and non-renewable case law. Although the power to tax remains broad and arbitral tribunals do not sit as appellate bodies to national taxation authorities and courts, the power to tax is subject to limits. Such inherent limits may be incorporated in the definition of a tax (e.g., "bona fide inquiry") or in the interpretation of the application of the treaty (e.g., "to what extent customary international law applies"). In any event, the limits are essential for the legitimate exercise of the state power to tax and building confidence in the regulatory actions of the state.

CHAPTER 6
Proposals

§6.01 OVERRIDING CONCERNS

The cross-fertilization between taxation and investment energy disputes highlights the need for delineating best practices, identifying cautionary tools and setting clear demarcation for certain actions and omissions. The sub-inquiry for this section is whether the points of tension arising out of the existing case law may be streamlined to modernize the current language in the ECT, set out a benchmark for tax legislation against investment commitments, and further improve the taxation chapters in investment treaties.

In investment arbitration, tax matters constitute some of the most complex treaty exercises, especially in the case of extensive drafting and difficult compromises. How a state comes to act in relation to these provisions may be difficult to assess, unless there is an identification of detrimental and unlawful practices. In the 2008 ASIL Annual Meeting, the late Professor Wälde underlined, specifically with regard to taxation, the importance of focusing on "red flags" to distinguish ordinary taxation measures from potential unlawful taxation measures, as follows:

> The challenge for tribunals, counsel and scholars is to develop a system of standards or "red flags" which, within the context of overall balancing, rather suggest a breach of the treaty disciplines distinct from "normal" taxation that has to be accepted as the regular risk of doing business in a country. Discrimination, arbitrariness, undue surprise, conspicuous deviation from international taxation practices and an identifiable intention to hurt foreign investors for the benefit of government or domestic competitors provide such "red flags"; they build up a presumption of breach of the relevant treaty disciplines.[1133]

1133. Wälde, *supra* note 30, para. 59. *National Tax Measures Affecting Foreign Investors Under the Discipline of International Investment Treaties*, Proceedings of the Annual Meeting, ASIL, vol. 102. Apr. 9-12, 2008 at 59. *See RosInvest* Final Award, para. 4 (where claimant argued for the shifting of the burden of proof due to the presence of certain flags). *See also* Thomas Wälde and Abba Kolo, *Coverage Taxation under Modern Investment Treaties*, *in The Oxford*

Professor Wälde's observations predated the current initiatives to update the ECT by more than a decade. Common criticisms, specifically aimed not only at ECT but also on the investment arbitration regime in general, center on the fact that the treaty does not reflect the needs of a modern society by protecting investors at the cost of struggling developing countries. Despite some valid criticisms, the investment arbitration regime including the ECT as a multilateral treaty may be improved, but it must not be scrapped.

Subject to the previously reviewed case law, the following analysis sets out to: identify the red flags and map them up for regulators, propose points for improvements in the ECT Taxation Article, and present meaningful changes in the treaties to avoid ambiguity and confusion.

§6.02 RED FLAGS AND PROPOSALS TO LEGISLATORS

[A] Overview and Identification of Red Flags

The first step is to identify "red flags" that may transform a lawful exercise of taxation power into an unlawful exercise. However, the red flags carry the implication of a binary effect: a measure is either problematic or not. A red flag does not necessarily presume a breach; it only asserts a presumption of some sorts, as suggested by late Professor Wälde. A demarcation, based on red flags, may be helpful in shifting the burden of proof but it may inevitably trigger an outcome-determinative inquiry.

Sufficient case law has already been examined to go beyond a presumption-based analysis toward an attempt to document best practices and extrapolate general principles. However, a state's obligations will vary depending on its treaty commitments. Despite a variation in treaty commitments, certain general principles may still be discerned that apply to different stages of the tax process. Such general principles are the first step toward guiding national authorities, whether they be finance ministries called upon to provide input on new tax initiatives, or administrative entities responsible for investment protection called upon to opine on existing tax initiatives. The general principles draw primarily on existing customary international norms and existing jurisprudence, but may not be deemed as codifying customary international law. For this reason, the five red flags delineated below: (1) bona fide; (2) expropriation; (3) discrimination; (4) arbitrariness and (5) enforcement are further divided into two categories: for the first two (bona fide and expropriation) where the consent of the state is not outcome-determinative, as to for the last three (discrimination, arbitrariness, and enforcement) the language in the treaty may have a substantial effect in determining the effects of the limitation to the state's power to tax.

Handbook of International Investment Law, 305-58 at 346 (Peter T Muchlinski, Federico Ortino, Christoph Schreuer eds., 2008).

Wälde, *supra* note 30, para. 59.

While the "red flag" analysis remains essential for identifying the risks, the toolkit below aims to address common situations likely to occur.[1134] Drawing on the methodology incorporated in the International Bar Association (IBA) Guidelines for the conflict of interest, the following analysis is divided into two parts: (1) general principles and (2) a practical toolkit applying such general principles. The practical toolkit incorporates a color-pattern resembling a traffic-light for purposes of distinguishing between various red flags depending on the degree of severity.

[B] General Principles

The general principles are delineated in terms of the lifecycle of a tax and without a particular priority in order. The headers are meant only as a classification instrument.

[1] Bona Fide

Red Flag Nr. 1: The implementation or application of a fiscal measure, impacting foreign investors, that is *not* reasonably related to a legitimate state interest, or that is *not* directly made to the state.

Comment: This red flag builds on the precedent from the *Yukos* award, namely that a tax measure needs to be bona fide in order to be valid. In principle, the matter is straightforward and could be deemed even a *pleonasm*. To be valid, a tax needs to be a tax; not a purported tax. There is a degree of consensus over the requirement that a tax shall meet its definitional requirements; however, what those definitional requirements actually are may be subject to debate. Fundamentally, both the OECD/IBFD and the emerging definition from arbitration awards point to a tax being a payment (whether an unrequited or compulsory) to the general government.

Inherent in the payment to the general government is the logical link that the payment needs to be related to a legitimate government purpose. A point of confusion is the seemingly illegitimate aims communicated in respect of a legitimate aim, namely the presence of an ill motive and a reasonable link to a legitimate public purpose. The consensus arising out of the case law reveals a low threshold for bona fide requirement. Hence, the existence of a reasonable legitimate aim would validate a bona fide tax measure in a manner that ill motives may be addressed in the context of the breach of individual standards: expropriation, FET, non-discrimination if such avenue is possible under bilateral treaties. What remains in dispute are instances when the ill motive overshadows the reasonable link. The basic example is the ruling authority enacting tax measures that curb offshore tax evasion but substantially affect a political opponent. Curbing tax evasion by the use of offshore practices may be a legitimate state aim and the measure could then be reviewed under the individual investment protections mechanisms granted by the state if any. However, when the sole purpose of the tax measures is to sideline an opponent, the tax measure loses its legitimacy and fails to be

1134. *See generally* International Bar Association, IBA Guidelines on Conflicts of Interest in International Arbitration, Oct. 23, 2014; http:// www.ibanet.org (Accessed: May 30, 2020).

bona fide. The standard of proof for such findings is, of course, very high. The moving party needs to establish that the sole purpose of the measure is linked to an illegitimate aim; that is, it is not reasonable. An illegitimate aim may extend beyond sidelining political opponents and may refer to measures that curb basic fundamental human rights such as those covered by the European Convention on Human Rights, or those that aim to forcefully remove foreign investors from the country.

General Principle Nr. 1: A state shall not implement, execute or enforce any tax measure against foreign investors that is *not* reasonably related to a legitimate state interest, or that is not directly made to the state.

[2] Prohibition Against Expropriatory Taxation

Red Flag Nr. 2: A tax affecting foreign investors that: (1) has no proportional relationship to the public benefit, or (2) is implemented without adequate due process or legal support, or (3) substantially deprives the investor of its property without prompt, adequate, and effective compensation.

Comment: The prohibition against unlawful expropriation is generally acknowledged in customary international law and the prohibition extends even to taxation matters. The link between taxation and expropriation is complicated by two issues. The first complication is derived from the states having the right to expropriate. What is prohibited, under customary international law, is unlawful expropriation. A general consensus emerges in favor of four cumulative criteria that need to be met for an expropriation to be deemed lawful. In order for an expropriation to be lawful, the taking must serve a public purpose, not be arbitrary and discriminatory, follow due process, and it must be followed by prompt, adequate, and effective compensation. The absence of any of these criteria would invalidate the lawfulness of a measure. The second complication arises from the fact that a tax in its very nature is a "taking" or "expropriation," in the ordinary sense of the word but not always in the legal sense of the word.[1135] A tax is a mandatory contribution to the government's coffers. In exercising their fiscal policy, governments need to retain broad flexibility to achieve their goals, reforms and when needed implement austerity measures. Often such reforms may cause substantial hardship on domestic and foreign investors. When such measures rise to the level of a "taking" or "expropriation" in the legal sense, a tax automatically has to automatically fulfill the definition of a lawful expropriation. Putting the burden for the state to defend every fiscal measure is administratively costly and burdensome, which is not the aim of BITs to achieve. Nonetheless, it remains good practice for the states not to deviate from a measure to be reasonably related to a public purpose, however broad such purpose may be, nor should the implementation of a tax

1135. *See generally* Weston, *supra* note 12, at 111 ("Consider, for example, the word 'taking' or, if preferred, the civil law term 'expropriation.' As every ordinary person might rightly suppose, these words can be understood to mean an act of sovereign power which, with or without compensation, results in an actual divestment of all or part of one's property. As every lawyer knows, however, they can refer also to the exercise of a special kind of sovereign power ('the power of eminent domain') which, if constitutional and other strictures are carefully followed, generally results in payment of 'just' compensation").

measure depart from basic guarantees of due process and basic legal processes, be it in a legislative, fiscal or administrative format. The prohibitions against discrimination and arbitrariness are taken separately below.

General Principle Nr. 2: In the presence of treaty commitments not only against non-expropriation but also as means of good practice, a state shall not implement or enforce a tax that departs from serving a public purpose and following due process guarantees, or that substantially deprives a foreign investor of its property or causes the abandonment of the property without prompt, adequate, and effective compensation.

[3] Discrimination (Primarily Treaty Based)

Red Flag Nr. 3: Any discriminatory tax or any seemingly narrow tax that applies only to one person or group, even when it is drafted in broad terms.

Comment: A tax may lawfully distinguish between tax subjects based on their innate differences. For example, excise taxes by their function are applied to the manufacturing, processing or use of a particular product that may distinguish between these based on their distinct effect on health, environmental or social costs. An excise tax on hydrocarbons serves as an example of an indirect tax that may distinguish hydrocarbon producers from producers of, for example, renewable energy. Absent treaty commitments to the contrary, a state is not restricted from treating foreigners (a.k.a. aliens) in a manner that is different than its citizens or permanent residents. However, states commonly extend the right against non-discrimination, along with the national treatment standard, to foreign nationals. When such treaty or similar commitments are made, a tax becomes unlawfully discriminatory when it singles out or "targets" foreign investors based on their nationality, or based on a protected group. The basis for such a comparison is a comparable group ("similarly situated group"). In the energy sector specifically, such distinction may be difficult to find as economics of scale may yield in favor of natural monopolies. In such case and only in the event that the unique feature of the tax subject is of relevance for the taxation measure,[1136] the group closest resembling the affected entity may serve as the basis of comparison. When such group is not available, a different group may be used, subject to the exclusion of the distinguishing characteristics between the groups. Discriminatory intent may further accentuate the unlawfulness of a measure, but discriminatory intent is not a prerequisite, especially in the event of a track record from the investor that it has in a timely manner objected and notified the state of the likely discriminatory impact of a particular measure.

General Principle Nr. 3: In the presence of treaty commitments against non-discrimination, a tax shall not single out a foreign investor, whether a natural or a juridical person, or a group of investors in a discriminatory manner. When the tax

1136. *See, e.g., Occidental I* Award, at 173 ("'in like situations' cannot be interpreted in the narrow sense advanced by Ecuador as the purpose of national treatment is to protect investors as compared to local producers, and this cannot be done by addressing exclusively the sector in which that particular activity is undertaken").

applies to only one natural or juridical person, or group of entities, due to the specifics of the market, such tax shall be narrowly tailored to address reasonable state goals.

[4] Arbitrariness of a Tax or Contradictory Commitments (Primarily Treaty Based)

Red Flag Nr. 4: An arbitrary or nonsensical tax that is patently unfair, lacks substantial link to or any proportional application for the scope it is passed, or that blatantly contradicts prior commitments made by the state.

Comment: Two distinct inquiries emerge: first, on the arbitrariness of a measure in its general sense and, the second, a measure that contradicts prior commitments made by a state. On the former, some overlap exists between an arbitrary tax measure and a tax measure that breaches the bona fide standard. In many cases, an arbitrary tax measure would not qualify as a bona fide tax measure. However, in many cases, the bona fide standard may address a tax, which may not be arbitrary in itself, but that it may have an unlawful purpose (e.g., singling out political opposition or racial minorities). In a similar manner, a tax may still be bona fide but be arbitrary in its application. Such an example would cover a VAT on oil in the context of a PSC covering exportation abroad of materials when VAT would not ordinarily apply.

The latter standard (contradictory commitments by the state) covers such instances where the state retracts its existing commitments and rejects its prior binding commitments to foreign investors. A mere contractual repudiation, albeit without any grounds, does not automatically qualify as being arbitrary.[1137] Most commonly, a contradiction would involve a stabilization agreement or a clause where the state commits to retaining the status quo for a number of years but due to political or economic changes fails to live up to such commitments. In all, the starting point is that a state enjoys broad powers to tax and it does not need to limit its own powers. In fact, a state will often require flexibility in its fiscal policy for purposes of raising revenue to meet existing, past, or future commitments. However, when a state does limit its taxation power, it needs to do so cautiously. Whether through its actors and its successors, the state needs to live up to any commitments on stabilization clauses. In the event that it chooses to renounce these commitments, it shall not do so unilaterally and without compensating the investors unless extraordinary events such as economic or political conditions dictate a sense of necessity, distress, or similar extreme measures to be taken.[1138] Dire economic necessity requires that the state departs from regular practices. Even in the event of necessity and emergency, the presence of the necessity or emergency has to be evident, and such state does not grant the state a carte blanche to trample on previous commitments. The state may not be deemed to have

1137. *See Duke Energy* Award, at paras. 381 ff. *See also* Dolzer & Schreuer, *supra* note 54, at 193.
1138. *See generally* United Nations General Assembly, Responsibility of States for Internationally Wrongful Acts, A/CN.4/L.602/Rev.1, July 26, 2001, Art. 25; UN International Law Commission (2008), Draft Commentaries. Responsibility of States for Internationally Wrongful Acts, A/56/10, Yearbook of the International Law Commission, 2001, vol. II, Part Two, at 80-4 [hereinafter "ILC Articles on State Responsibility"].

caused the state of necessity, or prior commitments expressly exclude necessity, in order to implement a fiscal measure in the event of a state of necessity.[1139] Likewise, the state fiscal measure must be the sole means for "the state to safeguard an essential interest against a grave and imminent peril" in such manner that the fiscal measure "does not seriously impair an essential interest of the state or states towards which the obligation exists, or of the international community as a whole."[1140]

General Principle No. 4: In the presence of treaty commitments to the contrary, a state shall ensure that a tax measure is not patently unfair or devoid of a substantial link to a state purpose, lacks any proportional application for the scope the tax was passed, or that the tax blatantly contradicts prior commitments made by the state.

[5] Unlawful Tax Enforcement (Primarily Treaty Based)

Red Flag Nr. 5: A targeted enforcement mechanism such as enforcement of taxation measures that are not consistent with the police powers of the state or that are structured in a manner to cause the abandonment of the property or the sale of the property at a *significantly* below-market level.

Comment: This red flag builds on the Restatement's formulation that focuses on the enforcement powers of the state.[1141] Enforcement of tax measures may be linked to other sovereign powers of the state, mainly the police power, which follows closely the sovereign power to tax and to lawfully expropriate (e.g., eminent domain). In order for a state to exercise the power to tax efficiently, it needs to ensure not only that tax offenses are criminalized but also that it retains effective powers to "freeze, seize and confiscate assets."[1142] Enforcement commonly occurs through "forfeitures" determined as "the loss of a right, privilege or property because of a breach of a crime, breach of obligation, or neglect of duty."[1143] Inherent in the transfer of assets or property to the state[1144] is the proper exercise of the police power of the state. The principles of non-discrimination, protection against arbitrariness and a link to legitimate exercise of government interests apply for determining the legality of enforcement mechanisms, much like the application for determining the legality of a tax. Tax measures often do not cause damage to foreign investors until they are *ripe* for a challenge, which occurs only through enforcement of the tax measures. Enforcement of an unlawful tax does not necessarily make the enforcement process unlawful. In a similar manner, enforcement procedures, even of lawful tax measures, may themselves be unlawful on their own. However, it is often the case that an unlawful tax

1139. ILC Articles on State Responsibility, Art. 25(2).
1140. ILC Articles on State Responsibility, Art. 25(1).
1141. *See* Restatement §712. *See also* Viñuales, *supra* note 389, at 336.
1142. *See generally* Organisation for Economic Co-operation and Development, *Fighting Tax Crime: the Ten Global Principles* 13-18 and 37-42 (2017); at http://www.oecd.org (Accessed: May 30, 2020).
1143. *See Forfeiture, Black's Law Dictionary* (11th ed. 2019).
1144. *See id.* (defining "civil forfeiture" as "an *in rem* proceeding brought by the government against property that either facilitated a crime or was acquired as a result of criminal activity" and "criminal forfeiture" as "a government proceeding brought against a person to seize property as a punishment for the person's criminal behavior").

measure may follow in parallel with an overly aggressive enforcement mechanism adopted by the state. Serious cases may be, in fact, referred to criminal tax enforcement. When tax enforcement by criminal law occurs, it may exacerbate the effect that tax enforcement process would have on foreign investors, such effects being difficult to redress through international arbitration alone whose remedies are often limited to civil remedies. What distinguishes the inquiry into the enforcement procedures from the inquiry into the legality of a tax is the *oppressiveness* of the enforcement procedure. Unlawful enforcement may take, in essence, two forms: it may cause for a foreign investor the abandonment of the property or relinquishment of the property through market conditions (e.g., sale at an auction). When exercised to enforce a lawful legal right, seizure of property even through auctions would be legal when such measures are conducted with sufficient due process safeguards under a reasonable period of time. Often the line between oppressive and non-oppressive enforcement mechanisms is difficult to draw, especially when prompt measures may be warranted to preserve dilution of value or squandering of assets in, for example, tax evasion cases. However, even in cases where ex parte intervention may be justified, some form of a review or appeal mechanism may be necessary to ensure that no abuse of power has occurred.

General Principle Nr. 5: Enforcement of taxation measures may be accomplished within the common practice of the police powers of the state, so that the measures do not cause the abandonment of the property or the sale at a distress price without sufficient due process, or in an otherwise unreasonably oppressive manner.

[C] Practical Toolkit

[1] Red List

[i] Bona Fide Tax

(1.i.a.) A tax measure[1145] that is not payable to the government or government actors.
(1.i.b.) A tax measure that is not compulsory for a well-defined group, or is compulsory for some but not others in the well-defined group.
(1.i.c.) A tax measure that, despite being levied by and paid to the government, is directly rerouted to private representatives or third parties.
(1.i.d.) A tax measure that is linked to no legitimate state interest, or whose *sole* purpose is to advance illegitimate aims such as removal of political opponents, banishment of foreign investors or curbing basic human rights.

1145. A tax measure is meant to encompass a formal tax and a tax subsidy such as relief from taxation.

[ii] Expropriatory

(1.ii.a.) A tax measure that lacks any possible link to a legitimate public purpose.
(1.ii.b.) A tax measure, including the removal of a tax benefit, that is passed under a substantially limited period of time without any possible explanation for the actions taken (e.g., immediate risk of squandering of assets or imminent risk of disappearance of assets).
(1.ii.c.) A tax measure that deprives a foreign investor of all of its property without any sort of payment of compensation.

[iii] Discriminatory

(1.iii.a.) A tax measure that is subjectively isolating political opposition, or racial, gender, or religious minorities, under vague and ill-defined purposes.
(1.i.b.) A tax measure that, under the guise of curbing tax evasion, is subjectively isolating political opposition, or racial, gender, or religious minorities, under vague and ill-defined purposes.

[iv] Arbitrariness/Contradictory

(1.iv.a.) A tax measure that has no relationship to the matter being taxed.
(1.iv.b.) A tax measure that has no relationship to the subjects being taxed (e.g., taxing foreign nationals without any link to the state).
(1.iv.c.) A tax measure that stands in direct contradiction to a tax stabilization clause in a law or investment contract that is in effect, or another commitment made by the state such as a binding DTT.

[v] Enforcement

(1.v.a.) Enforcement of a tax measure without any meaningful due process that causes the abandonment of the property or relinquishing of the property.
(1.v.b.) Enforcement of a tax measure by means of unreasonably oppressive means (e.g., threat to life or limb, including torture and criminal coercion) that causes the abandonment of the property or relinquishing of the property.
(1.v.c.) *Interim* enforcement of a tax measure by means of ex parte action without any due process review after the fact or by means of unreasonably oppressive means (e.g., threat to life or limb, including torture and criminal coercion).

[2] Amber List

[i] Bona Fide Tax

(2.i.a.) A tax measure that, despite being levied by and paid to the government, is ultimately rerouted to third parties.
(2.i.b.) A tax measure that, despite an alleged compulsory and mandatory provision for a large group of tax subjects, applies disproportionately to political opposition, or racial, gender or religious minorities.
(2.i.c.) A tax measure, including that, despite a purported legitimate interest, disproportionately affects political opposition, or racial, gender, or religious minorities.

[ii] Expropriatory

(2.ii.a.) A tax measure that has a tenuous legitimate government purpose.
(2.ii.b.) A tax measure that deprives a foreign investor of all or substantially all of its property without any sort of payment of compensation.
(2.ii.c.) A tax measure that while serving a legitimate government interest and depriving a foreign investor of all or substantially all of its property pays prompt compensation but does not grant either just or adequate compensation.
(2.ii.d.) A tax measure that while serving a legitimate government interest and depriving a foreign investor of all or substantially all of its property pays just and adequate compensation but does not do so efficiently or speedily.

[iii] Discriminatory

(2.iii.a.) A tax measure that, in the presence of commitments against non-discrimination, singles out foreign investors and treats them differently than other comparable actors on the market.
(2.iii.b.) A tax measure that, in the presence of commitments against non-discrimination, singles out foreign investors on a basis that could not be assessed against a controlled group; however, on its basis, the tax retains discriminatory elements that would otherwise not apply to other entities when excluding for the differences for such entities.
(2.iii.c.) A tax measure that, despite its broad application, disproportionately affects political opposition, or racial, gender or religious minorities, or foreign nationals in the event of treaty commitments to the contrary.
(2.iii.d.) A tax measure that, despite its claim to apply with the purpose of curbing tax evasion, disproportionately singles out political opposition, or racial, gender, or religious minorities, or foreign nationals in the event of treaty commitments to the contrary.

(2.iii.e.) A tax measure that, in the presence of commitments against non-discrimination, suddenly and disproportionately is imposed on a narrow range of subjects, in a time event of economic or political distress.

[iv] Arbitrariness/Contradiction

(2.iv.a.) A tax measure that expands the scope of application of a particular tax beyond a reasonable application of such measures (e.g., VATs on exported goods, import duties on domestic goods, excise duties for dangerous materials or materials that are not dangerous).
(2.iv.b.) A tax measure that is applied during the temporal application of such stabilization clauses and commitments but that may in principle fall outside of the scope of tax stabilization clause or prior commitments made by the state.
(2.iv.c.) A tax measure that suddenly and disproportionately is imposed on a broad range of matters or subjects without a clearly justified need.

[v] Enforcement

(2.v.a.) Targeted enforcement of a tax measure with some degree of due process that causes the abandonment of the property or relinquishing of the property.
(2.v.b.) Targeted enforcement of a tax measure without any meaningful due process that causes a significant devaluation of the property.
(2.v.c.) Targeted enforcement of a tax measure by means of intimidation tactics (e.g., blatant use of force, presence of military personnel) that causes the abandonment of the property or relinquishing of the property.
(2.v.d.) *Interim* enforcement of a tax measure by means of ex parte action without adequate due process review after the fact, or by means of intimidation.

[3] Green List

[i] Bona Fide Tax

(3.i.a.) A tax measure that aims to curb tax evasion through clear and reasonable means.
(3.i.b.) A tax measure payable to the treasury/state accounts held in various currencies.
(3.i.c.) A tax measure that is broad and legitimate in its application that affects a large population, without singling out political opponents or specific groups either directly or indirectly.

[ii] *Expropriatory*

(3.ii.a.) A tax measure that does not deprive the foreign investor of a substantial part of its property.
(3.ii.b.) A tax measure that is linked to a clearly defined public purpose.
(3.ii.c.) A tax measure that follows due process guarantees, including timely notice of the measure and is implemented in accordance with prescribed constitutional and administrative frameworks.
(3.ii.d.) A tax measure that, while passed for legitimate public purpose and subject to due process and substantially deprives a foreign investor of its property, pays just, efficient, and adequate compensation.

[iii] *Discriminatory*

(3.iii.a.) A tax levied on subjects or goods in the same sector without distinguishing between these; if distinguishing between these, it does so, on the basis of non-material criteria or on criteria that are reasonably related to an inherent gradation (e.g., incrementally different excise rates on the octane level of gas).
(3.iii.b.) A tax levied on subjects that treats tax subjects in different sectors differently based on reasonable criteria.
(3.iii.c.) A tax levied on goods that treats different goods differently based on reasonable criteria.
(3.iii.d.) A tax levied on a single foreign investor or a group thereof when the market specifics foresee consolidation of resources in one entity (e.g., natural monopolies) and such tax would not otherwise discriminate actors in comparable markets.
(3.iii.e.) A tax levied on a single foreign investor or a group thereof when the market specifics foresee consolidation of resources in one entity (e.g., natural monopolies) and if comparable actors could not be identified, does not discriminate against the single foreign investor or a group thereof based on a characteristic inherent to said investor or group.
(3.iii.f.) A tax levied on foreign investors in the absence of treaty protections against discrimination, but when such treatment does not rise to abuse of power nor unlawfully targets the foreign investors on the basis of otherwise protected criteria.

[iv] *Arbitrariness/Contradictory*

(3.iv.a.) A tax measure that is fair or has substantial cause for its application.
(3.iv.b.) A tax measure that is proportional to the aims it seeks to achieve.
(3.iv.c.) A tax measure that is passed after the expiration of any tax stabilization clauses or commitments, even when they run in contradiction to the express provisions of the stabilization clauses that have expired.

(3.iv.d.) A tax measure that, when passed in times of political and economic necessity or emergency, is supported by a clear justification for the measure, and is passed in a manner that is not disproportionate from addressing the circumstances arising for such necessity.

[v] *Enforcement*

(3.v.a.) Enforcement of a tax measure with adequate degree of due process that proportionally relates to the delinquent tax bills and any additional sanctions with the aim of punishing or deterring unlawful conduct.
(3.v.b.) Enforcement of tax measures within ordinary limits of police powers (e.g., enforcement by police or law enforcement personnel) with the aim to punish or deter unlawful conduct but not intimidate an individual.
(3.v.c.) Enforcement of tax measures through civil measures that do not cause the abandonment of the property or the relinquishment of the property.
(3.v.d.) *Interim* enforcement of a tax measure by means of ex parte action with reasonable due process mechanisms, such as appeal after the fact or alternative funding to secure the risk of forfeiture.

[D] Summary

The general principles set above and the specific examples are by no means exhaustive, nor do they aim to regulate all possible scenarios covering tax measures. Their aim is simply to contextualize, in a humble manner, the notable remarks of Professor Wälde delivered in the midst of the *Yukos* proceedings, and to drive the discussion further. Given the direct and vast implications of tax measures on foreign investors, tax law is far too important to be left exclusively to the sole realm of tax lawyers. In many ways, the investment arbitration lawyers have developed useful tools that may be easily extended, if not to tax law per se, at least to the area where tax law and investment law converge. From the investment arbitration regime, the IBA Guidelines, with the "traffic-light"-like ranking of permissible and sanctionable conduct, emerge as a useful tool for categorizing the Wälde red flags. Unlike the IBA Guidelines that regulate conduct between private parties, the specific examples above define the relationship between the state, which in nearly all cases is the sole authority to exercise the taxation power, and an individual. Due to the state-private actor relationship, the methodology did not bifurcate the red list into one that could be waived by the parties and one that could not.[1146] In taxation terms, a red list remains a red list. The nuance for simplicity shall remain a much-needed requirement of tax law that is further described in the context of treaty drafting below.

1146. *Cf.* IBA Guidelines at 17 (distinguishing between waivable and non-waivable red lists).

§6.03 TREATY-DRAFTING PROPOSALS

[A] The Need for Simplicity

Treaty drafting occurs often solely at a high level between the states with varying degrees of sophistication. As with the ECT, the drafting could be conducted by specialized representatives from, for example, finance, treasury, or energy departments and foreign ministries, alone or in a joint effort. In the past, the treaty drafting of the taxation chapters often enjoys little public debate and retains a technical characteristic. The initial drafting of the Energy Charter provides helpful insights on the journey of balancing a multitude of interests. In the example of the ECT Taxation Article, representatives from finance departments of the respective Contracting States determined the main text of the chapter. In recent drafts, there have been some tendencies for overemphasizing some key points that have been contentious or left unsettled by recent tribunals. Often, these are prefaced by "for greater certainty."[1147] In general, these initiatives are useful particularly to memorialize the intent of any Contracting States; however, such tools should be used restrictively and cautiously, since in its exercise to clarify certain issues, the language may be restrictive and interpreted in a manner that would contradict the original intent of Contracting States, thereby invalidating certain critical provisions and most importantly, stripping away the treaty text from the much-needed flexibility that may, in fact, address actual experience resulting from the challenges of the real world.[1148] Negotiating countries may opt to enter a reservation with the effect that the provision reserved shall not be binding on the state in order to ensure that its interests and potentially the ramification processes are secured.[1149]

Treaty drafting per se may be lengthy unless some alignment between the countries may occur beforehand. Model treaties are a prime mechanism to facilitate the discussion between negotiating parties before actual discussions commence. They set the bar from which states would commence their negotiations. States with low bargaining power may choose to set the bar pretty low in such model treaties, to be opaque in what they are ready or not ready to concede. In contrast, countries with high bargaining power may reveal a large degree of their position and anchor their position at a specific level in negotiations. In all, tax chapters in investment treaties introduce little new and reflect an existing adage of already reviewed and recognized terms. In structural terms, the four main elements are retained in a tax chapter in bilateral tax treaties: (1) exclusion; (2) inclusion; (3) limitations and exceptions; and (4) definitions and clarifications (Figure 6.1). In regard to the last point (definitions), drafters may

1147. *See, e.g.*, CETA Art. 28(8).

1148. *See generally* Morgenthau, *supra* note 2, at 260("the laymen were much quicker to recognize the gap between the rules of international law as represented by science, and the rules of international law as they exist in actual experience").

1149. *See generally* VCLT Art. 2(d) and 19. *See also* United Nations International Law Commission, Guide to Practice on Reservation to Treaties, Yearbook of the International Law Commission, 2011, vol. II, Part Two. A/66/10.

include further clarifications with the aim to clarify the definitions or set priority rules for treaty interpretation.

Figure 6.1 Structural Diagram for a Taxation Chapter in Investment Treaties

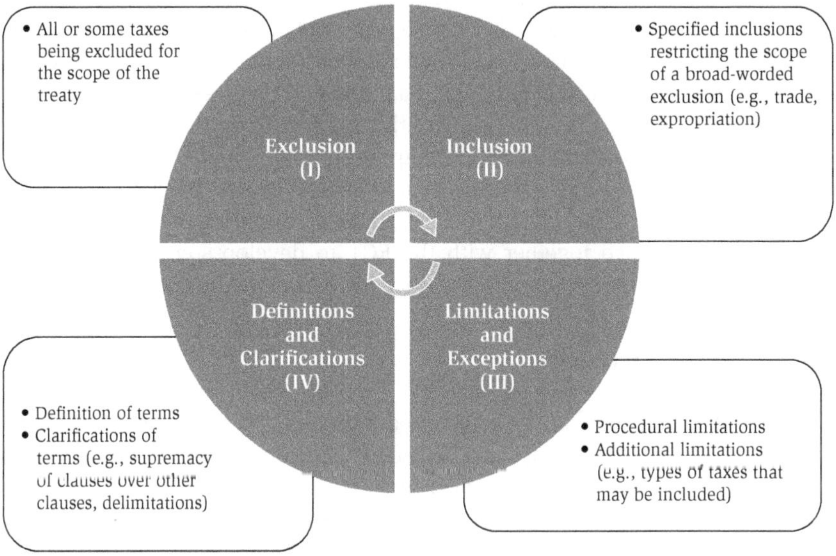

Source: Author's Own.

[B] Individual Elements

[1] General Presentation

Investment treaties do not require a taxation chapter. In the absence of a taxation chapter, taxation matters would generally be treated as any other measure by the state, thus, falling under the scope of application of investment protection regime. Taxation chapters thereby serve as a *clarification* of the state's intention to limit or not the consent of arbitrating the impact of taxation matters on investment protection. On the one hand, such limitation of consent may be *broad* as excluding *all* taxation matters from the treaty, or substantially *all* without an identified inclusion ("carve-out").[1150] However, any such broad approach in treaty drafting may run in contradiction to customary international norms that cover unlawful expropriation. On the other hand, a highly restricted tax exclusion (i.e., a tax exclusion with broad inclusions) may render the tax exclusion itself obsolete.

1150. *See, e.g.*, Indian Model BIT.

The following proposal reviews the previously analyzed provisions of the ECT against the background of three model BITs (US, Dutch, and Indian) and two multinational treaties that are under ratification after signature (CETA and US-Mexico-Canada Agreement). The aim of the analysis is to assess the relative strengths of the ECT and to see whether the text could be improved for purposes of developing a functional tax chapter in investment treaties. The US Model BIT was chosen due to its prevalence, and particularly as US BITs have commonly been invoked in tax matters. The Dutch BIT has been addressed, as Dutch BITs are routinely listed as the second or third most commonly invoked BITs. The Indian Model BIT has been analyzed due to its specifically restricted anchoring point that critically addresses the interests of Indian state, as it is still perceived as a net capital-importing state. Both CETA and US-Mexico-Canada treaties serve as prime examples of multilateral treaties that have been drafted and signed but remain to be ratified. As such, these five instruments provide an ideal platform when examined together with the ECT to develop some benchmarks for tax-related provisions for an investment treaty (be it bilateral or multilateral).

[2] The Tax Exclusion

Unlike the reservations on clarifications and definitions, which may not benefit from being overly inclusive, exclusions need to be clear and concise. Unlike definitions that aim to clarify, tax exclusions limit the state's consent to refer certain matters to arbitration. If the state were to restrict the scope of a treaty, it shall do so overtly, clearly and concisely; otherwise it runs the risk of the matter being misinterpreted.

[i] Form

In the simplest form, the tax exclusion may look as follows:

> Nothing in this treaty shall apply to taxation measures [...]
>
> or:
>
> [...] nothing in this treaty shall create rights or impose obligations relating to or in connection to tax measures.

However, a broad exclusion is not mandatory. Instead of having a broad exclusion with a list of long inclusions, a tax exclusion may also be limited in its form, so it only applies to certain types of taxes being excluded ("frontloaded").[1151] For example, CETA has opted for an approach where only certain types of taxes are excluded[1152] and certain types of actions to be excluded (e.g., measures aimed at

1151. *See, e.g.*, CETA Art. 28.7(4).
1152. CETA Art. 28.7(4) states:

> Nothing in this Agreement or in any arrangement adopted under this Agreement shall apply:

curbing tax evasion).[1153] In the CETA example, the broad exclusion is not counteracted with a list of exclusions but instead the inclusions are built in. In all, a broad exclusion may better set a clear exclusionary rule and then work backward on the type of matters that could be included.

[ii] Procedure

There are three possible methods by which a tax exclusion could be incorporated in a tax treaty, each providing for its own benefits. The first method, slightly long, is to have it expressly in a tax article to the article.[1154] The second method, slightly short, involves incorporating the tax exclusion in the "exceptions" section of the treaty. Such method could adequately exclude tax matters, or some tax matters, from the treaty without a full article being dedicated to it.[1155] The third method could involve an indirect/implied exclusion; however, such rule may lead to linguistic differences arising out of different legal traditions. Take for example, the Dutch Model BIT that extends national treatment (NT) protection to taxation, but excludes any benefits arising out of: (1) DTT, (2) customs union treaties, and (3) reciprocity with a third state (e.g., MFN).[1156] What may remain ambiguous is whether the NT is the *only* permissive standard applicable to fiscal matters, or whether it further supplements the other investment protection substantive standards such as those relating to expropriation, FET and non-discrimination and clarifies that NT applies to tax matters.[1157] Such drafting retains a degree of ambiguity and uncertainty to what extent a particular provision does or does not apply to tax matters. It may also require a degree of sophistication from the treaty negotiations (e.g., on the interplay of NT with other investment standards) to ensure an adequate balance between included and excluded provisions applicable to taxation measures.

[3] Inclusions

An inclusion counteracts any tax exclusions in the treaty by permitting certain claims. In most cases, an inclusion or some provision for the inclusion of investment protection against *unlawful expropriation* would be required.[1158] In such case, the tax exclusion

(a) to a taxation measure of a Party that provides a more favourable tax treatment to a corporation, or to a shareholder of a corporation, on the basis that the corporation is wholly or partly owned or controlled, directly or indirectly, by one or more investors who are residents of that Party; ...

1153. CETA Art. 28.7(2).
1154. *See, e.g.*, ECT Art. 21.
1155. *See, e.g.*, IISD Model BIT, Art. 25.3.
1156. 2018 Dutch Model BIT Art. 11.
1157. *Id.* Arts. 8-10 ("With regard to taxes ..., the Contracting State shall ... . Accord").
1158. *See, e.g.*, ECT Art. 21(5); NAFTA Art. 2103(6); US-Mexico-Canada Agreement Art. 32.3(8).

discussed above needs to be prefaced with a restriction such as: "except as otherwise provided in this treaty" or "subject to."[1159]

In addition to the expropriation inclusion, a state may include one or several specified inclusions for purposes of restricting the general tax exclusion so that investment protection obligations would extend to tax matters for certain topics (Figure 6.2). The list of relevant topics depend on the priorities of the state; some of the topics are: (1) transit;[1160] (2) transport; (3) trade matters, including interim provisions;[1161] (4) national treatment;[1162] (5) MFN;[1163] (6) collection of taxes[1164] and combatting tax evasion;[1165] (7) performance requirements for investments;[1166] and (8) market access, including export provisions.[1167]

Figure 6.2 The Spectrum of Tax-Related Matters Covered in Investment Treaties

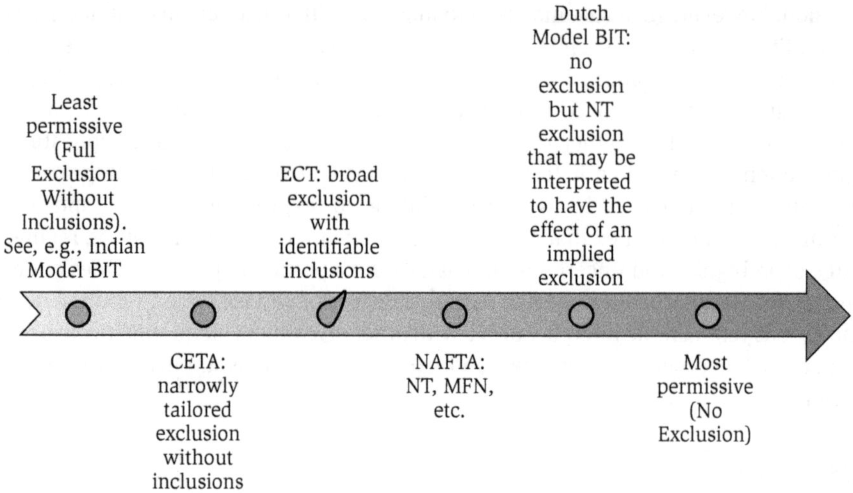

Source: Author's Own.

1159. *See, e.g.,* ECT Art. 21(1) ("*Except as otherwise provided in this Article,* nothing in this Treaty shall create rights or impose obligations with respect to Taxation Measures of the Contracting Parties") (emphasis added).
1160. *See* ECT Art. 21(2).
1161. *See* ECT Art. 21(4).
1162. *See* ECT Art. 21(3) by reference to *id.* Art. 10(2)-(3).
1163. *Compare* NAFTA Art. 2103.4(b) and US-Mexico-Canada Agreement, Art. 32.3(6)(b) extending the application of MFN provisions to taxes *with* CETA Art. 28.7(6). *See also* ECT Art. 21(3)(a) and (b) where MFN clauses are an added exception to the NT inclusion.
1164. *See* ECT Art. 21(6).
1165. CETA Art. 28.7(2).
1166. NAFTA Art. 2103.5.
1167. NAFTA Art. 2103.3.

In all, the inclusions would benefit from being grouped together, especially in the event that further limitations or exceptions are applied to one type of inclusion. For example, it would be reasonable to apply the inclusion on unlawful expropriation and national treatment to *all taxes* in order to curb the state's ability to wield its full taxation power in breach of these two standards. However, when it comes to other provisions relating to transit and transport, it may make sense to clarify that that state's power to tax shall be limited only to certain types of taxes (e.g., all taxes except certain direct taxes).

Combatting tax evasion is a legitimate and justified exercise of the power to tax and the police powers to tax. These principles are incorporated in the Tax Exclusion. It need not be expressly repeated in the treaty, as it may not cure the defect for when a state may enact measures that are not bona fide under the cloak of its use of taxation powers to curb tax evasion, thereby, putting in doubt the rule of law and a state's legitimate regulatory capacity or police powers.

[4] Limitations and Exceptions

Limitations and exceptions are other means by which Contracting States may restrict their consent to arbitrate tax-related matters. A Contracting State may choose from several limitations and exceptions, the difference between limitations and exceptions being mostly formalistic (albeit with the proposal that the limitations and exceptions could be relevant for determining whether a specific matter should be subject for jurisdictional review or on the merits).[1168]

[i] Common Exceptions

Despite certain inclusions, states may still indicate that certain types of tax matters will be subject to exceptions falling outside the scope of inclusions. The most common exception would be that applicable to direct taxes.[1169] The exception could vary in its specifics. It may only exclude taxes on income and capital[1170] or even refer to an appendix of specific taxes that would be excluded.[1171] For example, NAFTA excepts general taxes on income and capital but the list of excepted taxes covered "asset tax" specific to Mexico[1172] and even "excise tax(es) on insurance premiums" levied by Mexico when the latter would enjoy similar treatment by Canada or the US.[1173]

1168. *See supra* §4.04.
1169. *See, e.g.,* ECT Art. 21(2)-(4). *See also* NAFTA Art. 2103.4(b) and US-Mexico-Canada Art. 32.3(6)(b).
1170. ECT Art. 21(2)-(4) (uses "other than those on income or on capital").
1171. NAFTA Art. 2103.4 ("other than those on income, capital gains or on the taxable capital of corporations, taxes on estates, inheritances, gifts and generation-skipping transfers and those taxes listed in paragraph 1 of Annex 2103.4"). *Cf.* US-Mexico-Canada Art. 32.3(6)(b) ("other than a taxation measure on income, on capital gains, on the taxable capital of corporations, or taxes on estates, inheritances, gifts, and generation-skipping transfers").
1172. NAFTA Art. 2103(4), Annex 2103.4(1).
1173. *Id.* Annex 2103.4(2).

Although the direct tax exception has been preserved in the US-Mexico-Canada Agreement, the exception relating to "specific taxation measures" has since been removed. Given that expropriation may occur by means of direct tax matters, the use of exceptions in the tax chapters should be exercised cautiously particularly on detailed descriptions of taxes.

[ii] Review by CTAs

In DTTs, there is a tangible need for CTAs to opine, often jointly, on the treatment of a particular tax provision in order to: (1) align the Contracting States on the treatment of complex cases and (2) have a final determination of which state would tax any disputed incomes. In investment tax-related cases, the need for CTAs' opinions is disputed, as there is seldom a joint interest in determining a case of expropriation by one Member State. In investment sphere, the probability of the joint decision is highly unlikely. However, there remains one clear benefit for CTAs' review. The benefit centers on the possibility of CTAs to promptly dispose of non-meritorious claims. For this reason, referring matters to CTAs could be beneficial, as long as it is supported by short time frames for response with the aim of disposing of non-meritorious claims. In any event, the referral to CTAs should be made mandatory subject to a safety mechanism for urgent and exceptional cases where immediate relief from an emergency arbitrator may be required.[1174]

The proposal would include:

> Nothing in this Treaty, other than article * on expropriation, shall apply to taxes or taxation measures.
>
> Article * on expropriation and non-discrimination shall apply to taxes or taxation measures unless the competent tax authorities of the Contracting Parties, no later than six months after being notified by an investor of the disputed taxation measure, jointly determine that the measure is not an expropriation or discriminatory. The decision by competent tax authorities on discriminatory practices, when rendered within six months, shall be binding.

[iii] Definitions and Clarifications

The final section covers two interrelated issues: definitions and clarifications.

Definitions related to tax may be introduced at the beginning of the treaty (in the general section) or in the tax-related chapter. In the case of the latter, it shall clearly state its limitation and application. The definitions ought to be clear, concise, and avoid ambiguity. It shall include the critical elements of the definition: (1) the compulsory nature of the payment; (2) to the government, be it local, regional or national; (3) the "unrequited" nature of the payment, namely that an individual does not receive any direct benefit in return; and (4) there is a public purpose, however, remotely associated with the measure:

1174. *See, e.g.*, 2017 SCC Rules Art. 37(4) and Appendix II. *See* 2017 ICC Arbitration Rules Art. 29.

> A "Tax" or "Taxation Measure" shall mean "any compulsory unrequited payment to the government, levied for a public purpose."

Besides the formal definition of the term, the definition ought to also address the relationship between the definition and national law; namely that a measure defined under national law as a tax shall be presumed to be a tax unless proven otherwise:

> The term shall specifically include any provision relating to taxes of the domestic law of the Contracting Party or of a political subdivision thereof or a local authority therein unless determined otherwise.

Where common terms are being used, they should be clearly defined but a level of flexibility should be preserved in the event of reorganization:

> Competent Tax Authority shall be the relevant administrative authority under the Ministry of Finance, Treasury or related authority with prime responsibility over taxation matters. At the time of the drafting of the treaty, the relevant tax authorities are defined in Appendix *.

Regarding clarifications, there are of two types: clarification of terms and clarification of interpretative rules.

For the former ("term clarifications"), the definitions ought to define all the relevant terms without leaving any key terms undefined (e.g., "tax" versus "taxation measures") and resolve any conflicts between overlapping terms ("tax" and "customs" versus "tax" and "taxation matters"). In addition, the definition should clarify how it interprets customs duties and the link to excises, with excise duties being generally included in the definition but other customs duties being excluded:[1175]

> For greater certainty, "Tax" and "Taxation Measures" are used interchangeably.
>
> For greater certainty, Taxation Measures include excises but not customs duties.

The line between clarifications of terms and Interpretative clarifications is a fine one with a great degree of overlap between the categories. In many instances the clarification of terms may touch precisely on interpretative rules. When it comes to the definition of tax, it is critical that the relationship between the domestic measures and the treaty definition is properly addressed:

> For greater certainty, the determination that a measure is a tax under domestic law does not conclusively determine that a measure is a bona fide measure under this Treaty.

An important feature of taxation chapters, as seen with the initial drafting of the ECT, has been to resolve any conflicting interpretation arising out of: (1) other provisions of the treaties and (2) other treaties covering taxation matters (e.g., double taxation treaties). A provision in the investment treaty limiting its scope of application

1175. *Compare* NAFTA Art. 2107 *with* US-Mexico-Canada Agreement, Art. 32(3)(1), signed Nov. 30, 2018 (not in force). The US-Mexico-Canada Agreement has expressly added the phrase "taxes and taxation measures *include excise duties*, but do not include" (emphasis added).

so as not to conflict with existing tax treaties may sufficiently avoid any conflicting interpretations from DTT and BIT/MITs, including on matters falling under the MFN clause. Another possible point that could be introduced is how any such conflicts could be resolved. For example, the 2012 US Model BIT has vested the authority to resolve any conflicting terms with the competent authorities.[1176] This may cause various problems, including injecting uncertainty into how interpretative issues would be actually resolved by a third party and divesting arbitration tribunals of authority to resolve such conflicts. In such case, the proposal would be not to delegate the interpretative authority of the treaty to other agencies (e.g., CTAs) but retain it within the competency of the arbitral tribunals, as below:

> In the event of any inconsistency between this Article and any other provision of the Treaty, this Article shall prevail to the extent of such inconsistency.
>
> However, nothing in this Treaty shall affect the rights and obligations of either Party under any bilateral or multilateral tax agreement. In the event of any inconsistency between this Treaty and any such agreement, that agreement shall prevail to the extent of the inconsistency.

Inevitably, the tax of the treaty becomes lengthy. Especially in the context of taxation matters, there is a tendency to over-include and over-clarify. As not all alternatives can be reasonably anticipated the overinclusion may be susceptible to misinterpretation, especially after substantial time has passed altering the expectation of the drafting parties.

[C] ECT Modernization and Implications for the Taxation Article

Finally, on the ECT provisions specifically, the ECT is under modernization but the tax provisions of the treaty have not been taken up in the modernization efforts.[1177] The Taxation Article is currently not subject for the current modernization mandate of the ECT, despite containing major problems on several key considerations including the translation of the Italian text. Even though tax issues are not subject for the review, the right to regulate and the definition of "indirect expropriation" are part of the approved topics.[1178] Taxation is too important of an issue not to be taken up in the current ECT modernization efforts. Correction of errors, in accordance with VCLT Article 79, could be made where the parties agree. A few of the issues, perhaps with the exception of the Italian translation, could be corrected with the assistance of VCLT Article 79. In the instance of large deviations in the various translations, the Contracting States could in fact agree to correct the translations with the assistance of VCLT Article 79(3), particularly considering that the Russian and English versions were the primary languages for purposes of the contract negotiations and these are in sync with each

1176. *See, e.g.*, 2012 Model US BIT art. 21(4) ("In the case of a tax convention between the Parties, the competent authorities under that convention shall have sole responsibility for determining whether any inconsistency exists between this Treaty and that convention").
1177. Bucharest Declaration, Resolution.
1178. *See* Energy Charter Secretariat, Approved Topics for the Modernisation of the Energy Charter Treaty, Nov. 29, 2018.

other. Amending the treaty may be inevitable to rectify some confusion over terminology. Based on the existing case law, three initiatives could be extrapolated: (1) alignment and clarification of the definition of tax and taxation measures; (2) simplification and streamlining the inclusions; and (3) clarifying the scope of the competent national authorities. In parallel, any translations need to take account of the subtleties in these versions, most notably on the distinct use of the term "tax" and "taxation measures."

On the issues of different terminology, confusion over "tax" and "taxation measures" may be mitigated by clarifying the overlap between these two terms: that the term "tax" cannot be interpreted more restrictively than "taxation measures" and that the two definitions work in parallel. Further simplification and reorganization of the terms of the inclusions could be accomplished as per the proposals below. By adopting the classification of the terms in exclusion, inclusions, and limitations/exceptions, it becomes easier to draft the treaty and group these into building blocks in respective categories. Such language could follow clearly after the tax exclusion, clearly marking the existence of the inclusions and grouping these limitations. Finally, the scope and purpose of the review by the CTAs could be clarified.

§6.04 CONCLUDING REMARKS ON THE PROPOSALS

From this chapter, two distinct proposals emerged. The first proposal pertained directly to states in the routine task of implementing tax legislation: it directly addresses the gap between the implementation of taxation matters and investment arbitration regime. Inspired by the first findings of Professor Wälde, the proposal provided a practical toolkit. It developed a similar dual-structure of the IBA Guidelines to develop a principle-based approach supported by a practical application in the form of a "traffic-light" guidance to individual states on how to proceed. As the scope of the analysis concerns the relationship between the individual and the state, instead of two private parties, the proposed "traffic-light" regime excluded a waivable non-permissive category (e.g., "waivable red list") that is otherwise present in the IBA Guidelines. The work's proposal incorporated a top-down exercise of authority as it is with all tax matters, rather than a horizontal relationship observed with procedural matters such as those governing conflict of interest.

The second proposal focused on the tax-specific provisions in investment treaties. A tax provision is not required in investment treaties. However, when a tax provision is implemented, tax provisions ought to be understandable in terms of what matters are included and what matters are excluded from the application of the treaty. The starting points for the proposal are the provisions of the ECT that provide, against the background of new initiatives, a firm platform for determining the state's power to tax. Model treaties are now experimenting with several approaches, including narrowing the tax exclusion, as is the case with CETA, and omitting tax inclusions. The previous analysis reviewed some common model treaties, which may carry some subjective bias to address the interests of the drafters. Moving toward an objective model treaty, the text of model treaties was presented in two forms: short version and full version. These treaty improvements may be helpful even in the initiative to modernize the ECT: although taxation matters are not currently part of the scope of the modernization initiatives, they may relate to the "right to regulate" and the "indirect expropriation" definition. The ECT Taxation Article may be further improved by: (1) incorporating a definition on taxation and clarifying the relationship between tax and taxation measure; (2) simplifying the language on inclusions; and (3) further simplifying the procedure for competent authorities. In all, these proposals sought to increase awareness on the intersection of tax-related matters and investment protection and to provide helpful toolkits to address some of the most common problems. They are intended for states, but they may well serve claimants in assessing whether a taxation matter objectively rises to the level of an investment treaty breach.

CHAPTER 7

Conclusion

§7.01 THE RESEARCH QUESTION AND THE SUCCINCT ANSWER

At the outset, this book set out the following overall research question: what are the outer limits of a state's power to tax in the investment energy arbitration regime and specifically in the context of the ECT? During the course of this book, an answer has emerged. The outer limits to the state power to tax are specific limits to the national sovereignty of the state, either agreed by the state or applicable to state practice by virtue of public international law by which the fiscal power of the state may be restrained. Such outer limits obligate states to observe binding treaty commitments and to refrain from exercising the power to tax in a confiscatory or discriminatory manner, or in any manner that amounts to an abuse of rights scenario.

§7.02 THE THREE CORE POINTS OF THE POWER TO TAX

The outer limits follow from three core points of the power to tax. First, a state enjoys a broad power to tax. The power to tax constitutes a fundamental sovereign power anchored in the right of a state to decide over its own fiscal policy and economic values. In the energy context, the power to tax is further linked to a state's permanent sovereignty over natural resources, including the state's ability to dispose of and regulate depletion of the natural resources as best deemed fit.

Although the impact of BITs on attracting foreign investment is disputed, there is little debate on whether tax policy directly attracts foreign investment. The power to tax provides the state with its mainstream of revenue, but it also builds an interconnection between the taxpayer and the state. It incorporates an interdependency between taxpayers to share responsibility over key utilities, including at the state and national government, over education, healthcare, and social security. The power to tax involves determining *whom* to tax, *what* taxes to apply, and on *what* goods or activities, as well as *how* to apply them.

Second, the broad power to tax is not absolute. The power to tax is subject to limits under domestic and international law. On the domestic side, strict limits may be found in the national constitutional and administrative regimes of the state. The domestic limits remain confined to the national level. Beyond the domestic framework, two additional limits emerge from treaty obligations entered into by the state and from public international law. As to the treaties, a state may enter into international agreements to limit the broad taxation power; such willingness to curb its power may be motivated by various factors, including the commitment to preserve certain standards in exchange for attracting investments. As to public international law, this final constraint acts as an ultimate check on the state conduct not to abuse its powers even when no domestic limits are upheld or found. Peremptory norms may rarely materialize in the power to tax, unless a particular facet of the state's power to tax (e.g., enforcement of the tax law) is linked to an extreme act of the state (e.g., torture at collection of taxes or when property is seized) that would violate a peremptory norm. Customary international law rules on expropriation, minimum standard, and denial of justice may lay additional limits to the power to tax; however, how these rules interact with the express powers of states may require further fine-tuning. In fact, the rapid rise in investment law jurisprudence cause "general rules of international law," including laws of customary law to find "major practical expression in foreign investment law."[1179] The focus thus turns to three main limits, whether codified in the treaty or as part of customary international law: unlawful expropriation/confiscation, discrimination, and abuse of rights and process. In the presence of bilateral or multilateral treaties, these standards will be incorporated into the treaties themselves, but the argument of this book is that existing cases have gone further and have revealed a pattern where these standards are embraced as customary principles and are binding on the states *as standalone principles*.

Third, whereas the outer limits to the power to tax fall under the review of investment arbitration tribunals, the proper balance between the exercise of national sovereignty over taxation and any limits arising thereof retains the state as the central decision actor. Recent case law has identified the broad contours of the limits to the power to tax under international law. ECT case law has directly addressed the limits derived from expropriation and has even contextualized such limits in relation to similar provisions in other investment treaties. Other non-ECT investment cases have revealed similar limitations in other bilateral treaties. In all these investment cases, states remained in the proverbial "driving seat" when entering into treaties, providing commitments, or when passing legislation that may adversely affect outcome. States retained national sovereignty over what fiscal solutions they implement for stimulating investment (e.g., in the renewable sector) and how specifically they treated domestic taxation (e.g., by excluding it from the jurisdiction of an investment tribunal). In cases involving Spain, the Czech Republic and Italy, recent case law has revealed that *cost-based* subsidies, as opposed to market-based or fair sales value solutions, should be adopted with a high degree of caution. Nonetheless, on pure taxation issues,

1179. *See generally* Dolzer and Schreuer, *supra* note 54, at 17.

tribunals have preserved the state's power to tax when clearly defined under national law. Unless these taxation measures were not actually taxation measures in their own right (e.g., not being bona fide), they would be generally upheld and excluded from the review of the tribunal.

§7.03 DERIVING THE OUTER LIMITS

In reaching these findings, the work has explored seven sub-inquiries addressed in individual chapters. The first sub-inquiry focused on the origins of the ECT with regard to the rapid rise of investment arbitration jurisprudence; namely: *what are the origins of the ECT and specifically the Taxation Article?* The origins of the ECT are in the final vestiges of the Cold War when an attempt to level the "playing field" between the East and the West has been introduced: with the West providing the capital and the East providing the resources. The lengthy negotiations and the misalignment of interests have produced a complex treaty whose key driving actors have reneged on their obligations: the US has refused to sign the treaty and the Russian Federation, as the successor of the Soviet Union, has withdrawn from the treaty after *Yukos*. The Taxation Article, in its main form, was introduced by the US and resembles closely the same principles found in NAFTA. It incorporated a "tax filter" for winnowing out non-meritorious complaints by means of referral to tax authorities. The negotiations surrounding the Taxation Article remained at the level of the finance experts in the respective governments, and it served as a technical chapter to ensure the mitigation of any potential conflicts with DTTs. However, in the aftermath of the *Yukos* award, it was later revealed that taxation measures themselves could adopt an expropriatory character; a fact that it may be reconciled with the current version of the treaty where the term "tax" is left undefined but the term "taxation measures" is defined by reference to domestic law.

The second sub-inquiry explored *the key elements of a tax and how they have materialized in the first investment cases*. The definition of a tax remains an elusive concept with pure finance-based and investment arbitration-specific definitions containing analogous but slightly divergent elements. Both definitions recognize tax as a mandatory payment to the state. Whereas the finance-based definitions focus on the unrequited or non-reciprocal nature of the payment, the investment-based definitions have adopted a requirement that the payments to the state contain certain *elements*, rather than fixed criteria. At its core, taxation is an exercise of the state's fiscal policy at subnational, national and international level. The power to tax remains subject to four limits: national constitutional law, customary international law, treaty limitations, and administrative considerations. Investment arbitration tribunals rarely opine on national constitutional issues, as this is the purview of domestic courts. These tribunals most commonly address treaty limitations, based on the jurisdiction that they derive; however, customary international law and even administrative considerations may be relevant in reviewing the conduct of the state.

The early investment arbitration cases, linked to taxation, set out the broad contours for defining what a tax is and the limits to the power to tax. The early cases

(*Brewer*, *Cook*, *Kügele*, *Revere Copper*, and *Too*) point toward a high degree, but not an unrestricted level, of deference to the state. In *Kügele*, taxation is expressly defined as a taking with the clarification that loss of income alone does not qualify as a breach. After *Kügele*, the outer limits of the broad deference to the state have been further elaborated: in *Cook*, tribunals held that states may freely modify and repeal taxation legislation, while in *Revere Copper* and *Too*, tribunals deemed that states may not breach earlier commitments such as the obligations not to expropriate or pass discriminatory or unlawfully burdensome measures.

The third sub-inquiry investigated the formal structure of the ECT Taxation Article and *whether there are means to systematize the various elements of the Article*. The complexity of the ECT Taxation Article demands a formalization of the taxonomy or cartography of the tax provisions of an investment treaty. *Yukos* adopted the colloquial "carve-out" and "clawback" terms that describe the scenario when the state's consent to arbitrate tax measures is restricted ("carved out" from the treaty) but nonetheless remains within the purview of investment tribunals ("clawed back"). The use of this terminology, despite being colorful, may inadvertently trigger confusion as to the extent of the so-called clawback. Instead, the work offers an alternative to the classification of the various tax provisions that builds on vertical layers rather than horizontal concepts. In reviewing the complexity of the ECT tax chapter, it groups the various tax provisions in three categories: (1) exclusions, (2) inclusions, and (3) limitations and exceptions. The work also introduces the term "levels" by which terms at a level above may narrow, expand, clarify, or supplement the provisions at a level below. The methodology derived from the ECT Taxation Article may, due to its complexity, serve to facilitate the understanding and categorization of other multilayered provisions in treaties, not only tax treaties.

The fourth sub-inquiry investigated the BIT and the ECT case law and whether they yield any points of tension; it investigated whether such emergent points of tensions are ECT-specific or as part of a particular pattern linked to taxation and if such pattern arises, what are this pattern's contours and if there are any means of reconciling these tension points.

The limited but detailed review of BIT case law reveals a pattern where the definitional challenges over the ordinary meaning of the term "tax," the determination of a confiscatory tax and the determination of a bona fide tax remain consistent topics even in the BIT contexts. The BIT cases reveal that the tax-related inquiries are treaty-specific. For example, in the Ecuadorian cases, arbitral tribunals have upheld the application of tax exclusion/carve-out in the Canadian-Ecuadorian BIT but not in US-Ecuadorian BIT, leading to different results on substantially similar circumstances. Even considering potential arguments that confiscatory taxation breaches customary law, the inquiry in those early BIT cases remained squarely at the treaty level. The non-ECT *Yukos* cases established for the first time the inquiry into the bona fide nature of a tax, forging an important precedent for the ECT cases. However, this inquiry was initially developed for purposes of determining any breaches of the expropriation substantive standard, particularly indirect expropriation, not for jurisdictional purposes.

The forty tax-related ECT cases rendered to date reveal a distinct pattern of increasing importance of tax-related issues. The categorization of the ECT tax-related case law may be divided into renewable and non-renewable cases, with the non-renewable cases taking a distinct transformation after the rendering of the *Yukos* award. Prior to *Yukos*, tax matters were a peripheral issue. *Yukos* upheld the bona fide inquiry, and in doing so, it rotated the taxation-related kaleidoscope of the taxation-related case law to put the bona fide inquiry at the outset of the application of the Tax Exclusion/carve-out. The subsequent tax-related cases that followed arose out of the renewable energy initiatives in Spain, Italy, and the Czech Republic. In all these cases, state-adopted taxation measures were challenged when these were reduced. The ECT cases reveal a set of consistent issues: definitional concerns in the treatment of "tax" versus "taxation measure"; the jurisdiction to tax, burden of proof, treatment of taxation under domestic standard, the meaning of a bona fide taxation measure and the presence, if any, of a presumption in favor of validity. Investment tribunals have addressed these issues on the factual basis in the case; however, out of these cases, a pattern emerges that may be reconciled as per the sixth inquiry of this book. What becomes evident is that the shift toward renewable energy has put increasing strain on states to find prompt solutions. This pressure from the European Union or other similarly situated bodies is defensible, considering the challenges associated with climate change. States need to retain flexibility in adopting tax matters, which is inherent in the state power to tax. However, states cannot see the broad power to tax as a unrestricted justification for making and then reneging on far-reaching commitments on which reasonable investors, after completing due diligence, would rely.

The relationship between jurisdiction and the merits, where the determination of whether a tax is excluded from the review of an investment tribunal, falls within the jurisdictional inquiry of a case. Some risk of conflating or introducing through the expropriation "gateway" allegations of other breaches could be triggered for those extreme cases where the state conduct is "exceptional." During such inquiry, the burden of proof may be perceived to shift partially between the parties. States inevitably carry the burden to prove that an asserted measure falls within the scope of a treaty exclusion ("carve-out"). The states shall do so by first unequivocally establishing that a measure is a tax under domestic law. Upon such determination, it would be the investor who would have to assert the grounds for why the domestic valid tax measure is not bona fide. The presumption of validity may equally be refuted by establishing that certain conduct of the state falls outside of those outer limits to a legitimate exercise of the power to tax: expropriation, discrimination, and abuse of rights. In such case, the burden shifts back to the state to invoke any defenses or justifications. The initial burden of proof need not be high, given that the threshold that the state needs to meet is that the invoked tax is a valid domestic tax. The confusion is predicated on the various levels of exclusions, inclusions, and limitations and exceptions: the ultimate burden remains solely with the party asserting the defense regarding the shifting between the various strata of items falling within or outside the tribunal's jurisdiction.

The scrutiny of the ECT and non-ECT (BIT) case law against each other revealed that the observed points of tension may indeed be reconciled with regard to four inquiries: (1) ordinary meaning of the term "tax," (2) the inquiry under domestic law, (3) the inquiry under the treaty, and (4) overriding inquiries such as the bona fide inquiry, rooted in abuse of rights doctrine and good faith. In all, the focus of this inquiry is to what extent "taxes" or "tax measures," validated under the domestic regime, may be second-guessed in determining whether "a tax" is in fact a tax, namely, that the "tax" or the "taxation measure" contains certain characteristics that make the measure/state act a "tax." The underlying assumption, as the Czech cases reveal, is that an alleged tax must *unequivocally* qualify as a domestic tax in order for the state to assert it as a defense. The qualification under domestic law is a necessary prerequisite that seldom is not met. However, the Czech cases reveal one such rare instance where justifiable doubt may be present in the nature of the tax, even in the domestic setting. Once a tax qualifies as a domestic tax, investment tribunals may be called to rule on whether a tax is adopted in good faith. The Spanish renewable cases have revealed a high standard for refuting the presumption that a qualified domestic tax measure is not bona fide, with *Novenergia* suggesting a presumption of validity of a qualified domestic tax is well rooted in state sovereignty and to a certain extent the state's regulatory freedom.

While the contours of the tax-related case law are yet to be firmly outlined, the emerging consensus from the Spanish cases indicate, by drawing on the *Yukos* decision, that where the tax measures' main objective is unrelated to "raising general revenue" the measure may be deemed to be in breach of the bona fide standard. This reference to "raising general revenue" is a step in the right direction to clarify the legitimate requirement of a tax but is not without problems. In relying on such standard focusing on "revenue generation" or the revised standard presented in the negative in the *Voltaic* cases and *Antaris* "where the main purpose is other than generating revenue," a decision-maker may inadvertently exclude other otherwise legitimate taxes (e.g., Pigouvian taxes). Pigouvian taxes are an oddity in the bona fide inquiry because by their nature they are aimed to curb negative externality. The bona fide inquiry needs to account for instances where the state, while acting in good faith, may pass taxes even in instances where the main aim is not to generate revenue. But such conduct may not overreach previous commitments or the aforementioned outer limits otherwise imposed on the state's power to tax: arbitrariness, expropriation, and discrimination. If the *Yukos* standard in the original or the *Antaris/Voltaic* standard were to continue to apply, "raising general revenue" should not be interpreted restrictively and should permit for other relevant public purposes that may, for example, fall under legitimate regulatory or police powers of the state.

The glaring use of the term "tax" in the expropriation inclusion/clawback found in ECT Article 21(5) but not in the tax exclusion/carve-out need not be seen as an issue of concern, except perhaps when the actual term appears in different languages differently and all those languages are binding. The position that the undefined term "tax" is meant to encompass a broader, not narrower, scope than the term "taxation measure" is not only defensible but reasonable. These are two synonymous terms: one that is defined and one that is not defined under the treaty. The term "taxation measure" includes any tax-related provision under domestic law and under a DTT. By preserving the term "tax" for purposes of the expropriation inclusion, the ECT drafters preserved the integrity of the investment tribunals to examine a tax measure under international law without straining the implications for domestic provisions or DTTs. A tribunal need not give effect to the term under the tax exclusion/carve-out (be it under the bona fide inquiry or general principles of espousals), hence, not opining or invalidating the tax under the domestic law. Such approach is consistent with tribunals not serving as appellate courts to domestic courts and certainly not tax courts. Even in the rare instances when the tax measure may be linked to a DTT, the use of the term "tax" permits investment tribunals to find a tax to be confiscatory without necessarily prompting negative ramifications for the DTTs and the DTT jurisprudence. By preserving the term "tax" in ECT Article 21(5), the ECT drafters ensured not only that a finding of a confiscatory tax does not unduly strain the relationship of the ECT jurisprudence with national law but also that it does not unnecessarily strain the possible conflict right of tribunals to rule that a tax is confiscatory. Even when any ambiguity arises from the various equally authoritative translations, case law (particularly involving Italy) was able to reconcile the text reasonably; otherwise, any discrepancies in the various language translations may be reconciled by reliance on VCLT Article 33.

Finally, the last sub-inquiry focused on a prospective review with several recommendations into *whether the points of tension arising out the existing case law may be streamlined to modernize* the current language in the ECT, set out a benchmark for tax legislation against investment commitments, and further improve the taxation chapter in investment treaties. The driving force for the recommendation section and to a certain extent the entire book has been a speech by the late Professor Wälde in which he highlighted the importance of documenting, organizing, and dissecting systematic patterns ("red flags") in the practice of the states that deviate from "normal" taxation practices. Eleven years after the speech, sufficient case law has emerged to discern the broad contours of state practice with regard to taxation as reviewed through the eyes of investment tribunals. The outcome of the inquiry has been an affirmative yes, existing law provides a valuable outlook on the provisions of the existing treaties and tax legislation. The section provides a proposal for the modernization of the ECT, as well as model texts for the taxation chapters of other investment treaties. Finally, the work develops a set of key principles and a semaphore-type scale for state practice when passing taxation measures that builds on Professor Wälde's call for cataloging red flags.

§7.04 FUTURE INQUIRIES AND FINAL THOUGHTS

Between the start of this research project and its completion, the investment arbitration regime, including the energy-related sector, has confronted several developments, often of a conflicting nature. At a methodological level, the work incorporated the rapidly growing case law emerging from the renewable sector. Since 2015, the number of decisions has doubled (from forty-six to ninety-two awards and decisions). A large focus of these cases, concerning Spain, for example, involved the renewable sector with direct ramifications for taxation investment issues. There are now forty tax-related decided ECT cases.

At a conceptual level, the research has observed the rising tide against investment arbitration and a deep scrutiny into the purpose of the ECT. Climate change has become a decisive, albeit contentious, issue on both sides of the Atlantic. The *Achmea* decision has struck at the heart of the intra-EU BITs, sending deep reverberations into the disputes between two EU Member States. In addition, the EU Commission has fostered a great deal of debate on the transition toward a multilateral investment court, or at least a multilateral tribunal appointed by the states only.

These conflicting forces impose on states incredible pressure to act quickly, often without regard for the implications for foreign investments. Nowadays, public international law confronts unparalleled challenges often shaped by fragmentation and disagreement on the nature of these challenges, not to mention the solutions needed to address the challenges themselves. As already materialized in the numerous renewable cases against Spain, Italy, and the Czech Republic, these forces merge into a catastrophic storm when states develop "ill-thought" plans under the stress of meeting ambitious targets. The devastating consequences of climate change only increase the pressure for states to act and to do so quickly. In the sea of change and conflict, the topic of taxation and specifically the extent of the state power to tax remains the critical filament for the authority of the states to affect foreign investments and to preserve control over national financial policy. New proposals on addressing climate change almost invariably involve some tax elements: be it tax credits for renewable energy such as solar and wind, a carbon tax, or excises and tariffs on products from countries "without robust climate policies."[1180] The "trial-and-error" approach of the first wave of renewable initiatives is likely to cause greater concern in the future in comparison to what we have observed in the past.

At the core of the taxation power is the element of "confidence" or "trust": trust between the taxpayer and the state (be it in the role of the legislator or the tax authority).[1181] Capacity building inadvertently involves the establishment of "mutual trust" in the national tax system: establishing "a fair tax system," developing "well-functioning service oriented tax" and "spending taxes carefully."[1182] The establishment of a robust national tax regime is only half of the battle. Building a moat could protect against invading land forces, but it will not keep the dragons out. For investments to succeed, funds need to cross swiftly across borders, and tax regimes ought to account for how they will treat foreign investments. For developing countries, foreign investment is a scarce lifeline, particularly when confronted with climate change, such investment may be the only source of additional funding to change deeply ingrained economic activity. Investment protection by means of investment arbitration seeks to safeguard long-term trust: trust between the state and the foreign investor.

In its analysis and review, this book aims to serve as a theoretical and practical "spring board" for further inquiries into the outer limits of the power to tax, the

1180. *See generally "The Obstacle Course,"* The Economist, Sept. 21, 2019, 47-8 (detailing the detailed proposals of the Democratic candidates to the 2020 US presidential election).

1181. *See* Magdalena Andersson, Speech by Minister for Finance Magdalena Andersson at Stockholm Tax Conference concerning capacity building, May 30, 2018; https://www.government.se/speeches/.

1182. *Id.*

interplay with constitutional law and separation of powers, procedural mechanisms that may safeguard due process and even the potential linking of bilateral and MITs with DTTs and other relevant topics. The contribution of this book is to explore tax practices and to consolidate existing case law into discernible solutions: improving existing treaty texts, identifying red flags for the legislator, and offering proposals for future investment treaties. The proposals offered by this book are a mere first step in the lengthy journey of the transformation of the energy sector. Such transformation may only happen with robust tax tools being unleashed by governments. Regardless of the future of investment arbitration, states shall retain a broad but not unlimited power to tax. Does the state enjoy a broad power to tax? The answer is yes. But such power is accompanied by limits. The proper balance is not in what the state could have done better. Instead, the limit stands for the state *not* crossing a red line. The outer limits of such power remain squarely rooted in the limitations against expropriatory and discriminatory taxes, as well as protection against abuse of rights state practices. In the investment context, the broad contours of the outer limits of the state power to tax remain to be fully shaped, but their edges are starting to become clearer, as presented in this book.

Appendices

APPENDIX I

Timeline of Uncontested Events in the *Yukos* Disputes

Date	*Act/Event*
1993	Yukos incorporated as a joint stock company by Presidential Decree.
Late 1990s	Low-tax regions established exempting taxpayers fully or in part from taxes. Company rises to be one of the largest entities in Russia.
July 2003	Criminal proceedings commenced against Yukos officials: in July Platon Lebedev, CEO of Menatep; in October, Mikhail Khadorkovski, CEO of Yukos is arrested.
2003-04-28	Russian Tax Authorities conduct a field tax audit for the years 2000 and 2001 finding no breaches. Oct-November, tax authorities issue certificates that Yukos has no tax arrears.
2003-12-08	Russian Tax Authorities order a tax reaudit for the year 2000.
2003-12-29	Russian Tax Authorities issue a tax reassessment for the year 2000 ordering payment of USD 3.5 billion.
2004-04-14	Demand for retroactive payments (deadline for payments was 2 days). Subsequent request for payments followed on Sep. 2, 2004, Nov. 16, 2004, and Dec. 6, 2004.
2004-04-15	Asset freeze ordered
Nov. 17 – Dec. 1, 2004	RosInvest acquires shares in Yukos in two separate transactions.
Dec. 19, 2004	Baikal Finance Group acquires Yuganskneftegaz, the crown jewel of Yukos, at an auction. Four days later, RosNeft purchases the shares from Baikal for the undisclosed amount.

Date	*Act/Event*
May 2005	Platon Lebedev and Mikhail Khodorkovsky convicted of fraud and tax evasion. New charges of embezzlement followed in February 2007 with further convictions in December 2010.
Nov. 21, 2007	Complete liquidation of Yukos.

APPENDIX II

RES Timeline for Ecuador and Disputed Interests Triggered by the Respective Cases

Period	*Act/Event*
1970-1990s	Hydrocarbon Law introduced in 1991. Service contracts as the primary model for investments.
Early 1990s	Energy and power distribution crises in Ecuador.
1992-1995	Privatization efforts. BITs negotiated and signed starting with 1993.
1993	Hydrocarbon Law amended to allow participation by foreign investors and profit-sharing.
1999	Article 69A to the Ecuadorian Tax Law introduced affects VATs claimed. VAT rate increased. Banking crisis.
2001	SRI Resolution denying VAT refunds. VAT cases that followed (2002-2003).
2006	Law 42 amended for increased state participation.
	Decree 1672 implements Law 42, increases the share to 50% of windfalls.
Oct. 2007	Decree 662 increase the share to 70% on all new contracts and 99% on extraordinary income. PSC Cases followed 2008-present.
Feb. 2009	Enforcement proceedings for back taxes ("Coactiva").
Sept. 2009	Unilateral termination of PSCs by Ecuador ("Caducidad").

Nr	Case	Interest	Interest
1.	*Oxy II*	In 1985: Occidental entered into a service contract with Petroecuador's predecessor (Corporacion Estal Petrolera Ecuatoriana). Production began in 1993. Participation contract signed: May 1999.	Block 15. Amazon Region.
2.	*Burlington*	Between 2000 and 2008: Burlington acquires ownership interests in four blocks in the Amazon Region. Where Burlington held a minority interest, Perenco owned a controlling interest as consortium lead.	Block 7: minority (42.5%). Block 21: minority (46.25%). Block 23: 50% (settled before merits). Block 24: 100% (settled before merits). Amazon Region.
3.	*Murphy I* and *II*	1985: Conoco-led consortium enters into a service contract with Ecuador. 1987: Murphy's subsidiaries acquire a 20% interest in the service contract. 1996: participation contract entered into with the same 20% interest. 2009: Murphy Ecuador sells the interest to Repsol that, by then, is a Consortium operator.	Block 16. Amazon Region.
4.	*Perenco*	Same two blocks as with Burlington; Perenco is the consortium lead. Perenco was not part of the original concession. It becomes part of the Participation contracts for the respective blocks in 2002.	Block 7: majority (57.5%). Block 21: majority (53.7%). Amazon Region.

APPENDIX III

RES Timeline for The Czech Republic

Act/Order	*Implement*	*Effect*	*Scope*
Act 586/1992			**Act on Income Tax** introduces the first step to encourage RES, including: (1) tax holiday (exemption from income tax for the year of establishment plus five years thereafter) and (2) accelerated depreciation period for photovoltaic installations.
Act 180/2005	Mar. 31, 2005	Aug. 1, 2005	**Act on Promotion** adopts an incentive scheme for RES that includes: (1) preferential treatment for RES producers; (2) feed-in-tariffs; and (3) green bonuses. Ensures a stable tariff and guarantees that the feed-in-tariff would not decrease by more than 5% from the previous year.
Reg. 475/2005	Nov. 30, 2005		**Technical Regulation** empowers the Czech Energy Regulatory Office (ERO) to set technical and economic parameters to achieve a 15-year payback period in line with the Act on Promotion.
Act 330/2010		Jan. 1, 2011	Abolished all incentives related to photovoltaic plants with installed output, exceeding 30 kWp commissioned after March 1, 2011.
Act 346/2010		Jan. 1, 2011	Income tax exemption for RES repealed.
Act 402/2010		Jan. 1, 2011	Introduces the **Solar Levy**: applies for years 2011-2013 for plants put into operation in 2009-2010. The Solar Levy was set at 26% and 28%.

Act/Order	*Implement*	*Effect*	*Scope*
Act 165/2012	Jan. 30, 2012	Jan. 1, 2013	**New Act on Promotion** repeals Act 180/2005 (Act on Promotion); terminates all existing contracts between RES producers and grid operators, obligation to pay the "negative electricity hourly price" in instances of surplus of electricity, and even introduces recycling fees for disposal of photovoltaic panels.
Act 310/2013		Sept. 13, 2013	Extends the Solar Levy to apply past 2013 for plants put into operation after 2013. Cancels all other incentives after Jan. 2014. Reduces the Levy to 10% for feed-in tariffs and to 11% for green bonuses.

Appendix IV

RES Timeline for Italy

Act/Order	*Impl.*	*Effect*	*Scope*
Leg. Decree 387/2003	Dec. 31, 2004		Implemented EU Directive 2001/77/EC of 27 Sept. 2001, on the Promotion of Electricity from Renewable Energy Sources ("First Renewable Energy Directive"): simplifies the authorization procedures for RES projects and obligates states to set targets for energy consumption from RES. Also, adopts a remuneration system based on feed-in-tariffs (FiT)s.
Ministerial Decree	July 28, 2005		FiT remuneration system was first implemented in 2005 by means of the First Energy Account; later modified through the Second, Third, Fourth and Fifth Energy Accounts. Decreto Ministeriale 9 febbraio 2007 (Ministerial Decree of February 19, 2007) (the "Second Energy Account"); Decreto Ministeriale 6 agosto 2010 (Ministerial Decree of Aug. 6, 2010) (the "Third Energy Account"); Decreto Ministeriale 5 maggio 2011 (Ministerial Decree of May 5, 2011) (the "Fourth Energy Account"); and Decreto Ministeriale 5 luglio 2012 (Ministerial Decree of July 5, 2012) (the "Fifth Energy Account" aka *Conto V*).

Act/Order	*Impl.*	*Effect*	*Scope*
Law Decree No. 112/2008, Article 81(16), June 25, 2008, converted into law by Law No. 133/2008, Aug. 6, 2008 "Robin Hood Tax"	June 25, 2008	Aug. 6, 2008	Windfall profits tax applied to oil, gas and other energy companies. Initially excluded RES. Corporate income tax with gross annual income of over EUR 25 million was 27.5%; then 33% following by 34% in 2009. 2011: (1) RES producers no longer exempted; (2) gross annual income reduced to EUR 10 million and taxable income of EUR 1 million, and (3) rate increased to 38%. 2013: Threshold reduced to gross annual income of EUR 3 million and taxable income of EUR 300,000. 2015: On Feb. 11, 2015, the Italian Constitutional Court upheld that the tax applied prospectively on RES producers (*ex nunc*) and not retrospectively from the date of extension (*ex tunc*).
Leg. Decree 28/2011 Romani Decree		Mar. 29, 2011	Implement EU Directive 2009/27/EC (amend and repeal 2001/77/EC and 2003/30/EC). Established that FiT adopted by the Third Energy Account applied only to plants that entered into operation before May 31, 2011 (not Dec. 31, 2013). Limits eligibility for plants built on agricultural land only to 1 MW and occupied less than 10% of the parcel.
Law Decree 1	Jan. 24, 2012	Jan. 24, 2012 (ratified by Law 27 of Mar. 24, 2012)	Scales down the incentives from Romani Decree.

Act/Order	*Impl.*	*Effect*	*Scope*
Conto V or Fifth Energy Account "administrative fee"	July 5, 2012		See above Ministerial Decree for general evolution of the Energy Accounts. Conto V or Fifth Energy Account: 1. Introduced an administrative fee of EUR 0,00005 kW/h ("***Conto V* administrative fee**"). 2. Modified the tariffs bases: – PV plants under 1 MW received an "all-inclusive tariff" that combined: (a) the price of the electricity, (b) the value of the incentive premium, and (c) a specific tariff for self-consumed energy. – PV plants over 1 MW received a fluctuating amount between the all-inclusive tariff and hourly zonal price if such difference was positive. 2013: After Electricity Authority resolution of June 6, 2013, the tariffs provided by Conto V were withdrawn for PV facilities after that date.
Resolution 281/2012/EFR Again Resolution 522/2014/R/EEL "imbalance costs"	July 5, 2012		Resolution 281 terminated the exemption of PV producers from paying imbalance costs for oversupply of electricity. Since 2006 (Resolution 111/06) energy producers were required to project the amount of electricity that it would supply/inject into the grid.
Circular No. 36/E; further amended by Law No. 208/2015 "IMU/TASI charges"	Dec. 19, 2013 (Dec. 28, 2015)	Law No. 208 in effect Jan. 1, 2016	Circular reclassified PV plants as immovable property: affecting the depreciation rate and increasing the municipal property tax obligations. 2016: Further modification in the rule of determining which property is immovable, reducing what portions of PV plants were deemed as immovable property.

Act/Order	*Impl.*	*Effect*	*Scope*
Law Decree No. 145/2013, *Destinazione Italia* Decree	Dec. 23, 2013		The *Destinazione Italia* Decree altered the existing regime by introducing two options for PV producers: (1) *Shortening the period*: continue receiving the *Conto Energia* incentives at the same rate for the remainder of the 20-year period, but to foreclose the possibility of receiving additional incentives thereafter; or (2) *Reducing the incentives*: accept reductions to the Conto Energia incentives but to receive them for 7 additional years, for a total of 27 years.
Law No. 91/2014 *Spalma-incentivi* Decree	June 24, 2014	Jan. 1, 2015	Modified the *Conto V* administrative fee based on capacity, not production: ranged from EUR 1.20 per kW (for 1 MW) to EUR 2.20 per kW for plants with capacity of between 3-6 kW. Introduced three options for calculating new tariffs: (1) A new reduced incentive tariff over 24 years instead of the original 20 years. (2) The 20-year period remained the same, but the tariff rate would be reduced between 2015 and 2019, then increased in subsequent years. (3) The 20-year period remained the same, but the tariff rate would be reduced by a fixed percentage based on a PV plant's nominal capacity (e.g. a 6% reduction for plants with 200 kW and 500 kW nominal capacity; a 7% reduction for 500 kW – 900 kW plants; and 8% reduction for plants with 900 kW+). Tariffs previously granted to PV facilities over 200 kW were modified.

Appendix V

RES Timeline for Spain

Act/Order	*Implement*	*Effect*	*Scope*
Law 54/1997	Nov. 27, 1997	Promotion	Transposed EU Directive 96/92/EC on internal market in electricity; liberalized the energy production and supply; and established "special regime" for incentives
Royal Decree 2818/1998	Dec. 23, 1998		Sets out two options for the special regime: (1) FiTs based on kWh produced or (2) a premium to the market price.
Royal Decree 436/2004	Mar. 12, 2004		Replaced RD 2818/1998, which specified *inter alia* that any rate revisions in the CPI index shall apply "only to new facilities, and would 'not have a backdated effect on any previous tariffs and premiums.'"
Royal Decree 661/2007	May 25, 2007		Repealed 436/2004. Applied equally to CSP and PV. Introduces: (1) fixed FiTs, based on the plant's capacity, for 25 years of the facility (reduced to 80% for the remaining life of the facility). To be adjusted annually based on CPI. Review to occur every four years; and (2) priority for dispatch and accessing the grid. Requires registration in local registry for the special regime and a final commissioning certificate.

Act/Order	Implement	Effect	Scope
Royal Decree 1578/2008	Dec. 26, 2008		Introduces a regime for PV only for registration after the closing of Royal Degree 661/2007: (1) sets out a pre-assignment register for planning PV developments and (2) reduces the remuneration for these production entities.
Royal Decree 1565/2010	Nov. 19, 2010	Alterations/Reductions in the Existing Regime	Absolute cap on the right to receive a guaranteed tariff past 25 years of operation, later extended to 30 days.
Law 14/2010	Dec. 23, 2010		*Access toll*: Implements urgent measures: capping operating hours based on location and introduced an "access toll" of 0.5 EU/MWh.
Law 15/2012	Dec. 27, 2012		The Law introduced: – TVPEE: the 7% energy production value tax on all revenues, including FiTs derived from the production of electricity regardless of the source; and – Water Levy: a 2.2% tax on the use of continental waters for the production of electricity, applies to facilities of less than 50 MW.
Royal Decree 2/2013	Feb. 1, 2013		*Amended CPI*: Introduces the Amended CPI on which the FiTs were based; excluded price change in food, energy products and tax effects linked to inflation

Act/Order	*Implement*	*Effect*	*Scope*
Royal Decree 9/2013	July 13, 2013	**New Regulatory Regime**	Terminated the special regime, including the FiTs. Introduced the New Regulatory Regime by which the sale was subject to the wholesale market that may be supplemented with specific schemes.
Law 24/2013 et al	Sept. 12, 2013		New Support Scheme introduced based on the remuneration from wholesale market and a very detailed list of factors. Subsequent orders introduce minimum operating hours.
Royal Decree 413/2014	June 6, 2014		Introduces "reasonable rate of return" based on: "investment incentive" and "operating incentive." Sets out the specific remuneration based on a reasonable rate of return as calculated for a standard installation. Sets a target based on the 10-year Spanish T-bonds.

APPENDIX VI

Deep Dive into the Spanish Cases

Case	*Type*	*Fac.*	*Bifurcated*	*Domestic Standard*	*Bona Fide*	*Yukos Ref and High Standard*	*Gen. Revenue*	*EnCana test*	*Public Purpose*	*CTA*	*Relevant for Other Standards*
Charanne	None	PV	No: request denied	–	–	–	–	–	–	–	N/A
Eiser	TVPEE	CSP	No: request denied	–	Yes	Yes	Yes by quoting *Yukos*	Yes but not referred as such	–	Referred deemed as necessary	No
Isolux	TVPEE	PV	No: request denied	Tax under Spanish and intern. law	Yes	Yes	No	–	Referred to but no	Referred, complied but late. Relevant for costs	No

Case	Type	Fac.	Bifurcated	Domestic Standard	Bona Fide	Yukos Ref and High Standard	Gen. Revenue	EnCana test	Public Purpose	CTA	Relevant for Other Standards
Masdar	TVPEE	CSP	No: request denied	No	Yes	Yes	–	–	–		No: expressly excluded from damages
Antin	TVPEE	CSP	No: request denied	Yes (legislation only)	Yes	Yes	–	Yes	Yes		Considered but not addressed.
Novenergia	TVPEE	PV	No	Yes	Yes	Yes	No: BOP issue	No	No	No	–
Greentech	TVPEE	PV	No	Yes: Spanish and EU law	Yes	Yes	–	Yes, agreed by the parties	–	–	–
Cube Infrastr-ucture et al	TVPEE	PV	Yes: but only partially on quantum	Treaty; not domestic or EU law	Yes	Yes	–	Yes; includes “without any benefit to the taxpayer”	–	–	No
	Water Levy	Hydro			Yes		–		–	–	–
NextEra	TVPEE	CSP	Yes: but only partially on quantum	–	Yes	No	–	Yes	–	–	Some ref. that are possible

Case	*Type*	*Fac.*	*Bifurcated*	*Domestic Standard*	*Bona Fide*	*Yukos Ref and High Standard*	*Gen. Revenue*	*EnCana test*	*Public Purpose*	*CTA*	*Relevant for Other Standards*
9Ren	TVPEE	PV	No	Yes, relied on Supreme Court ruling	Yes	No	Yes	Yes	Reduction of tariff deficit is a public purpose	–	TVPEE omitted from quantum computations
RREEF	TVPEE	Wind and CSP	Yes: jurisdiction and quantum (defer. to merits)	Yes by reference to *Novenergia*	Yes	No: parties refer to *Yukos*, but the Tribunal does not take it up in either of the awards	Yes by reference to *Novenergia*	–	–	–	Yes
SoldEs	TVPEE	PV	No	Yes	Yes	Yes	Yes	Yes		–	–
OperaEd	TVPEE	PV	No	No: int'l law	Yes	No	No	No	Yes	–	Likely no
PV Investors	–	PV	Yes for jurisd.	–	–	–	–	–	–	–	Yes (gross up)
Infra Red	TVPEE	CSP	No: req. dismissed	Not discussed	Yes	Yes	Yes	Yes	Yes	Objection withdrawn	–

Case	*Type*	*Fac.*	*Bifurcated*	*Domestic Standard*	*Bona Fide*	*Yukos Ref and High Standard*	*Gen. Revenue*	*EnCana test*	*Public Purpose*	*CTA*	*Relevant for Other Standards*
RWE	TVPEE Water Levy	Wind Hydro	Quantum bifurcated	Not: but Supr. Court endorsed	Yes	Not directly, only in footnote	Not expressly	Yes	Yes	N/A	–
Stadtwerke	TVPEE	CSP	No	Not addressed	Yes	Yes	No	No, but standard adopted	Yes	–	–
BayWa	TVPEE	Wind	Quantum bifurcated	No, but Supr. Court endorsed	Yes	Yes	Not directly: but *Eiser* approach endorsed	Yes	Yes	Discussed	–
Hydro Energy	TVPEE Water Levy	Hydro-facilities	Quantum bifurcated	No: “not conclusive” for purposes of int’l law	Yes	Yes	Yes – but not directly	Yes as the test for the carve-out	Yes – but not directly	Not addressed: claim made the submission	No, but followed RREEF
Watkins	TVPEE	Wind	Not requested	Not raised	Yes	Yes	Yes	No	Not directly, but *Isolux* approach endorsed	–	–

APPENDIX VII

Summary Figures for ECT Cases

Type of Cases		Forum	Jurisd. (Not Tax)	Merits	Art. 21 Invoked	Exclusion Applied	Inclusion(s)	Gross Up
Non-renewable								
Non-Yukos	5	SCC = 2; ICSID = 2; UNCITRAL = 0.	Yes = 5; No = 0; N/A = 0.	Yes = 2; No = 3; N/A = 0.	Yes = 1; No = 4; N/A = 0.	Yes = 1; No = 0; N/A = 4.	Yes = 0; No = 0; N/A = 5.	Yes = 0; No = 0; N/A = 5.
Yukos	3	SCC = 0; ICSID = 0; UNCITRAL = 3.	Yes = 3; No = 0; N/A = 0.	Yes = 3; No = 0; N/A = 0.	Yes = 3; No = 0; N/A = 0.	Yes = 0; No = 0; N/A = 3.	Yes = 3; No = 0; N/A = 0.	Yes = 0; No = 0; N/A = 3.
Subtotal	8	SCC = 2; ICSID = 3; UNCITRAL = 3	Yes = 8; No = 0; N/A = 0.	Yes = 5; No = 3; N/A = 0.	Yes = 4; No = 4; N/A = 0.	Yes = 1; No = 0; N/A = 7.	Yes = 3; No = 0; N/A = 5.	Yes = 0; No = 0; N/A = 8.
Renewable								
Spain	20	SCC = 4; ICSID = 15; UNCITRAL = 1.	Yes = 20; No = 0; N/A = 0.	Yes = 17; No = 3; N/A = 0.	Yes = 18; No = 1; N/A = 1.	Yes = 18; No = 0; N/A = 2.	Yes = 0; No = 5; N/A = 15.	Yes = 0; No = 3; N/A = 17.

Czech Rep.	6	SCC = 0; ICSID = 0; UNCITRAL = 6.	Yes = 6; No = 0; N/A = 0.	Yes = 1; No = 5; N/A = 0.	Yes = 6; No = 0; N/A = 0.	Yes = 5; No = 1; N/A = 0.	Yes = 0; No = 0; N/A = 6.	Yes = 0; No = 0; N/A = 6.
Italy	6	SCC = 3; ICSID = 3; UNCITRAL = 0.	Yes = 6; No = 0; N/A = 0.	Yes = 2; No = 3; N/A = 1.	Yes = 4; No = 1; N/A = 1.	Yes = 4; No = 0; N/A = 2.	Yes = 0; No = 0; N/A = 6.	Yes = 0; No = 0; N/A = 6.
Subtotal	32	SCC = 7; ICSID = 18; UNCITRAL = 7.	Yes = 32; No = 0; N/A = 0.	Yes = 20; No = 11; N/A = 1.	Yes = 28; No = 2; N/A = 2.	Yes = 27; No = 1; N/A = 4.	Yes = 0; No = 5; N/A = 27.	Yes = 0; No = 3; N/A = 29.
Total	40	SCC = 10; ICSID = 20; UNCITRAL = 10.	Yes = 40; No = 0; N/A = 0.	Yes = 25; No = 14; N/A = 1.	Yes = 32; No = 6; N/A = 2.	Yes = 28; No = 1; N/A = 8.	Yes = 3; No = 5; N/A = 32.	Yes = 0; No = 3; N/A = 37.

Bibliography

Books, Collected Works, Articles and Periodicals

Abba Kolo, *Tax "Veto" as a Special Jurisdictional and Substantive Issue in Investor-State Arbitration: Need for Reassessment?*, 32 Suffolk Transnat'l L. Rev. 475-92 (2009).

Achim Börner, *Investment Law and Energy, in International investment law* 1644-76 (Marc Bungenberg, Jörn Griebel, Stephan Hobe, August Reinisch and Yun-i Kim eds., 2015).

Adam Smith, *An Inquiry into the Nature and Causes of the Wealth of Nations*, Book V Chap. II Part II (Edwin Cannan ed., Methuen & Co. 1904) (1776); at https://www.econlib.org/ (Accessed: May 30, 2020).

Ali Lazem, *The Treatment of Tax in Investor State Arbitration of Expropriation and National Treatment Protection*, PhD Dissertation, Brunel Law School (2014); http://www.bura.brunel.ac.uk (Accessed: May 30, 2020).

Ali Lazem and Ilias Bantekas, *The Treatment of Tax as Expropriation in International Investor–State Arbitration*, Arb. Int'l. 1-46 (2015).

Andrea J. Menaker and Heather van Slooten Walsh, *The Energy Charter Treaty and U.S. Investment Treaties: an Overview of Key Contrasts, in Investment Protection and the Energy Charter Treaty* 307-18 (Graham Coop and Clarisse Ribeiro eds., 2008).

Andreas Ziegler & Jorun Baumgartner, *Good Faith as a General Principle of (International) Law, in Good Faith and International Economic Law* 9-36 (Andrew D. Mitchell, M Sornarajah, and Tania Voon eds., 2015).

Andrei A. Konoplyanik, *Lubbers Plan: Soviet Energy as a Standpoint for Improving Economic Reforms in the USSR*, The Energy J. 13(3), 281-94 (1992).

Andrei A. Konoplyanik, *Russia-EU, G-8, ECT and Transit Protocol*, 4 Russian/CIS Energy & Mining L. J. 9-12 (2006).

Andrei A. Konoplyanik, *Professor Wälde: in Memoriam of the Friend, in Liber Amicorum: Thomas Wälde Law Beyond Conventional Thought* 121-32 (Jacques Warner & Arif Ali eds., 2009).

Andrei A. Konoplyanik, *A Common Russia–EU Energy Space: The New EU–Russia Partnership Agreement, Acquis Communitaire and the Energy Charter*, J Energy & Natural Res. L. 27(2), 258-91 (2009).

Andrei A. Konoplyanik and Freidrich von Halem, *The Energy Charter Treaty: a Russian Perspective, in The Energy Charter Treaty: an East-West Gateway for Investment & Trade* 156-70 (Thomas W. Wälde ed., 1996).

Andrei Belyi, Sophie Nappert & Vitaliy Pogoretsky, *The Energy Charter Conference Road Map and the Russian Draft Convention on Energy Security*, 29 J. Energy & Natural Res. L. 383-99 (2011).

Andrew Newcombe, *Yukos Universal Limited (Isle of Man) v The Russian Federation: An Introduction to the Agora,* 30(2) ICSID Review—Foreign Inv. L. J. 283-92 (2015).

Andrew Mitchell, *Good Faith in WTO Dispute Settlement*, 7 Melb. J. Intl. L. 339, 345 (2006)

Andrew P. Morriss and Lotta Moberg, *Cartelizing Taxes: Understanding the OECD's Campaign Against "Harmful Tax Competition,"* 4 Columbia J. Tax L. 1 (2013).

Anne K. Hoffmann, *Indirect Expropriation, in Standards of Investment Protection* 151-170 (August Reinisch ed., 2008).

Antonia Layard, *The European Energy Charter Treaty—Tipping the Balance between Energy and the Environment*, 4(5) Eur. Energy & Envtl. L. Rev. 150-6 (1995).

Arbitrating for Peace: How Arbitration Made a Difference (Ulf Franke, Annette Magnusson & Joel Dahlquist eds., 2016).

Arno Gildemeister, *Investment Law and Taxation, in, International Investment Law* 1677-91 (Marc Bungenberg et al. eds., 2015).

Asid Qureshi, *The Public International Law of Taxation: Text, Cases and Materials* (1994).

Asid Qureshi, *The Public International Law of Taxation: Text, Cases and Materials* (2nd ed., 2019).

August Reinisch, *Legality of Expropriations, in Standards of Investment Protection* 171-204 (August Reinisch ed., 2008).

Ben J. M. Terra and Peter J. Wattel, *European Tax Law* (5th ed., 2008).

Black's Law Dictionary (7th ed., 1999) and (11th ed., 2019).

Christopher S Gibson, *Yukos Universal Limited (Isle of Man) v The Russian Federation: A Classic Case of Indirect Expropriation*, 30(2) ICSID Rev.—Foreign Inv. L. J. 303-14 (2015).

Christopher Staker, *Jurisdiction, in International Law* ch. 10 (Malcolm Evans ed., 5th ed. 2018).

Clare Shine, *Environmental Protection under the Energy Charter Treaty, in The Energy Charter Treaty: An East-West Gateway for Investment and Trade* 520-45 (Thomas Wälde ed., 1996).

Commentary on the Energy Charter Treaty (Rafael Leal-Arcas ed., 2018)

Constantine Partasides and Lucy Martinez, *Of Taxes and Stabilisation, in The Guide to Energy Arbitrations* 46-62 (J William Rowley, Doak Bishop and Gordon Kaiser eds., 2015).

Craig S. Bamberger, *Overview, in The Energy Charter Treaty: an East-West Gateway for Investment & Trade* 1-34 (Thomas W. Wälde ed., 1996).

Craig S. Bamberger, *Epilogue: the Energy Charter Treaty as a Work in Progress, in The Energy Charter Treaty: an East-West Gateway for Investment & Trade* 591-602 (Thomas W. Wälde ed., 1996).

Craig S. Bamberger, *The Negotiation of the Energy Charter Treaty, in Investment Protection and the Energy Charter Treaty* xxxix-l (Graham Coop and Clarisse Ribeiro eds., 2008).

Crina Baltag, *The Energy Charter Treaty: The Notion of Investor* (2012).

Dan Engstrom and Cornel Marian, *The Swedish Yukos Saga: RosInvest's pyrrhic victory over Russia and the fortunate correction of previous Swedish case law under which Swedish courts lacked jurisdiction over challenges against awards in the absence of any connection to Sweden*, IBA Arb. Newsletter, 79-82 (2011).

David William Williams, Geoffrey Morse & Sandra Eden, *Davies: Principles of Tax Law* (8th ed., 2016).

DC Blaisdell (1929) *European Financial Control in the Ottoman Empire: A Study of the Establishment, Activities, and Significance of the Administration of the Ottoman Public Debt* (Columbia University Press 1929); https://archive.org/details/in.ernet.dli.2015.216049 (Accessed: May 30, 2020).

Eddie Tobis, *Avoiding Double Taxation on International Arbitration Awards*, J. Damages in Int'l Arb. 4:2, 15-39 (2017).

Emmanuel Gaillard and Mark McNeill, *The Energy Charter Treaty, in Arbitration Under International Investment Agreements: A Guide to the Key Issues* 37-62 (Katia Yannaca-Small ed., Oxford University Press, 2010), pp. 37-62.

Energy Dispute Resolution: Investment Protection, Transit and the Energy Charter Treaty (Graham ed., 2011).

Eric De Brabandere, *Yukos Universal Limited (Isle of Man) v The Russian Federation: Complementarity or Conflict? Contrasting the* Yukos *Case before the European Court of Human Rights and Investment Tribunals*, 30(2) ICSID Rev.—Foreign Inv. L. J. 345-55 (2015).

Evan Criddle, *The Vienna Convention on the Law of Treaties in U.S. Treaty Interpretation*, 44 Virginia J. Int'l L. 431-500 (2004).

Frank D. Dawson and Burns H. Weston, *"Prompt, Adequate and Effective": A Universal Standard for Compensation*, 30 Fordham L. Rev. 727-58 (1962).

Fred R. Shapiro, *Yale Book of Quotations* (2006).

Frederick N. Judson, *A Treaties on Power of Taxation, State and Federal, in the United States* (The Lawbook Exchange 2007).

G. Kaeckenbeeck (1935) *The Character and Work of the Arbitral Tribunal of Upper Silesia*, 21 Transactions of the Grotius Society: Problems of Peace and War, Papers Read before the Society in the Year 1935, 27-44 (1935).

Georg Schwarzenberger, *The Inductive Approach to International Law*, 60 Harv. L. Rev. 539-70 (1947).

Georg Schwarzenberger, *The Inductive Approach to International Law* (1965).

Gloria Alvarez, *Taxation, in Commentary on the Energy Charter Treaty* 288-98 (Rafael Leal-Arcas ed., 2018).

Graham Coop, *The Energy Charter Treaty: More than MIT, in Investment Arbitration and the Energy Charter Treaty* 3-22 (Clarisse Ribeiro ed., 2006).

Graham Coop, *Energy Charter Treaty and the European Union: Is Conflict Inevitable,* 27(3) J. Energy & Natural Res. L. 404-19 (2009).

Gregory E. Maggs, *A Concise Guide to the Federalist Papers As A Source of the Original Meaning of the United States Constitution*, 87 B.U. L. Rev. 801 (2007).

Ina Kotova, *A Treaty à la Carte? Some Reflections on the Modernization of the Energy Charter Process*, J. World Energy L. & Bus. 2016:9, 357-69 (2016).

International Bureau of Fiscal Documentation, *IBFD International Tax Glossary* (7th ed., 2015).

Investment Arbitration and the Energy Charter Treaty (Clarisse Ribeiro ed., 2006).

Investment Protection and the Energy Charter Treaty (Graham Coop and Clarisse Ribeiro, eds., 2008).

Irina Pominova, *Risks and Benefits for the Russian Federation from Participating in the Energy Charter: Comprehensive Analysis* (Energy Charter Secretariat Knowledge Center, Occasional Paper ISSN: 2295-9440, 2014); at http://www.energycharter.org (Accessed: May 30, 2020).

J. Gillis Wetter and Stephen M. Schwebel, *Some Little-Known Cases on Concessions*, 40 Brit. Y.B. Int'l L. 183-232 (1964).

Jacobus Gijsbertus de Beus, *The Jurisprudence of the General Claims Commission, United States and Mexico* (Martinus Nijhoff 1938).

James Crawford, *Brownlie's Principles of Public International Law* (7th ed., 2012).

James Crawford and Martti Koskenniemi, *Introduction, in The Cambridge Companion to International Law* 1-21 (James Crawford and Martti Koskenniemi eds., 2012).

James M. Buchanan and Roger L. Faith (1987), *Secession and the Limits of Taxation: Toward a Theory of Internal Exit*, Am. Econ. Rev. 77:5, 1023-31 (Dec., 1987).

Jan Klebbers, *International Institutions, in The Cambridge Companion to International Law* 228-44 (James Crawford and Martti Koskenniemi eds., Cambridge University Press 2012).

Jan Paulsson, *Arbitration Without Privity, in The Energy Charter Treaty: an East-West Gateway for Investment & Trade* 422-40 (Thomas W. Wälde ed., 1996).

Jeswald Salacuse, *The Energy Charter Treaty and Bilateral Investment Treaty Regimes, in The Energy Charter Treaty: an East-West Gateway for Investment & Trade* 321-48 (Thomas W. Wälde ed., 1996).

Jeswald W. Salacuse, *The Law of Investment Treaties* (2nd ed., 2015).

JHH Weiler, *The Interpretation of Treaties – a Re-examination Preface,* 21(3) Eur. J. Int'l L. 507 (2010)

John F. Avery Jones et al., *The Legal Nature of the Mutual Agreement Procedure under the OECD Model Convention – I*, 1979(6) Brit. Tax Rev. 333-53 (1979).

Jorge Viñuales, *Sovereignty in Foreign Investment Law, in The Foundations of International Investment Law: Bringing Theory into Practice* 317-62 (Zachary Douglas, Joost Pauwelyn & Jorge E. Viñuales eds., 2014).

Julia Doré, *Negotiating the Energy Charter Treaty, in The Energy Charter Treaty: an East-West Gateway for Investment & Trade* 137-54 (Thomas W. Wälde ed., 1996).

Julia Dore and Robert De Bauw, *The Energy Charter Treaty: Origins, Aims and Prospects* (Royal Institute of International Affairs 1995).

Kaj Hobér, *The Energy Charter Treaty—An Overview*, 8 J. World Inv. & Trade 323-55 (2007).

Kaj Hobér, *The Energy Charter Treaty – Awards Rendered*, 1 Disp. Resolution Int'l 36-57 (2007).

Kaj Hobér, *Investment Arbitration and the Energy Charter Treaty*, 1 J. Int'l Disp. Settlement 153-90 (2010).

Kaj Hobér, *The Energy Charter Treaty: a Commentary* (2020).

Katja Yafimava, *The Transit Dimension of EU Energy Security: Importance of Russian Gas Transit Across Ukraine, Belarus, and Moldova* (2011).

L.F.L. Oppenheim, Robert Y. Jennings & Arthur Watts, *Oppenheim's International Law* (9th ed., 1996).

Lena Hiort af Ornäs Leijon, *Tax Policy, Economic Efficiency and the Principle of Neutrality From a Legal and Economic Perspective*, Uppsala Working Paper 2015:2 (2015).

Liber Amicorum: Thomas Wälde Law Beyond Conventional Thought (Jacques Warner & Arif Ali eds., Cameron May 2012).

Louis T. Wells, *Backlash to Investment Arbitration: Three Causes, in The Backlash Against Investment Arbitration* 341-52 (Michael Waibel et al. eds., 2010).

Lucy Reed and Lucy Martinez, *The Energy Charter Treaty: An Overview*, 14 ILSA J. Int'l & Comp. L., 405-32 (2008).

M. Sornarajah, *The International Law on Foreign Investment* (3rd ed., 2010).

Malcolm Shaw, *International Law* (8th ed., 2017).

Marc Kantor, *Valuation for Arbitration* (2008).

Martins Paparinskis, *The International Minimum Standard and Fair and Equitable Treatment* (2013).

Maurice Mendelson, *The Formation of Customary International Law*, Hague Academy of Int'l L. Collected Courses 155-410 (1998).

MENA Chambers, *Note 13—Making Sense of the Taxation Provisions of the Energy Charter*, Series of Notes on the ECT, July 22 (2015); at menachambers.com (Accessed: January 1, 2017).

N. Gregory Mankiw, *Macroeconomics* (10th ed., 2019).

Nathalie L. J. T. Horbach, *Nuclear Protocol of the Energy Charter Treaty*, 13 J Energy & Natural Res. L. 163-77 (1995).

Patrick Dumberry, *The Formation and Identification of Rules of Customary International Law in International Investment Law* (2016)

Patrick M. Norton, *Back to the Future: Expropriation and the Energy Charter Treaty, in The Energy Charter Treaty: an East-West Gateway for Investment & Trade* 365-83 (Thomas W. Wälde ed., 1996).

Patrick Riley, *Social Contract and Its Critics, in The Cambridge History of Eighteenth-Century Political Thought* 347-75 (Mark Goldie and Robert Wokler eds., Cambridge University Press 2006).

Peter D. Cameron, *International Energy Investment Law: the Pursuit of Stability* (2010).

Peter Dietsch, *Rethinking Sovereignty in International Fiscal Policy*, 37 Rev. Int'l Studies 2107-120 (2011).

Peter Harris and David Oliver, *International Commercial Tax* (2010).

Reuven S. Avi-Yonah, *International Tax as International Law*, 57(4) Tax L. Rev. 483-501 (2004).

Richard D. Blau, Bruce N. Lemons & Thomas P. Rohman, *Excess Passive Investment Income—Passive Investment Income Defined Generally—Royalties*, 1 S Corp. Fed. Taxation § 8:65 (2019).

Richard Happ, *Dispute Settlement under the Energy Charter Treaty*, 45 German Year Book of Int'l L., 331-62 (2002).

Rosalyn Higgins, *The Taking of Property by the State: recent developments in International Law*, 176 Collected Courses of the Hague Academy of Int'l L. 332-8 (1982).

Rudolf Dolzer, *ConocoPhillips v Venezuela and Gold Reserve v Venezuela: Expropriation: A New Focus on Old Issues*, 30(2) ICSID Review—Foreign Inv. L. J. 378-83, 378 (2015).

Rudolph Dolzer and Christoph Schreuer, *Principles of International Investment Law* (2nd ed., 2012).

Ruth Mason, *Federalism and the Taxing Power*, 99 Cal. L. Rev. 975-1035 (2011).

Ruth Mason and Michael S. Knoll, *What Is Tax Discrimination?*, 121 Yale L.J. 1014-116 (2012).

Ruth Teitelbaum, *What's Tax Got to Do With It? The Yukos Tribunal's Approach to Motive and Treaty Interpretation*, 5 Transnat'l Disp. Mgmnt. (2015); http://www.transnational-dispute-management.com/ (Accessed: January 1, 2018).

Rutsel Sivestre J. Marta, *The Jurisdiction to Tax in International Law: Theory and Practice of Legislative Fiscal Jurisdiction* (1989).

Ruud Lubbers, *Foreword, in The Energy Charter Treaty: an East-West Gateway for Investment & Trade* xiii-xviii (Thomas W. Wälde ed., 1996).

S. Avi-Yonah Reuven, *Advanced Introduction to International Tax Law* (2015).

Sandra Wappelhorst, Peter Mock & Zifei Yang, *Using Vehicle Taxation Policy to Lower Transport Emissions*, Int'l Council on Clean Transportation Eur., Dec. 2018; http://www.theicct.org (Accessed: May 30, 2020).

Sébastien Manciaux, *Changement de Législation Fiscal et Arbitrage International*, 2001 Revue de l'Arbitrage, 311-42.

Sébastien Miroudot, *Investment, in Preferential Trade Agreement Policies for Development: a Handbook* 307-26 (Jean-Pierre Chauffour and Jean-Christophe Maur eds., World Bank 2011).

Simon P. Anderson, André de Palma, Brent Kreider, *The Efficiency of Indirect Taxes Under Imperfect Competition*, 2001 J. Pub. Econ. 231-51.

Sophie Nappert, *Square Pegs and Round Holes: The Taxation Provision in the Energy Charter Treaty and the Yukos Awards*, 2015 Paris J. Int'l Arb. 7-28.

Sophie Nappert, *Russia and the Energy Charter Treaty: the Unplumbed Depths of Provisional Application*, 6(1) Transnat'l Disp. Mgmnt. 1-8 (2009); http://www.transnational-dispute-management.com/ (Accessed: May 30, 2020).

Stephan Schill, *Ordering Paradigms in International Investment Law: Bilateralism-Multilateralism-Multilateralization, in The Foundations of International Investment Law: Bringing Theory into Practice* 109-141 (Zachary Douglas, Joost Pauwelyn and Jorge E. Viñuales eds., 2014)

Stephan Schill, *Sources of International Investment Law: Multilateralization, Arbitral Precedent, Comparativism, Soft Law, in The Oxford Handbook of the Sources of International Law* 1095-115 (Samantha Besson and Jean d'Aspremont eds., Oxford University Press 2017).

Stephan Schill and Heather L Bray, *Good Faith Limitations on Protected Investments and Corporate Structuring, in Good Faith and International Economic Law* 88-116 (Andrew Mitchell, M. Sornarajah and Tania Voon eds., Oxford University Press 2015).

Stephen Smith, *"Green" Taxes and Charges* (Institute for Fiscal Studies 1995).

Sunita Jogarajan, *Double Taxation and the League of Nations* (2018).

Tarcisio Gazzini, *Energy Charter Treaty: Achievements, Challenges and Perspectives, in Foreign Investment in the Energy Sector Balancing Private and Public Interests* 105-29 (Eric De Brabandere and Tarcisio Gazzini eds., Brill Nijhoff 2014).

Thomas Cooley, *Remedies of Illegal Taxation*, American L. Register 29, 1-16 (1882).

Thomas Rixen, *From Double Tax Avoidance to Tax Competition: Explaining the Institutional Trajectory of International Tax Governance*, 18(2) Rev. Int'l Pol. Econ. 197-227 (2010).

Thomas Roe, Mathew Happold & James Dingemans, *Settlement of Investment Disputes under the Energy Charter Treaty* (2011).

Thomas W. Wälde, *The Energy Charter Treaty: An East-West Gateway for Investment & Trade* (1996).

Thomas W. Wälde, *International Investment Under the 1994 Energy Charter Treaty, in The Energy Charter Treaty: An East-West Gateway for Investment & Trade* 251-320 (Thomas W. Wälde ed., 1996).

Thomas W. Wälde, *International Investment Under the 1994 Energy Charter Treaty: From Dispute Settlement to Treaty Implementation*, 12(4) Arb. Int'l 429-66 (1996).

Thomas W. Wälde, avundsjuk, 102 Am. Soc'y Int'l L. Proc. 55-9 (2008).

Thomas W. Wälde and Abba Kolo, *Investor-State Disputes: The Interface Between Treaty-Based International Investment Protection and Fiscal Sovereignty*, Intertax 35(8/9), 424-49 (2007).

Thomas W. Wälde & Abba Kolo, *Coverage of Taxation under Modern Investment Treaties, in The Oxford Handbook of International Investment Law* 305-58 (Peter T. Muchlinski, Frederico Ortino & Christoph Schreuer eds., 2008).

Thomas W. Wälde and Kaj Hobér, *The First Energy Charter Treaty Arbitral Award*, J. Int'l Arb. 22(2), 83-103 (2005).

Tullio Treves, *Customary International Law*, Max Planck Encyclopedia of Public International Law, November 2006.

V. Veeder, *The Lena Goldfields Arbitration: The Historical Roots of Three Ideas*, Int'l & Comp. L. Q. 47(4), 747-92 (1998).

Vladimir Vladimorovich Putin, *Strategic Planning of the Production of the Mineral-Natural Bases in the Region under the Development of Market Economy Conditions* (PhD Dissertation, 1997, K. Hobér trans., Uppsala Y.B. East Eur. L., 2006).

Walter Hellerstein, *Jurisdiction to Tax Income and Consumption in the New Economy: A Theoretical and Comparative Perspective*, 38 Ga. L. Rev. 1-70.

William Fox, *The United States and the Energy Charter Treaty: Misgivings and Misperceptions*, *in The Energy Charter Treaty: an East-West Gateway for Investment & Trade* 194-200 (Thomas W. Wälde ed., 1996).

William Park and David R. Tillinghast, *Income Tax Treaty Arbitration: A Study* (Sdu Fiscal & Financiële Uitgevers 2004).

William Park, *Tax Arbitration and Investor Protection*, *in Investment Protection and the Energy Charter Treaty* 115-47 (Graham Coop and Clarisse Ribeiro eds., 2008).

William Park, *Arbitrability and Tax*, *in Arbitrability: International and Comparative Perspectives* 179-205 (Loukas Mistelis and Stavros Brekoulakis eds., Wolters Kluwer 2009).

Reports, Speeches, Conference Proceedings, Shorter Pieces and Electronic Resources

Alison Ross, *Russian Withdrawals from Energy Charter Treaty*, Global Arb. Rev., Aug. 7, 2009.

Amsterdam Compensates Jews After the Revelations of a Temporary Worker (Dutch "Amsterdam compenseert Joden na onthulling door uitzendkracht"), Radio N1, May 17, 2016; at https://www.nporadio1.nl/radio-eenvandaag/onderwerpen/356547-amsterdam-compenseert-joden-na-onthulling-door-uitzendkracht (Accessed: May 30, 2020).

Cara Downing, Discussing the Energy Charter Treaty – Q&A with Dr Urban Rusnák, Secretary-General, Energy Charter Treaty Secretariat, Norton Rose Fulbright, Oct. 2018; at: https://www.nortonrosefulbright.com/ (Accessed: May 30, 2020).

Christer Söderlund, 10 Years of Energy Charter Treaty Arbitration – a Step Towards Consistency, Minutes of the ECT Conference, June 9-10, 2011.

Christopher Greenwood, Sources of International Law: An Introduction, Outline of the UN Library Presentation, 2008; at: http://legal.un.org/avl/pdf/ls/greenwood_outline.pdf (Accessed: May 30, 2020).

ConocoPhillips, ConocoPhillips and the Ecuador Agree to Settlement of ICSID Award, News Release, Dec. 4, 2017; at http://www.conocophillips.com/news-media/ (Accessed: May 30, 2020).

Damien Charlotin, *Natland v. Czech Republic (Part 1 of 2): Tribunal Jurisdiction over Claimants under Three Out of Four Treaties and Declines to Apply ECT's Tax Carveout to Contested Measure*, Inv. Arb. Rep., July 26, 2018.

Damien Charlotin, "Natland v. Czech Republic (Part 2 of 2): On the Merits, Tribunal Finds Stabilization Commitment in Czech Legislation and Breach of that Commitment with Introduction of the Solar Levy", Inv. Arb. Rep., July 26, 2018.

Deloitte LLC, International Tax Saudi Arabia Highlights 2019, April 2019; http://www2.deloitte.com (Accessed: May 30, 2020)

Diana Jean Schemo, *Political and Energy Crises Foil Ecuador's Hopes*, N.Y. Times, Nov. 7, 1995, at 3.

Ecuador Denounces its Remaining 16BITs and Publishes CAITISA Audit Report, Inv. Treaty News, June 12, 2012.

Ecuador Opens Bidding for Oriente Blocks, Oil & Gas J. 93(28), July 10, 1995; at http://www.ogj.com (Accessed: May 30, 2020). .

Energy Charter Secretariat, Fiscal Policies for Improving Energy Efficiency: Taxation Grants and Subsidies (ECT Report, 2001).

Energy Charter Secretariat, Taxation Along the Oil and Gas Supply Chain: International Pricing Mechanisms for Oil and Gas, 2008; at https://energycharter.org/ (Accessed: May 30, 2020).

Energy Charter Secretariat, *Blue Book: Making Investments in Energy Charter Member Countries Exceptions to the Principle of non-discriminatory Treatment* (2016); https://energycharter.org/ (Accessed: May 30, 2020)

European Commission, Reasoned Decision on State Aid, SA.40348 (2015/NN), C(2017) final, 10 Nov. 2017; http://ec.europa.eu/competition/state_aid/cases/258770/258770_1945237_333_2.pdf

G. Zandanshatar, *Kapla and Mongolia: Whose Game is this Case that Has Violated Human Rights?*, Ulan Bator Post, Feb. 25, 2015; at: http://ubpost.mongolnews.mn/?p=13561 (Accessed: May 30, 2020).

International Bar Association, IBA Guidelines on Conflicts of Interest in International Arbitration, Oct. 23, 2014; http://www.ibanet.org

International Centre for Settlement of Investment Disputes, Contracting States and Measures Taken by them for the Purpose of the Convention, ICSID/8C/, 2018.

International Law Association, Committee on Formation of Customary (General) International Law, Final Report, 2000; at http://law.umich.edu (Accessed: May 30, 2020).

Julie Bedard et al., *The "Law 42" Arbitrations Against Ecuador and the Importance of BIT Language*, Skadden 2015 Insights-Global Litigation (2015); http://www.skadden.com/insights. Accessed 31 October 2019.

Julie Makinen, *American, 2 Others Pardoned in Mongolia Tax-evasion Case*, L.A. Times, Feb. 26, 2015; at https://www.latimes.com/world/asia/la-fg-mongolia-mining-tax-evasion-20150226-story.html (Accessed: May 30, 2020).

Kyriaki Karadelis, *Italy to Quit Energy Charter Treaty*, Global Arb. Rev., Apr. 23, 2015.

Luke Eric Peterson, *In Shadow of Mass Solar Claims, Another UNCITRAL BIT Arbitration Quietly Moves Forward Against Czech Republic*, Inv. Arb. Rep., Jan. 10, 2014.

Magdalena Andersson, Speech by Minister for Finance at Stockholm Tax Conference Concerning Capacity Building, May 30, 2018; https://www.government.se/speeches/ (Accessed: May 30, 2020).

Nicola Slawson, Mossack Fonseca Law Firm to Shut Down after Panama Papers Tax Scandal, The Guardian, Mar. 14, 2018.

Organization for Economic Co-operation and Development, Negotiating Group on the Multilateral Agreement on Investment (MAI), Expert Group No. 3 Expert Group No.3 on Treatment of Tax Issues in the MAI, DAFFE/MAI/EG2(96)3, Apr. 19, 1996.

Organization for Economic Co-operation and Development, The Multilateral Agreement on Investment: Report by the Chairman of the Negotiating Group, DAFFE/MAI(98)/17, May 4, 1998.

Organization for Economic Co-operation and Development, *Addressing the Tax Challenges of the Digital Economy,* 2014; at https://www.oecd-ilibrary.org/ (Accessed: May 30, 2020).

Organization for Economic Co-operation and Development, the Multilateral Agreement on Investment: Addressing the Tax Challenges of the Digital Economy, Action 1 – 2015 Final Report, OECD Publishing, Paris, 2015; at http://www.oecd.org/ctp/tax-challenges-digital-economy-discussion-draft-march-2014.pdf (Accessed: May 30, 2020).

Organization for Economic Co-operation and Development, *Fighting Tax Crime: the Ten Global Principles* (2017); at http://www.oecd.org (Accessed: May 30, 2020).

Pigouvian Taxes, Externalities: What to do when the interests of individuals and society do not coincide?, The Economist, Aug. 19, 2017.

Procuradura Generalo del Estado Ecuador, End to Oil Dispute: Ecuador and Burlington Reach a Settlement Agreement, UCS/36, Dec. 4, 2017.

Russia Becomes WTO Member After 18 years of Talks, British Broadcasting Company (BBC), Dec. 16, 2011; at http://www.bbc.com (Accessed: May 30, 2020).

Sarah Keay-Bright and Steivan Defilla, *Energy Charter Treaty Review Should End Protection for Fossil Fuels*, Energy Post, Mar. 20, 2019.

Sören Amelang, "Power Grid Fees – Unfair and Opaque,", Clean Energy Wire, January 26, 2017; https://www.cleanenergywire.org (Accessed: May 30, 2020).

The Tax Man Scoffs at Genocide: Amsterdam Holocaust Survivors Were Forced to Pay Back Taxes, Washington Times, April 19, 2014; https://www.washingtontimes.com/news/2014/apr/19/amsterdam-holocaust-survivors-were-forced-pay-back/ (Accessed: May 30, 2020).

Tom Jones, *Academics Urge Trump to Ditch ISDS in NAFTA*, Global Arb. Rev., Oct. 27, 2017.

Tom Jones, *EU States Give Green Light for ECT Renegotiation*, Global Arb. Rev., July 17, 2019.

Transnational Institute, Ecuador Terminates 16 Investment Treaties; at: https://www.tni.org/en/article/ecuador-terminates-16-investment-treaties (Accessed: May 30, 2020).

Troy Segal, Monetary Policy v. Fiscal Policy: What is the Difference, Investopedia, Apr. 10, 2019; at: http://www.investopedia.com (Accessed: May 30, 2020).

United Nations General Assembly, Responsibility of States for Internationally Wrongful Acts, A/CN.4/L.602/Rev.1, July 26, 2001.

United Nations International Law Commission (2008), Draft Commentaries. Responsibility of States for Internationally Wrongful Acts, A/56/10, Y.B. Int'l L. Commission, 2001, vol. II, Part Two (2008.

United Nations International Law Commission (2011), Guide to Practice on Reservation to Treaties, Yearbook of the International Law Comm'n, vol. II(2) (2011)

United States Embassy Quito, Government of Ecuador Whipsaws Oil Companies by Ambassador Linda Jewell, WikiLeaks Cable: 08QUITO351_a, Apr. 18, 2008.

United States Energy Information Administration, Country Analysis Brief: Ecuador, Oct. 5, 2017; http://eia.gov (Accessed: May 30, 2020).

United States Trade Representative, Request for Comments on Negotiating Objectives Regarding Modernization of the North American Free Trade Agreement With Canada and Mexico, 82 FR 23699, May 23, 2017.

World Bank, A Better Investment Climate for Everyone. World Development Report 2005; https://openknowledge.worldbank.org (Accessed: May 30, 2020).

World Trade Organization, World Trade Report, 2013; http://www.wto.org (Accessed: May 30, 2020).

World Trade Organization, Report of the Working Party on the Accession of the Russian Federation to the World Trade Organization, WT/ACC/RUS/70WT/MIN(11)/2, Nov. 17, 2011; http://www.wto.org (Accessed: May 30, 2020).

Table of Authorities

Cases

Statutes

Other Authorities

Rules

Constitutional Provisions

Treaties

Domestic Cases and Decisions

Index

1. Moshe Hirsch, *The Arbitration Mechanism of the International Center for the Settlement of Investment Disputes*, 1993 (ISBN 07-923-1993-1).
2. Aida B. Avanessian, *Iran-United States Claims Tribunal in Action*, 1993 (ISBN 18-533-3902-4).
3. Isaak I. Dore, *The UNCITRAL Framework for Arbitration in Contemporary Perspective*, 1993 (ISBN 18-533-3573-8).
4. Vesna Lazić, *Insolvency Proceedings and Commercial Arbitration*, 1998 (ISBN 90-411-1115-8).
5. Joachim Frick, *Arbitration in Complex International Contracts*, 2001 (ISBN 90-411-1662-1).
6. Katherine Lynch, *The Forces of Economic Globalization: Challenges to the Regime of International Commercial Arbitration*, 2003 (ISBN 90-411-1994-9).
7. Christoph Liebscher, *The Healthy Award: Challenge in International Commercial Arbitration*, 2003 (ISBN 90-411-2011-4).
8. Hamid G. Gharavi, *The International Effectiveness of the Annulment of an Arbitral Award*, 2003 (ISBN 90-411-1717-2).
9. Abdulhay Sayed, *Corruption in International Trade and Commercial Arbitration*, 2004 (ISBN 90-411-2236-2).
10. Gabrielle Kaufmann-Kohler & Thomas Schultz, *Online Dispute Resolution: Challenges for Contemporary Justice*, 2004 (ISBN 90-411-2318-0).
11. Christopher R. Drahozal & Richard W. Naimark (eds), *Towards a Science of International Arbitration: Collected Empirical Research*, 2005 (ISBN 90-411-2322-9).
12. Ali Yeşilirmak, *Provisional Measures in International Commercial Arbitration*, 2005 (ISBN 90-411-2353-9).
13. Christian Bühring-Uhle, *Arbitration and Mediation in International Business*, second revised edition, 2006 (ISBN 978-9-041-12256-8).
14. Bernard Hanotiau, *Complex Arbitrations: Multi-party, Multi-contract and Multi-issue – A Comparative Study*, Second Edition, 2020 (ISBN 978-94-035-1261-7).
15. Loukas A. Mistelis & Julian D.M. Lew (eds), *Pervasive Problems in International Arbitration*, 2006 (ISBN 978-9-041-12450-0).
16. Julian D.M. Lew & Loukas A. Mistelis (eds), *Arbitration Insights – Twenty Years of the Annual Lecture of the School of International Arbitration, Sponsored by Freshfields Bruckhaus Deringer*, 2006 (ISBN 978-9-041-12606-1).
17. Mark Kantor, *Valuation for Arbitration: Compensation Standards, Valuation Methods and Expert Evidence*, 2008 (ISBN 978-9-041-12735-8).
18. Christoph Brunner, *Force Majeure and Hardship under General Contract Principles: Exemption for Non-Performance in International Arbitration*, 2009 (ISBN 978-90-411-2792-1).

19. Loukas A. Mistelis & Stavros L. Brekoulakis (eds), *Arbitrability: International & Comparative Perspectives*, 2009 (ISBN 978-90-411-2730-3).
20. Sam Luttrell, *Bias Challenges in International Commercial Arbitration: The Need for a 'Real Danger' Test*, 2009 (ISBN 978-90-411-3191-1).
21. Monique Sasson, *Substantive Law in Investment Treaty Arbitration: The Unsettled Relationship Between International Law and Municipal Law*, Second Edition, 2017 (ISBN 978-90-411-6103-1).
22. Ileana M. Smeureanu, *Confidentiality in International Commercial Arbitration*, 2011 (ISBN 978-90-411-3226-0).
23. Won Kidane, *China-Africa Dispute Settlement: The Law, Economics and Culture of Arbitration*, 2011 (ISBN 978-90-411-3674-9).
24. Karel Daele, *Challenge and Disqualification of Arbitrators in International Arbitration*, 2012 (ISBN 978-90-411-3799-9).
25. Crina Baltag, *The Energy Charter Treaty: The Notion of Investor*, 2012 (ISBN 978-90-411-3428-8).
26. Alexandra Diehl, *The Core Standard of International Investment Protection: Fair and Equitable Treatment*, 2012 (ISBN 978-90-411-3869-9).
27. Manuel Indlekofer, *International Arbitration and the Permanent Court of Arbitration*, 2013 (ISBN 978-90-411-4766-0).
28. Günther J. Horvath & Stephan Wilske (eds), *Guerrilla Tactics in International Arbitration*, 2013 (ISBN 978-90-411-4002-9).
29. Albert Badia, *Piercing the Veil of State Enterprises in International Arbitration*, 2014 (ISBN 978-90-411-5162-9).
30. Nadja Erk, *Parallel Proceedings in International Arbitration: A Comparative European Perspective*, 2014 (ISBN 978-90-411-5264-0).
31. Simon Vorburger, *International Arbitration and Cross-Border Insolvency: Comparative Perspectives*, 2014 (ISBN 978-90-411-5419-4).
32. Ahmad Ali Ghouri, *Interaction and Conflict of Treaties in Investment Arbitration*, 2015 (ISBN 978-90-411-5417-0).
33. Reto Marghitola, *Document Production in International Arbitration*, 2015 (ISBN 978-90-411-5159-9).
34. Alfonso Gómez-Acebo, *Party-Appointed Arbitrators in International Commercial Arbitration*, 2016 (ISBN 978-90-411-6671-5).
35. Jonas von Goeler, *Third-Party Funding in International Arbitration and Its Impact on Procedure*, 2016 (ISBN 978-90-411-5015-8).
36. Dean Lewis, *The Interpretation and Uniformity of the UNCITRAL Model Law on International Commercial Arbitration: Focusing on Australia, Hong Kong and Singapore*, 2016 (ISBN 978-90-411-6700-2).
37. Stavros Brekoulakis, Julian D.M. Lew & Loukas Mistelis (eds), *The Evolution and Future of International Arbitration*, 2016 (ISBN 978-90-411-7004-0).
38. Rémy Gerbay, *The Functions of Arbitral Institutions*, 2016 (ISBN 978-90-411-6217-5).

39. Maximilian Clasmeier, *Arbitral Awards as Investments: Treaty Interpretation and the Dynamics of International Investment Law*, 2017 (ISBN 978-90-411-8357-6).
40. Tony Cole (ed.), *The Roles of Psychology in International Arbitration*, 2017 (ISBN 978-90-411-5921-2).
41. Pietro Ferrario, *The Adaptation of Long-Term Gas Sale Agreements by Arbitrators*, 2017 (ISBN 978-90-411-8232-6).
42. Jacob B. van de Velden, *Finality in Litigation: The Law and Practice of Preclusion – Res Judicata (Merger and Estoppel), Abuse of Process and Recognition of Foreign Judgments*, 2017 (ISBN 978-90-411-8342-2).
43. Dolores Bentolila, *Arbitrators as Lawmakers*, 2017 (ISBN 978-90-411-8354-5).
44. Giacomo Marchisio, *The Notion of Award in International Commercial Arbitration: A Comparative Analysis of French Law, English Law, and the UNCITRAL Model Law*, 2017 (ISBN 978-90-411-8391-0).
45. Csaba Kovács, *Attribution in International Investment Law*, 2018 (ISBN 978-90-411-9675-0).
46. Mary Mitsi, *The Decision-Making Process of Investor-State Arbitration Tribunals*, 2019 (ISBN 978-90-411-9600-2).
47. Ahmet Cemil Yıldırım, *Interpretation of Contracts in Comparative and Uniform Law*, 2019 (ISBN 978-94-035-1130-6).
48. Beata Gessel-Kalinowska vel Kalisz, *The Legal, Real and Converged Interest in Declaratory Relief*, 2019 (ISBN 978-94-035-1244-0).
49. Maximilian Pika, *Third-Party Effects of Arbitral Awards: Res Judicata Against Privies, Non-mutual Preclusion and Factual Effects*, 2019 (ISBN 978-94-035-1273-0).
50. Yulia Levashova, *The Right of States to Regulate in International Investment Law: The Search for Balance Between Public Interest and Fair and Equitable Treatment*, 2019 (ISBN 978-94-035-0931-0).
51. Flavia Marisi, *Environmental Interests in Investment Arbitration: Challenges and Directions*, 2020 (ISBN 978-94-035-1723-0).
52. Martina Magnarelli, *Privity of Contract in International Investment Arbitration: Original Sin or Useful Tool?*, 2020 (ISBN 978-94-035-2020-9).
53. Xu Qian, *Water Services Disputes in International Arbitration: Reconsidering the Nexus of Investment Protection, Environment, and Human Rights*, 2020 (ISBN 978-94-035-2203-6).
54. Nobumichi Teramura, Ex Aequo et Bono *as a Response to the 'Over-Judicialisation' of International Commercial Arbitration*, 2020 (ISBN 978-94-035-2073-5).
55. Bruno Guandalini, *Economic Analysis of the Arbitrator's Function*, 2020 (ISBN 978-94-035-2265-4).
56. Zena Prodromou, *The Public Order Exception in International Trade, Investment, Human Rights and Commercial Disputes*, 2020 (ISBN 978-94-035-2031-5).
57. Jürg Künzle, *Multiple Contracts and Coordination in International Construction Projects: A Swiss Law Analysis*, 2020 (ISBN 978-94-035-2024-7).

58. Cornel Marian, *The State's Power to Tax in the Investment Arbitration of Energy Disputes: Outer Limits and the Energy Charter Treaty*, 2020 (ISBN 978-94-035-1752-0).

www.ingramcontent.com/pod-product-compliance
Lightning Source LLC
LaVergne TN
LVHW020644300926
849161LV00004B/800